American ★
songwriter
magazine

Song

the world's best songwriters on
creating the music that moves us
_____

edited by J. Douglas Waterman

W

WRITER'S DIGEST BOOKS
www.writersdigest.com
Cincinnati, Ohio

11 10 09 08 07   5 4 3 2 1

Distributed in Canada by Fraser Direct
100 Armstrong Avenue
Georgetown, ON, Canada L7G 5S4
Tel: (905) 877-4411

Distributed in the U.K. and Europe by David & Charles
Brunel House, Newton Abbot, Devon, TQ12 4PU, England
Tel: (+44) 1626 323200, Fax: (+44) 1626 323319
E-mail: mail@davidandcharles.co.uk

Distributed in Australia by Capricorn Link
P.O. Box 704, Windsor, NSW 2756 Australia
Tel: (02) 4577-3555

Library of Congress Cataloging-in-Publication Data

Song : the world's best songwriters on creating the music that moves us / edited by J. Douglas Waterman. – 1st ed.
    p. cm.
  ISBN-13: 978-1-58297-424-8 (pbk. with flaps : alk. paper)
  ISBN-10: 1-58297-424-1
  1. Composers–United States–Interviews. 2. Popular music–Writing and publishing–United States. I. Waterman, J. Douglas.
  ML390.S6634 2006
  782.42164092'273–dc22
                      2006004660

Editor: Amy Schell
Designer: Claudean Wheeler
Production Coordinator: Mark Griffin
Photographers: See photo credits on page 390.

Additional assistance provided by Alethea Beeker, Robert Clement, Julia McClelland, and Matthew Shearon.

F+W PUBLICATIONS, INC.

Acknowledgments

We set out in the summer of 2004 to compile—from *American Songwriter* issues dating back to 1984, as well as other sources—a thorough, resonant compilation of conversations with the best songwriters around. We hope you get as much out of this as we have. I'd like to thank a truckload of people who have helped to make this mega-volume a reality. We couldn't have pulled it all together without the cooperation, support, enthusiasm and wild-haired spirit of some passionate musical individuals. Here goes, in no particular order: Thanks to all of the songwriters who have passed on and left us with their timeless work; the writers who contributed their interviews; the photographers who contributed their art; all of the songwriters featured and their publicists, record labels, management and legal representatives; those who have provided editorial assistance, including Robert Clement, Matthew Shearon, Joey Hood, Julia McClelland, and Jay Steele; Evan Schlansky, Jewly Hight, and Phil Sweetland for writing introductions; Michael Kosser; Lisa Wysocky and the HitWriters.com staff; Greg Hatfield, Scott Francis, Amy Schell, Jane Friedman, and the F+W Publications staff; Laura Crookston; Tom Clement; Boutros Boutros-Ghali; Rodney Crowell; and the songwriters and music fans who buy this book.

Until the next edition,

—*J. Douglas Waterman*

About the Author

J. Douglas Waterman is the Editor-In-Chief of *American Songwriter* magazine, a bi-monthly publication which has covered The Craft of Music© since 1984. He is also a freelance journalist who has contributed to such magazines as *Blues Revue, Country Music Greats, Goldmine, Harp, Mojo, Relix,* and *Spin,* and has written for RollingStone.com and Nashville alternative weeklies *All the Rage* and *The Nashville Scene.* He resides in Nashville, Tennessee, and can be reached at dwaterman@americansongwriter.com.

the interviews

preface

When doing interviews, the inevitable question about how one goes about writing songs arrives in all its chain-letter glory. I have often invoked this line: "Talking about songwriting is like doing card tricks on the radio." In truth, I owe this bit of wit to Emmylou Harris, who in her ever-the-indulgent-big-sister-ly way giggled the words to me in a show of solidarity for a rant I was on about some rookie journalist who posed the question, "Which comes first, the words or the lyrics?" At the time, Emmylou was relying on songwriters such as myself for the bulk of her recording material and, perhaps out of kindness—more than gratitude for the good songs—opted not to point out the fact that I should have been grateful the guy wanted to speak to me at all. (Apart from my desire to emulate Bob Dylan's cool reticence to talk to journalists, I recognized the glaring truth that were I to button my lip on the subject of my songs, no one would care.)

In recent years Emmylou has proven what I long suspected… the soul of a poet, such as hers, would not long sit silent. As I've watched with heartfelt admiration my friend's triumphant foray into the added dimension of singer/songwriter, I have—when it came to my attention—done quick readings of her press clippings for the sole purpose of gathering whether or not she herself had used the line I'd adopted. Truth be told, I felt a twinge of guilt every time I used the line without giving credit where it was due. Clear conscience notwithstanding, the line still holds true.

When I heard that a book of interviews on the process of songwriting was being compiled by *American Songwriter* magazine—and that the honor of my take on the subject was being included among so many artists whose work I wholeheartedly admire—I was strangely reticent. My thought process went something like this, "Damn, songwriting is so hard to talk about, and the interview I've given to *American Songwriter* was for the purpose of promoting a new record… and the absolute truth about songwriting, as I know it, is if there is an agenda such as style or genre—pop, folk, blues, rock or anything else—dictating the process, the cart is before the horse and the potential for a good song finding its way into this world is in serious jeopardy… no way could I have gotten to the core truths about songwriting, as I know them, with the purpose of selling a CD in the forefront of my tiny brain." Luckily I got the mental hydrant turned off before the editors decided to withdraw the invitation to participate.

Alas, as songwriting goes, I stand by the card trick analogy. Lucky for you, the reader, as fortune would have it, there is a wealth of artists contained herein who—also á la Emmylou Harris—are blessed with the souls of poets and are beautifully capable of articulating the mystery that is songwriting. I can't wait to read the interviews.

Rodney Crowell
Nashville, Tennessee
July 2006

introduction

Clarity. I think most songwriters are just overgrown music fans first and foremost, striving for some sort of clarity in their musical creations. They're always itching to unfold lyrics and melodies that haven't yet been created—a new twist to an age-old theme, a crisp hook to a fresh theme, an innovative melody to a title that hasn't been accessed. It's just a natural progression for those who realize that they too have a gift to write songs.

Bob Dylan studied and internalized the language of Woody Guthrie and, over time, found out that he himself had some new things to say; he truly found his own voice. Merle Haggard imitated the vocal and writing styles of his heroes—Lefty Frizzell and Wynn Stewart to name a couple—and through this process of taking his fandom to another level, he has come to construct a classic repertoire of tunes that can easily be spotted as Hag's.

Like other art forms, the craft of music involves a delicate balance of inspiration and perspiration—inking the muse with hard work. The songwriters in this book have all taken their love of music into another realm—by writing (and for many, recording) songs themselves—and they've all been able to etch out a living in this endeavor. You can be sure that those included in this volume don't take their gift for granted. Songwriting is something they continually work at, and they view themselves as purely fortunate for the opportunity to do what they love as a profession.

There are literally tens or even hundreds of thousands of songwriters around the world today putting the pen to paper. There's always something new to say, a new way of looking at life, a new melody that hasn't been hatched. Songwriters—and other writers for that matter—thrive on observing, diagnosing, digging, discovering, uncovering, dwelling on, interpreting, and reflecting on ideas and music that is worth their time and their listeners' time.

Just what does the year 2100 hold in store for us musically? Maybe a bit of folk electronica-meets-alt. African country, or vaquero balladry-meets-Native American chants, or even better, Tin Pan Alley-meets-Tin Pan South with a subtle touch of power pop. Who knows?

If you've bought this book, you're probably hoping to stir some brain cells and be inspired… inspired to write your first song, or to write better songs (if you're already on your way and want some fine-tuning with the masters), or maybe you just want to read about how the writers create the music that both you and they love.

In any case, this book provides some revealing insight into songwriters' creative processes from the creators themselves. Those included run the gamut of musical styles, genres, approach, expectations, lifestyles, worldviews, inspirations, and more. There's a lot of meat in here, so don't consume it all at once or you'll ruin your digestive system. Take it in little by little, here and there, and *American Songwriter* magazine will keep you updated in the meantime.

Like many a music enthusiast, I recently paid homage to the King of Rock 'n' Roll in my first-ever visit to Graceland. While I was combing through a plethora of amazing photos and artifacts, Elvis's voice of conviction drew everyone's attention to the loudspeaker as he quoted songwriter Paul Whiteman's classic, "Without a Song." He began, "When I was a child, ladies and gentlemen, I was a dreamer. I read comic books, and I was the hero of the comic book. I saw movies, and I was the hero in the movie. So every dream I ever dreamed has come true a hundred times… I learned very early in life that: 'Without a song, the day would never end; without a song, a man ain't got a friend; without a song, the road would never bend—without a song.' So I keep singing a song."

And we keep on listening to the songs…

J. Douglas Waterman
Nashville, Tennessee
July 2006

Deborah Allen

*Interview by
Lisa Wysocky*

HitWriters.com, 2005

Deborah Allen was born with the gift of music coursing through her veins, cutting a path in her life as relentlessly as the Mississippi carves through Memphis, the place of her birth.

Her incredible voice, beauty, and always handy confidence quickly landed her a job at Opryland. As a regular cast member of the theme park's *Showboat*, Allen was invited to join Tennessee Ernie Ford as a part of a cast production he was taking on tour to the Soviet Union. It proved to be an invaluable experience. When safely back home in the States, her career momentum picked up speed. Veteran songwriting genius Shel Silverstein took Allen under his wing, and considering the sea of pretty faces and new singers vying for their own star in the skies over Music Row, he had one important piece of advice for her: "Write songs!"

While establishing herself as a major recording artist during the eighties, Allen's incredible string of successes as a songwriter were fast establishing her as one of the hottest young writers in town. In addition to becoming a major country hit, "Baby I Lied," from her first RCA album, *Cheat the Night* (1984), achieved huge success on the pop charts as well. This tremendous recognition in both fields garnered Allen two Grammy nominations as a singer and songwriter. Her first recording project for Giant Records, *Delta Dreamland* (1993), included the hit singles "Rock Me (In the Cradle of Love)" and "If You're Not Gonna Love Me," spurring a welcomed re-emergence of Deborah Allen on the charts. Her CD *All That I Am*, on Giant Records, further displayed the passionate intensity of her singing and the lyrical beauty of her songwriting. Here was the heart of Deborah Allen.

Now in the new millennium, with her talents culminating in international performances with world-renowned symphonies, Allen remains as current as tomorrow morning's news.

—LISA WYSOCKY

Tell us how your career began after moving to Nashville.

When I first moved to Nashville, I was like everybody else and had a day job—except my day job was a night job. Actually it was the graveyard shift at IHOP on Twenty-first Avenue. I felt like I had a family of friends there: the waitresses and cooks. Even when I quit working there, I would always go back because I knew that I could get some good breakfast. One morning, I was sitting there, trying to plot my strategy of how I was going to break in [the music business]. I noticed, in a booth across the restaurant, this guy with real black hair and these big sunglasses on, and another guy with salt-and-pepper hair. I thought, "I know those guys have to be in the music business." Don't ask me why I did this, but I got up from my seat, walked across the room, and said, "Excuse me, but um, are you in the insurance business?" They go, "No darling, we're in the music business." I slide into the seat next to them and I go, "That's what I thought. I'm a singer and trying to get started." They were amused by my tenacity and listened to every word I had to say. They were just really sweet to me. It turned out to be Roy Orbison and Joe Nelson, who, of course, wrote "Oh Pretty Woman."

Did that encounter lead to a first break?

Well after that, let's see, I believe Joe took me on a tour of the studio. I was really impressed. They said that they would ask me to sing on something. But, you know how it is… how is someone going to get in touch with you if you don't have a phone? I was living in a little one-room apartment, no phone, but I was working on getting a phone. Finally, I got a phone and got a call from AFTRA [the American Federation of Television and Radio Artists], which I had finally gotten the money to join. They said, "We are so glad you got a phone because Roy Orbison and Joe Nelson have been looking for you. They want you to record a song." And I said, "They have?" And she said, "Yeah." I ended up singing on two tracks of Roy's. It was really incredible that they allowed me to do such a thing. It's just an example of how, when you live in Nashville, you just never really know who you are going to bump into—who is going to be in the booth next to you. You never know how just a casual hello and a little enthusiasm can change your life. It sure got my life off to a great start here.

Could you tell me a little about "Baby I Lied," and how it came about?

Well, "Baby I Lied" is a really special song for me. It's ended up taking me around the world. I'll always be thankful for it. It came at a time when I had some records out, and I was really writing a lot. I was also hoping people would send me their great songs to sing, but my recording career wasn't at quite the level where writers wanted to pitch me their songs. You know, they would rather pitch them to artists who were number one on the charts at the time. So, I knew that it was really going to come down to me coming up with that song. So me, Rafe VanHoy, and Roy Burk got together one day and decided to give it a shot. Well, Rafe and I wrote a lot together at that time. We had such a great creative connection. It was almost like we had telepathy. So it was almost unfair for that third party, be it Roy or whoever, because it took a little while to break into the connection. I'll never forget it. Roy was sitting there and he says, "Well, I have an idea but I'm not really sure if you are going to like it, and if you don't, don't worry about it. It's not gonna hurt my feelings." So we both kind of looked up to hear what he had to say. It must not have really struck us because we started looking back at each other again. And the next thing you know, Roy speaks up and goes, "Wait a minute, did I say I wouldn't be hurt? I lied." When he said that, we looked at him. I started going, "Did I say that I wouldn't be hurt if our love just didn't work? Baby, I lied." And I'm telling you, from that moment forward, we were all synched up together, and it was like the song just wrote itself.

What do you most enjoy about being a songwriter?

The best thing about being a songwriter is that you can do it anytime, anyplace, asleep, awake, wherever you are. You know, my songwriting mentor was Shel Silverstein. I hung out with him and learned as much as I possibly could from him from day one. He's just a genius.

Did Shel inspire you to get into songwriting more seriously?

I was playing the Hall of Fame, which we call the Hall of Shame here. Don't ask me how it got that reputation, but it did. Anyway, I was playing a happy hour and I wanted Shel to come in and hear me sing, 'cause again, as a singer, I was waiting for that moment to get discovered. So he comes down and he listens to me sing. And afterwards, I go and sit down beside him and go, "What did you think?" He goes, "Well, you got a good voice." And I was like "Alright, I'm getting ready to get discovered." Well, he went on to say, "You know, there are a lot of great singers around." So I started feeling the

> *…you just never really know who you are going to bump into—who is going to be in the booth next to you. You never know how just a casual hello and a little enthusiasm can change your life.*

air come out of my bubble. It was like, "Oh, this isn't going to be good." But he just went on to explain to me how. He said, "You know how great you feel when you are up there on stage?" And I said, "Yeah." And he goes, "When you get off

that stage, that feeling kind of fades away, right?" And I said, "Yeah." I had no idea where he was going with this. Finally he just said, "You know, I really think you should consider writing songs. That way, you could design your own music. You could be much more a part of your music. You know what? The sun doesn't shine on the same dog's back everyday. Even if you were to have a successful singing career, it's not always going to be that way. And with songwriting, it's a creative outlet; it's something you can do and keep forever. And no one can take it away. It'll keep you from going crazy." Well, I don't know about that last part, but it sure has kept me busy.

What kind of satisfaction comes with writing a great song?

To me, the greatest thing about writing a good song is that it sort of surpasses all the different styles. I have a song called "You Never Cross My Mind." I cut it. Conway [Twitty] and Loretta [Lynn] cut it. And Isaac Hayes and Millie Jackson cut it. Talk about three different kinds of cuts on one song. The Loretta and Conway [versions were] kind of similar to mine. But the Isaac Hayes and Millie Jackson one… I almost didn't recognize it at first, except for a few pieces of the melody and, of course, the lyrics. But it was all open to their interpretation. That was what was great about it. Then, there are a couple of songs that always fall into a certain genre. For instance, "You Do It"—it's sort of dance-y, and luckily enough, I got Diana Ross and Sheena Easton to cut it. And they both brought out that pop element that was built into the song. But I betcha some country artist could cut it and it would sound completely different. Also, sometimes, those kinds of cuts happen via personal relationships. Like Billy Burnett is a really good friend of mine. Because of my writing with Billy, two of the songs that we wrote ended up on a Fleetwood Mac CD. So, to me, every song has a life of its own. It may take a couple of months, a couple of days,

> *The best thing about being a songwriter is that you can do it anytime, anyplace, asleep, awake, wherever you are.*

or even a couple of years for it to find its rightful owner or its birthright, you know? But they usually do if they are really good songs. I've been really lucky to have some success in the pop field. To me, the biggest success is just writing a great song. And once it finds its home… to me… that's like icing on the cake.

How are singing and songwriting different for you?

When I perform live, I like to give the audiences a piece of my heart and soul. Those are the songs I like to sing as well. I mean, I've written a lot of songs… about a thousand songs. And you know, not all of them are songs I feel really fit me. That's another neat thing about writing songs; you can write one, and maybe it doesn't fit you but it fits another artist. But [there are the ones that fit me], that I put on and wear. I don't put them on and wear them unless I can do them with all my heart and soul. To me, that's what music is all about. It's like a form of expressionism. The main goal is to touch someone's heart and bring them in, so they feel the same thing—maybe not in the same way, but the same thing at the same time.

What's an example of one of your big cuts for another artist, and how was it written?

There's a song I wrote with Rafe VanHoy and Kix Brooks ["I'm Only in It for the Love"]. It was right after we'd gotten this Prophet-5, which was one of the real early synthesizers. It was a pretty exciting time to have that piece of gear. I had been fooling around on the piano and I came up with this lick. So when we all got together, Rafe and Kix and I, I was like, "Hey y'all, let me show you this new lick." And I showed it to them on the Prophet-5. And all of a sudden, it kind of had this real pop flair like Michael McDonald but you know, not really… because nobody's Michael McDonald. But anyway, it was inspired from some of that. We just started writing this song, and the next thing you know, it was done. I mean, it just finished itself really quick. We all were kind of excited about it. We had visions of… I don't know what we had visions of, but the person who wound up cutting it was John Conlee, who was a wonderful country singer. I love John. But [he and his producer] took that song in a direction I never thought of. I mean, it blew my mind. It had horns, and I never would've envisioned this song turning out that way. But I am not complaining because it was like a big ol' number one hit, and it's a big song in the show I do, so it was just funny. You never know what's going to happen with a song, especially when you turn it over to another artist to do, because everybody has their own way of expressing music.

Nic Armstrong
IV Thieves

Interview by
Josh Baron

American Songwriter,
May/June 2005

Nic Armstrong and the Thieves, his merry band of garage rock revivalists, ply meaty British blues and ballads with a sharp lyrical bite. After burning through a series of dead-end bands in his native Newcastle, Armstrong was ready to give up his dreams of a music career. But a demo of his songs won him a talent competition conducted by *Dazed & Confused* magazine, and Armstrong earned a management and record deal as a result. With his newly formed band, the Thieves, the twenty-four-year-old Armstrong recorded his debut album, *The Greatest White Liar*, released in the United States on New West Records in 2004. That album featured the thunderous "Broken Mouth Blues," a song compared by one critic to "Bob Dylan fronting the mid-sixties Stones." The album won the admiration of British rockers Oasis, who brought Armstrong on their U.S. tour in 2005. The current incarnation of Nic and company is IV Thieves. They recently finished a successful tour with the Pretenders and released their debut album, *If We Can't Escape, My Pretty*, in fall 2006.

—EVAN SCHLANSKY

Your lyrics are accessible, grounded... dare I say blue collar. I wouldn't have guessed you were so young.

I didn't really want to push it. I really wanted to make a record that people would still be able to listen to in thirty years' time. And people could empathize with. The songs are from my heart, you know? The situation I came out of. I was struggling to find where I was going, relationship broke down, I had no money, and I was doing bum jobs. It's just honest, you know?

What do you think are qualities that contribute to a timeless sound?

It's just sort of the music I grew up with and have a real passion for. Stuff in my mind which is timeless like fifties rock 'n' roll. Elvis and Chuck Berry. I like the Beatles stuff, ahead of its time, but it still sounds as good today as it did then.

I read about your early musical influences—the Beatles, Gene Vincent, and Chuck Berry. What were some of the first records to truly change you? Early live performances?

I think one of the best concerts I ever went to see was Rage Against the Machine when I was a kid. They had just broken over here and I went nuts. That was a live show. But I sort of remember picking up "Strawberry Fields" and the [Beatles'] blue album, the red and blue compilations, and talking about it in music class. I wasn't interested in music at all but for some reason... this is when I was eight or nine or something and going through my dad's records and just picking [things] out and putting [them] on and I was like, "Wow, what's this?" Queen was the first ever record I bought. It was like the *Greatest Hits* but that was just sort of forming information in my head. I had no plans to become a musician at that time. So I almost just stumbled upon it for some reason. Sometimes I got to check myself to see what I'm doing.

When did you first pick up a guitar or sing?

It was when I about fifteen. I was a visual artist ever since I was a kid, always sort of drawing and painting and stuff. That's where my future lay. I can't remember the exact reason I picked up a guitar. My family has no musical background at all. It was like, I'll stick my fingers up and I'll show you how to do this. And just over time it became more exciting. I remember the very first time I tried to sing in front of someone I was completely stupefied with shyness. I got to go play in front of people and see what happens. And then it was like, alright, let's try a song.

How do you think you translated your visual art experience into the audible one?

I've always been about getting rid of the crap in my head. Just getting it... isn't every creative person? It became more direct and immediate. I'd be spending three hours on a drawing or a painting for days, two days, a week... but... but with writing and singing other people's songs you get that rage, that anger out of your system.

Were you an angry kid growing up at all? What were you like?

At one time I was a little bully, then I got bullied and I went into a shell. It took me years to get out of that. So I pretty much always felt like an outsider or a loner. I sort of still feel like that but the music has been sort of a therapy to become a different person. It's allowed me to change who I didn't like, what I didn't like about myself. There's still a lot of stuff I don't, but...

Your music has an undeniable integrity to it. Yet there are a lot of bands out there trying to do similar things that sound like crap or gimmicky. What's the trick to making it work in your opinion? How do you do it?

Because I'm genuine. I'm not trying to cheat anyone, you know? It's from my heart and I'm brought up in Newcastle which is sort of… it's a real down-to-earth area. If you try to bullshit people, you'll get slapped down.

Were you ever slapped down early on trying to this kind of music?

For a prolonged time it was just me and a mate trying to write tunes. We didn't have a clue what we were doing. We thought we were great at the time but… it's just getting up those steps with self-confidence and what you're trying to do. There's always been moments, always been people telling you, "Why don't you get back into painting again?" If someone tells me you can't do that, I'm probably going to end up trying to do it. I've found it really hard to put into words what I've been doing. I struggle to order a drink at a bar, mumbling around. Music gives me a little bit of voice. Clarity and stuff.

There seems to be a whole movement of British Invasion sounding bands cropping up… in particular Little Barrie and James Hunter, who sounds like Sam Cooke. Why is the time so ripe for revitalization like this?

Maybe because there's so much bullshit in the world, everything is fake. Maybe that's a reason. People have subconsciously grown up listening to the stuff their parents listened to when they were kids. Or maybe it's just a movement against this sort of plastic, artificiality of everything.

How do you walk the line between paying tribute and overindulging?

For me it's most important where the song comes from, my little bubble, my little unit I live in. Songs that I write in my head first, I try and remove excess. That record was made the first time I'd ever been in a studio. It was really suited to that sixties sound. I'm so up for trying to figure out how to make out first than trying to push limits. It's just trying to get to that stage and being able to do that. Just a little foundation that record laid down.

Your first studio experience must have been interesting; from the bedroom to this serious studio in relatively no time.

Yeah. It was quite nuts, that whole round that time. The record company said they wanted to sign me and put me in the studio where The White Stripes had just finished recording *Elephant*. And I was like, "Christ almighty! What's going on here?" The record company said, "Do what you like." You go in and have creative control. I had to go and find a drummer, luckily I found a great one in my local [area]. I took it in my stride but the first day we go there, the producer was like, "Okay, what's the first song we're doing?" And I was like, "What the…" Because we hadn't even rehearsed the songs or anything. I had my demos as a reference point and the drummer just jammed out to a lot of decent backing tracks. It was pretty tense at times, but it's all experience. Next time I get into one, I might muck it up, I might twist it, it might lose that jagged edge it has to it.

Do you think those beginner dynamics added to that jaggedness?

I don't really think so. The characters there originally… three of us. Complete strangers trying to make some madman's music. I was so rusty as well. I had only been using an acoustic guitar for about a year and a half before that. It's taking a long time to get back into the swing with jamming with a band and stuff.

Tell me about the band.

I had met Johnny a few times with his original band around Nottingham. I asked, "Do you want to come do the record?"

Me and him do all the parts. And then he knew a guy who had been playing in his band as a bass player, he's joined now. So we're all mates now. We all feel like we've known each other for twenty years. I can't believe how easygoing everyone is as well.

In relation to your earlier comments about the plastic nature of current music, was it a conscious decision to record in analog?

For those years when I was sitting in a bedroom or jamming down at the local pubs with my friends, all we used to listen to were fifties records. Eddie Cochran nonstop, Coasters and stuff. We were all art students that didn't want to touch a computer, you know? I mean, people do some great stuff with computers but why don't people do *this* kind of stuff anymore? I was given the opportunity one day and I was like, "Let's go for it." That equipment is great. You can still… as The White Stripes have done, made such… the *Elephant* record, it is sharp sounding. Very contemporary, so you definitely push the limits with analog.

I love the more ballad-like "In Your Arms on My Mind," "I'll Come to You" and "She Changes Like the Weather." Are those the tunes that initially got noticed?

There were three. I think it was "I Can't Stand It." "I'll Come to You," which everyone says that demo version is better than the album recording, the one I did in my house. I'll have to play you those demos and you'll go, "Why the hell did you ever get a record deal?"

As far live performances, in relation to the slower numbers, you have some real rippers like "I Can't Stand It," "On a Promise," "Back in That Room," "Mrs. the Moraliser," and "I Want to Be Your Driver." Do you like playing those better?

I've been on tour for months now and I think the band is pretty cooking at the moment. I'm definitely, slowly, more comfortable with my presence as a front man. We're playing loads of new songs at the moment and everyone is singing their own songs as well when we get to play longer than a half hour. Four songwriters, four singers. It's morphing in different directions. I'd quite like to do a show reproducing ballads and stuff, like a more low-key show.

Are there any one or two songs that you're particularly proud of?

I don't know about patting myself on the back, but "Too Long for Her" has some special memories behind because it was co-written by my songwriting buddy at the time. And "Mrs. the Moraliser" because it came out of one of the first songs I ever wrote. And maybe "You Made It True" as well.

It wasn't so long ago that you were going to give up on music, right?

Yeah. I was right down on my luck, you know? And no job. I couldn't hold down a job. I couldn't really decide between art and music. Just bumming around with no cash. All the equipment was stolen and my band had broken up. I was sort of in the wilderness with this. That Christmas I had really sort of made a decision. I had a job and I was going to keep it as I'd already lasted three weeks and stuff. So I made this decision to work on this job and it feels like making this decision and my girlfriend sent off my demos and something happens, you know… I got that call one day.

Burt Bacharach

Interview by
Paul V. Griffith

American Songwriter,
January/February 2006

Some may know him as the man behind the swinging sounds of the *Austin Powers* soundtrack, but composer Burt Bacharach, along with partner and lyricist Hal David, has been placing songs in the pop charts for four decades. Bacharach, revered for exquisitely crafted melodies and lush arrangements, first hooked up with David in the late fifties at the Brill Building, where they were both working as songwriters. After joining forces, the pair would go on to craft a slew of memorable hits for artists such as Dionne Warwick, Gene Pitney, Tom Jones, Neil Diamond, and the Carpenters. A sampling of the Bacharach songbook includes "Raindrops Keep Falling on My Head," "Walk on By," "That's What Friends Are For," "(They Long to Be) Close to You" and "(There's) Always Something There to Remind Me." In 1998, Bacharach's collaboration with Elvis Costello on *Painted From Memory* helped reintroduce him to a younger generation of fans. In late 2005, Bacharach released *At This Time,* his first album to feature self-penned lyrics.

—Evan Schlansky

How does the process of songwriting work for you?

Well, this whole album is different than anything I've ever done. It's not to be compared to "This Guy's in Love With You." You see, I'm not writing songs; I'm writing music. These are not songs. These are statements. Some are political statements, some are… you've got to look at the titles. These are not songs, these are not normal songs. There are no songs here, nobody's singing from the beginning of the song to the end here. They are vocal interjections; they're instrumentals. They have vocal lines coming in. They're not to be compared to either an instrumental album or a song with a singer.

That said, you seem to be quoting yourself a lot on this record. Did you intend for it to be so self-referential?

There's a direct quote from "What the World Needs Now Is Love." I would like to think that it's a love record, and not a protest record, but that's how it is right now for so many of us in this world. These are excursions. These break forms. These break rules. Not that I haven't always broken rules writing songs. Whether it's five-bar phrases, three-bar phrases, or changing bar lines in popular songs. On this album we set out to make it adventuresome, make it passionate, and I didn't want it to sound like somebody else was writing besides me. I don't think about it.

This is your first album where you wrote lyrics; was there something you needed to get out?

There's something I've got to say at this point in my life. I'm not a twenty-four-year-old kid. I've never been political in my life; never written political songs. There are years that went by where I never voted. I just kept writing songs and music. The fact is that at this time in my life, I can't think whether somebody's going to like it. It happens to all be true. And this is the first time I've written lyrics. Of course I had something to say lyrically, too.

How did this project develop?

The record was made for Sony UK. That was the starting point. Robert Grant said, "Don't give me an album of ten pop songs. I don't want that. Here's some different stuff I've done from the past. It's exciting that you're doing these things with Dr. Dre." So that's where we went. If I was a writer, I'd be writing an op/ed piece, but music is my thing. And you know, if I turn off some people, I'd rather they be turned off than to turn off my feelings.

What influences your musical direction when you're writing songs?

It's not called songwriting; this is called composing. It's calling on all the craft you have, all the resources. From my exposure to jazz, my exposure to classical music, my classical study. So the rules are basically thrown out as far as the way one would be advised to write a song: You have a hook, you have a verse, and where's the chorus? I never abided by that anyway. Somebody would say, "Where's the chorus?" I don't care what part is the chorus. It's the third section, I call them "sections."

How did you come to work with Dr. Dre?

I didn't work with him; I worked with his loops. It was very inspirational to work with Dr. Dre's drum loops. The songs would never have been written without the loops. They restricted me and inspired me. They have a form. They have a structure. It's a four-bar loop. It's a bass line. You write over it. It governs what chords you use, where you go. It's very good discipline for me [to write like] that. The first things we wrote, "Please Explain" and "Go Ask Shakespeare," melodically, form-wise… they never would have happened without Dre's drum loop and bass. It's a different way of writing. It's not writing songs; it's writing music. [Dre and I] were going to make an album three years ago, and we never got to make it until we started two months ago. He gave me about seven drum loops and said, "See

what you can come up with." When I played it for him, they were just Polaroids of what it might be like.

So your inspiration was a combination of these loops with your dissatisfaction with the way things are in this country?

All you've got to do is listen to the first song on the record, "Please Explain." That was the first thing written. What is that saying to you lyrically? Where is the love, where did it go? That's not pointing the finger, really, at anybody. Not the President, not the Vice-President. All it's doing is saying, "These are not good times."

Walk us through your writing process for a piece on the new album, where you took a loop and wrote around it.

The last thing I wrote, "Where Did It Go?" It's got a drum loop that Prince Paul from the Black Eyed Peas gave me. So that was a foundation to work with. Then you structure it and you play with it and you get an instrumental theme and you see where it might be going, and you realize that you let the drum loop guide you through this process. See, the fact that I can orchestrate, the fact that I hear all these things in my head—when I write I hear what's playing it. I hear when the strings are going to play and when they're not. It's always been that way.

Is it different writing for yourself, for your voice, than it is writing for, say, Dionne Warwick?

I always wrote for Dionne because she was a fine singer. And we were recording her… every month, it seemed. Knowing what Dionne could sing, you'd write what Dionne could do. I [would've liked] to have made one album with her before it was all over, you know? You write for your artist when you can, but sometimes you just write a song. I wrote what was comfortable for my own voice.

I have a sixteen-year-old son, and I worry about what kind of world he'll be inheriting. Are those the kinds of thoughts that inspired this record?

When I was a young boy, growing up in New York City, I could ride the subway all by myself. It's all true! It all happened. The fact that I've got a nine-year-old and a twelve-year-old and a nineteen-year-old, and there's validity and honesty [with what I'm doing]… Probably, the end of the month, when I'm doing concerts with the Buffalo Symphony, I will name the people [I'm singing about] in "Where Did It Go." And if they throw things at me on stage, they throw things at me. Better that than to offend yourself. The support for the way this country's being run is pretty low.

I hear you asking lots of questions, but I don't hear any answers. What can be done about the violence and the other problems you see?

I don't have solutions to this situation. You could take "Who Are These People?" and look at it backwards and you may come up with, "Hey, we're talking about Al-Qaeda here, too." People pretending to pray and getting away with it. Like the Christian Coalition in this country, it's the same with Al-Qaeda.

Aaron Barker

Aaron Barker was born in San Antonio, Texas, and began his musical career in a "variety band" at the awkward age of thirteen. He stayed with his band for many years and played everything from Bob Wills to Bob Seger covers. His first attempt at his own song, "Baby Blue," recorded by George Strait on the *If You Ain't Lovin' You Ain't Livin'* album, went to number one in *Billboard*. Not knowing what this meant to his future, Barker continued to work in the band and played his original songs for anyone who would listen until he got his first check. One night after a long father-and-son talk, he wrote "Love Without End, Amen." Barker decided to see what would happen if he sent it to George Strait. Strait recorded it, and it stayed at number one on the *Billboard* country chart for five consecutive weeks.

After an unsuccessful record deal with Atlantic Records, Barker began writing again and landed two number one singles in a row on George Strait's *Easy Come Easy Go* album: "I'd Like to Have That One Back" and the title cut. Doug Supernaw released "Not Enough Hours in the Night." George Strait released "I Know She Still Loves Me," which can only be found on his boxed set along with four other great songs of Barker's. "I Can Still Make Cheyenne" (co-written with Erv Woolsey) was released by George Strait and went straight to the number one position. Barker has had several other artists cut his songs, such as Clay Walker's releases "Watch This" and "You're Beginning to Get to Me," Neal McCoy's "Love Happens Like That," Aaron Tippin's "I'm Leaving," and Lonestar's "What About Now."

—LISA WYSOCKY

Interview by Lisa Wysocky

HitWriters.com, 2005

Could you describe your musical background?

I started off playing in a rock band in San Antonio, Texas. San Antonio is a big military community… a lot of Air Force. My band played at the Air Force base. We had a great time with the basics down there, had a great audience—a captive audience every six weeks… about twenty thousand new kids. They liked us. As they went on to their tech schools, they would ask us to play. Over the years, that just expanded into playing nationally. But after eighteen years of that, I woke [up one day], thirty-five years old with spandex and big hair. I thought maybe I ought to try something different. And just in time, George Strait had heard some of the songs I was writing that I thought were more adult contemporary [than country]. I had grown up with a country background. I thought my songs were more A/C. But George liked them and started recording them. That was how I got out of the big-hair business and came up to write songs in Nashville.

What compelled you toward music?

First of all, I got married when I was sixteen and had a kid about a month and four days later. So I had a little boy and I was raising a family and I went to work at this truck stop, because it was open twenty-four hours so I could get the hours I needed to pay the rent and finish high school. I did finish high school, did a little bit of local college… community college in San Antonio in the fields of advertising and broadcasting, which I still enjoy a lot even now. But when a band came through the truck stop one night looking for a bass player, I jumped at it because changing truck tires all night in the rain is not a fun thing at all. So I joined that band soon as I could after high school, hit the road, and never looked back.

How did your career develop when you moved to Nashville?

When I came to Nashville, I came as an established songwriter. I already had two number one hits before I actually came to

Nashville. George Strait's management company had been trying to get me a record deal for years as an artist. I was pretty confident in that, because I had made a pretty good living singing for many years. But when I got into the record-making thing, I made the worst record ever made on Atlantic Records. In fact, myself and the Titanic both fared the same on the Atlantic thing. When they got into dying my hair, and dying my beard, and highlighting my hair, and buying my clothes at Banana Republic, I was *not* comfortable with the artist thing. And it was then that I felt so fortunate to be a songwriter—an established songwriter—because it's the best job in the whole music business. I didn't have to go out on the road anymore. When I go out now, it's to sing the songs I wrote that were hits and people recognize them. It is nothing but fun to perform. So being an artist was not supposed to be for me, and it took me a while to swallow that because that's what we all dream about—getting a record deal and being a star somewhere. I made a bad record and I knew it was bad and I knew that I could never work in country music. I'm not good at that. But I love writing and I have had the best singers in the business sing my songs. I feel like I'm in the best place for me, and exactly where I am supposed to be.

Who are some songwriters that influenced you early on?

I was highly inspired in the early seventies by Neil Diamond. He's the best singer/songwriter. He sings great, but he also writes great songs. Another writer [is] Paul Williams. They were both A/C writers, but I loved how they played words with melodies. It intrigued me. Playing in this rock 'n' roll band, we were singing everybody else's music. I realized that I was missing the chance to say something in these songs. All of my music had an undertone of rock 'n' roll or pop. It was what I was the most familiar with performing. But lyrically, I was saying a little more than what rock and pop was open to. And country has always been a great musical field for lyrical content and substance. So

I guess that's why it caught on so well. And George Strait was looking for some music with substance to it. So this music that I thought was A/C turned out to be pretty good country music.

Tell me about "Baby Blue," the George Strait hit in 1988.

I wrote the song "Baby Blue" on a band bus coming out of Oklahoma. It was just a melody that got in my mind and the

> *And it was then that I felt so fortunate to be a songwriter—an established songwriter—because it's the best job in the whole music business.*

words *baby blue* seemed to go with that melody. There were songs in my musical history growing up called "Baby Blue" by other bands and it's always been a magical term for me. I won't go into detail over the subject that inspired the lyrics, but it was what ultimately led me in the pursuit of finding the cure for cancer. It had a lot to do with that. In fact, performing, writing music—pretty much any income I have now—is used to support finding a cure for cancer. And "Baby Blue" has a lot of relativity to that subject, and I'm still very dedicated to that pursuit. That's what I do with 85 percent of my time now. That's as far as I'll go into where it came from.

How about "Love Without End, Amen?," another Strait hit in the late eighties?

When my son—the son I had when I was seventeen—turned sixteen, I gave him this sixty-nine [Chevy] Chevelle. It had a great engine, and he helped me [work on and restore the car] since he was fourteen so he would understand the

importance of the car and what made it work… so he would have a lot of respect for it. So his sixteenth birthday came and I put him in that car. And all the rules about "don't go farther east or west than that…" went in one ear and out the other. And before I knew it, I got that phone call that said, "Dad, I'm okay but I had a car wreck." Nobody got hurt but the tire came off and landed in the hood of a brand-new Porsche. It was just a mess. And I was pretty young and inexperienced about fathering. But that night, it occurred to me that I needed to be the dad. So that night we sat down and had our first real heart-to-heart father and son talk. So he went to bed and I stayed up on my knees somewhere between looking for guidance and asking God for help in this particular subject. And as usual, working with a guitar in my hands is kind of like therapy. I wrote this song, which I thought would be a bedroom song between myself and my son… and maybe the grandkids one day.

So it didn't hit you right away that this song could be commercial?

I had already had "Baby Blue" cut, and someone suggested I send that to George Strait. I thought never in a million years he would sing this song. It's between me and my son, and it's very personal. It turned out that maybe George could relate to it with his own son, and with a little alteration on the lyrics, it suited him just fine. I was actually writing it because I was wondering, "How do you be a father? Where do you learn it from?" I mean, you learn it from your father, but when it comes down to you and yourself, where does all this strength come from? So I wrote this song and the chorus to "Love Without End, Amen." I needed to say that, because I wanted my son to know that I really loved him and the restrictions I

placed on him were because I loved him. I just associate that with the melody and the song. I came up with a story that had profound impact on a lot of people. The mail I get back from it is what [makes] me proudest as a songwriter because it made me realize the power of what we're doing here. I like writing songs that get into people's cars and people's homes. It can be a powerful, powerful instrument.

Do you have any advice for aspiring songwriters?

If somebody came up and asked me, "How do I become a songwriter?," whether it was my son or somebody off the street, I would tell them the same thing: "Whether you write poetry or something musical, just do *something*. So many people are afraid of rejection, or having their copyright stolen, and the logistics of writing that they are afraid of taking the first step. I would encourage them to do *something*. Contact NSAI, BMI, ASCAP, SESAC… *somebody*… and get started. And

Did you have mentors to help you in the beginning and along the way?

I had so many friends to help me along the way… friends down in Texas who believed in me more than I did. They've all been a big help. Of course, the Woolsey Company, who got me the record deal and these songs to George Strait, has been a big help. As a writer, there's always someone out there whom I'm lucky enough to have connected with and still connect with once in awhile. Probably my closest friend [who is a songwriter] is Dean Dillon. We've gone through a lot together. We had a lot of good times and bad times together, so we write really well together. We connect really well when we write. The other one is Whitey Shafer, who is such a well-versed and disciplined writing genius. To be in his presence was one of the greatest gifts in my life. Dean Dillon and Whitey Shafer have been my songwriting mentors. They've been a big influence and help to me.

And as usual, working with a guitar in my hands is kind of like therapy.

study the craft. To be consistent for a long period of time, one should learn the craft of songwriting. It is a craft. It's a craft that's been practiced and improved upon for many, many years. [I'd tell them] to come out here to Nashville and get involved with the songwriting community and learn how to be consistent and learn what really makes a hit song. And not to rely so much on luck and just stumbling upon some inspiration that leads to a hit song. I've been very blessed to be a part of this community and to get involved with some of the best songwriters of our time. But that's what I would tell them to do—to pursue it and *do something*!

Beck

Musical chameleon and perpetual man-child Beck Hansen is one of America's most eclectic and imaginative songwriters. Born July 8, 1970, into a creative family (his father is string arranger David Campbell, and his grandfather Al Hansen was an important figure in the modernist Fluxus art movement) in the multicultural climes of downtown Los Angeles, Beck spent his early childhood messing around with tape machines and dabbling in poetry and collage. He developed a deep love for the blues and dropped out of high school in tenth grade to become a street performer.

He began writing his own material in earnest after a stint in the New York anti-folk scene in the late eighties. In 1993, he released the single "Loser," which grafted a surrealist rap to a Delta blues guitar riff. The song became a runaway hit and a subsequent slacker anthem. He signed to Geffen Records to release his debut album, *Mellow Gold*, which saw him offering surrealist portraits of the down-and-out life. In 1996, he teamed with Beastie Boys producers the Dust Brothers, who helped him craft his masterpiece, the block-rocking party record *Odelay*, featuring hits like "Where It's At" and "Devil's Haircut." Radiohead producer Nigel Godrich helped him compile an album of gently psychedelic gems, 1998's *Mutations*.

Beck switched tacks with 1999's decadent *Midnite Vultures*, which brimmed with futuristic party music. 2002's *Sea Change* was the hangover, a collection of somber, tear-stained relationship songs that featured his most straightforward lyrics to date. He returned to the barrio in 2005 with *Guero*, reuniting with his *Odelay* beat masters to produce another fine album of summer anthems and melodic mash-ups.

—EVAN SCHLANSKY

Interview by
Evan Schlansky

American Songwriter,
March/April 2005

People are calling *Guero* a return to *Odelay*.

Who's saying that? Journalists? Really? It's probably people who haven't heard it. I think they just hear that I'm working with the Dust Brothers and assume that. It's probably a bit of old and new. You can never really re-create the past. I mean, there's a certain way I sing, or play keyboard, and there's a certain kind of beat that me and the Dust Brothers like. But there's plenty of new stuff. I was trying to put more of an emotional layer on it. I wrote them over the last three or four years.

How would you describe the album?

Um… a makeshift, heart-and-soul record with big beats. I hope a few of the songs make people move, and a few of them… make them pause. Music should be pleasurable, you know? Hopefully people will enjoy it. If not, I'll try again on the next one. Maybe someone can get some ideas from it and take it somewhere "better." That's a big part of music. It's a big relay race, a big hand-off, sometimes. You take some old ideas and make some new ones.

What do you get out of collaborating with others?

There's this intangible thing, something happens when we work together. I enjoy it. It takes two to have a conversation

---

Music should be pleasurable, you know?

---

sometimes. One of the biggest things I get out of working with the Dust Brothers is it helps me not self-edit so much. Most of the time, I know what I want to do, or when I'm going in the right direction. But it's nice to bounce something off of somebody, whether it's a stupid idea or not. There are certain things that I would do that I'd say, "Oh, this is stupid. It's simple. It's too cute, it's trite." And they'd say, "No, it's great." And so I'd leave it there. Also they're just great with beats.

Was making this album a more enjoyable experience than making *Sea Change*?

It was a good experience… really easy. There were a lot of long hours in the studio, but we all know each other really well, so we're all speaking the same tongue. We did all the hard legwork with Odelay, getting to know each other. There are certain things we don't even have to say. I also worked with Tony Hoffer on a couple of songs, [but] mostly with the Dust.

You played most of the instruments yourself?

Yeah, mostly. That's the first time I've done that since *Odelay*. That may have something to do with the haphazard bass playing. It's somewhat reminiscent of the bass playing of yore. I played acoustic guitars, electrics, bass, not a lot of keyboards, vocals, a lot of percussion, a lot of hand clapping. Half of the songs have handclaps going all through them. I was into this idea of including more human sounds. In "Scarecrow," there's a haunting, high-pitched sound that goes through the whole thing. That's me singing through the echo effect. All the percussive-type stuff on there is just me yelling through the delay peddle *[he demonstrates, making some weird squawking noises into the phone, without a hint of self-consciousness]*, using the voice a lot on this record. Timbaland does a lot of that, too. A lot of the sounds, people are asking where he got that, what synth module was he using, but he just did it with his mouth. You hear something… it's easier to do it than try to find it.

Do you consider arranging a part of the songwriting process?

Yeah. They're all blank canvasses. So you're looking at a blank page, and you have to fill it in with something that's meaningful to you. You start with an idea of what the song's gonna be, and you usually end up somewhere else, like with "Rental Car." But I do want to do something that's just my own folly and directly coming out of me. That's probably gonna happen in the next year or two. It'll be pretty chaotic, messy, undisciplined. I think it's just gonna be a mess.

What's an "E-Pro"?

I don't know! I think it meant something at some point but no one remembers. We're working on songs, usually we're just working on stabs of ideas first, and they got called things for clerical purposes. Occasionally there's a fake name that stays. I had some other names for it, but that one lasted.

Tell me about "Que Onda Guero."

It's about growing up. It's a sort of watercolor, pen-and-ink drawing with a little bit of oil stick portrait of where I grew up. I grew up around Spanish-speaking people, billboards and radio stations. I was born down in the neighborhood, and the song relates to that. If you go to that neighborhood you'll see the song. The popsicle guys, the *vendorsa*, the ladies with the shopping carts, the peeled mangos. My friend Paulo does the voices. He would just say things you'd hear in the neighborhood. "Rental Car" started around the time of *Midnite Vultures*. The original idea was to take what was happening then, the Korn, Limp Bizkit kind of thing, and try to merge that with Austrian yodeling. Sort of Julie Andrews goes to Fred Durst's house. And then the song eventually morphed into this hand-clapping, summertime-on-the-road song. But there is that little bit when it just goes full metal and then ends up lederhosen.

I read you were into poetry as a kid.

We had a little thing we photocopied [that] we used to sell in stores. We were always doing projects… used to do performance stuff when I was around fourteen, my brother was twelve and we discovered the Velvet Underground, and Warhol and the Factory, so we were heavily influenced by that until we [got together with] a bunch of other kids. We'd get together to make art and record music. We had our own little Factory thing going on. I was more into lyrics, though, like Lou Reed and Sonic Youth. I liked Bukowski, Kerouac, Henry Miller… a lot of that stuff belonged to another time, but I definitely liked the aesthetic, the beauty of the raw imagery. There was something unpretentious about it. It was pretty romantic, but it had all this rough-hewn, down-in-the-grave kind of feeling—born out of experience.

How many songs would you guess you've written?

Definitely in the hundreds, multiple hundreds.

So, songs get stored in your head, and you use them later?

Yeah, it happens all the time. I had the title for *Guero* a long time, the concept. I file these things away. I think *Guero* has been there for years. It's just finding the right opportunity to come out.

What was your first song?

I think I had a song called "Bells Are Ringing." I was eleven, maybe. I wrote it on a calculator, a little Casio that had that sort of an electronic doorbell sound.

Do you remember what it was about?

[*Sings*] Bells are ringing, bells are ringing…[*sounds suspiciously like "Frère Jacques"*] Bells are ringing. I don't remember what else!

Do you write all the time?

Yeah, but a whole year can go by [without writing much]. When I have a spare moment, that's when I'll write. Like maybe half an hour, before I go to sleep.

Does it bother you if you're not writing?

I think things get bottled up. It was really frustrating at the end of the *Sea Change* tour; I was on the road for about thirteen months, and I was definitely feeling the need to get in and work on new things. It starts to weigh on you a bit. It's good to unload.

How do you come up with your imagery?

I think there are certain things you're trying to express, and then you try to think of the best way to express them. I'm usually looking for some way to do it where it's not something that's already been done to death. There's certain shopworn imagery that's really easy to use and gets the job done. But I look for ways to say probably the same things, but in different ways. I'll sort of file through my head and see what pops out. You just keep digging. It's like you put something into the computer and something comes out.

Do the words or music come first?

I do both. Sometimes I'll have a lyric idea and I'll just write it down. When I already have a melody in mind, it becomes a more finite situation, where you pick the words that work with the melody. It's like you're sticking a backpack on the song. You've got to get it so it's not too heavy, and it fits right.

How do you see your early lo-fi material when you look back on it now?

There are things I like. I like the sound a lot. Obviously I see a lot of humor in those songs. Mainly I was writing for friends of mine; they already knew my troubles. I didn't need to put *those* in songs. I mostly just wrote things that we all thought were funny. There was a rooming house I lived in with an old man, who was kind of curmudgeonly, kind of a loner, who just randomly berated people. [He was a] classic angry old man, and he burst into my room with a Taser gun one night. I'd write a song about that or something. Certain songs, I think, it kind of is what it is. Some of them were kind of half-baked, but that was the intention at the time. The idea was to just spew out things, see what happens. And I still try to hold to that, somewhat. I like a lot of it. Some of it's pretty wacky. I probably wouldn't do things quite the same way now. I usually try to scope a little farther and see what's behind the joke. I've found that even if you put something in a song that is sincere, and you put one or two funny lines in it, it probably means some people will dismiss it. They'll think you're not really being sincere.

Are you concerned with people getting your meaning?

I think maybe when I started I just thought everyone was gonna figure it out, and it was obvious. I started to realize some people thought I was being obtuse, or I wasn't saying anything. That's happened on a few occasions. There's definitely more to it. I mean what I say and I say what I mean. It's such a personal thing, it really is. There are songs that I've done that are very direct, but I do like that approach where you can take someone to a space, rather than just give them a laundry list of events. Make a bunch of colors and images and pictures and try to transmit an experience that couldn't really be explained in a situation where it's a direct basic line. Loneliness, or contentment—these kinds of things—to convey that, you can't always use traditional storytelling methods. You want words that cut through the basic experience and take you right to where that place is, mentally. That's what words are for; they're to be used. And you're always looking for ways to express things in a different way or a different combination of words and ideas. There aren't any rules. I just always did what felt right at the time.

On *Sea Change*, the lyrics became more straight-forward.

Yeah, I wanted to do that on that record, kind of like how a lot of the songs I was writing when I started out were. I started using certain sounds that turned on all these other images for me, and the lyrics started to reflect that, the sound of the record.

How do you view that album now?

I like it. It was the kind of record that I didn't feel totally confident about putting out, because I didn't think anyone would care about those kinds of things. I didn't want there to be anything selfish about it. But I had some encouragement, and it just eventually felt right. It was probably the right time to do an album like that. The songs were kind of

You want words that cut through the basic experience and take you right to where that place is, mentally. That's what words are for; they're to be used.

eating away in the background. Sometimes you have to put it down to get to the next thing, get it out of your pocket, your desk. Let it get outside and breathe.

Kind of feels like Bob Dylan's *Blood on the Tracks* in some ways…

Well… there's only one *Blood on the Tracks*, you know? I can't have my own. That one's more conversational. It has a real formal yet loose grandeur. There are a lot of dimensions to a record like *Blood on the Tracks*—it's got all these stories and mystery. I get a different feeling from *Sea Change* than that. I

see the songs as being more simplistic, like how Hank Williams can just wring so much pathos and intense feeling out of really simple songs.

Have you been able to talk to some of your idols about songwriting?

No, I wish. I've met some of them, but I've never gotten to talk to them about songwriting. It's usually an environment where there are a lot of people around and it's nothing more than a quick conversation, so it's not really the time or place. But yeah, I wish it were like that. I wish you could be the apprentice. I have mostly good impressions. Joni Mitchell… Neil Young I've done a few tours with—I find him to be so encouraging and generous, way more than anybody of that stature would need to be. He goes out of his way, and he's interested, you know? That's one of the things I've found; I met Dylan briefly, too, and I found [that both Neil and Bob] were interested, [but] they weren't being interesting. They were more interested in what you were doing, what was going on with you. It's a little strange.

John Bell
Widespread Panic

Interview by
Andy Tennille

American Songwriter,
May/June 2006

Widespread Panic's music incorporates a number of things, from bluegrass and southern rock to jazz, funk, and reggae. The band, comprised of vocalist John Bell, guitarist Mike Houser, drummer Todd Nance, keyboardist John Hermann, bassist Dave Schools, and percussionist Domingo Ortiz, dates back to 1983 and Athens, Georgia's fertile music scene. They released a series of records on the now-defunct Capricorn Records, from 1988's *Space Wrangler* to 1999's *'Til the Medicine Takes*, cementing a reputation as one of the hottest bands on the jam band scene along the way. In 2000 they formed their own record company, Widespread Records, and continued to release adventurous studio albums. In 2002, they were dealt a severe blow with the loss of founding member Mike Houser to pancreatic cancer. It was Houser's wish that the band continue and, with the addition of guitarist George McConnell, Widespread Panic continues to be a musical tour de force and one of the nation's top-selling touring acts. After a mediocre album, *Ball*, was released in 2004, Panic fired back in 2006 with the adventurous, well-recieved *Earth to America*.

—Evan Schlansky

Tell me a little bit about your own process as a songwriter. How do you work? Do you start with words or does the music come first when you're writing a song?

I'll take it whenever it pops up. Most of the time, I don't really try. Something catches my eye or my internal ear or internal eye and then, depending on where I am or what I'm doing, I might just jot it down so I won't forget it and then start building from there. Sometimes it's a melody line, sometimes it's maybe a catchphrase or a combination of words that just catches your ear. It could just be a theme, an analogy, or something like that that pops up in your head and you start from there.

Is it a multidraft process normally? I was talking to Jerry Joseph about this and he said that typically he writes the song and it's usually a first draft kind of experience, so he's always interested to talk to other songwriters who say they've been working on a song for seven years. I was interested to know what your process is as far as that goes.

Sometimes something will just pour right out of you and it's done in ten minutes, but I'd say for the most part, I go back in and examine the lyrics for more descriptive ways of saying things after my initial draft. For me, I'll normally get a feel of the song within the first half hour of sitting with it and then it's kind of a matter of putting the puzzle together in a way that's really reflecting the image of what I'm trying to convey—it's like there's an image or an idea or combination there coming through and then I want to report on it correctly. So for me, it's about listening to what I have and relaxing and letting other things pop in that are going to be slightly better ideas. If you're in a daydream kind of mode, the characters in the song start doing their own thing and you just report on that. There's a discovery process where you might have started out with one thing but it's really a door

leading to some other thing that's been bubbling in your subconscious. It's a little therapeutic along those regards.

Would you say that most of your songs are fiction or nonfiction?

They're fiction in the sense of you're working with metaphor and analogy. It's imagery that gets away from a narrative. It's more storytelling or a scene description as opposed to a narrative spewing an opinion. 'Cause for me, a song's dead if you're sitting there just giving your opinion in a pushy kind of way. I like songs with a story full of color and shapes and movement with music that supports the imagery—then all of a sudden you're giving people who listen to the music their own little picture to look at. It's like looking at a painting and getting to interpret it on your own. You can be attracted or repulsed. You keep the audience in the process there. I think if you're gonna actually explore the truth, it's best to do it… I don't even know if it's best but it's way more fun and, and I think there's a lot more life to the song if you do it through fiction.

Why is the word "I" so rare in your songs? I was trying to think of any first-person references in the Panic catalogue and could only come up with "Chilly Water."

Well, George Harrison kind of wrote the best first-person song with "I, Me, Mine" [*laughs*]. It is the starting place because basically your own personal storehouse of inspiration is all you really have to work with, but you can make a little effort to get away from *I* and *me* and *my* because it's a narcissistic way of presenting yourself and it leaves the audience a little farther removed. If there's a first-person perspective in my songs, it's usually assuming a character and not as opinion-filled as if you're taking on the exploration yourself. It's more like, "I'll go on this adventure and you can watch" kind of thing.

I wanted to get your thoughts about Mike Houser as a songwriter because one of the things I've found so interesting over the years is the two different approaches you guys had to songwriting.

Well, we went through our stages as a songwriting team. Basically, we started when we met in 1981. He had a few songs he had written. I had a bunch of songs I had written and I was performing in that little guy-and-guitar situation. So we started sharing those but immediately upon coming together we were writing songs together with either a piece shared from one of his songs and a piece there that I came up with. Sometimes, one of us would have a song without a bridge and we'd just kind of sit back and listen to it and the other one would offer up an idea to help finish the song or fill in the gap. Other times, Mikey might have some lyrics and I'd offer suggestions on what he had. So it was collaboration in its traditional form. We were very good about doing that. We were living together all the time, too, so that's where a tune like "Driving Song" comes from. It's a tune where it's hard to know where one of us ends and the other one takes over or something like that.

After a while, you do that enough and you get to a point where you want to start exercising your abilities individually and become hungry for a little alone time. With a little more success and being able to have our own places and our own families and stuff, some of the songs became more individualized. The collaboration would take place when we got the band together and would tweak the arrangement, make a few chord changes, or add a bridge. To me, that was pretty important, too, because there you get a taste of distinctive individual styles.

What about Jerry Joseph as a songwriter? When I talked with Dave [Schools] and Jerry, they said that collaborating on "Second Skin" and "Time Zones" was an experiment for them to write for you specifically in mind as the vocalist. It's an interesting proposition because Jerry Joseph is a songwriter who's very different in his approach to songwriting than you. Can you talk to me a little bit about your thoughts on Jerry as a songwriter and specifically these two songs—how you connected to them given that you didn't write the words but were going to be the one presenting them on stage?

After the time off we took, Dave said that he had a few tunes that Jerry had worked up with him with the idea that we could play them with the band. It was left open to me when the songs came to me to go ahead and fool with the words so they'd be comfortable for me to sing and so the image would come alive for me when I was singing them. At that point, the band jumped in on the arrangement and fiddled with them and lyrically I fiddled with the words just the way I would if I was editing myself.

With "Time Zone," which I thought was hip, there were references to *To Kill a Mockingbird*. So I went to the library and got the Cliffs Notes and the book because I thought that was really important and that some of the other verses should still tie in with that reference and I needed to discover what was going on there. So basically it was a collaboration where Dave and Jerry put something together and then brought it to the band and then we worked on it from there.

You guys cover a lot of different people's material, be it Jerry's or Danny Hutchens'; the list goes on and on. Is it difficult at times to sing someone else's words? What needs to be there for you to be able to connect to it?

When we do a Jerry tune like "Climb to Safety" or "North," it's like when you're a kid looking at somebody else's toy. When you go over to their house and play with their electric cars or something, you think how you'd really like to just jump in and experience that more than just watching. You want to get in there and experience it more subjectively and get behind the wheel and see how it feels. When it comes to covers, everybody in the band is like, "Yeah, let's get on that jungle gym and play, see what that's like."

I love listening to music and getting moved by the arrangement, the poetry involved, and wondering where the person's head was at the time they wrote it, or wondering if I'm getting the same meanings that they were getting when they were writing it. The next natural step to have more fun with the tune is to experience it by jumping into the driver's seat and taking it for a spin. You know, jumping into somebody else's skin, so to speak, and living that song from the inside.

Are there songs that you wrote early on in your career that you can't seem to connect to anymore when you sing them?

It's kind of like the way a kid draws. Adults can try but they're not going to be able to draw with the innocence that a little kid can. There are some tunes I've written that I still connect with because I see them as far as where they fell in the process of becoming the songwriter that I am. But they're in a form where it's not like I really have the urge to go back and edit them and tweak them and bring them up to the standard of songwriting that I would like to present now. They represent a place and time I was at in the past, so trying to change them wouldn't be right. It'd be like an adult trying to get back on the little kid's picture and embellish it, you know?

I've got a friend who did the *Ain't Life Grand* album cover—James Mickelopolis out of New Orleans. If you go back into his studio and you get to see some of his earlier stuff, the style is way different. Every time I step into his gallery, his technique is growing and flowing, and that's how you know he's evolving. That's kind of how I view some of the songs that have been around awhile.

There's one specific song that I've been enjoying off of _Earth to America_, and it's "From the Cradle." Can you tell me anything about the writing of the song? How it came together? Where did that lyrical inspiration come from?

That is 99, I'd say 100 percent, Todd.

Really?

Yeah, I remember I was transcribing the lyrics and really getting into the images that he had there. I did very, very little. I might have changed a couple words here and there just so I could fit them in rhythmically, but that one's all Todd. That's kind of neat that we are that kind of band where everybody can assume any role in the band. I probably can't play drums [*laughs*]…

But everyone's expected or at least given the opportunity to present ideas…

They're allowed the opportunity and nobody should feel pressed to be the only guy in a certain role, you know? Because that could put a lot of pressure on you, which might take a little fun out of the rock 'n' roll experience. When other people are out there having experiences and having their own take on things, when they can bring it to light poetically or lyrically, that should come out, too, because it just adds to the variety of moods and it's probably more reflective of the world we live in. Everybody's out there with their own experience.

One thing that freaked me out was when I was transcribing that song and really falling into the images, I asked, "Todd, did you write this after the hurricane in New Orleans, after the flooding?" And he said, "Nope." Maybe it was in my brain and it was being filtered through that, but that's what I was getting.

That's what I assumed, too, to be honest.

So there you go, it's happened before. Sometimes you'll write a song and be living it out five years later. It starts out

as fiction and then wow… it's right there standing next to you. Maybe there's some kind of premonition. I don't know where Todd was getting the images from, but that's what my little English report on it would have been like if I had to turn one in [*laughs*].

I really like the song and have enjoyed Todd's songwriting contributions over the last several albums. Was that a recent trend or has that been going on since he came on board twenty years ago?

Man, since the beginning. I remember before we even met him, when we knew he was coming to rehearse with us after Mikey had tracked him down and given him a call because they'd known each other in junior high school, Mikey still had something that Todd had written and I think it was more a free flow of words and ideas. But it was really heavy. I remember thinking, "Wow, there's some stuff here." It was one of those things where you go, "Okay, there's more to this guy than just a whiney drummer." Which he has never been.

If you could've written any song in music history, what would it be? I know it's a pretty daunting question…

It's an interesting question, though. Wow, you know as soon as I hang up I'm going to know [*laughs*]. There are some classics that I listen to because they're there for inspiration and because I'm just blown away by the way they come across with stuff. That'd be Van Morrison, Neil Young and Jimi Hendrix, Pink Floyd… you know, I'm more old school. Bob Marley. If there's one song that kind of blew me away lately, I think it's called "When God Made Me" off Neil Young's *Prairie Wind*. I just thought that was really hip.

What's the most personal song you've ever written?

That's the weird thing; they all feel more personal than others depending on how the mood is. Given certain circum-

stances—the time of year, that time of week, or what's going on in the world—all of a sudden, a tune will hit me and mess with me in a way that I never thought it would. We might have been playing the tune for ten years. I remember when Mikey passed away, all of a sudden there was something to read into every tune. Not just memories of playing them with him, but new meanings came out of a few songs that stirred new feelings. I guess at the moment, I'd say the last tune on this last record, "May Your Glass Be Filled." I put together a little Irish drinking song thing in memory of a good friend. It's fun when stuff comes through you. It's like you don't really feel like you wrote it. You kind of feel like it came through you and you were able to get out of the way. It's really hip because then you get to enjoy the tune like it's somebody else's. If you feel really good about it or proud about it, it's neat because it gives you the chance of feeling happy about yourself without worrying about it being an ego booster or something like that. I'm lucky when I can experience things in that way.

The Bellamy Brothers

photo courtesy Dean Dixon

Though Brooks & Dunn have surely given them a run for their money, the Bellamy Brothers remain the most successful country duo in country music history. Since the mid-seventies—when they clinched their first number one pop hit ("Let Your Love Flow")—the Florida-born and raised David and Howard Bellamy have been churning out everything from radio-friendly country and southern rock to reggae and traditional country fare. Growing up, in addition to the country music they heard in their house, the Bellamys were fascinated by the calypso music of the Caribbean islands. However, the Beatles and the Everly Brothers provided a solid rock 'n' roll foundation, and George Jones and Merle Haggard confirmed their love and devotion for country music, which they would draw on for inspiration for years to come. A decade after "Let Your Love Flow" broke through, the Bellamy Brothers penned a string of classics in the mid-to-late eighties, including "If I Said You Have a Beautiful Body (Would You Hold It Against Me)," "You Ain't Just Whistlin' Dixie," "Redneck Girl," "Sugar Daddy," and "For All the Wrong Reasons."

—DOUGLAS WATERMAN

Interview by
Vernell Hackett

American Songwriter,
January/February 1989

Where do you get your song ideas?

David: I think the best ideas I get are from observing and eavesdropping. I like to sit in a restaurant and hear people get into a fight or something because there's usually something that'll come out of it that I can use in a song. *Looking* for an idea is sometimes the worst thing you can do. The best things really are the ones you bump into.

Howard: My favorite thing to do is try and use a word that has never been used before. I used *priorities* and *naïve* on the latest album, which I don't think have ever been used before. It's not always easy to do.

David, is it true that you got your start in songwriting by making up lyrics to your sister's rock 'n' roll records?

David: I'd make up dirty lyrics or stupid lyrics, parodies of what I was hearing, which I think a lot of people do [starting out]. I remember trying to write, listening to Roger Miller when he first came out. "Dang Me" and "Chug-A-Lug." That stuff just killed me because he had a sense of humor—plus it was great music. Then I got into the Beatles and their songwriting, so that is some of the earlier stuff I remember about writing songs.

Do you guys always try to co-write with one another?

Howard: It really depends on the song. I think people end up co-writing because they need help; you have an idea, but you just can't finish it. So you could end up co-writing with anybody, not just your brother. Or David might show me a song, or I show him a song and one of us thinks it needs a bridge, so we'll write a bridge to it. A song is a very personal thing; it's like any kind of work. You don't want someone walking up going, "That's wrong, let's do it like this." So you don't interfere without being asked.

David: I contacted Don Schlitz and Bobby Braddock about co-writing. There are a lot of ways to write, and I don't think you should limit yourself to any one method. You might hit one that works better for you than another one. Co-writing was something that hadn't been done much… mainly because we have been touring for years and haven't been sitting in Nashville, so we've written more for our own way. I looked up some people I liked and we started talking and then got together to write. Howard and I wrote a song called "Get Your Priorities in Line," which was Howard's idea, but Don helped finish it. And then I had one called "Staying in Love," a kind of Spanish-sounding song that I just could not finish, and Don helped me finish that one.

And this song has had a special meaning for you with the death of your father?

Howard: It's a simple song but you look back and see the mistakes you've made and realize where you are now and wish you could correct those things, but no one can ever do that and no one can ever make your decisions for you. I took it to Don and David because I thought it was a great idea and I didn't want to screw it up. It was the first song the three of us wrote together and it was really fun. We wrote it [as well as] another song whose title I threw out to them in one afternoon. Things were really flowing that day and it was an interesting experience.

David: "Whistling Dixie" is probably one of my favorite songs but it was actually kind of spooky how I wrote it. I had not had much experience with what we call "channel writing." I later read an article where Merle Haggard talked about having a song happen to him like that. He said he had no idea where the idea came from, it just spilled out. He was on his bus and he just started singing it and Leona Williams wrote the words down. It came so fast. That's kind of what happened with "Dixie"; it just sort of fell out, and that was a real strange experience for me. I didn't really talk about it for a long time because I wasn't into metaphysics and I didn't know what was going on. I read a book on Van Morrison and he talked about the same thing happening. He called it "The Muse." Now I wish they would all happen like that!

Does your approach to songwriting differ drastically from your brother, Howard?

Howard: I've written things that weren't as serious but probably, in general, I'm more of a free spirit and when I feel good I'm out doing something else. When I get serious, I'll sit down and write a song. So in general that assessment is probably right.

David: I grew up listening to such a wide range of writers—Roger Miller, Ray Stevens, Bob Dylan, Van Morrison, Paul

> *A song is a very personal thing; it's like any kind of work. You don't want someone walking up going, "That's wrong, let's do it like this."*

Simon, Paul McCartney, Merle Haggard, Don McLean… I think all these people are unbelievable writers and I liked all of their styles. I don't see why you can't mix them together. It's like a good movie, a comedy-drama with a lot of different elements in it.

Are there some days where you are just too busy to write?

David: If you're going to endure as a writer you have to teach yourself that writing is the most important thing in your life and you have to discipline yourself to do that. Thank God for Sony Walkmans and that sort of thing, because you can just keep one by your side and go off and hum your melody and sing right into it so you don't forget it. I've gotten to the point where I'm kind of into "combat writing." That's where I just pull out a piece of paper and try to write any place, with no instrument. I find it easier to do under conditions where we are traveling or touring. It's something you have to adapt to. Songwriting is the one most important things for us creatively and financially, so it's become the real center of what we do and you just got to adapt it to the way you travel.

Are you open to outside material?

David: A lot of people are way off base when they pitch to us. We find that when you go around to publishing companies in Nashville, they just seem to play the same thing for everybody. But occasionally, you'll get somebody that really gets your direction. The worst thing is somebody who will pitch us songs that we've already done. One about a hippie or a tongue-in-cheek song. We haven't been around in awhile, but now I'd guess they would pitch us all Southwestern songs because of "Santa Fe."

Dierks Bentley

Interview by
Paul V. Griffith

American Songwriter,
September/October 2005

It's hard to imagine that just a few years ago, pitch sheets circulated to Nashville's songwriting community said of Bentley: "Yeah, Dierks is his first name and he's not changing it." The first name is a family one, and young Dierks was a Hank Williams and George Strait fan growing up in Arizona, where he began playing electric guitar at age thirteen.

When a friend of Bentley played him an obscure Hank Williams, Jr., album cut, 1990's "Man to Man," about a cosmic connection between a son and his late father, Dierks pretty much switched his allegiance from pop, rock, and disco to country. "That moment really changed my whole perspective," Bentley says today. "Everything just clicked. I just knew I loved country music."

By age nineteen, he had moved to Nashville, where he snagged an ideal day job—scanning old TV and film footage for country acts at The Nashville Network (TNN). He applied the knowledge he'd gained from watching his heroes on rare concert footage to his own music and songwriting. A publishing deal followed, then a recording contract with Capitol Nashville.

"What Was I Thinkin'?" was a highly successful first single on country radio and the album *Dierks Bentley* came out in 2003. *Modern Day Drifter* followed in 2005, and *Long Trip Alone*, with the single "Every Mile a Memory," in 2006.

—PHIL SWEETLAND

Do you remember the first song you wrote?

The first song I wrote… I was seventeen, and I put my words to a Charlie Daniels song. That's how it started. I remember the first time I had the nerve to play them for someone. I was answering phones for a publishing company in Nashville, and I had a bunch of songs I thought were pretty good. You know how you type your songs up and you think they're pretty good? You put them in a three-ring binder and you treat them like they're pieces of gold. At the end of the week, some of the songwriters that worked there invited me to come upstairs and have a drink. They were going to play some songs, and maybe I could play a song I'd written. So we all sat in a circle, and the guitar came around to me. And I played a song that had gotten a good response from my family, and my friends all thought it was pretty good. I got done, and one person said, "Man, I never really got the hook on that song; I never really got that." And another said: "Yeah, it took you forever to get to the chorus." And it was, like, semi-devastating. Then this guy said, "You've got a long way to go; you need to write about five hundred songs, then give me a call, and I'll write with you." Five hundred songs! I thought the guy was just being an asshole, but he was just trying to help me. You've got to write 'em and just throw 'em away. Don't take 'em too personally and be ready to let go of 'em. Let 'em be beaten up. Let people get on it and just let it go where it needs to go. That was a good lesson.

Who are your favorite songwriters and why?

One of my favorites is Brett Beavers. He's my producer, but he's my songwriting buddy first and foremost. First when we were getting together to write songs, we both really clicked songwriting-wise because we both had the same appreciation. The guys I write best with are the guys that have the same appreciation for the kind of country music I like. We like the same stuff that's out there, and it doesn't matter what genre as long as you're coming from the same spot. We both come from loving more traditional country music. We clicked together. I love his melodies and I love his ideas. We were making demos that sounded really good, and I wanted him to produce my records. That's how that came about. Another guy I write with a bunch is Deric Ruttan, and he's great. Mark Nessler has always been one of my favorite songwriters.

How did you meet Brett?

I made a record on my own in 1999. We were playing down in this little bar, and my drummer took my CD over to Sony/Tree Music. Long story short, I ended up getting a publishing deal with Sony/Tree and he wrote for them, so we met through the publishing company. The plugger said, "I think you need to write with this guy."

I notice a lot of songs on *Modern Day Drifter* are team-written. Do you write by yourself?

My first two records I wrote by myself. This record, I leaned more on co-writing. The stakes are a little higher [now], and there's no time to mess around. There are two or three guys you know you can get it done with. I never wanted to write a great song just to write a great song; it's got to fit me. I may be writing with someone and they think it's going to be a song on my record, but I know halfway through that it might be a great song, but it's not going to be for me. "Let's let the song take it where it needs to go," [but it might not be for me]. The second record we had about a year, but this time I had to lean on Brett a lot.

How do you start a song? Are they out there fully formed? Do they just fall on you? Do you piece them together?

My favorite songs are the ones that just start out of nothing and there's no plan. You get an idea, someone says something, or you just think of someone. A lot of my songs come from my emotions—emotions bring the first words. And

from there, I just try to write into a hook. I think Brett writes like that—he can kind of see the song out there—and I think I'm the opposite; I let the emotion take me where it needs to go.

Do you consider yourself an autobiographical songwriter? "Gonna Get There Someday," for example.

That song's a great example, because my mom's still living… she's doing fine. The health of my family is one of my greatest blessings. That song was not planned from the beginning. That line came to us, "We're gonna get there someday." We started off with that, and it kind of twisted toward the end. It's probably the least autobiographical song. The girlfriend stuff—that's autobiographical and emotional—but the stuff about the mom and dad, that's not. But it's in the vein of a great, classic country song, a well-written song. That's what makes country songs great… one of the things… that knife twist. It starts out that you lost your girl, but then the knife gets twisted around 180 degrees—it hurts.

Are you a geographical songwriter? How important is Phoenix to your writing? "Cab of My Truck," for example.

I think my sense of place is mostly Nashville. I've been in Nashville for eleven years. Most of my songs are written from relationships that I've been in, and those have happened in Nashville. I've always gotten my ass kicked in town. Struggles in relationships and music, like the Hank Jr. song—that's where most of my stuff comes from. In the end, most of my relationships have failed because of my passion for music.

Are there tricks to writing about sentimental stuff without coming off cheesy? Jamie Hartford, who contributes to your record, does this well.

The guys whose songs are on my records, the ones I didn't write, are guys that I hugely love. John Hartford is such a great songwriter. The songs I like—I put rock first, then country, blues, and folk. And that song doesn't have the perfect Nashville songwriter hook where every line connects to the line before it. But on a deeper level, every word is connected and works with what's around it. That song is a love song without being a love song. It doesn't spell it out like "Baby, I wanna"… whatever. You've got to listen to it. It's on a deeper level. "I see colors and I hear sound." It's a deeper level of the heart.

I know you're a fan of bluegrass. For people who might not hear it on *Drifter*, how has bluegrass influenced your writing? Is it a struggle to get Capitol to let you express your rootsy side? "Good Man Like Me," for instance.

I'm really lucky. I've got a record label that really lets me do my thing. But I'm sure if my thing wasn't working out very well, then there'd be some other influences coming in.

You're doing a lot of dates. Is it hard to write out on the road?

[Yes], it's hard to write out on the road. I put ideas together. I've got a book next to my bed. I've got a recorder in here [on my bus]. I've got my computer. I like to get it started, have 'em here, think about 'em, get 'em started, then take 'em back to Nashville and finish them. People put down the Nashville way of writing, but I really like it. I can call somebody and say, let's get together tomorrow; let's work on some stuff. You get time to think about it, then you go and make a new friend or see an old friend, get a cup of coffee, and just talk about life and fall into it and see where it takes you. I played the Opry with Bill Anderson the other night, and he's always in the mix. When it's all said and done, Bill has really made a place for himself. It's just incredible, the way he's kept his songwriting as current as he has. He's a great writer. And he's not getting cuts by telling his memories of the Grand Ole Opry, he's got Joe Nichols cuts.

Do you have any advice for our readers as far as picking a publisher?

Without being too choosy, you're trying to get somebody to pay you fifteen thousand dollars a year so you can quit your job. And [Sony/Tree] was the one and only company I visited. They offered me fifteen grand a year and I said, "Hell yeah." Give me anything so I can quit this other place and do music full time. Not just songwriting, but music—playing full time. I didn't have the luxury to pick and choose. There's always a trade off. With a big company you might be able to get paid a little more and there's a larger pool of people to write with, but with a small company, you might not get paid as much but you'll get a lot of attention and your songs will get more attention. When you're in a big place like Sony, you're competing with a lot of great songwriters who are on that label. It kind of goes both ways, and a lot of people I know move around. They'll have a big deal in one place then move to a smaller place. In the end it's really about the writer. Like with a record deal, just because you get a deal doesn't mean you're going to be a star. You've got to work even harder and push your agenda even more after you get a publishing deal or a record deal. You've got to keep writing songs and work with the song plugger. Offer suggestions about who you think the song would work for. You've got to work it, you know?

How do you get unstuck when writing?

Well, it happens to everyone—especially on the road. As I've said, it's hard out here. There's other business to be done. It's not just get up and play, then go back and be a gypsy and write songs. There are telephone calls to be made, radio stations to visit, signing with the fans, changing guitar strings, interviews... there's a lot of work to be done, and on top of that, you never sleep very well on the road anyway. I have to remind myself to write everyday, or at least tread water when it comes to my chops so that when I get back to Nashville and have a chance to write with other songwriters, [I'll have something to work with]. It's tough, because you never [have enough time], and you're always a student as a writer. It suffers on the road. It's like the musicians who are in town playing on demos. They're creating all the time and coming up with new ideas and sounds. You lose a little bit on the road, but I try to tread water by working on the craft and at least writing [some]. Probably not writing anything good, but at least writing.

If it wasn't your job, would you still write songs?

Yeah. It's a natural thing to do for me. Some people do it [as] therapy; I just like to write. Singing is my passion. I love to sing on stage. That's the fun part. But I like the work part, too. I like writing and singing stuff I wrote.

What are you reading?

I'm reading a C.S. Lewis book called *Mere Christianity*. It's really great because he writes the way you read. I also read Johnny Cash's biography, *The Man Called Cash*.

Is there a question I'm going to kick myself later for not asking?

I don't get a chance to talk about songwriting much, so that's great. It's usually like, "Where's Jake?" He's my dog. I'm just in awe that there are so many great songwriters in Nashville. People have different visions about what they see Nashville being, but for me, it's [about being among] the greatest songwriters in the world. Not guys who are just talented, but guys who are most driven craft-wise and are talented, too. They're all there; I love Nashville's songwriting community.

Matraca Berg

Interview by
Robert L. Doerschuk

American Songwriter,
May/June 2006

Matraca Berg was born and raised in Nashville, where creative juices were flowing at an early age. Her mother was a song plugger and session vocalist, and songwriters frequently visited the Berg household. She hooked up with Bobby Braddock ("He Stopped Loving Her Today") to write what would become her hit, "Faking Love," for T.G. Sheppard and Karen Brooks—which just so happened to reach the top spot in 1993. In 1990 Berg released her first album as an artist, *Lying to the Moon*, on MCA Records to critical acclaim, and she has gone on to release several other respected recording projects. Her primary success has come as an in-demand songwriter, writing hits for Suzy Bogguss, Patty Loveless, Trisha Yearwood, Reba McEntire, Pam Tillis, Deana Carter, Martina McBride, Gretchen Wilson, and a host of others. Berg is signed with Universal Music Publishing in Nashville, and her most recent cuts include "I Don't Feel Like Loving You Today" (Gretchen Wilson) and "That's Why we Call Each Other Baby" (Ashley Monroe).

—Douglas Waterman

Young writers come from far and wide to Nashville, but you started here, you left, and then you came back—perhaps for similar reasons but with fewer illusions?

Well, I was born here. My mother was in the music business. She was a backup singer, songwriter, song plugger… a jack of all trades. My aunt and uncle were also in the music business.

What was your mother's name?

Her name was Icie Calloway. Most of her friends were songwriters. She hung out with Sonny Throckmorton and Red Lane. I knew all these people when I was a very small child. Those were my heroes. I wanted to be them when I grew up. As soon as I was out of high school I knew enough people where I could hang out with my guitar and they wouldn't ask me to leave. Bobby Braddock heard me at a party. We were passing a guitar around. I played a song, and he wanted to write. He said, "We should write a song. I think you're good, especially for your age." So we wrote a song and it was a number one hit not long after that. So my first recorded and published song was a number one hit. The pressure was a bit much for an eighteen-year-old. I met a boy who had a band in Louisiana. I followed him down there and sang in his band and played keyboards—badly.

Did you watch your mother's friends write at your place?

They were just hanging out. Red Lane, who is a Hall of Fame songwriter, would put nursery rhymes to music and play them for me at the kitchen table. He'd make up the melodies as he went. But she was also a big fan of singer/songwriters. We had Kris Kristofferson and Mickey Newbury and Bobbie Gentry; I cut my teeth on all of them.

What early songs influenced you?

There was a Mickey Newbury song, I believe it's called "Sweet Memories." I could sing that one as a very small child,

in kindergarten and first grade. [Kris Kristofferson's] "Sunday Morning Coming Down." [Bobbie Gentry's] "Ode to Billie Joe" was a big one to me. I think [the Beatles'] "Yesterday" was the first song that really made me want to cry. I was too little to know why. It was kind of odd.

Do you remember the first time you tried to write a song?

I was in kindergarten. I was singing in the back seat of a car. My father was a grad student at Vanderbilt [University]. He was a physicist and he worked in the computer room they had there at the time. They used to have these big cardboard sheets, really thick paper, and he had some of it in the passenger side. I was singing in the back seat, making it up as I went, and he wrote it down.

Patsy Cline was your third cousin?

No, she was a distant cousin. My grandmother's mother was a Hensley. That was introduced very early in my career and it has sort of attained a mythical status. We're related, but I think it's more like fourth cousins.

Was there ever a time you wanted to do anything outside of music?

I wanted to be a journalist in high school. I also got into the theater. I moved back to Indiana for a couple of years in high school and lived with my father. I was involved with theater and I thought maybe that would be something, too. But writing has always been my passion. Singing is not. I was dragged kicking and screaming into singing.

When you came back from Louisiana, what steps did you take to get established? Were they different kinds of steps than a total stranger would have had to take?

Actually, I had to start over when I came back. I befriended a woman named Jane, who'd moved here from New York and

was just trying to get her foot in the door. We wrote some songs together. I just felt more comfortable being a little out of the main loop, because when I wrote that song with Bobby nobody really paid attention to me. They didn't think I was any kind of child genius and I totally understand why they would think that; I wrote it with Bobby Braddock, and he's a genius. I wanted to write with unknown people after that, just to get my own name out there.

You were obviously not intimidated by writing with famous writers.

No, they were friends of mine. Bobby is so generous. He has no ego. Writing with him is like *buttah*. He's fun and wide-open. I do remember writing with Harlan Howard in my early twenties, and that was very intimidating. Harlan pretty much takes the bull by the horns. You'd try to get a word in, but he was so incredibly fast that it was very intimidating to me because my process is very slow. I just felt better about having my name on something with somebody that nobody knew.

What were some of the songs that you and Harlan wrote?

Further down the road, in '99, we had a couple of years where we were writing some good stuff… when I was older and more established and I wasn't afraid to get my ass kicked by Harlan [*laughs*]. And he was still just as fast and just as sharp. You just had to paddle along and keep up. We had a song that Tricia Yearwood cut, called "Come Back When It Ain't Raining." I think that's the only thing we've had recorded, but we've got several out there.

What other writers affected your work?

I wrote most of my first record with Ronnie Samoset. We wrote "I'm That Kind of Girl" and "On Your Way Home," which was a Patty Loveless single a couple of years ago. We're like kindred spirits. We always said that if there's such

a thing as reincarnation with your brother and sister in another life… He was so encouraging and so open that I blossomed when I started writing with him. He was such a great cheerleader. He was struggling and I was struggling, and we were there for each other. That was the first time I felt comfortable going deeper into my experience as a writer, as opposed to just writing a hit song. He really believed in me as an artist and pushed me that way, too. That was the beginning of good work from me.

And some of that stays with you as you work today with up-and-coming writers and encourage them. Was there anyone else who left an impact on you?

Gary Harrison is so amazing. He's extremely fast, too. It's almost a stream-of-conscious way of writing. He's got this legal pad and he goes at it. He rips out a page and hands it to me, and I'm like, "Oh! What do we have here?"

He doesn't write with an instrument?

He can play, but yeah… it's hard to describe with Gary. It's almost like he channels stuff. You have to lift this and lift that from out of it. He's this "manly man" [*makes growling noises*]. The funny thing is, Ronnie's like that, too. But some of the words he puts together are pure poetry. I was enamored with some of his turns of phrase. When we wrote "Strawberry Wine" he said, "Just tell me what happened." I told him, and he wrote it down just to have it on paper. And he came up with "the fields have grown over now, years since they've seen a plow." It just blew my mind. It brought tears to my eyes because it was so dead-on.

One challenge with writing lyrics must be to keep the language colloquial or even conversational while putting just the right amount of poetry in there to elevate it a bit. Are you too easily distracted by a great metaphor?

I've done that. I've tried to write songs around a great metaphor—and failed. It's so odd, because it's such a strange thing that happens. It is almost a metaphysical process sometimes. And it takes care of itself, if you're committed to the song being what it's supposed to be; it seems to work itself out. When I try to be poetic [*laughs*], and romantic and dark, it just sounds like bullshit. But if you just write the song, you'll get that little gift, and it'll come out eventually.

"I Don't Feel Like Loving You Today," which Gretchen Wilson recorded, is about the most plain-spoken title you could imagine. In this song you take this mundane idea and, using everyday language that would be suited to someone like Gretchen to interpret, you come up with a powerfully emotional statement. When you write this sort of lyric, do you act scenes out in your head, as if two people were talking?

I don't have to act; I've lived it [*laughs*].

So it's based on life…

Absolutely.

…and characters. You create characters that any listener can identify with. It's personal, yet everyone should be able to put themselves into that picture.

Well, you know, I used to try to make sure it relates to everybody. But we're all human beings. We're all in our core—Dolly Parton called it "the God core"—the same. You don't have to try too hard to write about your experiences in such a way that other people can relate to them. The one song I thought nobody would relate to was "Strawberry Wine" because it was *so* autobiographical, right down to the farm. I

just thought, "That's my story. I'll have to record it because nobody else will." There you go.

So the songs on your albums are the ones that you feel are the most personal.

Yeah. The funny thing is that nearly every song on my first record was covered by somebody else.

When you came back to Nashville, what was it like as far as being a writer's community?

It was very different from what it is now. Marshall Chapman put it perfectly: She said the writing scene in Nashville in the late sixties and early seventies was like Paris in the twenties. It was beautiful. I lived it vicariously through hearing stories my mother would tell.

Maybe the food wasn't as good as it is now.

The food was *great!* That's a myth! That is not true! We just didn't have chicken in truffle and raspberry sauce, that's all. We had good Southern food. But it seemed like the songwriters had more of a vagabond/poet drive back then. Of course, people were crazier, too. I think it was more dysfunctional. They'd hang out and get drunk and pick each other's songs. They didn't come to work if they didn't want to. But the songs were really good.

Why did that change?

It was business—the corporatization of music. [*She gestures outside the door.*] Look at this building: We have cubicles. People come here from nine to five everyday. But they're also hardworking craftsmen. They go home to their children at the end of the day and make a decent living. It's a tradeoff, I guess.

The really influential writers, such as Kris Kristofferson, were far from corporate in their

mentalities. Even the very talented people today must be challenged to find whatever it is that might have inspired their forebears. You deal with that by writing mainly at home.

Yeah, I'm not good at coming to the publishing company and writing songs. A lot of younger people have told me they started dreaming of coming to Nashville back when Steve Earle and Nanci Griffith—Steve called it "the credibility scare" of the late eighties—were going on. A lot of these kids came here to be part of that. And when they got here, it wasn't here. That makes me sad.

It's like going to Haight-Ashbury in 1969.

Exactly [*laughs*], when the acid trips started going really bad.

Your songs are the standard for modern Nashville songwriting, whether you're being clinical or spiritual, whether it's about the meaning you can derive from the words or the strong hook or chord change that plants the music in the listener's head. Is it a double-edged sword to maintain commercial viability as well as artistic quality?

Well, my Gretchen single got only to twenty on the charts. The critics were raving about it. I'm really proud that I can do that, that I can write songs that I'm proud of and a good many of them are hits. Kristofferson had hits, too. Steve Earle had hits. People forget that Steve Earle was a hit act here in Nashville. It's getting harder. We're all feeling the pressure. But some great songs still slip through. And some great songwriters are doing commercials… It's getting to be more of a challenge because radio wants a lot of tempo, like Up With People [*laughs*]. There's a lot of that going on.

How much of what's going on in society, even in the news as well as in music, informs what you write?

World events are too overwhelming for me to write about right now. When I'm happy I write about the conflicts of my past because I can see them in a clear way. When I'm in the middle of a mess, I can't do it. I did write one song called "South of Heaven" with Sharon Vaughn and Troy Verges about the war, which is really more about mothers burying their children.

Has there been an evolution in your writing over the past ten or fifteen years?

It's changing a lot. I think "I Don't Feel Like Loving You Today" is a good indication. After Harlan died and Waylon died, and so did John [Cash] and June [Carter Cash], something happened to me. I just started digging in. I wanted a legacy. I wanted to make sure I was doing what I do in as pure a way as I can. I wanted to do some small part in keeping that music alive—not that this music is ever going to go away, but I want to at least keep a generation aware. That all sounds so pretentious, but I wanted to honor them and to explore the simplicity and the dignity of what they had done. I also wanted to challenge myself, because I was writing the same song over and over again for a while: up-tempo, woman power, whatever. I really loved it. I started listening to old Willie Nelson records and old Jessi Colter records and fell in love with that music all over again.

Was Cindy Walker an inspiration?

Well, the night I won my CMA Award for "Strawberry Wine" and I performed that night, she and Harlan Howard were inducted into the Hall of Fame. It was pure magic. I was levitating [*laughs*]. It couldn't have been more perfect for me.

Do you ever think about an artist who would do a good job of performing a song, even as you're writing it?

I never think about that while I'm writing a song. After "I Don't Feel Like Loving You Today," I was on the phone saying, "Gretchen Wilson needs to hear this. She's the only woman in town that can sing it." I rarely do that, but I knew that in my heart. Usually I just let it go where it's supposed to go.

When you do something as personal as creating a song, when you let it go, there's a bittersweet quality to that release because you don't know what's going to happen to it.

Yeah, a lot of my songs have my fingernail marks in them. That's where a publisher comes in handy, because I just give it to them and let them deal with it. I don't always know. I've been wrong about what I thought was the right casting for a song.

Do you have a typical work schedule? Do you wait for ideas to come to you, or do you set aside a block of time for work?

I do both. When I have a good pile of ideas, if I don't finish them I will have somebody in mind. If I'm stuck on something, I'll think, "You know, Gary would be great for this. He'd get me over this hump."

What do you do when the time has come to write?

I try not to talk on the phone. I try to freeze out the world for that morning or afternoon. I don't have any special rituals. I've read about writers that do, but I just walk my dog and drink my coffee.

Regarding Faith Hill's version of "You're Still Here," does that change your mood for the day?

It's a very painful song. Do you find yourself going into that character as you write?

Yeah, because I write about whatever happened to me, and you do have to relive some of that. You do carry it around with you for a little while. It's hard to break the spell of the song, especially that day. Jeff, my husband, says, "You've got that stare."

Maybe there's a tendency to shy away from that kind of stuff, considering what you have to go through?

Well, it's so gratifying to get it out, if you can. That's worth it. For years I've been trying to write a song about the death of my mother. Amy, whom I had written it with, had just lost her father, so it was just supposed to happen at that time. It's horrible. This is not even close to the pain, but I also lost my dog at thirteen, so it was heavy in the air. And it happened quickly. I'm real proud of it.

Do you write differently on that kind of material than you do on lighter material, such as "Eat at Joe's"?

It's different every time. I started "Eat at Joe's" when I was on a radio tour to promote my second record, in the backseat of a car while the promotion guy was driving. I saw a sign that said "Eat at Joe's" at some diner, and I came home and finished it with Gary. I wrote "I Don't Feel Like Loving You Today" in the car. I was having a hectic day. I think Jeff and I had a spat that morning. I was also missing Harlan really bad. I swear, that title just popped into my head. I wrote it down and I felt like Harlan was sitting in the car with me. I was missing him so bad, I probably was just holding on to that.

Big & Rich

*Interview by
Chris Neal*

American Songwriter,
January/February 2006

Who could have predicted the runaway success of Big & Rich?
Forgoing Nashville conventions in favor of doing whatever the
hell they feel like, the band has won over crossover crowds with
their mischievous sense of humor and harmony-laden hooks.
Big & Rich formed when ex-Lonestar singer John Rich hooked up with songwriter Kenny Alphin (aka Big Kenny) in Nashville in 1998. The pair saw one of their
early songs, "She's a Butterfly," recorded by Martina McBride in 2003, which
helped land them a deal with Warner Bros. Records. Their debut album, 2005's
Horse of a Different Color, turned heads for its contributions from hip-hop-and-
western pioneer Cowboy Troy. Big & Rich came back strong with 2006's *Comin'
to Your City.* Both albums reached the number one spot on the country charts and
respectable slots on the *Billboard 200.* Both artists continue to secure cuts with
other artists, produce albums, and publish music to keep their hands in nearly
every sector of the music business.

—EVAN SCHLANSKY

Your current single, "Comin' to Your City," includes the line "Put a little bang in your yin-yang." I've been wondering how I can, indeed, put a little bang in my yin-yang.

Big Kenny: I think, like religion, it's something that's kind of individual to everyone.

John Rich: Whatever gives you the biggest charge out of life is what you ought to do. For me and Kenny, what puts a little bang in our yin-yang is making music and performing, hanging out with our friends, and basically wringing every day out like a washrag. Pretty often nowadays, one of our friends or relatives is going six feet under, or something bad is happening to them—and something bad could happen to *us* at any time. So to put a little bang in your yin-yang means to kick your life up a notch. If you want to do that, come with us, because we've perfected that.

BK: We're comin' to your city…

JR: …to give you a little extra kick in the butt.

How do you sit down and write a song like that one?

BK: That was in that MasterCard "Priceless Edge" mentoring session we did in 2002. They brought fifty students from all around the world to Nashville. We sat down in rooms all over town with ten of them at a time, and they would observe John and I writing a song.

JR: We had two hours to write one.

BK: The way "Comin' to Your City" got started was, I'd ask everybody where they were from, and boom! Well, how about this: "We're comin' to your city?" And we took every town those kids were from…

JR: There are ten cities represented in the song. You can count 'em.

BK: And we talked about something special in those cities.

JR: Like this one girl was from Buffalo… I asked her, "What do you do in Buffalo for fun?" "Well, you go down to Chippewa Street. There're all these bars, and everybody gets drunk." I went, "Okay, so… 'Chippewa's where you go when you're up in Buffalo/Don't you know those Yankees drink enough to drown.'" Why would you talk about Jeff City, Missouri, in any song? Because there was a guy from Jefferson City, Missouri. Other than that, you would never write a song like that.

BK: Just like any song, it had a pretty real inspiration.

Given how busy you are, how do you find time to write now?

BK: Most of my writing just happens walking around, dreaming. Or I'll be in the shower, or I'll wake up with a song.

JR: I came up with an idea for a song last night. I think it's probably the same way for Kenny; you'll come up with a seed, a little fraction of an idea, a root, and you just kind of dwell on that for a while. Then one day when you've had enough rest, you'll write three or four songs in a couple of days—just knock 'em out. I can go for a couple of months without writing anything. All of a sudden, I'll start worrying: "God, I wonder if I can still write a song?" Then all of a sudden I'll wake up one morning, get a big cup of coffee, my brain wakes up, and it's like, *Wham!* I'll write ten or fifteen songs that month. It's always been that way with me.

BK: We write a lot on the bus, too. After a show, trying to chill out, we're just sitting around playing guitars and something happens. Or somebody brings up something that's been on their mind—one of those seeds John's been talking about. And all of a sudden, it just flies out.

JR: Kenny and I are a little bit different like that. After a show, that's how *Kenny* winds down. I can't. I have to wind down in a different kind of way.

BK: There's never any set way, though. We're definitely busy enough now that I don't write as much now as I did years ago, when all I had to do every day was try to get better as a songwriter. But the quality's definitely there now.

And it's always going on. There's always a song singing in my head. Always.

How do you know when a song is a Big & Rich song, or when you should pitch it to someone else?

JR: It's just an instinctive thing.

BK: I think if it grabs John and I both, it's a Big & Rich song.

JR: Plus a lot of the lyrics that we sing… there's no other artist in town that *would* sing them. I recall that at one point, "Wild West Show" and "Save a Horse (Ride a Cowboy)" were both pitched, hard, through Warner/Chappell [Music], and nobody would touch them. And thank God! We learned a lesson. I've gone through my catalog now, and there are about 140 songs I've put on hold and told 'em, "Do not pitch these songs, because they're potential Big & Rich songs." Having another hit in the bag is a lot bigger for us than having a hit on somebody else, as far as impact on the career.

How different is the demo of something like "Save a Horse" from the finished cut?

JR: "Save a Horse" *is* the demo.

BK: "Comin' to Your City" is the demo.

JR: "Wild West Show" is the demo, "Drinkin' 'Bout You" and "Deadwood Mountain" [both from *Horse of a Different Color*] are the demos. The demos were so good, we felt like they had magic on 'em, and we just remixed 'em. "Comin' to Your City" we didn't even re-sing, we didn't do nothin' to it. We just remixed it. It was tracked in probably a total of forty-five minutes to an hour… just *boom*.

Do you remember the first time you wrote together?

JR: Yep. October 9, 1998, would have been the first day.

BK: We wrote one the first day and were like, "Wow, that was pretty good. We ought to try that again."

JR: "How about tomorrow?" October 10 we wrote "I Pray for You."

BK: "I Pray for You" is the second song we wrote, and it's on this record.

John, I remember hearing "I Pray for You" on your [unreleased 2000] solo record. Why did you decide to revive it?

BK: It's a badass song.

JR: One, because it's one of our favorite songs we've ever written. Two, because it was released and never got its just desserts [Rich's version of "I Pray for You" reached No. 53 in 2000]. Three, it has a message to it that I think a lot of people kind of feel.

BK: And it's fun for us to sing together. It was one of the first times we realized the things we could do with our voices together, how his range and my range melded together. We played it at Merle Kilgore's funeral [at the Ryman Auditorium in Nashville, February 15, 2005]. Hank Williams, Jr., came up to us and went, "Man, what *is* that song?"

JR: He looked at us with a weeping look in his eyes and said, "Brothers, did you boys write that?" We said, "Yes sir, we sure did." He said, "I hope that's something you're thinking about putting out, because that got ol' Hank right here" [*puts a fist over his heart*]. We were like, "We've *gotta* cut this."

What in particular did you want to accomplish with *Comin' to Your City*?

BK: I think we wanted to do the same thing we'd done with the first album, and that was make an *album*. It's not just a collection of songs. We want it to ebb and flow; we want it to have a beginning and an end. This album definitely ends a whole lot different than it starts.

Song

There's something a little different on every track on the album.

JR: It's all country to me and Kenny, but there are little elements of all kinds of music that we like. It's like, you know, Johnny Cash was sitting around listening to Nine Inch Nails at one point. Think about it! It was okay for him to do it. He was a music lover. We're music lovers. We take little spices from here and there and make our own chili.

BK [*to Rich*]: That's nice.

JR: The album actually begins with probably the goofiest thing we've ever done, which is "Somebody's got to be unafraid to lead the freak parade" ["Freak Parade"]. That's for the kids. We've got a lot of little kids that love our music. I think they look at me, Kenny, Cowboy Troy, and [MuzikMafia's resident dwarf] Two-Foot Fred as cartoon characters, like living cartoons. And our music is so hooky and melodic, kids just love it. So we thought it'd be cool to put something on there for all the kids in the back of the car as they're heading off to school in the morning. They can just drive their parents crazy for about two years, until we do another album.

I'm hearing a disco influence on this record.

JR: Yeah, there is! [*Imitates four-on-the-floor disco beat with his mouth*] It's on "Comin' to Your City" and on a song called "Jalapeño." That has a breakdown that's a disco kind of breakdown. Hey man, the Bee Gees made some of the best music ever.

BK: Did they write some songs, or what? [*Sings*] "Ah, ah, ah, ah, stayin' alive, stayin' alive…"

JR: And there ain't a better groove alive.

BK: Rhythm is such a wonderful thing, a wonderful tool in writing. Rhythm alone can mesmerize.

JR: It's as good a hook as a lyric sometimes.

BK: If you find that right spot, it's like getting a full-body sonic massage.

JR: You just don't want it to end.

When other people cut your songs, do you ever worry that you might not like what they'll do with them?

JR: No, because I figure they're doing with it what they want to do with it.

BK: That's the risk you take as a songwriter. You know, "Yesterday," the Beatles song, has been recorded over a thousand times. Great songs typically stand on their own, although they *can* be messed up. But it never crossed my mind once.

JR: It's been rare for me to ever hear one of my songs recorded that I didn't like. The producers in Nashville, they don't *make* bad records, you know what I'm saying? I've heard some demos I didn't like—but not records. Like the Jason Aldean record ["Hicktown"], I think, sounds great. I would have done it a little bit different, but if we did *everything*, everything would sound like us.

How does it feel to have people eager to record anything you guys come up with?

JR: You come on our bus, first thing we're gonna do is make you a drink. If you don't like to drink, we'll pour you a Coca-Cola. We're gonna make you as comfortable as we can. We're hosts. We're helpers. So if some of our songs can help, if it's not something we're gonna record, if it's gonna help a new artist, man, they're welcome to it. I run into singers in this town that don't have record deals, hear 'em at a writers' night, and I tell 'em, "Look, all you need is some really good songs. Tell you what, I'll just send you a CD of about a hundred of my songs. Go through 'em, and if you like any of 'em, I'll have my engineer pull the Pro Tools file and you can go sing it and it won't cost you hardly anything." Just to help them out. People have actually gotten record deals that way, off some of my songs. I think that's being selfless and help-

ing people, and I believe that's why we're doing so well right now. It's coming back around.

What have you learned about the publishing business over the years?

JR: That it *can* be figured out. I've made some drastic errors in a couple of language things in contracts that, thank God, have been worked out now. But wow, it's really complicated. It takes a while to really understand how that money's getting split up and how it really works. Kenny and I have invested a substantial amount of money into new songwriters. He has some that he's signed on his own, I have some that I've signed on my own, and we have some that we've signed together—just people we believe in on one level or another.

BK: We've both gone through a bunch of contracts. We've both made a lot of mistakes and learned from them. So I would say we know over 100 percent more than we did at the beginning, just from jumping in elbow deep and going for it. In trying to help other writers, one of the things we do is try to keep it real simple. We make the contracts simple.

JR: Real simple. Like three pages.

BK: We can help out because we have a little money now, and that's a blessing.

JR: But you've gotta pull your weight. And if you don't, we can still be buddies, but…

BK: The ultimate lesson we learned here in Nashville is that it's up to the writers. Publishers can only do so much. The more relationships the writers make, the more they play their music, the more they expose their music, the better chance that something's gonna happen with it.

JR: Writers have gotta network.

BK: And the better you get, ultimately everything you want will come to you. You won't have to go out there trying to beat everybody's door down saying, "Look at me! Look at me!"

JR: I don't believe it's accurate when I hear writers say, "My publishing company sucks! I've gotten four cuts this year and they didn't get any of them! I got my own cuts!" Well, good, that's what you're *supposed* to do. Your publishing company is giving you a draw, giving you the ability to write songs for a living and not get a real job. They're working your catalog, but they're working a lot of other catalogs, too. It's like Kenny says, you've got to be proactive if you're gonna get the edge in this town.

Is there particular advice you usually give the people you sign?

JR: Work with people better than you. I've always tried to work with people that I considered better than myself.

BK: But you have to earn it. You've got to do something great yourself. You've got to get to the point where somebody better than you *wants* to work with you.

JR: It might be an incremental thing. Somebody better than me ten years ago was a baby writer, but they were still better than me.

BK: Everybody's learning stuff. You put any two writers together and I'll guarantee you there's a chord or a method of rhyming that one of them knows and the other one doesn't. Find a group of friends you're comfortable with, support each other, make music together—encourage each other. Write on your own… write with other people… stir it up every way you can possibly stir it up. Just focus on being great and let all the things you want come to you.

How many songs do you think you've written altogether?

BK: John knows *exactly* how many he's written.

JR: 908. I have them all in my computer, and I have them numbered.

How about you, Kenny?

BK: A lot.

JR: It's probably somewhere close to that.

BK: It doesn't seem important at this point to count them. What seems important is to create everything I can before I run into a tree.

JR [*to Kenny*]: Please don't do that, by the way. [*To me*] He rides his Harley everywhere, and every time I see him take off, I go, "God, please don't let Kenny run into a tree."

BK: One day about midway through the seventy-two Tuesday nights in a row that we played at the Pub of Love, I was driving through the intersection at Division Street and Twelfth Avenue when a car came flying through the red light, totaled my three-quarter-ton Dodge pickup truck, and busted my neck. I went through hell with that, but I realized that for some reason, something saved me. But you don't know when that meteor is gonna come out of nowhere and nail you, so I just think we have to make the most of the moments. I don't try to focus on that stuff, but I definitely realize it's there, and it affects the way I live my life. The moments to me are about creating and inspiring and love…

JR: …and getting a little bang in your yin-yang.

At this point, what goals do you have left?

JR: My goal is to have the biggest funeral ever. I actually had a dream about my funeral that I'll tell you about. I don't know how old I was when I died; I just knew I was dead. Could be tomorrow, but I think I would have to have been old. My funeral was at the stadium here in Nashville, and my casket was there and there were flowers everywhere. The whole funeral was a two-day music festival, and every artist that played, every song that was played, I had some impact on—whether it was somebody I helped get a record deal, a song I wrote, or somebody I introduced to somebody. They

all had a story. It was like a two-day musical eulogy. And I woke up from that and went, "Good God that was wild!" What a goal! Well, how do you get that funeral? You've got to help a lot of people make a lot of music.

Kenny, have you thought about your funeral?

BK: I know I want it to be a joyous occasion. I want it to be a celebration, and not a bunch of people getting together and crying about something.

JR: That's what I'm saying.

BK: Life ain't something to be mourned. You've gotta go through that, but get over it as quick as you can and be happy that we got this opportunity.

With that in mind, what's the most you can do? How far can you take Big & Rich?

JR: Tiananmen Square. We want to take our music around the world. We think that what we stand for, musically, could do that.

BK: And we want to create everything the great creator of the universe has in mind for us. Creative people—I think that's your caste in life: to make art in every form you can. I think music is the weapon of the future. I've never seen people get together around music and not be joyful about it, other than the occasional bar fight.

Clint Black

Interview by
Vernell Hackett

American Songwriter,
May/June 2004

When charismatic country musician Clint Black scored his first number one hit, "A Better Man," he became the first male country artist to reach the top of the charts with a debut single in fifteen years. Born in 1962 in Long Branch, New Jersey, Black grew up in Katy, Texas, where he began learning guitar and writing his first songs. He signed to RCA Nashville in 1988, and his debut album *Killin' Time* spawned the number one hits "Killin' Time," "Nobody's Home," and "Walkin' Away." The album went double platinum, and Black had similar success with the 1990 follow-up *Put Yourself In My Shoes*. He continued to record throughout the nineties, during which he was inducted into the Grand Ole Opry and won a Grammy for his part in the all-star collaboration "Same Old Train." 2004's *Spend My Time* collected Black's first batch of new songs in six years, followed by 2005's *Drinkin' Songs and Other Logic*. Black is a partner in Nashville's Equity Music, a venture which follows the "artist-friendly label" model that has been embraced recently by a handful of others.

—JEWLY HIGHT

Describe the process of picking songs on your album _Spend My Time_.

I had thirty-five songs I wanted to put on the album, then I narrowed it down to twenty, and from there I just had to start thinking about the song keys, tempos, and themes. I finally eliminated another eight from the running, which ended up getting it down to thirteen. Then it was just a matter of the thirteenth song I wrote by myself, [which] I decided to save for another time.

You continue your longstanding musical and co-writing relationship with Hayden Nicholas on this album. How did you meet, and what is your professional relationship with Nicholas like?

Hayden had an eight-track recorder in his garage and I needed to do a demo. The first song we did was "Nobody's Home" [from Black's debut album _Killin' Time_], so I took it and got a manager. Right about that time Hayden started playing gigs with me and he's been with me ever since. Together, we're a brain trust for all the songs I've written and recorded. So there's a shorthand there for thinking about what we don't have. I try not to repeat myself. There's a quickness there; we know what we have already, what I've recorded… so that's one thing. And I guess when you're doing something together for so long there is a comfort level with rejecting ideas. But a lot of it has to do with friendship—being real close with somebody after so many years and them being somebody you like to work with. It's a combination of all those things that make it natural.

What's important for an amateur songwriter to consider when co-writing?

It's a little awkward at first. Everybody has a different way of approaching writing a song, and a different bar for themselves as far as what is a great verse or line or melody. Some-times it's just a little bit of work to get into a groove. You have to be comfortable in saying, "That's good, but I don't know if it's great; let's keep trying."

What happens in a situation where your co-writer has a different songwriting approach?

I've written with some people who have different ways of approaching songwriting, and that really is challenging, which I don't mind. I enjoy a good challenge. But it takes a lot of work adapting to their style and getting them to adapt to my style. It's kind of like pulling myself toward the barrel and them toward the barrel so we can both get over it and be on the same page and be productive.

When you receive a song idea, where do you go from there? Do you have a notebook to record lyrics, or do you immediately begin picking on your guitar?

I've always got a notebook full of ideas, some fleshed out a little more than others. The way I approach a song is the way an actor approaches a scene in a movie. I have to find the truth of the "scene" and go from there. Also, the idea has to be profound enough to inspire the other ideas that have to come around it. I have to decide if it's an essential idea or is it just a starting point. And I'll look at the idea in those terms. Can it inspire the entire song or support something stronger?

Is there an example of a Clint Black tune that falls under those terms?

"A Bad Goodbye" was wide open for direction when I started writing it. When I started to think about it, I found the sadder meaning of a bad goodbye and started thinking, okay, if we're going to the sad part of a bad goodbye and somebody's leaving or not wanting to leave, there must still

be love there. I started thinking about what I would be feeling, and the emotions started to pour out and that's when the lyrics came.

What's a good example of a fun tune where you took this approach?

"If I Had a Mind To." We had written all these machine gun lines—those little two-line rhymes—without thinking of how they fit in. We decided that after we wrote them all down, we'd put them on index cards and lay them out on the table, and then start looking at them in relationship to how they would best work together. We didn't bog ourselves down in editing as we went; we just wrote them down as they came to us, sometimes laughing at some of the lines we came up with.

Does this approach work well with ballads?

With an emotional song... that needs to be about feelings, I tend to work more in trying to get myself to feel something. When Skip Ewing and I wrote "A Love She Can't Live Without," we tried to get to know this woman that was in that situation. She was fictional, so we had to create her back story.

Is it hard to keep your songwriting new and fresh?

That's the hard part. I think it has to start with a new way of saying things lyrically. And it has to feel like there's a spark in the room when you're writing it. There have been times when I was writing where it felt like something someone else had done, and I can't stand that. I have to try something else. I use different chords that will force my melody out of the box and give me a new inspiration for the song. If I'm trying to write G, C, D, it's hard to carve out a fresh melody. But I could add some color to those chords, by adding a ninth or sixth, instead of playing D, I'd play D7 or D11. By adding the different colors it helps to inspire a more unique sounding melody.

Do you have any advice to give to new songwriters?

Listen to everything from the past… listen to it all. Know how the great songs have said what they said, so you don't come around and say it again in the same way. At the same time, when you're writing a song, you just can't be thinking of other songs; you've got to get them out of your mind and concentrate on the song you are working on. Songwriters should look at song books and learn the different chords that people have used and different ways they used to get from one to the other and back again.

Everybody has a different way of approaching writing a song, and a different bar for themselves as far as what is a great verse or line or melody.

We had to define her in order to relate to her. We had to feel the sadness and the emotions of the relationship in order to tell the story of a woman who would no longer settle for less than love.

Black-Hawk

Like a comet, the trio BlackHawk came and went across the country sky far too quickly—particularly in the case of Van Stephenson, the Ohio native who died in 2001 at age 47.

The original lineup (Henry Paul, Stephenson, and Dave Robbins) first impacted country radio in 1993 with "Goodbye Says It All." That song only reached number eleven, perhaps because the band was still an unknown quantity. But those of us who had the privilege of seeing BlackHawk in those days won't soon forget them—the Civil War-style clothing worn by Henry Paul and the sheer musicianship and joy of Robbins and Stephenson on quirky hits that were always a little left of center but a joy to hear.

"Every Once in a While" came next, going to number two in the summer of 1994; "I Sure Can Smell the Rain," "Down in Flames," "That's Just About Right," "I'm Not Strong Enough to Say No," and "Like There Ain't No Yesterday" followed. In that period (1993–95), it appeared the band could do no wrong, yet they never quite got a number one at *Billboard*. By the time the post-"Achy Breaky Heart" and post-first Gulf War boom in country music ebbed in the mid-nineties, BlackHawk found it harder and harder to get on the radio.

All three members had been veterans of other groups—the Henry Paul Band for the leader—while Robbins and Stephenson were well-known Music Row songwriters when they teamed with the singer and mandolin player Paul to form BlackHawk. Their long-awaited comeback album is in the works.

—PHIL SWEETLAND

Interview by Kelly Delaney

American Songwriter,
May/June, 1997

What is the difference between writing for yourself now vs. writing for other recording artists?

Robbins: We used to say, "Hey, let's sit down and write a hit." You just try to write a commercial song without selling out too much. But writing for BlackHawk is a little different deal, trying to write stuff that lends itself to harmonies rather than just a wonderful melody that a solo artist can sing.

So there is more freedom and latitude in what you can write for yourself?

Paul: Most of what we've had success with has been on the cooler side of the fence. We just gravitate toward that because it satisfies a certain intellectual, musically speaking, sensibility.

That's more a characteristic of pop music, isn't it?

Stephenson: I think that's where we are coming from musically. We all have a good history in country music, but we all grew up listening to pop music. The two are intertwined in our songwriting. If it's a real traditional song, we can't sing it; you won't believe it if we sing it, because we're not that.

This really is a group of songwriters.

Stephenson: We sweat blood over what we record. We spend more of our energy writing and listening to songs [than anything else]. I have a little studio we take on the road and we do demos in our hotel room. We sit in hotel rooms 150 days a year with guitars, and writing is by far the most important thing when it comes to making a record.

Can you take more chances when you're writing your own songs to record?

Stephenson: I think you've got to. Look at "Strawberry Wine." That's a pretty chancy song. If you want to play it safe, you can. There are plenty of people who will let you do that. But I'm not afraid to take chances at all.

Talk about your early days as songwriters.

Robbins: When we started out, there were only a handful of artists who wrote their own material, or had anything to do with it. Everybody looked for songs. Very few people were involved with writing their own music. You sat down and wrote songs because everybody was looking for them. We also had a publisher, Bob Montgomery, who was very hands-on. He was a great song man and a writer himself, but we were just writing what we felt and all these people were recording them. That's what we did with BlackHawk; it was kind of a natural evolution.

What's an advantage of co-writing?

Stephenson: I used to write by myself when I first started. It would take forever. We get together and write a song in two or three hours. It would take two or three weeks by myself, and I still wouldn't know what I had. It's just really good to have other people there.

So, co-writing can speed up the rewriting process?

Paul: We wrote a song one day called "Good Love Gone Bad." I thought it was a great song. We came back the next day and Van says, "Let's call it 'Bad Love Gone Good'." As it turns out, that was a good call. We rewrote the chorus and John Anderson cut it, and we cut it on our second record. That's just part of learning how to write with someone—being sensitive to other people's ideas.

Are the great song men, publishers like Bob Montgomery, as prevalent today as they once were?

Stephenson: I don't think so. Most of the small companies have been swallowed up by the bigger publishers. You don't

> *If you want to play it safe, you can. There are plenty of people who will let you do that. But I'm not afraid to take chances at all.*

get that kind of personal attention. They also have song quotas now, which quite honestly are a damper on a writer's career—to have to boil his contribution down to numbers. I think it's the worst thing they ever did in this town.

That can result in mediocrity, because a writer is trying to meet his or her quota of completed and turned-in songs for the year?

Paul: If you compare Nashville to the National Football League, in a way, they just keep expanding. The talent pool is still the same, but there are more teams to go around and you're farming out songs to twice as many artists. Well, they all can't be good songs. People complain of stuff sounding alike—gee!

Giving writers song quotas is a bit like telling a traffic cop to give out so many tickets a month. Somebody might get one they don't deserve.

Robbins: When you love to write songs as we do and it's really a part of you, it can, to a certain degree, take the fun out of it. When you're under the gun, and it's November and you've still got ten more songs to write—I guess that's my biggest gripe about it.

So you guys must be pretty self-motivated to write great songs for yourselves.

Stephenson: Song quotas just add unneeded pressure to the whole situation. Nobody needs to stick a fire under us to get us to write. We know that in another fourteen months we're gonna be in the studio again. We want to be on our own records. If it doesn't add up to what's on a piece of paper in somebody's office, I'm sorry, but they're gonna get some last-minute tunes that ain't what they should be.

Is eavesdropping on conversations a good source of ideas for songs?

Paul: I've heard this said and I believe it's true. One of the most important qualities of being a songwriter is being a good listener. You'll hear great titles if you shut up and listen. People say them all the time.

Do you write down these ideas or trust your memory?

Stephenson: I write titles down. People give me business cards and I write titles down on them. My wallet's full of them right now. That's usually how songs come to me— in the form of titles.

Do you read much, and is that a stimulus?

Stephenson: Sure it is. Any time you put words in your head, you're gonna get stimulation from it. I read self-help books… because I need a lot of self-help!

Paul: It's awesome; it is to me. I read American literature. Dave is more up on the bestsellers.

Why don't each of you tell me what the hardest part of songwriting was for you early on.

Robbins: When I moved to this town, I didn't have a clue about lyric writing. I'd write all this keyboard stuff and just put anything I could think of to go with it that rhymed, but I

started listening and somewhere a light clicked on. I started contributing something that made the lyric clear or said it in a different way.

Stephenson: I used to write songs that wandered off into emotional things that probably only I was feeling and was going to get. To make it good is something I still chase.

> *One of the most important qualities of being a songwriter is being a good listener. You'll hear great titles if you shut up and listen.*

Paul: I learned that if you're going to be the character in a song, it's important to be someone who's likable. If you write a character into a song and his behavior is unattractive, basically, nobody's going to want to hear it anyway. That was a big breakthrough for me.

What about originality in a lyric?

Stephenson: There are just so many words and rhymes, like fire-desire and true-blue, that after you've written for a while and you've written so many songs with those words in them, you try to transcend that trap of using those easy rhymes.

Paul: Another thing, too… you don't want to write "cuts like a knife"… that's just a suggestion.

You've also been an outlet for great, unique songs by writers other than yourselves.

Robbins: "Just About Right" was Jeff Black's first cut. Hit songs sort of sit back, and a lot of people never get to hear them because they're just a little different.

Writing quality songs isn't easy, is it?

Paul: There's a very broad misconception of what Nashville will take for a song. People think country music is easy to write because they think in terms of history instead of the present or the future. Songs that are being written today are songs that are on the couches of every psychoanalyst in America. You've really got to go deep to get it over the fence.

Gary Burr

Sales on CDs that feature Gary Burr's songs tally over fifty million units. In his first band, his cronies said the guitarist had to write the songs. Burr was the guitarist… so he started to write some tunes. A recording artist in his own right, he has made an indelible mark as a songwriter in both the country and pop worlds. A few years after he had a hit with Juice Newton's "Love's Been a Little Bit Hard on Me"—and other cuts with Conway Twitty and The Oak Ridge Boys—Burr made the move from Connecticut to Nashville. He counts Ringo Starr, Desmond Child, Carole King, Richard Marx, Michael Bolton, Mary Chapin Carpenter, and Ed Robertson of Barenaked Ladies as co-writers/collaborators, and his songs have been recorded by Christina Aguilera, Clay Aiken, Kelly Clarkson, Ty Herndon, Tim McGraw, and LeAnn Rimes, among many others. Burr has garnered many accolades over the course of his career, including being named Songwriter of the Year—on three separate occasions—by ASCAP, *Billboard*, and Nashville Songwriters Association International (NSAI). A recent noteworthy Burr single is "Nothing 'Bout Love Makes Sense" from LeAnn Rimes' *This Woman* album (2005).

—DOUGLAS WATERMAN

Interview by
Kelly Delaney

American Songwriter,
May/June, 1995

What was the catalyst for you to pursue music?

The main reason I got into music was that when I was in high school, I broke my leg and was in a body cast for three months. I had to do something to keep the boredom away so I learned how to play guitar. When I got back on my feet, literally, I went to Woodstock. I sat there with a friend and we both sort of looked at each other and said, "We've got to do this." So we went back and started a band.

Talk about some of the first bands that you played in. Were you the sole songwriter in these bands?

I think I was lucky enough to have sort of a natural feel for it because the people I was emulating were very good at it. They were very structure-oriented. Those first bands I was in… I played with some people who wrote songs that were very unstructured and I felt the difference in which type the audience liked, which was easier to play and easier to remember, and that helped me stick to the more traditional format of writing songs. I was lucky. No one ever sat me down and said, "Here's how you write a song." It always struck me as obvious.

Is songwriting something that can be taught?

I think you can teach anyone to be a songwriter. But whether you'll like the songs, that depends… just because you have the tools doesn't mean you can build a boat.

You had some early success as a professional songwriter with hits for The Oak Ridge Boys and Juice Newton. But after that, things cooled pretty quickly. Did this deter your efforts at all?

The first song I ever had cut was a big pop hit and the second song was a number one country song. So after that I pretty much figured this is an easy industry—two out of the box, boom, two hits. No problem. Then I settled in for about two

years of dust on the telephone and realized you're only as good as your last chart position. That's when I hunkered down and figured it was going to be a job, not just a flash.

Did any one thing trigger this cold spell?

At that time, I was sort of moving up in technology and bought a whole bunch of toys I thought were going to make me a songwriter. I had all the drum machines, the sequencers and synthesizers, and basically for two years I just had an awful lot of fun recording these tiny nuggets of crap. That's all they were. There weren't any songs. I was so excited about the process and this whole new discovery that I was like Ben Franklin and the key just started sparking. I wasn't even finishing the songs before I was putting the bass parts on. My publisher [Bob Montgomery of House of Gold] at the time sat me down and said, "You know, since you put in that studio at your house, how can you see over the toilet rail?" He had a lot of colorful euphemisms for it, but basically he was telling me that I was not doing the level of work that he would have liked. Bob could be a very blunt man and he shook me out of that. Basically I scrapped all that stuff, picked up an acoustic guitar, and figured that if I couldn't write it and play it on an acoustic guitar, it shouldn't be [written].

What other kinds of direction did you receive from your publisher?

I wrote a lot of up-tempo songs, and if I had a ballad there was basically bizarre psychodrama like, "He loved her. He lost her. He shot her." My publisher said, "Just once, if you'd write a positive love song, you might have a career. Have you considered that?" Or, "Do you like wearing a hairnet and serving ice cream?" I said I'd give it a try. So I wrote one positive ballad and turned it in. It got recorded and went to number one. And I didn't write another positive ballad for about a year. He kept saying, "See, I thought we proved something here. I thought you would see that you did it. You made money. Do it again. Don't you want to make more money?" So I put away the psychodrama killer songs and started writing love ballads.

You stayed in Connecticut for a pretty good portion of your career. What prompted your move to Nashville in 1989?

I was really frustrated professionally up there because I knew that I was doing okay selling songs, but I also knew that there were a lot of facets of the industry that I wasn't able to tap into… that I would like to be a part of. I knew that I

> *I was lucky. No one ever sat me down and said, "Here's how you write a song."*

couldn't sing on other people's albums. I couldn't produce acts and I couldn't play at the nightclubs that I read about in the magazines. It's a very multidimensional business we're in, and I wanted to be a part of it all.

You've written a good bit with other top songwriters like Robert Ellis Orrall, Tom Shapiro, Don Schlitz, Victoria Shaw, and Bob DiPiero. When you consider a co-writing session, what qualities do you look for in a co-writer?

I've written some great successful songs with people where we've basically spent the afternoon playing Game Boy and sitting by the pool. There ain't nothing wrong with that. It's great to write with somebody who's really strong in all aspects of it because no matter what hurdle you run into, you know that somebody in the room is going to figure out a way to get over it. I try to be fairly structured in that I have to get out of the house otherwise I'll watch *Gilligan's*

Island all day. That's why I asked them to give me this office here at MCA. I was a solo writer in Connecticut and when I first came here I was a solo writer. I enjoy the process and I still try to set a certain amount of time a year aside to write by myself. The songs I write by myself are the ones I get up at three in the morning and jot down, or work on while I'm driving around.

Do you have any imparting words of wisdom for aspiring songwriters?

If you're really great and you're the best in your hometown, you owe it to yourself to come here. This is where everyone who is great in their town comes. This is the all-star game. The best players from every team come here and we try to play against each other. If you're the best—and it's not your Aunt Hilda telling you that you're the best—then you should come because you can't be a deep-sea fisherman in Kansas. If you want to be a songwriter, you should come to Nashville because this is where God planted the songwriter garden.

photo courtesy Rick and Janis Carnes

Rick & Janis Carnes

*Interview by
Lisa Wysocky*
HitWriters.com, 2005

During the Stax/Volt soul music boom in Memphis in the sixties, Rick Carnes found himself playing in an R&B band at every chicken joint and frat house in the southeastern United States. Determined not to have his career shortened by a stray bullet—he enrolled in Memphis State University. Rick met his future bride Janis, married, and somewhere along the way, he became enthralled with the idea that one could travel to Nashville and sell one's songs to music publishers; so that's what they did.

In 1983, Rick wrote Reba McEntire's first number one hit, "Can't Even Get the Blues No More," and co-wrote with Janis and Chip Harding three top ten hits for The Whites: "You Put the Blue in Me," "Hangin' Around," and "Pins and Needles." Rick also had success with album cuts on such artists as Conway Twitty, Karen Brooks, Loretta Lynn, Lacy J. Dalton, Johnny Rodriguez, Janie Fricke, Ronnie McDowell, T.G. Sheppard, Pam Tillis, and many others, in addition to three more Reba McEntire cuts.

In 1994, Rick signed an exclusive writing deal with peermusic. Some of his more recent activities include co-writing, with Steve Wariner, "Longneck Bottle," recorded by Garth Brooks; co-writing again with Wariner for the title track on Wariner's gold-selling album *Burnin' the Roadhouse Down*; and sticking to tried-and-true co-writing partners Wariner and Janis for a cut on Wariner's gold-selling 2000 Capitol Records release, *Two Teardrops*, entitled "If You Don't Know By Now."

—LISA WYSOCKY

What is your role at the Songwriters Guild of America, Rick?

Rick: I'm president of SGA. It's the nation's oldest songwriting organization. We've been around since 1931 and basically we're a songwriter protection organization. We lobby in Congress. We occasionally sue publishers when there's a dispute about royalty collections. That's basically what we do. We also have a Web site, songwritersguild.com, and we have forms where people can do song critiques, and we also have online chat sessions.

Where did you two meet?

Janis: We were living in Memphis at the time. I'm actually a Nashville native. I was born in Middle Tennessee, one of the few. I moved to Memphis and met Rick and actually got involved in a band. Rick had a band and we met at a party. And after the party, everybody was singing and he said, "Wait a minute, there's a voice in here." And then he went around and made everybody sing and then he said, "You're the voice; I want you to be in the band." So, we got started that way and eventually moved to Nashville. Why did we move to Nashville? Our dog was shot... I think that's it [*laughs*].

Rick: That didn't sit well with us. So we packed up and left.

Janis: We married in Memphis and moved to Nashville. My parents live here. It's a good place to come home to, so we started writing.

Were you writing songs at this point?

Rick: Actually, the way we ended up here as writers was that we were playing the Hyatt Regency in Memphis one night, and a guy came up to me. We were playing actually one of the few songs that we had written, and the guy waited until we took a break and came up to me and said, "Who has the publishing on that song?" And I said, "What do you mean?" And he said, "There are music publishers who own the rights

to songs." And I said, "Where are these people?" And he said, "Nashville." I got in the car and never looked back. At that point, I learned that you could sell songs to music publishers. I decided that's what I wanted to do for a living.

Janis: When we first came to Nashville to try it out, Rick had made two hundred tapes and was going to take them to every publishing company in town. He started out and said, "I'm going to leave"—I stayed at my mother's. Rick hit the biggest publishing companies first. He went to Tree. And he called me, I guess it was an hour later, and he says, "Janis, they want to sign me and they think that maybe they could get you a record deal." And I said, "Oh shut up." [*Laughs*]

Rick: She thought I was kidding.

Janis: I said, "When are you coming home?" He said, "No, I'm serious. They want to sign me." It was a real piece of luck with all of his tapes; he ended up at the first place he went.

How does the co-writing process work with you, and do you have a favorite song you've written together?

Janis: We call it co-fighting because when we sit down and write together...

Rick: Yeah, we sit down and open a book, start an argument. That's pretty much how it is. And if we can at some point get the argument resolved, we end up with a song. But most of the time, it just dissolves into an argument. We can't make up our minds or decide. That way, we come to a process where if we both agree on the song, it's going to be better.

Janis: There was a song Rick started... it [was] years ago... but I think that there was something going on maybe physically and I was in a lot of pain. Rick wrote this song—or actually started this song and we ended up finishing it together— called "Part of Me." It was sort of an I-hurt-when-you-hurt... I-feel-when-you-feel type of song. And that song still means a lot to me. And we did a duet on it when we were artists. It

was never released, but many of our things weren't. Anyway, that's mine.

Rick: I'll just go with hers 'cause it's easier. I've written so many songs it's impossible to think about one or the other. They are all really my babies and to distinguish between one or the other…

Janis: No, we've written a lot that I'm not proud about [*laughs*].

Rick: Well, there are some that I'm not proud about. I'll grant you that. And it's really embarrassing when you hear one on the radio. That's a problem.

So you started having some hits?

Rick: Well Janis got the first top ten record. She wrote a song…

Janis: Oddly [*laughs*], 'cause he was the writer, basically. But yeah, I got a song on Joe Stampley's album. It was called "After Hours." But our first song together…

Rick: Oh yeah. I got Reba McEntire's first number one song called "Can't Even Get the Blues No More." And that song has been really good to me. It just keeps earning money and people keep listening. And I think that it's because the song's based on a true story. You know the first verse… "I walked into the kitchen/The silverware's gone/ The furniture's missing/ Seems every time you leave me/You think of something worse." And apparently that must've happened to a lot of people because that song is very popular and has been going on for years. And then after that, we had a series of top ten songs together.

You had a lot of success with singles released by The Whites.

Janis: Oddly, we were on a label as artists and so when we wrote those, we would demo the songs. When we brought "You Put the Blue in Me" in, they said, "Nah, I don't think so. It's not going to be a single."

Rick: And then when The Whites put it out, it was a big hit. And then we brought them "Hangin' Around," and they said…

Janis: Nah, I don't think so.

Rick: And then The Whites put it out and it was a big hit. Then we brought them "Pins and Needles." And they said, "We've been wrong two times, so maybe you're right this time." And they took it out to California and played it for a bunch of people [there] who said, "That may be a hit." So they came back and they said, "We don't think it's a hit."

Janis: By that time, we had already pitched it to The Whites and Reba McEntire.

Rick: Well, Reba cut it and The Whites cut it.

Janis: And then, they told us that we should cut it. But by then, it was too late. We did do a record on it.

Tell me about the song "Longneck Bottle."

Rick: "Longneck Bottle" was a song that I had been working on for years. Janis and I wrote it a couple of times and could never get it done. It was one of those songs that we argued about and never finished. And then one day I was walking out the door to write with Steve Warnier and Janis says, "You know, I think you should run that longneck bottle idea by Steve."

Janis: I said, "I still think that's a hit song."

Rick: And I said, "Whatever." So Steve and I are sitting down to write, and we really couldn't think of anything to write. We really just wanted to go out and play basketball. And so I said, "You know, when Janis and I were walking out the door she said run this song by you." So I played him the chorus. And he instantaneously said, "You oughta do this for the verse." And I said, "Yeah, that's right." And so an eighteen-year-old problem was solved instantly, and a few minutes later we had a hit song. And it worked out when Garth cut that. That was the first single off the *Sevens* album, which sold something like twenty million copies. And recently, we had Alabama's "It All Goes South," which was the title cut. John Jarvis and Janis and I co-wrote that.

Janis: That was, as I recall, the first country-rap thing I remember anyone doing. We were trying to mess around with that in doing a rap song. We did a lot of research on that, too… read a lot of books on Southern-isms. Of course, with both of us being born and reared in the South, we knew quite a few already.

You have been on a lot of different labels, right?

Rick: We were on four labels. We were on…

Janis: I was first on RCA Nashville by myself. Then Rick and I were together.

Rick: Then Elektra/Asylum. Then Warner Bros. Then MCA.

Did being an artist take away from writing time?

Janis: Well, I think the reason we did the whole artist thing was [because] we thought it would *help* with our songwriting. But it didn't. It took so much of our time trying to be artists… We were with Jimmy Bowen for years. He was head of all the labels but one, and we once had a song that was going to be cut by Juice Newton.

Rick: Yeah, it was following "Angel of the Morning."

Janis: And it was one of his favorite songs on us. And we thought, gosh, we should have the Juice Newton cut 'cause we are nobody. And we thought it would actually help us as artists. And they were going in and they were actually writing charts on the song and Jimmy Bowen called us in and said that we were not artists if we were willing to give up our songs. And he took it back because of the licensing. And it didn't help us as songwriters.

Rick: It did, however, in terms of the writing process, make us understand the difference between writing a good song and writing a good song for an artist. The difference is that you can write a good song but it doesn't make them sound great.

So then it's not going to work. You have to tailor the song around what the artist wants to say and how they are going to say it, the vocal range, and so forth. So essentially, if you are pitching to a hardcore country artist, you are not going to write something that stretches the boundaries 'cause you don't want to step outside their usual genre. So you have to really tailor the songs and that gets to be a challenge.

Do you have any advice for upcoming songwriters?

Janis: We learned some good things from Jimmy Bowen. Some good, some bad [*laughs*]. But he told us to learn how to pick our critics. And that's very important. Find someone you admire or appreciate, and listen to them. And that helped a lot 'cause in the songwriting business, there are a lot of critics.

Rick: The world is full of critics.

Janis: And you do have to learn how to accept criticism…

Rick: Except between each other.

Janis: We've never been able to… [*laughs*]… we used to go into the studio and someone would be singing and Jimmy Bowen would call us in and say, "We've got to do something. Find some sort of way to mediate between you two because the musicians are afraid that you are getting a divorce and it's scaring everyone." I mean, we used to just fight like cats and dogs and then we would go to lunch.

Deana Carter

*Interview by
Kristi Singer*

The Wilmington Star-News, *2003*

Deana Carter is simultaneously sultry and girlish, sweet-voiced and innocent-sounding, yet unabashedly sensual, womanly, and not unfamiliar with heartache. It matters not whether the Nashville expatriate is churning out truly country music, like she did on her sparkling 1996 debut, *Did I Shave My Legs For This?*, or veering into fresh folk-pop territory, like she did on her most recent album, 2005's *The Story of My Life*. There remains something uniquely, sincerely, and pleasingly Southern about Carter's delivery, even when pedal steel and fiddles are noticeably absent. Having Nashville session guitarist Fred Carter, Jr., for a father ensured that she was thoroughly immersed in music from a young age, though she'd already finished nursing school and turned thirty by the time she got a record deal, a moment hastened by Willie Nelson's invitation to perform at Farm Aid VII in 1994.

—JEWLY HIGHT

I read that you've been through quite a lot since 1998—you moved to Los Angeles, got divorced, signed a new deal—how did all these changes affect you as an artist?

The artist and the person in me are the same. So, as a person there were some pretty scary times, there were a lot of uncertainties. A lot of change when you're in the face of that much diversity when you're going from point A to point F, and B, C, D, and E are flying by. You can become concerned with the outcome. But if you follow your heart and do what you feel is best for you, you're going to be fine. So as far as the music goes, I'm really happy about the positive vibe in this album. Having been through all those changes that you might think make an artist write really dark music, I'm really surprised and excited at how positive and fun my records can turn out.

That was part of my next question—*I'm Just a Girl* seems very upbeat for having gone through those types of experiences, and I wondered if that reflects your attitude on life? Or did the songs just come out that way?

Honestly, it's just conducive to where I'm at and how I am as a person. I try to function every day looking on the bright side, finding the good in people and the good in life. It really does reflect how I am as a person, really trying to make light of all the heaviness. I guess the album does that. It addresses issues that are real—some controversial and some life experiences—and it's nice to have a sense of humor about those things and not take ourselves so seriously.

Where did you go to write these songs? Did they accumulate over time or did you go somewhere in particular to get creative energy?

I wrote a lot of it in Nashville. Living in L.A., I have a lot of different influences there, which is nice. Just seeing what Tom Petty and the Eagles and all my favorite artists write about is great: landmarks in California, heading out West, and all those things. It really was important and cool for me to realize that they're real things and places. I hadn't really put two-and-two together before. I thought Reseda was a street, I didn't realize that it was an area of California. You see landmarks that have been very significant in American music and it's been nice to kind of put those things in my songs, too.

From your perspective, what are some of the main themes running through the album?

Well, the album title is real basic. It's saying that I've been through all this stuff and I feel I've seen and done just about everything you can do, but it just goes back to the point that we are unique and beautiful and we're just the core of who we are, is the blessing. And we have to work harder on recognizing that as opposed to tearing ourselves apart and being hard on ourselves. *I'm Just a Girl* is saying I've done everything for a living—I've been a bartender, a waitress, I've cleaned toilets—I don't have a maid, I do my own laundry. I'm your average guy, basically. Just like everyone else. No matter how grandiose our lifestyle might seem we need to be the core of who we are every day. To support each other and help the world turn a little smoother. It's so true.

This war is so scary for everybody. I try every day to wake up and make a difference in the people I come in contact with that day, just for myself—being courteous, being nice, holding the door open, being patient, biting my tongue, trying to just go the extra mile so that I can... just help things run smoother. It seems like it's not panning out too well now. I think if we all did that, look at the wonderful world we'd live in... I love people. I look people in the eye and I take in their spirit. I try to look at people as the kid in us, all of us. And living... it is extended high school anyways. It never changes. I feel like you can relate to people so much better when you can address the child, the kid, in their spirit. *I'm*

Just a Girl is really about that. And if you apply it, if you try to look at people like big kids, adults are just big kids. It's all we are and you can relate to that a lot more.

How does it feel to tour with a war going on? Is that difficult?

It's tough. I think the challenge is to continue to be grateful for where we live and to continue to be grateful for an industry that brings a lot of pleasure and happiness to people. The challenge is when you see all the footage and the concerns. We all feel very heavy over it, I think. Whether you're for it or against, it's a heavy time. The challenge is to keep positive… try to feel that we are part of a bright spot in somebody's day if they're going to go to a show that night, or a little bit of escapism to try to continue with their lives. It's a heavy time right now.

"There's No Limit"—when did you write it and what inspired it?

I brought half of this album to Arista from Capitol, so that was one of the new ones I wrote after I signed with Arista. Randy Scruggs had mapped out the first half of the song and I just helped finish out the bridge part and the California influences.

I try to function every day looking on the bright side, finding the good in people and the good in life.

Are you surprised by its success?

You can't control trends in the market, that's impossible. So you just have to be, for me personally, I just have to be honest in my approach to the production, the writing and co-writing. You don't know where you're going to land. You just don't

ever know where the trends are going to go. I've just been fortunate that my music seems to strike a chord with a lot of people, with a lot of different demographics, which is great.

Tell me about "Liar."

It's nice to approach those things with a sense of humor, as heartbreaking as they can be and as trying. Just singing what you feel, singing what you feel like screaming is really fun sometimes.

I really like what you said once: "It's amazing how in touch I've become with my strength and at the things I've realized because of all this. When the blindness is gone, the decisions all weigh heavier because you understand the cost and the pain. But you also realize that you have choices. I used to think happiness was like the lottery, either you had the numbers or you didn't, but that's not so. Everybody can be happy if you're willing to work at it every day."

It's true. It just dawned on me one day. I went through a lot of therapy with my husband and worked on a lot of individual therapy, too. It's such a good thing because you realize the root of our problems with people is in our childhood and all the answers that we need are in our childhood. Once you start facing that and you deal with it, you're able to own and peel away all the layers of denial and stuff that you pile on top of the pain or whatever you've gone through. Our present situations, all of them, are results of choices, of how we reacted to different types of stimulation—emotional and physical—and all those kinds of things. And when I started going to therapy with [my husband], it's painful to pull away the layers and realize that sometimes people that you love in your family can be the most damaging because you have an adult and a child trying to interact on totally different levels.

Song

Anyway, I just realized through therapy that I do have choices. I don't have to be abused by anybody and I can control the outcome of how I deal with that. And it slowly turns your world around; it's really neat. It's heavy. I didn't want you to think I was going through any physical or sexual abuse or anything like that. But I have lived through a lot of harsh emotional situations, I guess. Like we all have. It would be so much easier to duke it out and deal with it. Then there's no baggage as opposed to emotionally being tortured or toyed with.

How long did you go to therapy?

We started as a couple, then we both went as individuals, which was so great and helpful. I think parents—I'm getting off on a whole 'nother subject here, but briefly—parents are people too, and they're doing the best they can. I'm not a parent so I'm not going to be real judgmental, but they're trying the best that they can and they're human beings, so I try to be a little open-minded about it.

You have such a youthful spirit, and I know you're older than me, yet I connect so much with what you're saying.

I haven't had Botox or anything and we were talking about it and I was like, "Ew, does it hurt?" Thinking I don't know if I want to get it, maybe it's too soon. And that makes me feel good 'cause look at people like Sheryl Crow. Nowadays fifty is forty; and forty is thirty. People are living so much longer, hipper, and cooler that the age question is really less relevant… I had a girl ask me [my age] in the most creative way and I gave her a wink because it was very cute. I was at this "meet and greet" recently and she said, "Now, what year did you graduate from high school?" I went, "1984" with a big smile. The bottom line is I don't want to narrow my dating bracket by too much. It's so cool that I have a twenty-year swing factor in the age of people I can date.

I hope when I'm your age I can pull that off, too!

My manager was giving me some grief because… she was laughing at me going out with someone who was twenty-something, very young, like twenty-three barely. And she said, "Well girl, you go for it 'cause there will come a day when a twenty-two-year-old guy won't want to be kissing on you."

You will never end up dateless. That's nice to know that someone as beautiful and talented as you still has "girly complexes."

Are you kidding me? I've been in New York for two days and I love to go to little pubs and cool lounge bars and hang out. I've had Black and Tans the whole time I've been here. I haven't had any today. But it certainly does change the way your jeans fit.

Regarding the song "Liar": Do you know some liars or what?

Someday I'll tell the story about the nature of that song. It was written about a particular person in the music industry. It wasn't my husband. It was my vindication for being able to say how I felt about somebody.

Do you have a message you want to put out there for girls since this record is so girly?

Just that it matters so much that you feel worthy of walking in your life every day. I think girls go through—we have such image issues. I get really inspired when I see girls, especially young girls, confident. If they're a size twelve it doesn't matter. Confidence is so sexy and beautiful. And kindness, it has to go hand-in-hand. Confident and kind people, especially women, are very inspiring, so inspiring no matter what age or size or shape or color or whatever, it's just very important to be that.

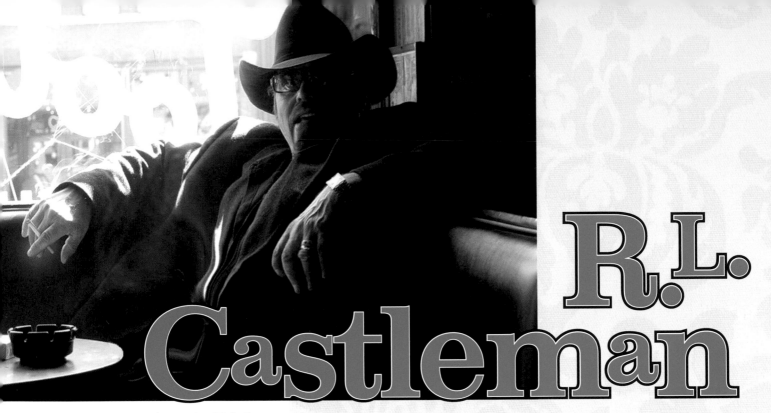

photo courtesy R.L. Castleman

R.L. Castleman

Interview by Doak Turner

American Songwriter, *July/August, 2005*

It's appropriate that a kid whose first and middle names are "Robert Lee" would grow up in a military family. Robert Lee Castleman was indeed the son of a military careerist, so he lived in lots of different places during his school years. This type of travel and separation often makes for great writing, and in Castleman's case, this appears to have happened.

He has paid his dues, working in a guitar store, playing bars and folk clubs, driving trucks, and working various other gigs before finally moving to Nashville to become a songwriter. "Sneakin' Around" was picked up as the title track for a 1991 album of duets by two of the greatest guitar players ever, Chet Atkins and Jerry Reed. He worked in road gigs for Suzy Bogguss and Eric Johnson before the bluegrass queen Alison Krauss heard his song "Forget About It."

Alison is on Rounder Records, based in Cambridge, Massachusetts. She liked Castleman's music so much that she arranged an audition for him at Rounder; he passed and Rounder released Castleman's first solo album, *Crazy As Me,* in the summer of 2000. Castleman secured the title cut on Alan Jackson's latest album, *Like Red on a Rose* (2006), not to mention three additional cuts.

—PHIL SWEETLAND

Tell me about writing your song, "The Lucky One."

I was at a guitar workshop in 1984—David Smallridge's Guitar Camp in Connecticut. They study all styles of guitar playing. I wrote that song at that particular workshop. A friend of mine, Buck Brown, did a guitar/vocal demo of the song. We even did a live version of the song at a club where Alison [Krauss] recorded. When I was touring with Alison years later, around the year 2000, Buck had moved to Washington, D.C. I called him and told him we were going to be playing at Wolf Trap in Vienna, Virginia. He stopped by and handed me a cassette that had what he considered great old R.L. songs on it. I was listening to the cassette on the tour bus. When it came to the song "The Lucky One," Alison asked, "What is that?" The rest is history. She changed it to second person. I had originally sung it in the first person.

You wrote the song "Forget About It," which Alison recorded a couple years earlier. Tell me about that song.

It was the title track for a previous album with Alison. I wrote "Forget About It" around 1985, maybe even earlier.

How did she hear that one?

Alison's husband had a surprise birthday party for her around 1999. That was the first time I had ever met Alison. Of course, at the party, I stuck a guitar in my hand and that was one of the songs that I sang that night. She said she had to record that song! She also recorded "Let Me Touch You for a While."

What is the story behind "Let Me Touch You for a While"?

That song was also written in the eighties. Someone even had a live recording of that when I recorded it at the famed Bitter End in New York City back in the eighties. That song was also on the cassette I mentioned previously.

Your original connection with Alison was with her husband, right?

I met Pat Bergeson [Alison's future husband] in Connecticut at the Guitar Workshop, and we got to be friends. He said we should put together a band and play The Bitter End. We did that as The Checkered Past Band. Chet Atkins had come to the Guitar Workshop with his friend John Knowles, who used to transcribe for Chet. John works for the Country Music Hall of Fame. I had a previous connection with Chet through an album that he had produced for Homer & Jethro called *Songs My Mother Never Sang*. Listening to Chet records was the inspiration for me to fingerpick a guitar. I brought that album up to Chet and Jethro, who was Chet's brother-in-law. We hit it off. I gave him a copy of a demo tape I had made, and Chet passed it on to his manager. His manager and I got hooked up and I moved to Nashville in 1989. After I was here for a while, Chet recorded an instrumental song of mine called "Sneakin' Around," which was the title track of the album. It was the first cut I ever had. Chet and Jerry Reed did the song on the album. I had played a song for Pat Bergeson. I took Pat to meet Chet. Pat ended up moving to town. He knew Alison's brother, who hooked him up with Lyle Lovett. Pat ended up marrying Alison, which ended up with me getting my songs cut to begin with, which led to other success in the business.

You had those songs that were twenty-years-old and Alison cut them. Now she has a new CD. What has happened for you on her new CD?

She recorded "Restless," which I wrote for her new CD called *Lonely Runs Both Ways*. Another song that I wrote called "Gravity" is also on the album. I wrote that song in 1990 or 1991. Then a funny thing happened on another

song. She called me from L.A. and says, "R.L., I got this idea for a song that I want you to write." I said I do not normally do things like this, but I'll take a whack at it. She said the title is "Doesn't Have to Be This Way." It is about two people who do not have a relationship that are breaking up. Of course, I asked what happened, and how does that work? I was sitting at the house one morning, about 6 A.M., picked up a guitar, and came up with this thing. I wrote it in about maybe twenty minutes, made a guitar vocal, and called her. She said she loved the song. She recorded that song on the album, making it a total of four cuts on the latest Alison Krauss CD! I went from one cut on an Alison CD, to two cuts on the next, to now four songs on the current album. I guess that the next challenge for me with Alison is for her to do a complete record of Robert Lee Castleman songs! [*laughs*] Her next CD will be great!

You've written these songs. You've played them. How did you end up pitching these songs to her?

"Restless" was on a CD I gave her, and I told her to listen to a bunch of songs to see if there was anything that she liked. She called me up and said she had to have "Restless" and "Gravity."

Did she help you get your record deal with Rounder a couple years ago?

Yeah—that goes back to the night at her birthday party I mentioned. I played for the crowd for about forty-five minutes to an hour with her husband Pat. She called Ken Irwin the next day at Rounder Records and told him that he had to make a CD with me. That happened real quickly.

So then you had a record and she took you on tour.

We had about thirty dates that I opened for her. It was her and I and a driver and a nanny to watch her little boy. Another bus had the road crew and the band. It was a barrel of laughs.

Can you tell me about writing a song or two, starting with "The Lucky One"?

It is just about a guy that has a positive outlook on life. He sees the glass half full rather than half empty. "I'm the lucky one so I have been told/free as the wind blowing down the road/loved by many, hated by none/You would say I am lucky if you know what I'd done." He has a checkered past and has been lucky. It did win a Grammy, so I *am* the lucky one.

What were you doing when you found out about the Grammy?

I was an OTR [over the road—long-haul trucker]. I started driving in 1985 to put food on the table. It has taken me fifty some years to receive any accolades in the business.

When did you first hear the song on the radio?

I was sitting in my truck in Sevierville, Tennessee, with a load of scrap metal that I was getting ready to unload. The cell phone rang and it was Alison. She was so excited, telling me that my song was nominated for a Grammy. Here I am in dirty, filthy clothes, been up all night driving from the coast of Alabama to get to Sevierville. I had been up about twenty hours when she told me I got nominated for a Grammy for Best Country Song of the Year. I near soiled myself [*laughs*].

Did you ever have any other artists call you when you were on the road?

Alan Jackson called me one day to tell me he wanted to record a couple songs of mine. He recorded "Maybe I Should Stay Here" and "Kind of Like a Rainbow," from my record. He put "Maybe I Should Stay Here" on his CD *When Somebody Loves You.*

What was your famous quote about your Grammy?

Peter Cooper from *The Tennessean* asked me what I was going to do with the Grammy. I told him it will look good on the hood of my truck. You are not supposed to have a job after winning a Grammy, you know. If you have eighteen Grammys like Alison, you really have to work hard at not working [*laughs*].

Let's talk about the new single, "Restless."

I was in jail in Martinsburg, West Virginia. I had been arrested for public intoxication and drunk driving… spent a wonderful evening in jail. My first wife-to-be decided that she did not want to be my first wife after all. I became emotional… drowned my sorrows. The lyric, "Honey I know that you've been alone some/why don't you phone some/'cause I love you" came from that night in jail. It was the first time that I had come up with a lyric without a guitar. I wrote the lyric for a simple music piece and added music later. I did a demo in Hagerstown, Maryland, and that is what she heard. That was written in around 1981.

How did you keep track of all these songs over the years?

There are a lot of songs that people have kept over the years. I have forgotten about many of them and maybe someday someone will bring an old tape to me from way back then. That is the way "The Lucky One" was heard! I do not have a system. If I write a song that is a hit at my house, for however long it takes me to wear it out, I just keep the tape around the house. I give it the whistle test. If I can whistle it, it's good. I remember hanging with Chet Atkins one night in Nashville. We were at The Cockeyed Camel, a bar out on Highway 100 around Belle Meade. We were walking out halfway during a guy's show that night and Chet asked what I thought of the guy's songs. I said that the music was so complicated that I could not remember any of it. Chet said, "Well, as long as he keeps doing that I won't go out of business." [*Laughs*]

What advice would you give to aspiring songwriters?

To always be tenacious… never give up chasing the dream. It is a great job if you can make a living at it. Reflect on the times and places that you have been. That is hard to get away with at times. I never write a song about sailing on a battleship, because I do not have any experience with that particular thing. Einstein said to make things as simple as possible, but never simpler. Every line should be as strong as the one before and after. The DJ on the song cannot play the song back to explain the songs. If I write a song and it is not that great of a song, but there is one [good] line in the song, I will keep that line for another song. Twenty bad songs may have the elements to write one great song. The trick is to write a song that doesn't say anything, yet says everything—to have someone say, "How did you know that I feel like that?" I hate direct things. If you notice, Alison very seldom cuts songs that talk about specific times or events or items. She does not say the name of a town or a truck or specific things. It has to be timeless. Her songs could be written today or in the twenties. She loves to be obscure, not current. She will not talk about computers, caller ID… she changed a line in one of my songs that mentioned caller ID.

When you are writing songs, do you ever write one and say, "This is an Alison song?"

I know her voice so well, and I can put her voice to my song and hear her singing it. I know her phrasing, what she likes and does not like, and I know how to channel it to her. She may not like [a particular] song, but she will listen to my songs, which is great.

photo courtesy Atlantic Records

Ray Charles

Interview by Kristi Singer

Singer Magazine, *2002*

Ray Charles is one of popular music's most beloved icons. A pioneer of early soul music, Charles became a constant hit maker in the 1950s and 1960s and charted a career that found him delighting audiences well into his eighties. Ray Charles was born September 23, 1930, in Albany, Georgia. He lost his sight to glaucoma at age six but began learning piano by ear. As a teenager, he learned to write music in Braille while attending the Florida School for the Deaf and Blind. Charles began making his first recordings in the late forties and scored his first top ten R&B hit, "Baby, Let Me Hold Your Hand," in 1951. But his trademark emotive, emotionally charged singing style went missing from his records until he was signed to Atlantic Records, where he was encouraged to let loose. Among the golden hits he recorded there were "Drown in My Own Tears," "Hallelujah I Love Her So," "(Night Time Is) The Right Time," and "What'd I Say." In 1963, Charles recorded the groundbreaking *Modern Sounds in Country and Western Music,* a unique country-soul hybrid that became one of his biggest selling albums and featured the hit single "I Can't Stop Loving You." Charles's career was revitalized in a major way in 2004 when, at the age of eighty-three, he released *Genius Loves Company,* a hugely successful album of duets. Charles died of liver disease in June 2004. In October 2004, the award-winning motion picture *Ray* reminded the world of his incredible story and resounding legacy.

—Evan Schlansky

How did you develop your distinct sound and delivery?

I just sing—what comes out of me is what comes out of me. It's not planned or nothing. I take a song I like and I put myself into it. If I can't put myself into it, it may be a great song, but I won't do it. If I can't make it do something for me, then I don't do it. And it may be a great song; someone else may come out with it and make a hit out of it. But I feel that if I can't really put myself into the song then I don't want to bastardize myself.

Of all of the songs you've recorded, what is your personal favorite and why?

I don't have any… I've been making records since 1948, it would be impossible to say a favorite song because I've done too many songs and too many different types of songs—I've done country music, I've done jazz, I've done the blues, I've done love songs. I mean, there's just no way to say, "This is the greatest song ever." If you're talking about some songs that made a lot of money you could take songs like "Georgia [on My Mind]" and "I Can't Stop Loving You" and "What'd I Say" and "Ruby" and things like that. But that's not necessarily saying those are my favorites. I've made a lot of songs that didn't make a hit but I loved the music, the way it was done and the way it came out. So I couldn't really answer that question, truly.

How has the music industry changed, for better or worse, since you started recording professionally in the fifties?

It's different. It's very different. When I was coming up in the business I was very lucky. I didn't have anybody to dictate what to do and what not to do, as opposed to kids today where they have a producer—he tells them what to do and how to do it, and I didn't have that problem. So that's one thing. On the other hand, the actual making of the music, the recording studios, the equipment is much better—you get much clearer music. On the other hand there's music that I think I'm much too old for, and I admit that. For instance, like rap. I don't know nothin' about that; I can't deal with it. I can't learn anything from it. It don't trigger my brain. I could say poetry to music when I was eight years old. So, basically all they're doing is talkin.' So I always tell the rappers, "I know you guys are making all this money, but can you hum me the melody?"

Do you like any of the music today?

A lot of the music today, I don't hear any originality, any creativity. I guess I got spoiled with people like Frank Sinatra, Ella Fitzgerald, Aretha Franklin, Gladys Knight, and Barbra Streisand. People that when they sing one note you know who they are. I don't see that. Or let's say Art Tatum or Oscar Peterson, or Charlie Parker… these were creators. These people had a sound of their own. You can even go back to Bing Crosby. He could sing two notes and you knew it was Bing Crosby. I don't see that today. I don't see anybody with a sound that I can say, "Wow," they sing one note and I know who they are. I don't see that and I think it's because the record companies just don't let people really do it themselves, be themselves. I'm not sure about that, but that's what I think. I think the last people who came along that I really liked were Michael Jackson and Stevie Wonder. I think they were both very talented people and they had a sound of their own. And that's what I try to preach to youngsters. Get a thing of your own; get a sound that's you. Don't let these people tell you, "Well, this last record was a big hit, they want you to sound like that." That's not creating anything. Or they have what they call these things that they use to… it's like a copy thing where they take two bars where they repeat them over and over. They might not create the two bars themselves. They may take the two bars from somebody's record.

Sampling, you mean?

Sampling. See, I don't like that. Because, to me, you got a brain. Can't you think of your own stuff? Why do you need to be sampling? It's just not my kind of thing.

I noticed that when a singer is really into a performance his eyes are closed, and he may appear to be visualizing something mentally—being inspired. What do you visualize when you're singing?

What I do is I try to put myself into the lyrics. In other words, what are the lyrics dictating? In other words, what is the story? Just like when you watch a movie, what is the story? A good actor or actress will make you believe what is happening. In other words, they can make you cry if it's a sad thing. The emotions come out in you from the way they're doing it. That's what makes a good actor or actress. They can make you become a part where you actually feel, although you know it's just fiction, but you still react to it. So when I sing I try to put myself into the lyrics of the song. What is the guy really saying? What is he trying to get over? What is his point? And I try to make it believable, so whatever I say I want people to feel it, and many times you sing some song sometime and people say, "You must have had that experience because there ain't no way in the world that you could sing that song like that unless that happened to you." That's the kind of thing I'm into. Have it so that people really think that it was a personal experience. When you do that then you know you're getting over.

I read that you said you were "born with music inside of you." I wondered if you could explain that feeling in more depth and how you knew that music was inside of you?

It's kind of hard to explain. It's like you were born and breathing is a part of your life, it's part of your bloodstream.

I mean, I had it; it was something that was very natural. It wasn't something that I was taught, although I was taught, but it was in me before I ever went to school and thought about a quarter note or a half note. Music was the one thing as a child, when I was three years old, that would stop me from playing. If I was out playing with my buddies, he would get his old man Wally Pittman and start to play that old piano. I would stop what I was doing and run in there and sit down and bang on the keyboard with him and he would stop me and try to show me, tell me, "Okay, you love music so well, I'm going to show you how to play a song with one finger." That's the way I started out. Music has always been something that totally fascinated me, and it still does.

Do you feel your struggles of poverty, blindness, and losing family members have inspired you to be the success you are today? And in addition to that, how can other singers and songwriters use their lives and struggles to inspire their music?

The thing is to believe in yourself. You have to start that way. Because people are going to try and discourage you and tell you don't have this… but you know because all you have to do is look out there and see what's out there and how do you stand up to what you hear out there? Do you feel that what you're doing is as good, or better? And look at your talent. It's just like if you were in sports. I tell the kids all the time, whatever you're doing, you got to practice. You got to practice and practice and practice. Even if you're good. I never met a good pianist who didn't practice. And he's good but he still practiced. So you have to, once you get there, you have to keep your fingers limber. You have to keep your mind active to tell your fingers what to do and how to do it and when to do it and the way you do that, you improve because you practice and you learn how to do things easier for yourself. So, I'd say to anybody in whatever you're doing, have faith in yourself. If you really believe in yourself, then you just work toward it at that end and don't let anybody discourage you and just keep on practicing. That's the key.

How important do you think it is that singers are able to accompany themselves on keyboard or guitar or another instrument?

It's nice if you can, but there are a lot of great singers that don't play an instrument, just like you have a lot of great people that play instruments that can't sing. It works the same. There are great singers who can't play music, can't play piano, saxophone—no kind of instrument. And there are great instrumentalists who cannot sing. So, when you sing, your voice is really like an instrument. You do have to practice as a singer, just like I said. Anything you do from an honest point of view, you still have to practice. Sing in the shower. You'd be surprised how good that is. People make fun of it, but it's a good thing to sing in the shower because you can hear yourself come back to you, your voice, you can hear if you're singing out of tune. It's a good thing. So the name of the game is, whatever you're doing, whether you're playing an instrument or you're singing, whatever you're doing in the music business, you got to stick to practice.

As artists begin their careers, who do you think they should begin surrounding themselves with? What kind of people should they put their trust in?

I think that there are people who need that, but I wouldn't concern myself so much about managers and agents and lawyers. These people are very important, I think. But in the beginning, what you should focus on is what you're doing. Get yourself up so that you got something to offer, and that way you can have control of what happens to you. Of course, if you get something going, you're going to need a manager because you won't be able to handle all the ins and the outs of booking, and you don't want to. See, you want to concentrate on what you're doing. You need a good manager. And

like anything else you need to ask questions of people. You have to talk to people who've been there and done that. Just like if you hunt for a good doctor or you hunt for a good lawyer. You have to ask questions of people and talk to people you might know that would give you good advice as to which way to go. 'Cause you will need these people in the end if your career starts to go. You will need a good manager and you will need a good lawyer, you will need a good accountant. These are people that you will need like you need a good doctor. So in the beginning I wouldn't bog myself down with that type of thing. That will come. But the first thing you want to do is start with yourself. Let yourself become what you think you want to be. At least get on the right road to where you want to go. Then if you start seeing where you're getting some good reaction in what you're doing, you can start thinking about a manager or something like that. But in the beginning I wouldn't bother about that.

What have you found was the hardest part of entering the music business? Maybe the toughest hill you had to climb in your career?

The toughest time you mean? Anything with me was like a ladder. I started at the bottom. It wasn't like I was making five hundred dollars and the next thing you know I was making ten thousand. It didn't happen like that. Everything in my career started from point zero. And as time went on I kept climbing the ladder and climbing the ladder and climbing... and that's what I was recommending earlier about artists who want to be in this business. You can start with zero. But you have to build yourself up. You are going to run into pitfalls, but so what? Nobody promised you a rose garden. When you run into things, the stumbling blocks that get in your way, walk around them. Don't just stand there looking at them, go around and keep on stepping. Life is always going to provide adversity. You're not going to always have everything going great for you all the time because the wind

doesn't blow in the same direction all the time. So, you have to realize that. You're going to have some trying times because that's part of life. But if you believe in yourself and you think you know where you want to go, you say this is part of it and keep on stepping.

If you were going to tell an up-and-coming singer to never forget this:_____, how would you fill in that blank?

I think you just said it. You just got to start with yourself, as I said earlier. You got to believe totally in what you're doing and have a strong idea of where you want to go and keep on practicing. That's really the bottom line.

Do you have an accomplishment or contribution you think has been your greatest to soul music?

I wouldn't know that. 'Cause I don't think like that. It's not the kind of thing I go around asking myself, my accomplishments. I do what I do. I play music and I sing songs. My accomplishment is to be able to draw twenty-five or thirty thousand people. To me that's an accomplishment, especially when you start out at zero. So, the accomplishment is where I am today. You have to add all this stuff up over the years, all the trials and tribulations that you've gone through. And the accomplishment is where I am today. I'm very independent. I do what I want to do when I want to do it. To me, the greatest achievement of all is to be self-independent and not have to worry about anything, other than your health. If you stay healthy and you keep your direction straight, know where you're going all the time or where you want to go, that's the best accomplishment. To be really, truly independent means you don't have to accept anything that you don't want to accept. You can take what you want; don't take what you don't want. That's a pretty good life.

If you had a motto or something that gets you through each day, what would it be?

My motto is very simple, honey. With music or whatever artistry you're doing—whether you're singing or playing a horn. My motto is always, "Be sincere." Be honest with yourself. Don't cheat. If you've got five hundred people, play just as hard for those five hundred people as you would have played if you had five thousand. 'Cause you want those five hundred people to say, man, there weren't too many people there but he put on a hell of a show. That's what you want. You don't want them to say, there weren't too many people there and I'm sorry I went there 'cause it was a drag. You don't want that. You want people to really love what you're doing and appreciate what you're doing and talk about you to other people. That's the main thing. To answer your question, I'd say I want my motto to put on my tombstone, "One thing we can say about Ray Charles, he was always sincere."

I know that Nat King Cole was a great influence on you growing up. How important is it for singers to have someone to look up to?

Everybody's got somebody to look up to, whether they're a newspaper man or a television person or whatever it is. Somebody was doing it before you.

Kenny Chesney

Chesney's latest album is *The Road and the Radio*, released in 2005. If you have just become a Kenny Chesney fan because of his ever-so-contagious record *Be As You Are: Songs From an Old Blue Chair*, then you are missing out on a whole other part of Chesney's songwriting career—which goes as far back as his days at the University of Tennessee. Although this musical slant has fairly recently come to the lime-light of Chesney's career, he's always been drawn to the ebb and flow of its emotions, and his writing is infused with this personalized element—not merely an indulgence in the sea of its treasures. Since his early years with Capricorn Records in the early nineties to his current status on BNA Records, Chesney has created some of his deepest lyrics and painted endless, vivid pictures for his audience with songs ranging from "The Tin Man" and "You Had Me From Hello" to "I Go Back," "There's Something Sexy About the Rain," and "This Old Blue Chair."

As Chesney reveals a special part of himself with the *Be As You Are* record, he also opens those sacred places in his listeners' hearts. The album debuted at number one on the Billboard chart—not bad for an album without a planned single release. It followed 2004's *When the Sun Goes Down*, which sold more than three million copies, making it the number four best-selling record of 2004. In 2005, his album *The Road and the Radio* came out to great acclaim. The single "Summertime" rocketed to the number one spot in the summer of 2006.

—KEMP BUNTIN

photo courtesy Glen Rose

Interview by
Kemp Buntin

American Songwriter,
July/August 2005

Tell me how this career of yours began.

I got into the music business as a songwriter when I was young, and the guys I really looked up to and listened to were the singer/songwriters like Jackson Browne, Willie Nelson, Springsteen, Roger Miller, Mellencamp, Buffett, and Petty. They taught me that it was possible to paint a picture with words, and that turned me on to songwriting.

Do you remember one of the first songs you wrote?

One of the first songs I tried to write was a song for this girl… it's usually about a girl… it was a horrible song. She was in a persuasion class with me. I wrote her a song and threw it away—I could not even tell you the name of it. But that was where it all began.

Did you know from the beginning that songwriting was something you wanted to pursue?

I never really thought I was going to do anything with my writing. I was just doing it for fun… for something to do. Then, I started to play my songs for my friends and began playing them out around Johnson City [Tennessee]. People started coming up to me and telling me they liked them. I got a lot more confident about my writing. In January 1991, I decided to move to Nashville. I landed a publishing deal with Acuff-Rose [Music] in 1992 and a record deal with Capricorn Records in 1993. I was Capricorn's attempt at country music—they were more of a southern rock/college label. But it was also my attempt at recording my own songs, and it was a huge learning experience for me. I put out a song called "Whatever It Takes" on Capricorn. Then came "The Tin Man."

How did "The Tin Man" come about?

I was sitting in my apartment one night in 1991, and I had just broken up with a girl who moved back to Florida… no… actually we didn't break up… she just moved away. I was pretty upset about it and I happened to be watching *The Wizard of Oz* and I saw the Tin Man go through the whole movie… wanting a heart. Finally, he gets one. It is when Dorothy leaves. He says in the movie, "Now I know I have a heart because it is breaking." He only thought that there was a good side to having a heart. First thing he finds out is that there's a downside to it, too. That just hit me deep.

Have you always been a deep thinker?

I think a lot and read a lot. Some things just hit me completely differently than someone else. I try to dig deeper than I used to. That was one of the first songs that I was really proud of. It opened lots of doors for me. It helped get me my publishing deal and record deal.

Do you prefer writing by yourself or with a co-writer?

I've been writing a lot on my own lately, but it kind of depends on the situation. I used to use co-writing as a crutch. At times I was not as comfortable with my writing. But I have gotten much more confident with it over the past couple of years. I realize that nobody can tell the story like me because they didn't see it through my eyes.

Being more confident with your writing… what has changed?

I think it comes with growing up. I am more comfortable with putting myself out there… putting my heart and my feelings and emotions out there… and letting people see what I am thinking. I was never really like that before. I really believe that when people are listening to music, and I am the same way, they are suckers for the truth. I have really tried to become a more truthful songwriter and to let people pretty much have an open book into what I am feeling and how I am living my life.

You wrote "You Had Me From Hello," "Being Drunk's a Lot Like Loving You," and "There's Something Sexy About the Rain" with Skip Ewing. You must really be a good team.

Every time we've sat down we've written a great song. He and I write great together. Both of us love to paint those pictures and he is a great melody guy.

Are you more lyrical?

You know, I don't know. I can write a pretty good melody, too. But I don't know if I am better at one or the other. I just kind of write what I am feeling and let the melody take me

I realize that nobody can tell the story like me because they didn't see it through my eyes.

where it does. That is what I love about the island record, *Be As You Are*. I wrote those songs over about five and a half years. Nothing was rushed about it, and it all just happened like I said. It was really neat because it all really happened through my eyes. Every song on it was a real moment and every person is a real person.

I am so glad you are eager to talk about the new record. How did it all come to be?

Basically, *Be As You Are* is my journal from the islands put to words. I didn't think anyone was going to hear them except for me and the few people I wrote them for. They were just so personal. I had a guitar on my boat and forgot it was there until about three or four years ago. I put something in a closet one day and saw the guitar in there and pulled it

out and started playing it… and eventually wrote four of the songs that were used on the album. Then, one day I looked down and I had, like, twelve songs. I decided to go in and record them. I worked on the record for about two years. Really, it has been the most satisfying thing I've ever done, and usually the most satisfying things are the hardest. This record was for my fans and me. I wanted them to know this side of me.

What is it about the islands that gets you in the zone?

It is very ironic that the place I escaped to, to get as far away from my bus and the music industry, ended up being my most creative place. I've spent a lot of time in the islands over the last seven or eight years. It is just one of those places that draws me in like a magnet. I feel satisfied when I am there. When I look out into the ocean it reminds me of how infinite our possibilities are. The ocean really humbles me. My life is so fast-paced and hectic, one thing after the other… it's just a great change for me, because how I live my life down there is anything but the way I really live. It really is a place that opens me up.

Do you think certain circumstances led you to this point?

I don't know if there was one thing but I know the island record taught me so much about songwriting and being able to show all the emotions I felt in that record.

Do you regret not having put a single out?

No, I don't—because to me, not releasing a single made the album more special. And I had no idea what we were going to do with it when we released it. The fact that it went number one [on the *Billboard* pop charts] with no single is amazing. I never knew it would do something like this. So, no, no… no regrets.

Will you be playing songs from this album at your concerts?

This album is very laid back. My concerts are not. It is very much in your face. I like to keep the pace of my shows moving. I like people leaving there knowing they have completely been to a show… this album just doesn't really fit in. It fits in on a beach, on a boat, in a little funky beach bar, and little hideaway places. This is kind of where I like to keep it.

I know there are some who compare, sometimes criticize, the similarities of you to Jimmy Buffett. Are you okay with that?

That is going to be inevitable—especially when you release an album like this. As much as I love Jimmy, and he knows it (we've become good friends), Jimmy did not have anything to do with this record. The whole record is just how I grew up as a person and as a man during the periods I spent down in the islands. And I think this album reflects that. If people say, "Oh, he just wanted to write a Buffett album," that couldn't be further from the truth. Once they listen to the record, they will realize that this is not just a weekend in Margaritaville.

So if someone said, "We don't need another Buffett album," what would you say?

I didn't give them one!

Let's talk about some of the memorable songs on _Be As You Are_. I love the melody on "Boston." Did you write the melody on that?

That was me and Mark Tamburino. He really had the chords and I wrote the melody and the lyric around the riff. We wrote it on my boat… see, that is one of the great things about this record—every one of these songs was at least start-ed or finished on my boat. We'd just sit there, listen to music, drink, and write songs about it.

Explain the sexy "rock" in "Magic."

There is a part of an island I go to. They call it "The Rock." I do think in a lot of ways it has a lot of sex appeal. Lots of times, the things that are the least obvious are the things that make something magical.

Do you have time to write on the road?

It is hard to write on the road. And it is hard to bring writers on the road and just try and be creative. It just has to come to me. It comes when it comes… I can't really push it that much. But I wrote "I Go Back" on the bus one night. I stayed up all night and wrote it in bed. Mark Tamburino and I always go to this bar in the islands, and every time we walk in the bartender calls us the "Redneck Boys." I'm not from Alabama, but when we walk in he plays "Sweet Home Alabama" for us. We were on the bus one night and we heard "Sweet Home Alabama" and Tambo said, "Man, every time I hear that song, I go back to that bar in the islands." I said to Tambo, "You don't know what you have just done for me." I sat up and thought of all the songs that meant something to me.

How do you describe yourself?

I am a very laid-back person, I have a tenacious work ethic, I love life, I love love, and I love writing about it.

What is it about love that we can find so many ways of writing about it?

It is crazy that we can still write about love after all the times it has been written about. Everybody feels a lot of the same emotions, but not necessarily in the same way. People are going to paint different pictures. No two artists are going to sit there and look at a woman and paint the same thing. It is the same way for a songwriter. I'm no different either… I feel this stuff, too. Springsteen is going to write something completely different than somebody else. All those guys I love to listen to wrote about love and how it affected them. I think that is so great.

Right now you have the number one country song with "Anything But Mine," written by someone else. You sure keep a lot of Nashville songwriters happy by continuing to cut outside songs. Will you write more for this next album?

I'm not one of these guys that sits there and says, "I've got to write my own songs for my record." I've never done that. I'm

record. The island record was more hushed; this next one will be really rockin'.

Will there be any taste of salty sea air?

Maybe a touch here or there, but maybe not. I think I have done that. I've given people that side of me. It may go back to what really turns me on live—a bunch of guitars and a good lyric.

Any final thoughts?

I am just glad God gave me the gift of songwriting. I love it—I will always be a songwriter.

Everybody feels a lot of the same emotions, but not necessarily in the same way.

smart enough to know that there are some great songs out there and some great songwriters. I try to tap into as much as I can… I am in a very creative part of my life right now. I've been writing lots of songs. There are always going to be a couple that make it on the record. There is never going to be just a full album, other than *Be As You Are*, of Kenny Chesney songs. (Oh my gosh, I just spoke of myself in third person. Holy shit!) Right now the only song written for my next album is the song Sammy Hagar and myself started in Cabo at his birthday bash.

When will the next album come out? What are we to expect?

We're working on it right now. It is a hard process and I put a lot of stress on myself. I hope it will be out sometime in the fall. It is going to be completely different than the island

photo courtesy Walter Leaphart

Chuck D

Public Enemy

Interview by Deshair

American Songwriter,
January/February 2005

Public Enemy bears the distinction of being one of the most influential and infamous rap groups of all time. Their incendiary albums lit up the rap world in the late eighties and early nineties with their trademark mix of chaotic beats, military posturing, and revolutionary lyrics.

They formed in 1982 while students at Adelphi University in Long Island, New York, where Carlton Ridenhour and Hank Shocklee worked at the college radio station. Ridenhour assumed the name Chuck D while rapping over a track that Shocklee had created, called "Public Enemy #1." The track was heard by Rick Rubin, cofounder of Def Jam Records, who drafted the two for his fledgling label. Chuck D called on his old friend, William Drayton, to become his comic sidekick (Flavor Flav), and Public Enemy was born.

Their debut album, 1987's *Yo! Bum Rush the Show*, was largely overlooked, but the follow-up, *It Takes a Nation of Millions to Hold Us Back*, ignited hip-hop fans, making it to number one on the *Billboard* R&B charts. It is widely regarded as one of the best rap albums of all time. "Fight the Power," the theme song to Spike Lee's *Do the Right Thing*, became the band's calling card in 1989. In 1992, they released *Apocalypse 91… The Enemy Strikes Black*, their highest charting album, and toured with U2. The band went on hiatus until 1998, when they provided the soundtrack to Spike Lee's *He Got Game*. Legends in their own time, Public Enemy continues to create vital music to this day, most recently with 2005's *New Whirl Odor*.

—EVAN SCHLANSKY

At what point in your life did you know that songwriting and reciting would be the ultimate way for you to get out the word?

During my first album, back in 1986, 1987. Rap albums didn't have liner notes and they didn't have lyrics printed. So once I was able to print my lyrics out on the album sleeves, I knew that I would make an impact.

Tell us about how The Bass (Chuck D) and The Treble (Flavor Flav) tackled the songwriting process together.

The songwriting process was based around Public Enemy. So when I wrote a song, everything else was mapped around it. I found the musicians, made the revisions, created themes, and carved out the lyrics. It was a total team process, but someone had to have the initial idea. When Flav wrote his tunes, he would either have an idea or he might take an idea and sit with it for a year in some cases.

Would you say that you are a more lyrically driven songwriter or a melody driven songwriter?

I'm lyrical, not [melodical]. It's more like a sound, a sonic noise, audio; that's what drives me. It's not melody. It's not really a beat. If I hear a sound that I haven't heard before, I would probably be more interested in an ugly sound than anybody else. I wouldn't necessarily take a pretty sound that anybody can get on. I've always liked to take something that nobody would ever pick—nobody would ever feel.

Let's look back on one of the greatest musical collaborations of our time, "Self-Destruction." When you think about the messages that were delivered in that heartfelt masterpiece, do you feel that we're still heading for it, or have we already reached self-destruction, and why?

What is seventeen years when a so-called civilized nation goes over a thousand, right? They've been talking about self-destruction for about a thousand or two thousand years.

Are there any artists from this generation that you feel are Public Enemy's descendents in the sense of carrying the torch?

Yes, there are plenty. Whether it's in rock, like Rage Against the Machine… you got groups like The Roots; you got Dead Prez; you got Nas. Public Enemy is a group, so our influence is always there, and it splinters into a thousand areas. Right now, you got Little Brother. But I mean hey, I'm proud of the fact that our influences have been felt in heavy rock as well as rap.

Let's do some song association. I'll give you a title to one of Public Enemy's greatest hits, and from there you can describe to us what you were going through at the time you wrote that song.

"Public Enemy #1": I was going through a time of establishing myself on radio stations and college radio stations, to help build rap music back in 1984.

"Welcome to the Terrordome": I was just finished with the 1989 controversy that summer. I took a long drive to Allentown, Pennsylvania, to let go of a lot of steam from the top of my head.

"Shut Em Down": It was the winter time, and we were trying to find some new angles. This young cat came up to me and was like, "Yo, Red Alert is shutting down everybody on the radio station. He's shutting them down; he shut 'em down." I'm like, "Wow, okay, boom, a song idea."

Has anything changed about how you attack songwriting since the release of Public Enemy's debut album, *Yo! Bum Rush the Show*?

A lot of things have changed. But then again, I say that the best thing that songwriters can do is keep their eyes, their ears, and their noses open to what is going on around them.

Do you ever rank the songs that you've written in the past, and if so, what would you rank as your best display of lyricism?

The number one thing that I was taught to do was to try to take a song that someone would probably hate—somebody probably would love, and not really give a fuck about either. "Welcome to the Terrordome" was a personal favorite, because I reached inside of me more than any other song.

Tell us about your new album, *New Whirl Odor.*

New Whirl Odor is another [phrase] for "Ball of Confusion." The world is a ball of confusion.

What can we look forward to with this release?

Fans of our music can be looking forward to a different album with *New Whirl Odor.* Public Enemy has never made two albums alike, and that's our goal. The funny thing is, we always come out with records where you'll have a whole group of people who would say, "Wow, this is the best shit in years," and then you'll have people that don't know what to say. But they shouldn't know what to say, because that's the goal. This album is a revisit to warm sound. People hear a warm sound with nice bass and feel that. But the next album might not be like that. You have to be a bold and daring artist to say that it's not about trying to make everybody feel good. It's about standing by what we do and believe and seeing people cross over to that walk. If they do, they're cool, and if they don't, they still gotta be cool because you gotta be *you.*

Tell us about the first single.

"Bring That Beat Back" is the first single, which was produced in our four studios that we have on this Slam Jamz label. All of our producers [a staff of fifteen] had to get over the philosophy that they should share, and know what everyone was doing. They also passed around their works to each other. It was a double-checking establishment, and that has worked on the Public Enemy albums. How long that will take place? I don't know, but I'm against having one producer captain an entire album. It's hard to convince cats today, so I try to convince them with philosophy.

Is there a universal accomplishment that you hope to achieve with every release?

Yes, it's [like] that when you write; your words and your sentiments are frozen in time. So when people pick it up, it's like thawing out food in the freezer. It should be fresh enough for them to eat, because the freezer should protect it. Now it doesn't work all the time for every artist, if someone comes along that is just writing for the sake of following a trend, such as a negative trend; once it is thawed out, it can only create negativity, which could be cancerous and poisonous to your mental existence. Why do you think that if Billie Holiday can make a song in 1942, if we hear it in 2005, it still parallels what's going on right now in some cases? It's because the song is freezable, you can thaw it out, and you can get some goods from it—some nutrition. I'm not saying that all songs must be mentally stimulating, but even if you talk about having a good time like Sam Cooke, if you thaw it out, he's having a good time. I think that you just gotta be diversified with your approaches and point of view. I think that artists, when they are writing music, should write music that they feel totally confident [with] in the outcome. I think that they should take chances and be totally bold in their approach.

Guy Clark

Guy Clark is a long, tall Texan and songwriting genius who was born in the small town of Monahans, Texas, on November 6, 1941, and was raised in Rockport.

Clark's catalog is almost endless, with classics like Ricky Skaggs's "Heartbroke," Jerry Jeff Walker's "L.A. Freeway," Bobby Bare's "New Cut Road," John Conlee's "The Carpenter," and Steve Wariner's "Baby I'm Yours." He is one of Nashville's most influential tunesmiths and has been for decades.

Transport yourself back to the early sixties to a club in either Houston or Austin; Guy Clark is playing, and so are Townes Van Zandt, K.T. Oslin, and Jerry Jeff Walker. Late in the sixties, Clark moved to San Francisco, where he witnessed first-hand the early days of the Grateful Dead and Jefferson Airplane. Tiring of that scene, he bolted for L.A., where he built Dobros for a living for eight months. He then split for Nashville in 1971 with his wife Susanna, an accomplished songwriter herself ("Easy From Now On").

No matter how far Guy Clark moves away from Texas, he often returns there in his music. Songs like Jerry Jeff Walker's "Desperados Waiting for a Train," Johnny Cash's "Texas 1947," and Asleep at the Wheel's "Blowin' Like a Bandit" all refer to either Monahans or Rockport. Clark's latest album, *Workbench Songs*, was released in 2006.

—PHIL SWEETLAND

Interview by
Kelly Delaney

American Songwriter,
May/June 1990

You once told me you had to go sit in front of a window for two or three days in order to get in the right frame of mind. Is that still true?

I do that coming off the road and trying to regroup. It takes a while to focus on what you're trying to do. At least it does for me. Of course, sitting and staring out a window is also one of my favorite pastimes. But I think that is especially true if you write about things that happened to you in the past. You kind of re-create it.

Do you think it is better to write about things you're familiar with?

Yeah, I mean, I've never driven a [tractor], but I know about that feeling. There's a lot of leeway in that, but I've found over the years that's true. The songs written about things I really know about, that really happened to me, are much better songs.

You've done more co-writing lately, haven't you?

Yeah. I used to write by myself; I just didn't have any reason to write with anybody else. But the last four or five years I have. Before, when I got stuck, I just didn't write. One time I went a year without writing a song. So, I started co-writing to keep the juices flowing when I couldn't come up with anything.

So co-writing is a way to overcome writer's block.

One way is co-writing. I've also found that it's nice to have something else to do. Writing is kind of a real cerebral, introspective, strange thing. It's good to balance that with something that requires real hand-to-eye coordination, using the other side of the brain. Sometimes I'll set up two tables. On one I'm writing and on the other I'm building a model airplane at the same time. Playing golf is that kind of thing. Painting… that's another one. Balancing those two things. Anything you can do to trick yourself into writing.

After years of writing by yourself, was it hard to co-write?

It's a different discipline than writing by yourself, but I enjoy it. The last two or three years, I started writing with other artists for their projects. They'll come up with an idea for something they want to do, and I'll help them write it. That's fun.

Were there any adjustments you had to make?

I don't know if there are any real adjustments. You have to write with someone you can trust, but sometimes it sparks and sometimes it doesn't. I've tried to write with people I've known for twenty years and not get anything and then somebody will walk in that I've never met and bingo—there it is.

What about when you come up with an idea that you're keen on and your writing partner isn't? Do you have to stick to your guns?

With co-writing there are a couple of givens. One is that co-writing is cooperating and finding a trade-off. A lot of the stuff I come up with I know is off the wall in left field, because that's me. But that's not always good for the sake of the song. If it is really good, usually it'll wind up being in there. Maybe you just don't have it turned around right. If you have another person to bounce it off of, they've got to get it at least.

That's true. If your co-writer doesn't know where you're coming from, maybe it's too far out.

How else can you expect anybody else to get it? But if you come up to an impasse, maybe you shouldn't be writing together. And there's no rule against having two versions of the same song. I do that a lot. I'll write with somebody, and he'll say, "I'm gonna do it this way," and I say, "Fine, I'm gonna do it this way." We demo two versions of it. Nothing is set in stone. It's like "I'm All Through Throwing Good

Love After Bad." That song was written in a 6/8 Ray Charles kind of waltz. I couldn't sing it like that, so I turned it into a bluegrass song. I do that all the time. I just went back and changed a line on a demo; I do that all the time.

And sometimes your co-writer might come up something that doesn't ring true to your ear. So it works both ways.

Maybe you try it a while later and say, "Look, I think this is hanging this song up. Let's have another run at it; let's write it again." That's just part of the process. They're never finished.

That's true with many tunes.

I've got songs I'd love to go back and rewrite. They were just too inside, too hip for their own good. A lot of lines in my songs… it was just that I didn't take the time to figure them out. Most of them I knew weren't good at the time.

I think it was Danny Dill who once told a young Kris Kristofferson that his songs were wonderful but that he needed to dummy them up a little bit.

Well, it's just that you don't have to compromise your intelligence, but you also don't have to dazzle them with your knowledge of the English language, either. One hot lick in a song is a whole lot more effective than a whole stretch of hot licks. It's what you leave out. Kris's songs are real literate and in a lot of them, it's what he left out [that makes them stand out].

Didn't you once say that Townes Van Zandt influenced your writing?

He approached it in a way that appealed to me—a poetic, if you will, approach to the song. I don't how he writes, but you get the sense that a lot of it is from that alpha state. A real dream kind of thing.

He has some lines that stand up with any poetry.

It's not real crafty, but you don't sit down and think up "His horse as fast as polished steel, his breath's as hard as kerosene." That's from a strange place. He's really good with the English language and he's a well-educated guy.

I guess songs are today's poetry, in terms of mass appeal.

They've always been. I personally like lyrics with a poetic flow, but they obviously don't have to be that way. All you gotta do is listen to the radio to know that. But I think you can have it both ways if it makes a difference to you.

Are there certain words you like the sound of and try to use when and where you can?

You bet. All the time. I've heard, "Oh, you can't use that word, it's too literate." "Heartbroke," for example, has a lot of those words and phrases in it that you would think would not be standard country fare. I write words down that really have a ring to them as well as whole thoughts.

Ricky Skaggs asked you if he could change a line in that tune, didn't he?

Yeah. It doesn't matter to me if people want to change stuff. I mean, I know exactly why he can't sing "Pride is a bitch and a bore when you're lonely." The point is he really liked the song; it sounded like a hit to him, and he knew it was going to be a problem when he got ready to take it to the radio guys. It was a problem for his personality as well, and man, that's fine with me. I can do it the way I wrote it anytime I want to.

It doesn't really change the meaning.

It might, but I don't really have that kind of artistic chip on my shoulder… "You can't do my songs unless you do it exactly the way I say." I don't do that with other people's songs.

I recorded Townes's "To Live Is to Fly" and left out the whole first verse and used the same chorus every time. I went to him and said, "Look, man, I want to do the song but this is the way I would do it." He said okay.

What about an instance where an artist wants to make a few changes in your song and wants a writer's credit?

That's all negotiable. I find it real tacky myself and I don't think I would do it. But still, if I were presented with that situation, I would consider it, if it were a valid change. I mean, why not. It might be better.

Has that ever happened to you?

No, but if it did it would be a business decision, not an ego decision. What is one line worth? Ten percent? Let's negotiate here, especially if you knew it was gonna be a hit—if you knew it was gonna be a single by a well-known artist. There are situations where it could be unethical. But the way I look at it, that's a sell-out by them; it's not a sell-out by me. They're the ones who gotta live with that kind of karma.

You mentioned before that you file ideas.

I wouldn't call it filing, but I try to write them down in one place and refer to them when I'm looking for something. A lot of times it works. You always get an idea and think, "Oh, this is great, there's no way I'll forget it." Five minutes later it's gone. That's the way I wrote "L.A. Freeway." I was coming back from a gig at four in the morning from San Diego to Los Angeles, in the back of the car asleep. I woke up, looked around, and thought, "If I can just get off this L.A. freeway without getting killed or caught." Light bulb! I scrambled around and wrote it down. I carried it around in my billfold for a year. But I would not have remembered that. So, that's a valuable piece of discipline you can do. I still don't do it every time, but at least I try.

Are there any common mistakes aspiring writers make?

Everybody's different. Some try to write just like what's [on the radio] and some try to be different. But they're all things I've thought myself. I don't know if there are any common mistakes.

But there are some guidelines to songwriting.

Sure. There's a real world. If you want your songs on the radio, that means they have to be under three minutes long. The Western ear—by that I mean Western civilization—is attuned to certain sounds. The reason there are choruses and refrains is because it's fun to hear them again. There are a lot of formulas you fall into.

But the real bottom line is that writing sure is fun.

Oh yeah. It's because you never conquer it or learn it or master it. It gets more mysterious the longer you do it. I don't know near as much about writing songs as I did twenty years ago. I'm not near as convinced I know exactly what I'm doing. That's part of the appeal of it. The more you learn the less you know.

Earl Thomas Conley

Ohio native Earl Thomas Conley had a massive impact on country radio in the 1980s. From "Fire and Smoke" in the spring of 1981 to "Love Out Loud" in the winter of 1989, Conley (whose friends and family call him "ETC") racked up an astounding seventeen number one *Billboard* country singles.

Born in 1941 in southeastern Ohio, Conley's family was traumatized when Earl's father lost his railroad job. Conley and his seven brothers and sisters barely scraped by in the postwar years, in the area of Ohio near the West Virginia and Kentucky borders known as "the Little Smokies." (Conley later wrote about this region in "Smoky Mountain Memories.") Conley served a tour of duty in the Army, and upon discharge went to work for the Pennsylvania Railroad in Xenia, Ohio, then for a steel mill. Conley tired of these dead-end jobs, so he split for Huntsville, Alabama, where he met a studio owner named Nelson Larkin. Soon after he started digging his heels into songwriting, Conley hit pay dirt; Conway Twitty cut his composition "This Time I've Hurt Her More (Than She Loves Me)," and it went to number one.

Conley is a classic example of hard work paying off for a songwriter. He didn't even take the job until he was twenty-six, and like Merle Haggard, his voice and songs resonated with honesty. "Fire and Smoke," came out on tiny Sunbird Records; RCA quickly signed him and six months later worked his first major label single, "Tell Me Why," to country radio.

—PHIL SWEETLAND

Interview by Vernell Hackett

American Songwriter,
July/August 1985

87

Do you have a good idea about what people want to hear, and then go from there in your writing?

I went through a period where I had a "save myself" attitude, and I was trying to find out what in the world I liked about music and what I liked about myself during the time. I was writing stuff that, from a writer's point of view, was great. It was total creativity in motion. Since then, I've learned that being on the road and performing is an art form in itself. Since that time, I've gotten a better idea of what mass appeal is, and I've become comfortable aiming in that direction. I'm not making that many compromises… it feels natural to me.

How do you feel about co-writing?

Around the time I wrote "Smoky Mountain Memories," I knew my stuff was commercial. After that, I [didn't] really need to write with other people. Sometimes it helps, because you can bounce ideas back and forth, and I think sometimes it's faster, but then it got easier for me to go over and close the door and go inside of myself and do my own thing. I started believing in myself to the point where I would know whether it was good or not. I'd always have to ask someone else. And sometimes the opinions I got did more harm than good.

Do you write much on the road?

When you're working hard on the road, you don't have time to go that far in yourself, and that may be a problem. I just don't know. I've never done all that together. Maybe you can. I'll have to wait and see.

You and Randy Scruggs write some great songs.

Time is involved. Time is important. But I just think that co-writing is much more a pleasure than spending a lifetime alone in my own head. It's nice to have Randy Scruggs to write with. Sure I get in his head and he gets in my head… and it's real natural—what comes out. And nice, too.

What about singing other people's songs?

I'm probably the hardest singer in this town to write for, not because I'm so different or because of my style, but for my emotions… my feelings. I have to be able to feel the song and believe in it. It's along the same lines that Hank Williams had the feelings and the emotions he could put into a song.

What about living your songs?

I still live with that struggle inside myself every day. One minute I'm destroying myself and the next minute I'm saving myself. I can see the need to take care of yourself and push forward without any help, except the help inside the God-Self and the creativity—the war of losing and winning—destroying yourself and saving yourself. Sometimes I destroy myself just to display the need of freedom and just to take it. I go in two different directions, sometimes too extremely. When I'm serious, I'm too serious, and when I'm having fun, I'm having too much fun, when I'm sad, I'm too sad… "As Low As You Can Go" is a song about that, saying, "Hey, it's time to slow down in this direction, 'cause this direction is not going to be good for you. So instead of throwing it away, grab the best that life has to offer you and do this."

How did "Blue and Green" come about? That's one of my favorites.

I'm going to say what this is about, but I'm not going to say it happened to me. It's about a young boy and an older woman. I don't know how it is for a woman, but lots of guys fall for older women. A lot of people say that happens because the baby falls in love with their mother and there's a strong possibility that this is the case. Anyway, I was always infatuated with older women, and that's what this song is about. I think I came up with the title line after I had the idea for the song. I do that a lot. I think if you sit around and wait on a line like that, you'd only have one song in your career. Those are nice, happy accidents that you work toward after you start a verse, and when they come out you say, "Wow, I knew I was having inspiration for some reason or another!" By the way, that's one of my favorite songs, too.

Did you draw from personal experience?

I had a bunch of aunts and I knew a bunch of people back in my teens, and I always felt sorry for the women back then. We're talking the fifties and sixties, because if this happened to a particular couple, well, the guy could go ahead and leave and get a divorce or run off and cheat, and the woman was degraded and everything happened to her except being stoned in public… and she was never allowed to do anything and still isn't allowed to do anything. If she follows her heart she still gets no respect. The song was written to say, "Hell, if it's alright for him, it's alright for you to search out your heart and find happiness for yourself." And the song hopefully gives her this freedom, and yet it makes everyone aware of the connotations involved.

How about "Somewhere Between Right and Wrong" and the controversy with it?

I'll spend my eternity there, I guess. This has to do with a girl who's saying, "I'll probably do this and I'd rather do this, and if I do this, I'd rather it be for love." And people were saying, "Well, this guy is talking about sex." Well if I was, and that's the question, I redeemed it by saying, "Yes, but I prefer to do this for love." But people always take the negative when they don't even see the positive aspect of it. But yeah, I got some controversy over that song a little bit. I love controversy. I don't dwell on it. I don't live for it. If people are bitching about something, they are questioning something, so the question itself will lead you to the truth. So if you cause someone to think one way or another, they're at least listening.

"I Have Loved You Girl (But Not Like This Before)" is a very sincere love song.

It was one of my first positive love songs and I hope there are many more to come. I wrote that out of a need to write a positive love song—and it is. I did it poetically and it's kinda romantic, and I like it. I wouldn't even want to work with a song like that every time. But it's real; I see starlight every time I hear that song… a full silvery moon.

What was the inspiration for "Fire and Smoke"?

That song was motivated strictly from a craft point of view, and then that didn't work, because the bridge was all I had written for a long time. Again, I put myself into a potential situation where this guy is out gallivanting around too much and he's lost the best thing in his life. Anyway, the bridge lay around for two years and I couldn't get any verses that would add or do anything for it. So I wrote "Silent Treatment," and immediately after "Silent Treatment," the words to "Fire and Smoke" started to make sense. So this is one of those songs that stretched over a few years.

Bryan-Michael Cox

Interview by
James Kendall

American Songwriter,
January/February 2005

Looking for a smash R&B hit that will rule the charts all summer long? Why not have Bryan-Michael Cox write it for you? The prolific producer and staff writer for Jermaine Dupri's So So Def label has been cranking out hit songs since the late nineties and was recently honored as SESAC's Songwriter of the Year for two years in a row. His co-writing and production work on Mariah Carey's comeback effort, *The Emancipation of Mimi*, helped land her the top-selling album of 2005. He also co-authored Mary J. Blige's breakout single "Be Without You" for her 2005 album *The Breakthrough*. Cox also scored big with songs on Usher's multiplatinum *8701* and has written for a who's who of urban artists, including Destiny's Child, Fantasia, Chris Brown, Christina Milian, Li'l Bow Wow, Aaliyah, and Jagged Edge. In terms of both songwriting quality and creative output, Bryan-Michael Cox retains a Midas touch.

—EVAN SCHLANKSY

Why songwriting?

Because it's something that is a passion of mine. I've always wanted to do it. I've been writing songs as far back as I can remember. Writing little poems and writing little diddies. I had this nickname when I was really little; it was "n BUMP" because my mom played the stereo real loud and I used to crawl up toward the speaker and stand myself on the speaker and bump to the speaker.

Do you think that's necessary for somebody to be successful? Does it have to go that far back?

It doesn't have to go that far back. Some people discover they want to do music when they are teenagers, it just depends. I have a friend who was an athlete, and then he got hurt and discovered that he could write songs. Now he's an accomplished songwriter. The music bug can bite you whenever. For me, that's all I've ever known.

What is it about your songs that makes you consistently successful?

Number one, I do believe in God. That is the main thing; everything comes from Him. It keeps me going. Also, it's melody. Melody and the chord progressions the people feel. Each chord progression gives you a different kind of feeling. A lot of records nowadays lack progressions. Or chord progressions are really just influenced by the beat. It's just not as chord influenced as it used to be. I think that's [melody and chord progressions] what makes it easy for me to write to my records. Harold Lilly or the other songwriters I collaborate with, when I give them a track they automatically get it melodically because of the progressions. You can follow it vs. getting an open track that you kind of have to create melodies on because there is no melody on it.

Do you write more music or lyrics?

Right now I'm a little bit of both. When I first started making records I was really into the composing/producing side of it. Then when I started working with Jermaine [Dupri] a little more. I was a little shy about my writing because I was surrounded by so many talented writers—like Brian and Brandon Casey from Jagged Edge. In the past I was like, "I'm gonna compose my music and give them melodies, I'll let them do what they need to do because they're so incredibly talented." When I started working with Jermaine, he opened up my eyes to my writing ability. So I was doing double time. I was working for him, then I would run up the street in the afternoon to work for Toni Braxton, Jagged Edge, whoever, then go back and work with him on Mariah. I'm still double-timing, really.

How do you go about writing songs for somebody like Toni Braxton or Mariah Carey? How do you write a woman's point of view?

To tell you the truth, I have the most success with writing when the artist is there—when I wrote for Keke Wyatt, she was there so we were able to interact with her. We kind of got her vibe and from her telling us stories, we began writing songs.

What do you think is more successful—writing from your own experience, other people's experiences, or just from your mind?

It just depends on the circumstance. It depends on the vibe, like when we wrote "Burn," it was just a vibe going. We were actually talking about a personal relationship or personal situation and we were like, man, you should probably just let it burn, it was like, "Yo, that's a song." We started talking back and forth and I started singing, he sung the first line, "It's gonna burn for me to say this." Then we did the hook and the second verse. Jermaine and Usher did the break part and it just kind of came together organically. It came from personal experience where all of us kind of meshed our other personal experiences together.

What makes a good song? What does somebody need to do to write a good song?

I think the main thing is story lines. If you can tell your story, that's the first step, but the attractive thing about a song also comes in the melody. Can I sing along with it? Is there ear candy in the record—do I want to hear it over and over again? I think that is the key, like parts on "You Got It Bad." That's the ear candy, something you can just drop in and make people feel the song. And that's a formula that I learned from Jermaine. There's always a part we have to do that's the ear candy.

As far as lyrics and "ear candy," what's more important?

They're equally important.

How does a songwriter just starting out take it from their home out to where it gets noticed?

There are different ways to go about it. The main thing is to try to make some contacts. Try to call up labels, try to figure out who's the A&R person—who's the intern for the person—try to figure out the channels. Because nine times out of ten you're not going to be able to get that record directly to the A&R person, but find out the channels, figure out who is who.

What do you mean by channels?

When I say channels, I mean figuring out the chain of command. In every situation there is a chain of command. That's what I think a lot of people misjudge in the music industry, the fact that it is a business, an industry. You've gotta start at the bottom of the totem pole and go up. For me in Atlanta, the chain of command was using my talent to engineer records. I knew how to engineer, but even with that there was a chain of command in engineering. In my mind, it was a well-thought-out plan. I didn't know if it was going to work, but I

thought, let me get with a company that's inclusive—so either they're their own label, or they're their own production company. I didn't want to work at a big studio because it's really hard to get with the artists or producers at an open studio like that. I wanted to work for a production company that was also a production house so I could leverage my work, learn the production aspect of it and the writing. It's not easy. Find out whatever you can find out. Every plan is different.

I would think that a lot of songwriters think of their own stuff as good as anything else that's out there. Do you think that's a misconception?

It is. A lot of times when CDs get sent to the A&R reps, they don't listen to them. When I worked at a label, we had boxes and boxes of CDs, filled to the brim. You know what they do with those CDs? They throw them away. It's too much music to go through. It's not personal, but I'm going to listen to this CD that my man brought me face-to-face. I'm going to listen to the CD that the intern brought me and put on my desk. That is what I mean by chain of command.

So, even if the only person you can get in contact with is an intern—

That's way better than [just] sending it. Think about it—an intern wants to be an A&R rep someday, so this intern bringing somebody a hit record could be his key to success.

Say you do know an intern and he brings your CD up, but it only has one or two songs. Are they going to say, "This has only two songs" and laugh at you and not even put it in? Are they going to even bother with one song?

If it's one song and they put it in, and it's a hit record, they're going to move it. They're going to get that record in the building. There are politics, but at the end of the day it's about a hit. If somebody gets his hands on a hit record, it doesn't matter if you sent half of one. They're not going to laugh or say, "This guy is crazy; he only sent me one song." If the song isn't a hit record, they're going to say, "He only sent me one song. It was cool, but it's not a hit record." That's all they care about up in there. It is personal opinion and pure chance.

For someone trying to be a songwriter, what do you think is the biggest misconception?

The biggest misconception is publishing. I think that, secondly, they think that every song they write is a smash. A lot of writers I meet say, "I have fifteen smash hits here" and you know, I don't even have fifteen smash hits. I know you're only as good as your last hit record.

How many songs would you write to get that hit song?

I might write five songs, and my ratio's probably two out of five.

So what did you mean when you mentioned misconceptions about publishing?

I think people don't realize how you get paid. I don't think they understand the whole point of full rate vs. three-quarters rate. I don't think people understand that the lyrics and melody are 50 percent, music is 50 percent, that's what makes 100 percent of a song. I don't think people understand that when you do a publishing deal that your publishing deal is actually supposed to be a 50/50 deal—not a 75/25… and there is no class you can take that will teach you that.

This is kind of an odd question, but why should somebody not be a songwriter? Who's the person who shouldn't be a songwriter?

The person that doesn't want to grind, who thinks it's going to come easy, who thinks that every song he writes is a hit, who thinks, "I'll take the easy way out and be a songwriter." This is not an easy job. You've got to be built for this because this game is crazy, there's so much shit that goes into it. It's not like a nine-to-five [job]. If you don't work, you don't eat. In the beginning you're not gonna be making any money until you make your first hit. So, a person who's not patient or diligent, and who doesn't understand the meaning of working really hard… you're not going to see that money. When I first started writing songs, I didn't know anything about it. I couldn't see that money. I didn't even know what kind of money I would make, but I had faith that it was going to lead me to something good—something great.

What's going on in Atlanta?

Well, it's popping. It slowed down a little bit when L.A. [Reid, cofounder of Atlanta's LaFace Records] left, but now it's popping. Jermaine is getting it going up here. There are a lot of producers up here, a lot of songwriters up here, a lot of artists up here. The scene is getting thick again. People are making music again, and the studios are paying again.

What inspires you?

Everything, man. My mother. My girlfriend. I draw from everything around me. I listen to all kinds of music. Throughout the day, to start my day, I may listen to some James Brown and then listen to some Jay-Z and then listen to some Maroon 5. I get inspired by everything that gives me drive to be better.

Wayne Coyne
The Flaming Lips

*Interview by
Benjy Eisen*

American Songwriter,
March/April 2006

There will never be another band quite like The Flaming Lips. Led by Wayne Coyne, the unapologetically weird and relentlessly experimental Lips have slowly become one of America's favorite acts. When they were properly introduced to the mainstream with their 1994 top forty novelty hit, "She Don't Use Jelly" (from the album *Transmissions From the Satellite Heart*), few people were aware they had already amassed a sizable body of work. The band was in danger of being forgotten as quickly as they'd been embraced (one of their follow-up projects, 1997's *Zaireeka,* required four separate stereos to be properly reproduced) until unanimous critical praise for 1999's psychedelic opus, *The Soft Bulletin*, helped lift them from cult status band to respected rockers. 2002's *Yoshimi Battles the Pink Robots*, featuring the hit "Do You Realize?," provided the perfect vehicle for the Lips's new message of spiritual uplift. In 2006, the band returned with the eclectic tour de force *At War With the Mystics.*

—EVAN SCHLANSKY

94

I'd like to talk about the process of songwriting. I know that what makes one song better than another can be a fairly elusive notion. But in your opinion, what makes the perfect song?

Well I think—you mentioned there is an elusion to the whole idea of what songwriting is. To me, it's not really just the song. Here's an example. Take Elton John's "Bennie and the Jets." When you listen to that song—it's on the *Goodbye Yellow Brick Road* album—it's a wonderful creation. You don't know, is that a song? Is that a production? Is that a performance? But you don't really care, it just comes out of the speakers and you enjoy it, you know? Now if you listen to Elton John play that song now, with the way his band sounds now and the way his voice sounds now, and you take away all that great production—I love Elton John but sometimes it's just too awkward to listen to. It's not a matter of songwriting. But sometimes the songwriting is just one element of it. It's performance, it's production, it's timing, it's enthusiasm, it's a billion different elements that make a song seem like it's doing all the work when really the work is being done by all kinds of little worker ants along the way. It sounds like it's just in the song, but it's rarely just in the song.

Don't get me wrong—you have to have great songs. But you have to have great production, you have to have great performance, and everything along the way has to be interesting.

I completely agree. What are some of your own songs that, looking back on them, you really feel that you hit what you were going for?

Oh yeah, I think all along the way you stumble upon these things and you just get lucky. But from the past five or six years, I don't think anybody would hear a song like "Race for the Prize" and not think, "Damn, you guys got lucky with that one!" It's something that feels triumphant and powerful, but human and fragile, all at the same time.

I even think "A Spoonful Weighs a Ton." There's an element to these songs… we went in to do them and we really thought they were going to be heavy, sad, these songs that are revealing the hard, sharp edges of a sad reality. When we started to hear these songs coming out of the speakers coming back to us, we thought, damn, these are really songs about the joy of living! And that really surprised us. It revealed something to us, that despite what we thought was our state of mind—gloomy and doomy and death colored—somewhere deep inside of us we were still enthusiastic and optimistic. I think our best songs do that despite our intentions.

And then there's a song like "Do You Realize?" that just touched so many people. Almost every time we play it at least someone comes up to me and [tells me] it was either used at their wedding or the birth of their son or daughter or their brother's funeral or one of these big moments in someone's life, and again, we just got really lucky.

I think you struck a very similar emotional chord with the song "My Cosmic Autumn Rebellion."

Oh, yeah! Well that song—to me, it's one of those powerful, sort of existential, sort of optimistic, defiant songs. I don't know if people will be able to understand exactly what is going on there, but it just rolls at you with such epic-ness.

It goes back to what you were talking about earlier, how a song that could be about suffering and drudgery actually ends up revealing deep joy. It seems to me that you really explore that whole yin-yang thing.

You see, there's an exuberance that comes out of music, which isn't necessarily found in song*writing*. I'm not saying that the two aren't woven together, but there's something in sounds and atmospheres that can take a melody and a chord structure and change it utterly into another realm. Even a song like "Feeling Yourself Disintegrate," I remember when

I wrote it in the back room here, I wasn't even sure what I was trying to say but as I sat there with the tape recorder on, I came up with that line of "Love in your life is just too valuable." The minute you don't feel love emanating from something in the universe, you almost realize how little life is worth living, and everything that you try to embrace is going to die and everything is slowly disintegrating including yourself, you know? But there are really only a few moments in your life when you ever feel that. Most of your life is just happening and you're eating breakfast or you're shitting or you're taking a shower or you're having sex with your wife or you're playing with your band, something is always happening to you and you hardly ever have a moment where you just really understand what is the true cosmic reality we're kind of floating through. In that song, I didn't know I was going to do that. And I sat there and the words that came out of me, I'm like "Fuck, that's wickedly truthful!" Almost to the point where it scared me.

I remember reading something from you a while ago where you said you thought of yourself as an entertainer and music was sort of just your vessel. A lot of people see music purely as entertainment, and then a lot of people see music as a very spiritual and powerful force. I'm wondering your thoughts on that dichotomy and on music's ability to be both these things.

Well, you really said it earlier when you said it's all so subjective. And if a teenager comes up to me and says, you know, the latest Blink 182 song changed his life profoundly and he thinks it's the greatest song that's ever been written, he's right. To his experience, if that song did that, then he's right. Whereas, you know, someone else might come up to you and say gosh, "Somewhere Over the Rainbow" when Dorothy sings that in that movie it encompasses all that's great about life—they're right, too! So it is all subjective. To me, I try to take it out of the realm of being something so precious like music and art is and think of it more like food. If someone comes up to you and says their favorite food in the world is Cap'n Crunch cereal, you can't tell them it's not. Music should have the same freedom.

A lot of times the people who think music is sacred and holy and changes the world, that's usually musicians and artists, you know? And the people who think of it as being dumb entertainment, I mean… it's neither one. I think at best entertainment can be a transcendental experience. We have a great art museum in Oklahoma City. On any given day maybe they have like twenty people show up, you know? The art that's in museums is usually visited by other artists. But you can see how many people are at home watching *Project Runway* on TV and how many people are going to rock concerts, how many people are going to these dumb wrestling shows, because they're just dumb entertainment! It's not necessarily that they're escaping in entertainment; it's just fun to have somebody else do the work for you. When I play, I guarantee people: You don't have to do anything here. All you have to do is laugh with us. You just relax and all the work is going to be done for you. And if people think that that's any less of a dignified stance to take as a profession, they're just wrong.

Your live shows are theatrical spectacles with multimedia elements and confetti and people dressed in animal costumes dancing all over the stage. Do you think the party atmosphere masks some of the seriousness and meaning of some of these songs?

No. I think there's an element of that thing you are talking about when people are dancing onstage with us and it becomes such a joyful moment. But you see how much the audience is doing it when you're up there with us on stage and they're singing along and I'm telling them, "C'mon, you've got to cheer louder!" It really is a great moment of some sort of shared experience. We're all there together making this moment happen. And I don't really know if we need to search any deeper than that. In a way rock concerts are supposed to be vehicles by which you get to have sex with your girlfriend. They're not designed to change the world; they're just supposed to be a little moment that we have together. I think if you want to go home and listen to the records and stuff like that, in the isolation of your own mind, you'll find plenty of questions and plenty of answers and plenty of different ways of thinking. But when we're all there together I kind of feel like the best thing that we can do is kind of share that sort of top level of love that happens at a concert like that where I'm saying "I love you" and they're saying they love us. We know it's just dumb rock 'n' roll, but it's a fun thing and it really does make you feel good about your fellow human beings, to share a moment like that together. And to me that's the greatest thing you can do.

When you come out with a new album, do you try to come up with a totally reworked live show or are you just going to integrate the new songs into the current show?

When we begin any kind of cycle where there are new songs and stuff we usually try to keep it familiar. What's liked about us is if you saw us play, let's say, last October [at the] Vegoose [music festival] and you see us this summer, I wouldn't want you to think, "Oh, whatever they're doing, it's completely different." I hope that there's an element of things that you like about us and hope to see about us and we'll do those things and then as it goes along we'll probably add some new things and, you know, maybe drop some of the old things, but I think for the most part we'll probably veer along looking similar enough that no one would be disappointed.

How does producer Dave Fridmann play into the songwriting process? Does he come in more for the production end of it or does he have an active role in the songwriting process?

If we're lucky, we get to work on records for quite a long time. We've worked with him since 1989, almost everything that we've done has been done with Dave, and only one record was done with Keith Cleversley. And so there's an intensity by which we can work because we're so familiar with each other. Sometimes I can walk in and I can have something almost completely finished and he can listen to it and he can know, "Oh, we should change this or that" because he's listening to it objectively and he knows that I'm obsessed with it and that I think everything about it is perfect. And he can easily listen to it and go, "Oh, that's too long," or "Let's change this," and I have to trust that that's going to work.

Other times I can come in with stuff that's very kind of, you know, just a sketch and say, "Oh, I've got a couple of ideas," but what I need is input from people to say we need some sounds here, we need atmosphere, and it really requires everybody to sort of be into this thing at the same time. And he lets you work however, whatever it is you're doing, he can make it work. So if we have a really thin sketch, he's part of the songwriting team and part of the production team that's actually creating it. If we have things that we've already created, he's part of the team that's letting it be recorded and letting it be arranged. So he really is just right there with you doing whatever has to be done. I mean, I say it all the time, but it's like if the toilet is backed up, he'll go and help you unclog the toilet. He's not necessarily just pragmatic but he just takes whatever is in front of him and says, "Look, what can I do here, fellas? Can I assist you?" And usually he's of great assistance. He's either patient or he's mad or he's something that's adding an energy to it and when we're all moving along in the unknown, a lot of times

as we are, you need people to be opinionated. Because if you don't like it, you better say something. Don't tell me a year later, "Oh, I never liked that part."

The music really fits the lyrics on this album, and it seems like they both were written with the other one in mind. "Mr. Ambulance Driver," for example, musically mimics an ambulance siren. Can you talk about that process?

That's exactly it. There's no clear way that you can do it. A lot of times it happens by accident and you say, "Oh! Whatever that was, go back to that, because that was perfect." It must be something like when the guy is walking on the hot coals and he's on his bare feet and he just looks up and says, "Fuck, I hope it all works out." There's just, sometimes, a momentum in the vagueness of what you're doing that helps you not be so precise. There is this idea that someone like Mozart just thinks of all this in his head and then he just simply writes it down and it's already in his head. And maybe that was true for him but I've never seen that to be true for anybody else, ever, that I've ever worked with. Usually what happens is you're simply fumbling in the dark and you have expressions and internal things that you want to get out of you but you just don't have the right vehicle to pull it out.

Suddenly you'll stumble upon something and this emotion and this line of thought is able to coast out of your mind and hopefully onto some computer somewhere or some tape machine somewhere and sort of be stranded there forever as evidence of what your mind was doing. Because it isn't just thoughts and lyrics, it's a whole atmosphere; it's like a whole life inside of your mind.

With something like that little segment "It's Dark…," I stumbled upon this little sound that I just thought, "Boy, that really sounds like you're in this mystery," yet you're curious about what's coming at you. And you're afraid yet you keep going forward. It sounds like this British teenage girl,

you know? Connecting that to "The Sound of Failure" was just perfect. Here she was searching for this darkness that she wanted to understand and embrace and suddenly she went into that and it really does become this thing that's all around you—almost like a psychedelic movie that's playing. We know when it's happening because it's happening to us and we try to trust that if we like it, probably you would, too.

The original concept for that album began as something different, with this naked star queen and this wizard…

Yeah, just drug-induced fantastical freaky imaginative thinking. It couldn't go anywhere. We never want to diminish the originality of something like the *Yoshimi Battles the Pink Robots* record or even something like the somber thing that's happening on *The Soft Bulletin*. So even though by accident we end up doing the same kinds of things over and over, we always try to catch ourselves like, "Fuck, we can't do that again." It isn't that we don't like it; it's just that we don't want to diminish the originality of those other recordings. And so we would just go off on these tangents, like, "I can sing songs about wizards and spaceships and shit," because it's fun and it frees you to be of another identity. But there are always three or four different colors colliding at the same time and if you're lucky you can get two or three themes running through your music at the same time. So while you can be singing about something supernatural and fantastical, you can also be talking about something that's actually humanistic and real, and doing both at the same time, if you're lucky. And I think with some of the better tracks you get a sense of I'm either totally hallucinating on twenty hits of LSD or I've discovered the undisputed absolute truth. Maybe it's both at the same time, and I love that, you know?

Sheryl Crow

photo courtesy Christian Lantry

Sheryl Crow's musical journey has taken her from backup singer to rock royalty. A talented song-writer—a capable lyricist with a knack for sunny melodies—Crow understands the fundamental goodness of sixties and seventies classic rock and strives to uphold the same traditions in her own work. Crow was born February 11, 1962, in Kennett, Missouri. Her parents were both musicians and encouraged her to play the piano. She studied music at the University of Missouri, and after moving to Los Angeles, found work as a backup vocalist for artists like Michael Jackson, Rod Stewart, Sting, and Sinead O'Connor. She was also busy writing songs; Wynonna Judd, Céline Dion, and Eric Clapton all recorded Crow's early compositions. Her debut album, 1993's *Tuesday Night Music Club*, was initially met with slow sales until the third single ("All I Wanna Do") caught fire upon release. *Tuesday Night* would go on to sell seven million copies and net her the first of several Grammy Awards to come. Outsider producers Mitchell Froom and Tchad Blake helped her craft an adventurous follow up, 1996's *Sheryl Crow*, whose singles "Every Day Is a Winding Road," "A Change (Would Do You Good)," and "If It Makes You Happy" all went on to become rock radio staples. 1998's *The Globe Sessions* spawned the hit "My Favorite Mistake," rumored to be about ex-boyfriend Eric Clapton. It also contained the track "Mississippi," a gift from Bob Dylan (he cut it himself on 2001's *Love and Theft*). 2002's *C'mon, C'mon* gave her another summer smash with the top twenty pop hit "Soak Up the Sun." In 2005, Crow released *Wildflower*, her most personal album to date.

—EVAN SCHLANSKY

Interview by
Michael Gallucci

American Songwriter,
September/October 2005

Are you the "wildflower" of your new record?

Thematically, that song seemed to be consistent throughout. No matter how chaotic it is in the world, there is goodness and beauty. We just have to be sure we don't become desensitized to it while we're being barraged with all these images. Part of that really is influenced by not only the chaos in the world but by my own personal search. Here I am in my forties, trying to find a way to exist with a certain modicum of peace, while everything outside is kind of in a heightened chaotic state.

How personal are the songs?

This has been an interesting experience. We had just toured the greatest hits record [*The Very Best of Sheryl Crow*], and it was a bigger success than any of us thought, with the advent of iTunes and the ability to make your own kind of greatest hits. We were surprised it did so well, and it gave me the opportunity to step back a little bit and say, "What direction do I want to go? That's the end of that chapter. It's time to turn a corner." Also, I think what influenced the record [is that] I'm older now. I'm not competing for radio time anymore, at least in my mind. My business has become so image-conscious and youth-oriented, it really felt to me that I had all this freedom to explore themes and ideas that are, for people my age and maybe ten years younger and ten years older, very prevalent on a daily basis.

Are you under any pressure to deliver these days? Back when you started, you had to get your name out. Now, you have obligations to your record company and fans.

I really don't feel any obligation to be successful for my fans or record label. Luckily, I'm on a label that put out *Sea Change*, and when Beck handed it in, nobody said, "Look, we don't have a hit. We're not even gonna work on this." Instead, they rose to the occasion and said, "This is a complete artistic state-ment. It's too silly to send this artist back in and say, 'We need a single.' So, we're going to find a creative and hopefully innovative way to get this out to the people that it would really relate to." It was a critically acclaimed record and a record that is now a staple of many people's record collections. Definitely mine. And I hope that mine will be received the same way. I certainly got the same reception from my record label. Nobody said, "Okay, we don't have a 'Soak Up the Sun.'" They said, "If you feel like this is complete, then let's go to work and everybody put your creative hats on."

In a way, it's the opposite of "Soak Up the Sun." It's a more somber, reflective record.

I always like having the comfort of a palette to choose from of records that, for me, seem to have some relevance. The only record I could really look at for this record before going in and recording was Neil Young's *Harvest*. I listen to that record still, and it always commands that I feel. And it also gives me the sense that Neil is singing personally to me, and obviously he's not. I think as a listener that's what you strive for in a record like this—that you have that interaction between you and the listener. There's nothing on this record to me that says I'm trying to get on the radio. And that wasn't even of interest to me. And the thing I loved, and still love, about *Harvest* is that… the songs are simple, but they transcend time and space. I think he accomplishes it through the melodies he writes and the lyrics and the fact that his voice is so much an important instrument on the record. I found that through the years that I've gotten bogged down with being the producer. I just wanted to have an experience where I felt like the main thing on this record was the voice, the melody, and the lyrics.

The title, *Wildflower*, even sort of reflects *Harvest* in that they're both outdoorsy.

I honestly didn't think of that aspect of it, but yeah… but ["Wildflower"] is my favorite one on the record; to me it's the song that encapsulated [the record] thematically all the way through—what I felt the record was about.

At this stage in your career, is it easier to focus on writing?

This musical experience to me was much more about writing the songs before going into the studio. I've always had this love-hate relationship with recording, because I would always wait until I got into the studio to write. And usually it follows a very strenuous, long tour, and I think I'm just gonna go in, be creative, make a record, and take some time off. And it never happens that way. There's always a certain amount of teeth gnashing and hair pulling before I ever come up with anything. And the thing that drives me to finish the record is that I know if I stick with it, I'm going to surprise myself and come up with stuff I've never done before. But it's just an arduous experience. So, this time, I went to Europe with [boyfriend] Lance [Armstrong] and just wrote on the guitar into a cassette recorder and didn't go in to record anything before it was finished. And it makes for a really peaceful and pleasing recording experience.

So, some of these songs were written in Europe? It's a very American-sounding album.

Most of them were written over the course of last year, between February and September, kind of all over the place. I wrote some of them in Austin, some of them in Los Angeles, and some of them in Spain, which is where we spent a lot of time last year. I wrote one of them while I was in [Gran] Canaria, which is a Canary Island. While [Lance] was training, I was kind of sitting at the top of a volcano. Wherever I was, I was writing.

Did the songs change much by the time you recorded them?

No, not at all. It really was a singer/songwriter record, where it was just about the melody and the lyrics and the voice.

Do you write differently now than you did when you started out?

On this record, there are a couple of songs that are written on piano, and that's the way they're recorded. There are more songs written on guitar. Sometimes I write on bass, because I find that the melody is better. Most of it was written on a guitar with a tape player. I set out with software and was gonna do some demos, but I just decided to not even do that. [I wanted to] just go in and record the best version of it and not get bogged down with big, fancy production.

How does your environment affect the songs?

Not only the location but also the relationship informs the tone of the record, in that I was a stranger in a strange place a lot of last year. I didn't speak the language and was really living in these places, not just visiting. Also, I was in a new relationship, which also creates this sort of vulnerability, this kind of open-heartedness, where you're really expressing acute feelings. A lot of that stuff came over the record much more introspective and much more personal. And I do think that socio-politically speaking, there were a lot of things going on in the world that definitely affected all people. This chaotic feeling. This feeling of uncertainty. To me, there are big questions that are kind of interwoven through the record. Like, this idea of, where do we stand in our beliefs? If our whole [faith] is based on a God that gets us into this place, heaven, and we're warring with people who believe their god is a god who gives them salvation… is that not in direct opposition with what we believe God to be? Certainly, we exist in America under the constraints of our policy being dictated by religion now. But also in bigger themes, like the Terri Schiavo thing and being out of the country and watching how Americans are being portrayed. All that stuff was a part of the consciousness of that record.

Like Dylan sang more than forty years ago in "With God on Our Side."

That's the beauty of getting to have the job I have. All those themes? They don't ever go away. Most wars have been steeped in religious overtones, if not overtly. And, certainly, you come into the world in your religious surroundings because of the clan you were born to, and you start to ask questions. And ultimately the main question is, "Where am I going to go when I die?" It's a question you ask when you're a child: "Where are you going to go, Mom and Dad, when you die, and am I going to see you there?" And then, in the end, you're laying on your deathbed in the final hours still saying, "Where am I going to go, and what do I believe?" Dylan asked it. Everyone asks it.

Are you religious?

I'm spiritual. And I definitely believe in a god. I have many friends who are agnostic, Jewish, following the Kabbalah. Everybody is in a search for what they believe, certainly during these times. What's happening in our country is really too much. Everybody's on that search. And to say that one way is the right way is arrogant. I think that's why we suffer the reputation we suffer outside of our country. We have leaders right now that are saying, "We are the ones who know. We need to police the rest of the world." It's a dangerous time to be a writer; it's a great time to be a writer. And luckily, and sadly, my business has gone the way it has gone, so I have this wide open-door policy that I get to write about things that I know aren't going to get on the radio.

Do you know what you're going to write about when you start writing?

I always have a notebook. I try to write every day, though I'm not religious about it. I don't edit myself, and then later on, I'll [look at the] themes, or if there's even anything in there that looks like a title or a beginning of a song.

Do you ever get writer's block?

I did on the last record, and that's only because I didn't have any business going in and making a record without songs and having been on the road and not having taken time off to kind of gather some stories.

Are you inspired more when you're happy or sad?

I'm not terribly productive when I'm sad. I'm not terribly productive when I'm really down and exhausted, either. [It's more like in between] when you have enough detachment to be able to have an idea about what's happening.

What inspires you as a fan?

I'm a purist. I believe what makes a good song is a memorable melody and universal lyric themes. I grew up with writers like Burt Bacharach in my house. On any given night, Burt Bacharach might walk into my house and have dinner with us. He was such a real fixture. I grew up with music by Cole Porter, real melody-oriented stuff, because that's what my parents played. Over time, I kind of got away from wanting to write melodies because it didn't seem so cool, and that's not what was getting played on the radio. But now that I'm older, I come back to it and I realize what really motivates me to continue to write songs is that somebody wrote the song "Yesterday," and it's possible to write a song like that. It was a human being that wrote it. In all of our imperfections, there is perfection.

Do you still strive for that?

Yeah, that's what keeps me interested in writing. I always feel like my best work is ahead of me.

Looking back, how has the past decade shaped you?

I think who I am as a person shapes what I put out. Realistically, the best you can hope for is that you allow yourself to be exposed on your record, and that the record documents something that is real. It documents who you are while you're writing it. But I think what's happened in my life, as far as my career goes… I've had the opportunity to see a lot of different things in the world, and it's given me a bigger overview, and it's made writing interesting for me. But it's also made me extremely devoted and aware of who I am and where I'm from, as far as, like, having grown up in a small town in Middle America and what that means to me as a writer.

Is that self-consciousness a good thing or a bad thing in a songwriter?

It depends. For me, my biggest curse was editing myself. But it's fun to write in an alter ego. The [most] fun record I've ever written was the *Sheryl Crow* record, because we were in New Orleans, and that had a lot to do with the feel of the

…The best you can hope for is that you allow yourself to be exposed on your record, and that the record documents something that is real.

record and the cinematography of the record. It was a lot of fun to make that record because there was a strong personality on it. On this record, there was none of that. It was all about introspection and analysis; not so much self-analysis, but analysis in general.

The *Sheryl Crow* record is my favorite of yours.

I hear that from more people. I think more people found things to relate to on that record than anything else.

What are you most proud of?

I think the songs you're always proud of are the ones you got your own way on and that wrote themselves top to bottom. You look back and go, "Gee, where did that come from?" "Home" is one of those songs. "Riverwide" is one of those songs, lyrically. And musically, it was more kind of adventurous. And probably "Redemption Day." It wasn't the song I set out to write, but it definitely summed up how I felt about the government's involvement, or lack of involvement, in Rwanda.

How often does that happen?

Not so often, because as a songwriter who knows how to craft a song, you get bogged down in that. You really beat it to death, trying to pull it together, knowing, "Okay, I'm going to make this song great, because I know how to do it." At which point, you finally just say, "Okay, I'm not gonna finish this." Sometimes, that's when the good stuff comes. And that's what "Redemption Day" was. It was meant to be a song about a relationship and it wound up being about a trip I just made to Bosnia. And it was written at the computer with no song, just a cadence, basically.

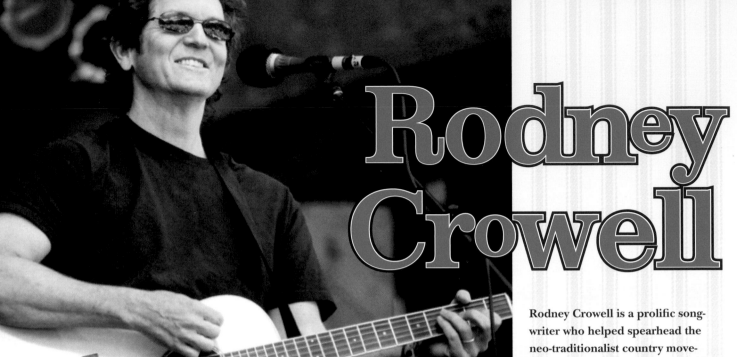

Rodney Crowell

Interview by
Brian T. Atkinson

American Songwriter,
May/June 2005

Rodney Crowell is a prolific songwriter who helped spearhead the
neo-traditionalist country movement in the mid-eighties. Crowell
moved from Houston to Nashville
in 1972, where he landed a publishing deal and palled around with Townes Van
Zandt and Guy Clark. Crowell scored his first top forty hit, "Ashes By Now,"
taken from his second solo album, in 1980. During the next decade, Crowell
also saw success with songs he'd written for others, penning number one hits for
The Oak Ridge Boys ("Leavin' Louisiana in the Broad Daylight"), Crystal Gayle
("'Til I Gain Control Again"), the Nitty Gritty Dirt Band ("Long Hard Road [The
Sharecropper's Dream]"), and Highway 101 ("Somewhere Tonight"). Crowell's
1998 album, *Diamonds & Dirt*, yielded five number one singles in a row, among
them "It's Such a Small World" and "I Couldn't Leave You if I Tried." His most
recent album, *The Outsider*, was released by Columbia Records in 2005. He also
turned in a solid rendition of Kris Kristofferson's classic "Come Sundown" for
the 2006 tribute album, *The Pilgrim: A Celebration of Kris Kristofferson*.

—EVAN SCHLANSKY

How did hanging around Townes Van Zandt and Guy Clark when you were young affect you as a songwriter?

It instilled me with the right attitude, which is that the craft, the process, and the creativity of songwriting is far more important than the material rewards. To illustrate that a little further, [in the early days] it was about late night song-swapping sessions, and that was always about: "What are you working on? Are you getting any better at this?" Now, you know, it's changed in Nashville. These days it's about who you can get to record the song. With Townes and Mickey Newbury and that crew, it was never about who you could get to record the songs. It was about if you're getting anywhere in your ability to communicate. And can you take the music away from this and have it stand alone as poetry?

Did one of them influence you more than another?

Guy Clark. More personally, Guy is probably the most influential on me, especially in terms of practical craft. By allowing me to be his friend and be close, I learned more from Guy about self-editing than anyone else. I'd say Guy is the best self-editor of all the songwriters I can imagine. There is just nothing wasted in what he does.

I know those guys were really influenced by the blues—especially by Lightnin' Hopkins and Mance Lipscomb. Were you as well?

I think it was more lifestyle. I think Townes wishes he was Mance Lipscomb or Lightnin' Hopkins, so therefore he sort of emulated their lifestyle, their swagger, their free-wheeling. Both Townes and Guy were well-read, educated lads, Townes particularly. He was extremely smart. I think he just loved to live the lifestyle.

What's your background as far as musical influences?

I came from a musical household that was based in Appalachian folk music and Roy Acuff country music and, later on, honky-tonk. Country music came from my father, the records lying out of their dust jackets when I was a wee lad. There was Hank Williams. And I was just the right age for the British Invasion to sweep me up in its fashion and its romance. You know, the Stones and the Beatles and Dylan. The Carnaby Street persona really grabbed a hold of me. I'm equal parts—in terms of musical influence—Merle Haggard and Buck Owens and Lennon/McCartney and Dylan. It's just when I found my way into the actual practical world of being a songwriter, among other professionals, I was lucky enough to fall [in with] Townes and Guy and Mickey. In truth, study with masters.

Those writers would probably say that the lyric is what really counts the most. Is that what comes first when you write, the words?

Well, I think that's true with both Guy and Townes. That's the school of Bob Dylan, whereas with me, the band and the arranging are also important. I think it's that I'm ten years younger, and the band and the arranging are forms of expression that's used with the songwriting. Still, having said that, what's most important is what the song's saying.

Does the production affect the songs at all when you're creating them in the studio?

It will. But I'm usually very careful to see that the writing is done before I ever get to the place of production, because production is the soundtrack to the movie. So, I'm usually very careful to see that the writing of the song is complete before it ever gets to the production stage. Occasionally I'll fool myself and find myself in the middle of making choices about production when I'm realizing that I need to back up and solidify the thought that I thought I had captured in writing the song. Let me put it this way; I don't trust creating a track and building a record and then writing the lyrics. I feel I do a better job of writing if I do that before getting to the production stage.

Tell me about the title of your album, _The Outsider_. Where does that come from?

It came from a dream, actually. Without going too far into the specifics of the dream, I woke up and wrote it down. I went back to sleep, and then I got back up again and went into my studio and started writing [the title track]. It was the last song that I wrote for the record. I really thought I had finished it. Really, coming from the liberal viewpoint, I don't want to contribute to the media's catchall polarization of America. I was abroad during an election, so I was pretty angry all during the election campaign. To me _The Outsider_ was intended to balance, to walk right into the middle of the polarization and give both sides a voice. It's just my own personal opinion, and I'm always very careful of my ownership of my own personal relationship with the Great Spirit or God or whatever you want to call it. I have no reason to try to bring anyone to my point of view. It is my point of view that God, as we may or may not know it, is indeed _The Outsider_.

How important do you think it is for artists to offer social or political commentary?

It's a tradition. It's part of art's role in the evolution of mankind. Whenever the church finally released its stranglehold on art, when the Renaissance came and art was opened up and someone else started bankrolling the artists, it took another swing, and the artists actually started to express the hypocrisy that they saw. In the tradition of the artists that I've admired, even down to Merle Haggard, it's the artist's job to reflect back to those who'll listen to the truth of what they see. It doesn't mean you're right; it's just the truth of what you see. That's the artist's job, as far as I'm concerned. It's not just love. It's not just Hallmark pleasantries. It's the dank and dour aspects of humanity, too.

I just saw Steve Earle here in Denver the other night, and he's pretty overt with that idea.

There's a lot of political talk between songs. He takes some pretty hard hits from the conservative press because of that. Is there anyone else you see out there making such a stand?

I think Steve does it with a heavier hand than I do, and I admire him for that. I think Steve's important. His courage and his willingness to put himself up there and take those hard hits; it's like, "Hey, my hat's off, dear boy." There are other artists. To me, it's not just railing from my point of view. In fact, I'm really more interested in what unites human beings than what divides them. That was my real purpose in _The Outsider_, the song itself: "I don't have to be hip/You don't have to be losing your grip/I don't have to be white as a ghost/You don't have to be dumb as a post." All of those so-called polarized political positions—it's out there, it's true. But what's far more of interest to me is what unites us. This is a long-winded way of getting at the fact that I admire what Bono [of U2] does. He strives for a higher level, and he actually goes to the source. He goes to the conservative right and finds a way to communicate with those people. He tries to bring them in to make things better, to lift up the human spirit. Given that, I'd have to admire his approach the most.

You said you wrote most of the album in Europe. How did that influence the songs and your mindset? Was it actually being in Europe that made you mad about things, or did you just see them differently from over there?

I really felt like an expatriate watching something from abroad. What I saw is how absolutely adept the media is at creating a split right down the middle. Anybody who's ever studied writing—especially writing for television—knows it's all based on antagonism. I think they play the antagonism right down the middle. It's how they get their ratings, how they get their audience. I couldn't decide if

I was [angrier] at the hierarchy who controls the media or the rank and file out there in the middle of America who let themselves be swept up by it—including me. I'm talking about the American media. The British have a way of sidestepping the fact that they're in cahoots with our regime, but they're a lot more fair and balanced in the way they present it.

Tell me the story about "Don't Get Me Started." I read it came from a woman being verbally abusive toward you in a Belfast pub.

I had on this T-shirt that said "Security" on it. She gathered that I was American and she just started ripping into me. She took "Security" to mean our homeland security position, as in our global policy. She just ripped me. And I was just trying to get a hand up to tell her to stop. I was never able to get her to understand my point of view. What it left me with was the notion of political railings in a bar. I came back home and started creating my own rant from the point of view of an angry politico in a bar—just drunk and spewing. I chose that way to express it because it is truly my viewpoint, everything in that song, but I wanted to deliver it with a little humor. If you look a little deeper, you see that this guy owns up that he's a drag when he's drunk, and he's over the top with it, but, damn it, "I mean it."

"The Obscenity Prayer" is one of my favorites.

Mine, too.

Lines like "I can search for truth some other time/but right now I just want to get what's mine" seem to touch on a lot of different groups of the modern era. You've said something specifically about Enron relating to the song. Is that what inspired the song?

Enron is just a symptom of what I think is the really pervasive disease: greed without moral center. This debate in America about moral values—being about gay rights and other things—is just a smokescreen. The real moral decay is greed and profit at all costs. That's who I'm railing against. Shit, the hypocrisy of the "me, me, me." Reagan and Clinton set up the deregulation so it could escalate to the place that it is now, where corporations can own everything. Therefore, with power they can justify their selfish greed. "The Obscenity Prayer" is about trying to expose the greedy mindset, the selfishness, the lack of compassion. That is my favorite one.

When I first heard it, parts seemed to be about gangsta rappers.

Well, I have gangsta rappers in there. There's a certain slice of that whole thing that's motivated by greed. A lot of the NBA is motivated by greed. But Enron is sort of the illustration; it is my belief that the greed and its lack of a moral center will eventually bring about its own undoing.

The Dylan cover ["Shelter From the Storm"]: Why did you include that on the album?

It was something that I had recorded with Emmylou [Harris] and did for a television show [*Crossing Jordan*]. I liked how we sounded. Several of my trusted advisors said that I should put that out… that it should be heard. I felt the tone and the feeling of it fit the record.

John Denver

Known for his sweet, mellow voice and his deep love of nature, John Denver has authored some of the country's most wholesome slices of Americana. Born with the name Henry John Deutschendorf, Jr., Denver took his stage name as a tribute to his beloved Rocky Mountain region. In 1969, he made waves on the folk music scene with "Leaving on a Jet Plane," a hit he penned for Peter, Paul and Mary. After a stint in the Chad Mitchell Trio, Denver went solo, becoming one of the top-selling artists of the seventies. 1971's *Poems, Prayers & Promises* contained the future standards "Take Me Home, Country Roads" and "Sunshine on My Shoulders," and in 1974 Denver topped the charts with "Thank God I'm a Country Boy." In 1991, he released his last solo album, the uplifting *Different Directions*. Denver died in a tragic plane crash in 1997. In 2005, his songs were celebrated on Broadway in the stage show *Almost Heaven: John Denver's America*.

—EVAN SCHLANSKY

*Interview by
Deborah Evans Price*

American Songwriter,
July/August 1992

When did you begin writing melodies? Was it something that naturally occurred after you began playing the guitar?

I think it's natural for anyone who starts to play a musical instrument to start experimenting with melodies of their own. I was about twelve when I started playing the guitar. I think the first song I wrote… I was about thirteen. It was at a Presbyterian Church camp in Arizona. One day I went for a walk up the Colorado River and the song I wrote was called "Sittin' on the Banks of a Lazy Little Stream." It's interesting to me that from the very beginning nature was a big part of how I tried to communicate or articulate myself. The fourth song I wrote was called "For Baby (For Bobbie)." And the next song I wrote was "Leaving on a Jet Plane." That's about the fifth song I ever wrote.

And you got your start, so to speak, by singing your songs for Cherry Lane Music reps?

[Cherry Lane head Milt Okun] said it was good enough for the Chad Mitchell Trio and offered to be my publisher. And he has been ever since. I had never thought about signing with a publisher. I never thought about the business end of it. When it got to a point where a song of mine was going to be recorded, then it was appropriate to have a publisher. It was much smarter to have a publisher who knew the business and who could take care of me in an area where I have no talent or ability or knowledge than to try to do it myself. I was very lucky to have been able to sign with a very able, wise, and *honest* man. And I underline honest because there are a lot of crooks out there that will make every deal they can, hoping to sign some young kid who has the greatest song in the world, make a fortune, and pay the kid as little as possible. Unfortunately, that goes on out there. But you trust your heart and look for a guy who can't do the things you do.

We have now established a new company called Cherry Mountain Music, of which we share ownership. It was Milt's idea and his offer. He said, "John, it's appropriate you get a part of the business end of it, too."

Do you have a specific approach as a writer? Are you what they call a "structured songwriter"?

I don't sit down every day and try to write a song. For some people, it's like a job and that's what they do. They go in and try to write a song. For me it quite often begins with a phrase like "leaving on a jet plane" or "follow me" or "back home again" or "sunshine on my shoulders." What'll happen… there'll be a phrase or line that I've come up with. When I'm driving I'll start writing the song in my head. Then when I get to a guitar, I'll sit and play the guitar until the rest of the song comes. Some songs come very quickly. I wrote "Annie's Song" in ten minutes one day on a ski lift; that's how I know it was ten minutes. The other songs, like "Rocky Mountain High," took about seven months to write.

Do you believe in rewrites?

You take whatever time it takes and when it's done, it's done. I'm one of those that feels the song has a life of its own, and in my songwriting, I want whatever comes through to me to be true to my song. I try to be true to the song, true to the music.

What do you look for when cutting a song that has been written by another songwriter?

For me to say, "Gosh, I could have done that song." When I can relate to it easily and it makes me feel something and I wish I had written that song. It's just that connection you have with that piece of music.

Talk about your relationship with songwriter Joe Henry. Looking over your credits, he seems to be the only person you've collaborated with.

If I get stuck lyrically, he's the person I call. I've never gotten stuck musically.

You guys wrote "Windsong" together. How did the idea for that song come about?

We sat up one night and talked about the wind. Joe and I wanted to write a song about the wind and we talked and talked. I put out all these ideas and pictures I had in my head and he took notes. He stayed at my house that night and the next morning I got up and he had gone. The song was written out on a piece of paper on the kitchen table. So then the song was there and that gave birth to the music.

How have you progressed as a songwriter from the time that you were a thirteen-year-old kid writing songs at church camp?

It's more mature. It comes out of being able to look more honestly at the feelings, look a little deeper inside, articulate things in a broader way. "Annie's Song" is a great example. What that song makes me feel is what I felt when I wrote the song, not all the other stuff. It's a great love song and what it is about is being in love. That's what it makes me think about regardless of what happened between me and Annie [Denver's ex-wife]. When I sing "Annie's Song," and when I hear it, it's about being in love and that's what I think about. I don't think about hate or divorce, and see, that's why it's such a good song... because it brings that out of you. It opens up that inside of you regardless. There

was a time when I had a pretty hard shell around my heart in regard to Annie, but I could sing that song because that song made me think and feel about being in love.

Do you have any advice you would like to give aspiring songwriters?

I think that you can be taught the craft, the technical ability, the rhyme and meter. You can be taught all that... but I think songwriting is the ability to articulate in a musical way and lyrical way an experience, a feeling, a memory, a vision in such a way that someone else can hear that lyric or listen to that piece of music and have it mean something to them. I think it's a gift, and I don't know that you can learn how to do that. I think you can learn how to better communicate your ideas or feelings, but to really sit down and do that is a gift. But you shouldn't try too hard. Don't copy anybody. Just let it come through to you.

I think songwriting is the ability to articulate in a musical way and lyrical way an experience, a feeling, a memory, a vision in such a way that someone else can hear that lyric or listen to that piece of music and have it mean something to them.

Ani DiFranco

photo courtesy Righteous Babe Records

Ani DiFranco has created her own musical empire, built on her highly poetic feminist anthems and politically astute protest songs. Born in Buffalo, New York, in 1970, DiFranco began singing Beatles songs in bars at the age of ten. By fifteen she was living on her own and writing her first songs. In 1990, she launched her own record label, Righteous Babe Records, to release her self-produced albums and has remained fiercely independent, despite offers to sign with major labels. DiFranco's constant touring and high-energy live shows helped her grow a large, loyal, and reverent fan base. In 1996, her eighth album, *Dilate*, cracked the *Billboard* Top 100, and 2002's *So Much Shouting, So Much Laughter* reached the Top 30. The prolific songwriter generally releases a new studio album at the rate of one per year. Her latest effort, *Knuckle Down*, was released in 2005. Her Righteous Babe roster has expanded to include artists like Andrew Bird, Hamell on Trial, and Toshi Reagon. Her latest release is 2006's *Reprieve*, her 18th album.

—EVAN SCHLANSKY

Interview by
Nancy Moran

American Songwriter,
July/August 2006

111

How old were you when you got your first guitar?

Nine.

Do you remember what or who first inspired you to start playing music?

Michael Meldrum here in Buffalo, New York, a songwriter/folk singer… a community guy, an active member of the community, a man about town… everybody knows him. And I met him when I got my first guitar—at the guitar shop down in Allentown. We became friends, and for many years I just thought, "Oh yeah, that's my buddy Michael." It didn't occur to me that he would take me to his gigs—like from when I was single digits—and just sort of tote me around to bars and take me under his wing. This of course was my entrée into what would become my life. He loved the Beatles. And John Lennon was his hero. And he was very into Dylan.

But you're not?

No, but he was and so maybe I got that influence vicariously? [Michael] was sort of a sandalwood, vest-and-chapeau wearing, chain-smoking, philosophizing kind of songwriter.

Early in your career, besides learning from Michael, how were you influenced?

I started to make my own songs and even get my own work. I found myself luckily… suddenly… at folk festivals. Most of my early work was in Canada. They have this great series of festivals every summer and one of them in Toronto, near my hometown, hired me. Then the next summer they all hired me. Suddenly I was in front of lots of people and I was amongst lots of folk, roots, and especially world music musicians that were a great influence. At the folk festivals, there'd be parties every night at the hotel. And people from all over the world, who couldn't talk to each other but could *play* together, did so, all night long. That was eye-opening and musically expanding for me. I was introduced to instruments I'd never seen and the possibilities of roots music. You know, music without machines but with incredible array of tonal possibilities.

Did that affect your songwriting?

I think so. It's hard to quantify because I was just exposed to so many different things within a short span. So many different kinds of music. One of my more popular songs along the way or one that people have embraced, you know, one of the more anthemic ones, is called "32 Flavors." And when I listen to that now, it seems like a total African melody to me. And then, of course, it dissolves into hand drumming for like five minutes at the end of the song, you know, with doumbeks and djembes. So, I can definitely hear the "me hanging out at folk festivals" influence.

I remember seeing you at the Philadelphia Folk Festival in 1992, and it's safe to say that your music has changed significantly since then. Do you think this is because you like to experiment or because your influences have drawn you in different directions?

I think both. I'm a little experimenter and also I'm a sponge. I've been heavily influenced by people I'm close to. You know, people I'm hanging out with. When I was hanging out with Maceo Parker a lot, I invited him on tour with me and we just struck up a pretty close friendship for a while. I was like, "I want a horn section! Man, I want to get down and get funky!" [*Laughs*]. That was totally part of where I was at the time, which was really deep in funk music and hanging out with Maceo and sort of asking myself, like, why does every song have to tell a story? What if I just want to groove and sort of throw words out there musically? So that was definitely Maceo in my consciousness. And I think a really big one that I wouldn't want to leave out is Greg Brown.

How has he affected your work?

Greg Brown has been one of my favorite writers since I first heard his music. We've been corresponding since back then, too, probably around that same time—the early nineties. When I hooked up with Jim Fleming, he gave me a Greg Brown tape right out of the cassette deck in his car. He was like, "Here, check this out." It was a record he'd made called *Dream Café*. I loved it from the moment I heard it and over the years he's been my most consistent pen pal. For instance, I remember him saying he walks around the house when he plays guitar. I always just sat there in a chair… I was like, "Oh yeah, right. Why am I sitting here?" So now I put on my guitar and I walk around the house.

How are you affected by other songwriters? By listening to them, performing with them, or—

Mostly performing and hanging and inspiring each other. I remember I sort of orchestrated a tour once with Greg Brown and Gillian Welch and David Rawlings. And the four of us would sit on stage together and swap songs. And for the couple of weeks that we were on the road, everybody was writing a *lot*, because it was sort of a salon vibe. That was great. And I love hanging and touring with people like Dan Bern, who would write a new song *every day*. By the end of the tour he'd have a song about the tour, you know? [*Laughs*] He's just constantly throwing things out there. And *that's* really inspiring to me… people who don't obsess and sort of get all constipated with their writing but are always turning their life into song.

You've recently moved to New Orleans…

What comes to mind is that people are really *real* there. I think New Orleans music is affecting and keeping me in touch with what is important in music. It's like if you're in a song, you can convey it to anybody. If it's real and *you're* being real, the experience is universal… It's like, if you're straight up deep in your shit and just opening yourself wide, then it's like you're part of the family there.

Do you have someone whom you consider to be a role model?

My mom. You know, she's pretty huge. There's quite a similarly of nature, you know, spirit. I think I got a lot of my shit from her. Even that instinct… you know, right from when I was a little kid people would comment on my smile or my ability to put people at ease. I was a smiling kid and now I'm a smiling adult. That comes from my mother. I have memories of her that really strike me. Like, somebody telling her something that she already knew that I *knew* she already knew and she acted like she didn't know it because that was what would make the other person feel good. And I'm like, "Mom! We knew how to get there." And she's like, "Ahhh." That was cool.

How would you like to be defined?

I guess my go-to answer all these years has been I'm a folk singer. And then whatever kind of impression, confusion, or stereotype that is in somebody's mind… fine, perfect, go with it. Right from the beginning when I was entering the folk community, I looked around and I thought, "These are my people!" They're political, they're socially conscious, and they're making music with just wooden boxes and being themselves on stage. One of my friends who played saxophone in my band, Hans… we were in a cab one night going somewhere after a show and somebody asked [*in a slight foreign accent*], "What kind of music is it you make?" I looked at Hans and he looked at me and I said, "What is it, Hans? What's the music?" And he said, "Well, it's music with a story." And I thought, "Oh. That's good." I mean, for people who don't really know folk music too much, that may be an even better way of putting it.

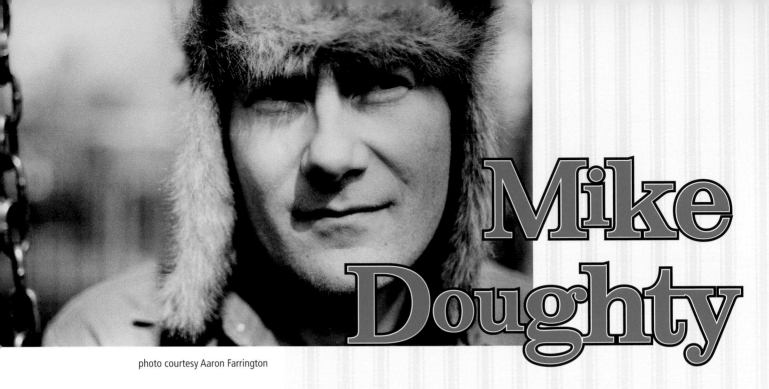

photo courtesy Aaron Farrington

Mike Doughty

Interview by
Jesse Jarnow
Relix Magazine, *August 2005*

Like many albums following the breakup of a singer's band, former Soul Coughing frontman Mike Doughty's *Haughty Melodic* (2005) had a long, twisted genesis. Following the demise of the beloved avant-pop quartet, and Doughty's recovery from his own heroin addiction, the songwriter began to rebuild. During the nearly five year process, Doughty hit the road with an acoustic guitar in a series of rental cars, sold a literally homemade album called *Skittish* from club and theater stages, and openly questioned the principles of songwriting.

In the bargain, he built himself a new fanbase, and—after financing the album himself—eventually found himself signed to ATO Records, a label co-owned by longtime fan Dave Matthews. Doughty's interests are wildly varied. Though he no longer publishes the type of poetry that comprised 1996's *Slanky*, Doughty is a regular blogger and world traveler (usually to Africa).

Doughty's musical tastes are omnivorous, to say the least, ranging from bizarre compilations of African pop to American Top 40 to the Grateful Dead. His guitar playing—a self-invented fusion of hip-hop and reggae rhythms known as the *gangadank* that's informed him since the Soul Coughing days—reflects this. In the end, though, Doughty most frequently hones his interests with incredibly accessible directness. A master lyricist with a deeply rhythmic delivery, Doughty stands out.

—JESSE JARNOW

You've spoken of wanting to make *Haughty Melodic* a "world within a world."

One of the most important things I ever learned [came from] a class in directing a Shakespeare play I took when I was in college. I directed Julius Caesar. The thing was that you had to cut it to half an hour. You had to cut it down to the essentials. You had a limited cast, just the people in the class, and you had to direct it. And it was something that the teacher of the class—Peter Wallace—kept talking about: the world of the play. What's the world of the play?

It was kind of a real foundation of my aesthetic: a record with a world has a limited bag—a limited number of hooks; there's kind of a philosophical stance to it. It's just the world of the record. I think subsequently you get something that everything kind of hangs together.

It was interesting with *Haughty Melodic*. I was doing it with [producer] Dan [Wilson] in Minneapolis. If I had my druthers, I would have had the same players, the same time period, but eventually what we came up with was the idea of me and Dan in a lab. And, as long as on the production side, it stays me and Dan, that's the world of the record, and we can use a different drummer, and we can use different people for different things.

The story of the process—flying out there, doing a week, coming back, wringing my hands for two months, going back for two weeks, getting into an amazing creative head, then being yanked back to New York for two months... I think you can really hear that stuff in the record. Maybe it's just my memory projecting itself on the songs.

What period of time was the record written over?

It really kinda started after September 11th. I sort of consider the *Rockity Roll* songs as being in the same period. I got clean in May of 2000, and then I didn't write songs for, like, a year. Sometime within the year, I had the chorus of "Grey Ghost." "40 Grand in the Hole," I wrote. I had the verse of "Ossining," the first verse. I just had little bits that I had no

idea how to expand. I was so messed up. I didn't know how messed up I was. Just listening to the stuff I recorded at the time... it was just pure slush.

Were you trying to write stuff this whole time?

I was journaling. I was journaling like a madman, it was what I focused all my energies on: journaling and pining away for my old junkie girlfriend. Then, like a year after it, I kind of started—it was the summer before September 11th, when things started to really come together writing-wise. I was going to the notebooks and picking things out and I was like "oh, that's an interesting title..." But after September 11th, I wrote "Madeleine and Nine" and "Down on the River By the Sugarplant." I immediately started this intensive demoing process. I did "Looking at the World From the Bottom of a Well," "Sunken-Eyed Girl," that's when things really started to bubble and smoke.

Do you see any reflection of the 11th in there? Or is that just an arbitrary date, where you just remember starting to work after that?

Well, "Madeleine" is addressed to my junkie ex-girlfriend, who has the unsingable name. The thing about the unsingable name is that it's really an unsingable name. It's such a beautiful name, this great name. You just look at and you go "it's just gotta be a song." I tried it a million ways, so "Madeleine" is... [sings melody with the unsingable name atop the melody]... you can't do it. The accent's in the wrong place.

She worked at a bar downtown, by the World Trade Center. It must be a miserable place. It's a bar, where daytraders go with their laptops, and they just get drunk all day and day trade. They look at the numbers.

Was it a gradual stopping of the creative process? Or was it just: got clean and then stopped?

I was way stopped before I got clean. Believe me. Just drivel. I have this great artifact from the bad old days. I used to

write on post-it notes. I've always been about little, discreet phrases. Nowadays, I go to the notebooks and pluck them out, but I went through a phase of writing them on post-its: have an idea, write it on a post-it, stick it on the wall. I have this post-it that's got one word on it: "column." And from then on, it's like "bluuuuuuuuuh… bluuuuh…" and it just turns into a child's drawing, and then into an ink stain. I found it, and it was just horrifying! I was physically unable to write. I wanna get that thing framed someday.

I just could not physically write, didn't have anything to write about, just channeled everything into the proliferation of pure misery.

When did you realize that acoustic music was something you wanted to do?

1990. I always anticipated that I would go into a heavy acoustic mode. I've loved it all my life. That kind of music has just always been the pinnacle for me—somebody performing solo, that kind of intimacy, that kind of focus. I've always thought that if a song sounded great, it would always sound better with just one dude and a guitar.

You've mentioned that you don't think Soul Coughing fans will like the new album.

I think *some* of them are gonna like it. There's a certain variety of fan I call the Zappa variety. They're not gonna like it. There's sort of a splatter effect thing. They like the messiness. They like things that sort of communicate the avant-garde, regardless of content. Which is fine. I worked at [experimental jazz club] the Knitting Factory! Don't tell me about avant-garde. I'll eat that shit up. The rapping thing isn't in there. A lot of people saw me as an MC.

A lot of the Soul Coughing stuff was done at a distance from myself. I think the best stuff we did was "True Dreams of Wichita," "Janine," and things that are really heartfelt. But a lot of it is sort of skirting around whatever it was that was both-

ering me, which I know a lot more about now. So somebody who was attracted to that, to us, was attracted to maybe the distance—sort of dealing with it, but keeping your distance.

Once you really delve into it, writing about relationships, and about emotions, some people are gonna be like "whoa, a little corny for me…" A lot of the time, from about the second Soul Coughing record on, I started feeling like this singer-songwriter trapped in this groove band, in this avant-garde experience, and I kept fighting my way out of it. Some of it was really interesting because of that struggle. On a personal level, I was really unhappy.

You spoke at Harvard recently about music and technology.

I was interviewed in a presentation at Harvard about my experiences with digital performing, my experiences with sample clearing. Mostly what I did was play the roots of songs that I had written and said "I took this little melody from here and expanded on it." Then I played the song that they stole it from, and sometimes the bit that *they* stole it from. I also did this thing which I thought was totally pedantic. I played them "Louie, Louie," "Wild Thing," and "La Bamba," and said, "These are the same three chords," and thought "they're gonna think 'you asshole, we know that,'" but all these lawyers were like "wow…" Harvard Law School. "Wild Thing." "Louie Louie." Same chords.

You once wrote that "music doesn't progress, it's not a fucking technology" that "new sounds can be found—very, very rarely—but not new feelings." While that's true, the technology used to express those feelings changes all the time.

Which is fascinating. I've always loved that, at one point, if you were on a 78, you had a certain amount of time, then a 45 you had a little longer, then an LP got even longer. You went from 24-track tape to hooking up two machines where you had 48-track tape, which seemed so excessive at the time. It was such a complicated process, and you needed an extra engineer. With ProTools it's unlimited.

One of the things I talked about at Harvard is that when you do a vocal, you do twenty passes at, and then you comp them. And what that can mean sometimes is listening to a word, a single word, on twenty different takes. Torturous for a singer to sit there listening to himself all day, more so the use of AutoTune to really go clickclickclick and put it in tune. If you sing it twenty times, you're bound to get that word in tune once. Those kinds of things have affected music.

The point I was making is that when you say, "This kind of music is progressive," I really think that feelings are feelings, and—ultimately—that's what we're about. We're not about "well, he's using…"

…a jungle beat.

Exactly. If somebody uses a jungle beat, it's more "progressive." It's very difficult to see us that way, because we came from the Knitting Factory, and everybody was like "Ooh, a pop band! We never get pop bands!" I was lectured by Marc Ribot—a fantastic experience, since I was such a huge fan. But he lectured me as to why we shouldn't fall prey to the temptations of the Knitting Factory, how there was one Knitting Factory in the whole world, but there was a CBGB's in every city in America and Europe.

Do you ever feel the desire to filter the weird stuff you listen to back into what you're doing?

Oh yeah. It happens all the time, but it happens skeletally. It happens in melodies, it happens in chords, or in chord progressions.

Do you have any internal references for songs that nobody would pick out?

I was lucky. When I was a kid, I had a couple of teachers who impressed on me that great artists steal. If you take something, you possess it. You don't have to feel like you're taking someone's thing. If you can make something beautiful, make it.

I did a radio spot recently and they sent me a free satellite radio, which I adore, there's a Norteño channel. It's this insane Mexican music, which is tubas, drumlines. I guess they just overdub snare drums a million times. The singers sound so drunk and sad and freaky. It's some of the weirdest music I've ever heard, swear to God. And sometimes it is tempting to think "Oh, I'm gonna pull a David Byrne and do a Norteño record," but, no… it's more likely that I'll take a melody, take a pattern rhythmically.

There are certain types of words and phrases that seem to recur in your songs. Are you conscious of what might be called, for lack of a better phrase, "Doughty words"?

When I was studying, I was told to have a style, don't be ashamed of it, steal, have a style. And then, as the years went on, I thought "I wanna let go of this style, I just wanna write completely natural." Now I'm at the point, after having done that for a couple of years, where I'm like, "Oh, I have a style!" I guess I notice when I think "that's very Doughty…"

At Harvard, there was this other band on the conference from Milwaukee called Beatllica. They do Beatles covers. The singer was there, the guy who does James Hetfield. We were having dinner the night before the conference, and one of the guys said, "Hit us up with a little Hetfield," and he said "Somebody give me a word with an O-sound," and I said "rope," and he goes "rooooope," and he just did it. Hetfield has a style, but he just thinks he's singing.

Jermaine Dupri

Interview by
Deborah Evans Price

American Songwriter,
September/October 1993

When Atlanta's own Jermaine Dupri, the twenty-year-old production Svengali behind teenage rappers Kris Kross, hit the scene in 1992, few realized how far he would go in the R&B game. While Kris Kross—with their backwards clothing and ubiquitous, Dupri-penned hit "Jump"—would eventually fade into obscurity, Dupri had no trouble transferring his talents to more mature artists such as TLC and Mariah Carey, whom he helped guide to multiplatinum heights. Dupri, a childhood performer himself, got his first break at age ten, when he hopped onstage to dance with Diana Ross during a TV show his father produced. Soon he was performing at malls and festivals across the country, opening for acts like Cameo and Herbie Hancock. He became a bona fide producer while still in his teens, working with the female dance music trio Silk Tymes Leather, and at age sixteen he launched his own label, So So Def (home to artists like Li'l Bow Wow, Jagged Edge, and Da Brat). Dupri has also written and produced for megastars like Usher and Janet Jackson. In addition to a decade's worth of guest appearances, Dupri has released a handful of successful solo records including 1998's *Life in 1472: The Original Soundtrack* and 2001's *Instructions*. His latest album, 2005's *Jermaine Dupri Presents… Young, Fly and Flashy Vol. 1*, features several new Dupri jams and showcases the talents of So So Def's newest stars.

—EVAN SCHLANSKY

You've had a successful career at a young age; did you know you wanted to be in music as a teenager?

At that point in time I thought I wanted to be a dancer. I was also doing other things like playing drums. But I let my parents know music was what I wanted to do.

Do you enjoy being the artist or the producer most?

At first I was an artist. I'm at another position now, and I'm glad that I went through both things, seeing the artist side and seeing this side. What I'm doing now is hard, but it's easier than getting out there. I've been on the road with Chris and Chris [from Kris Kross] and I see the responsibilities of being a star. Chris and Chris can't even walk out of their hotel room without people wanting autographs.

How did it come about—you teaming up with Chris and Chris?

At first they weren't really with it. I got the chance to produce the whole album. I think they wanted some other people to produce, but my father [who manages Dupri as well as Kriss Kross, Arrested Development, and other acts] talked them out of it. It didn't really hit, but it was a good experience to do a whole album by myself at that early age. I'm real thankful for that.

How would you categorize yourself?

Basically I'm a hip-hop producer. I've got my own label now [So So Def Recordings]. The first act coming out on my label, Xscape, is like an R&B hip-hop group—like an En Vogue with rap beats. I'm letting people know I can do R&B cause I'm [producing] Shanice Wilson. I [produced] El De-Barge. I've got a couple R&B projects getting ready to jump off that'll let people know I can do R&B [as well as rap]. You get bored doing the same thing all the time.

Tell me about working with hip-hop pioneers Run-DMC.

Run-DMC came to Atlanta for me to do something with them, and I was real excited because that's *Run-DMC* and they wanted *me*. I was really excited about it and they were like "Jermaine, we don't want you to hold back. We want you to give us the same treatment as you give Chris and them. Produce our record like how you did theirs. If not, there ain't no reason for us to be down there." When Run told me that, that just gave me a whole other attitude as far as all these other groups like Shanice and El DeBarge. Now when I work with them, I don't look at it like they're a higher status then me. I look at it like I have a job to do, regardless of who they are. If I have an idea, I'm going to take it to them. I'm not gonna hold back. They opened my eyes. If they're there to work with me, they're there for a reason. So I should act the way I usually act and don't hold back.

When do you write most of your lyrics?

Sometimes I can be on an airplane and start writing lyrics. Other times I'll be thinking about a beat and I can hardly wait till I get to my house and start putting the beat down and then write the lyrics. It just depends.

What are the advantages of playing on the road?

It helped me develop my rhythmic skills. If I messed up the original phrasing, I'd catch myself and pull it off in different ways. That's one thing that I'm high on. I really like to phrase stuff in ways nobody else does.

Do you approach writing for R&B differently than rap?

I write my R&B songs like I would write a rap song. I try to use little catchy phrases and that type of stuff. Raps have more lyrics than [other] songs. You can write a couple of

lyrics for a song and the verse will be finished. With raps you have to write stories and they have to make sense. You can't put down just anything. Raps are a little bit harder, but it's easier when you do it everyday. I did Kris Kross's album in two weeks. Some musicians might say, "That ain't nothing… he can do an album in two weeks… it's got to be easy." But it's just because once I start writing something I'm really into it, it just goes like that. That's how I vibe. That's what it is with this rapping thing. Raps are like nursery rhymes, like Dr. Seuss [that] every kid used to know. They learn it quick; that's the way rap is to us. We learn it so fast that it doesn't take any time. It doesn't take long to learn the craft. It looks so easy because we know the craft.

Do you think rap is getting the recognition it deserves?

A lot of musical producers are coming around now, but back in the early days when rap was first out, they felt like it was hip-hop be-bop and just a couple of words. But if you are a real listener of music, period, you shouldn't be so shallow. You should listen to all rap just to find out what's really going on.

So you think rap has a lyrical distinction that's more in-depth than most songwriting?

Rap music is the type of music where we get to express ourselves. Everybody's human. Everybody has cursed in their life. If I have a group, and if there's a part of a song where they are vibin' and "damn" might come out, you've got to be real. You can't hold back on your feelings. If you feel it in your heart, there's nothing wrong with that. I can't really say if I would ever write something like that because I write what I vibe. I'm a writer. Just like in poetry, all poems can't be like flowers and the sun. All my music won't be like Kris Kross. I wrote to what the group is. If I had a real underground rap group and they say they want to be underground, I know how to write that.

What is your take on controversial acts like Ice Cube and N.W.A.?

I listen to those artists and they are speaking their mind. I can't really fault them 'cause they say they're telling us how they live. That's their life. A lot of things they say are true, like getting stopped by police—that happens. Like with me, Kris Kross hit two years ago. I was eighteen and got a chance to buy a couple of cars. I got me a Beemer [BMW]. I looked so young and I got stopped so many times by the police thinking I was a dope dealer. So some of those things they are saying, I can relate. A lot of people can relate. I listen to that, and if they are real about what they are talking about… if all this is real, then I ain't got no problem with it. I can overlook the profanity.

Many producers use sampling in their production of beats. How do you get the sample you want?

At first when I [produced] Silk Tymes Leather, you could sample anything you wanted to. Rap wasn't that big and wasn't making as much money as it is making now. Now if you sample an old record, the publishers are coming after you. You got to pay for the samples or get sued—if it's big. Big samples [will] take your whole record off the shelf. If you want to do an old track, it's best to get musicians in the studio to replay and do it like that. Now my lawyers are saying, "Now [that] you have money, you can say whatever." Some samples I don't want to get a live band to come in on, so I just sample it and have to pay like five thousand dollars for the sample and not really worry about it. There are certain things you have to do. If you're gonna sample now, you have to pay for it.

So do you often find yourself in a tug-of-war with the publishing community?

EMI, Jobete… all the old publishing companies… they've just got old music and they know we're going to pay for it. They set traps now for the younger rappers that are coming up putting out CDs of all the old music so you ain't got to look for it no more. They know you're gonna sample, and then they're gonna take your money. It's a game. They're setting traps for all the young rappers coming up that ain't hip to the sampling issue and how all this stuff works.

How did you first become turned on to sampling?

That's a tradition in rap. Before rap [artists] started making records, kids used to go to the park and rap over people's records, funky instrumentals or whatever. That's where [rap] deejays were coming from, rapping over old records. That's how it started. Then people would sample them and make their own records.

You talked about rap artists speaking *their* mind; do you think that quality leads to rap only catering to a certain audience?

Rap music is for everybody. I think at first a lot of people were looking at it and thinking it was about things they couldn't relate to. But it's not just black people's problems. A lot of white people have the same problems.

When you begin producing each song, do you go in trying to create a hit?

I don't really think of any of my songs as hits. They sound good. That's all I can say. After that I turn them in, if people like them, that's cool. Then I go on to the next song. [All I want a record to sell] is 2,500 records. If I can sell 2,500 records, I'm cool. Now 25,000 records, I'm straight, as long as the record gets heard. That's what's important.

Do you have any advice for young artists trying to make it in the business?

Don't stop. Get a good manager who can help you and talk to people and talk your material up. Don't worry about the business side, just worry about your material, and getting it done the best way you can and make it sound as good as possible. Let them worry about the business and then you should be straight.

What part do you most enjoy about your job?

Coming up with ideas and seeing if people are into it—that's the part I like. The producing and arranging is a little harder 'cause you've got to get them to do it how you hear it. They might not hear it like that. But writing, that's when you're off on your own, in your own world, and you can just go for it. Write what you want to write and feel it how you want to feel it.

You can't hold back on your feelings. If you feel it in your heart, there's nothing wrong with that…Write what you want to write and feel it how you want to feel it.

Steve Earle

Interview by Caine O'Rear IV

American Songwriter,
November/December 2004

Steve Earle is what one might describe as a "potent" artist. There is little about him that toys with subtlety; from his corrosive-turned-redemptive personal history and no-holds-barred political activism (that includes a wealth of anti-death penalty work), to his visceral, untamed country-rock repertoire, Earle is one of those treasured American songwriters who takes on his work and art with full commitment. The Texas-born singer/songwriter helped propel the progressive country movement—which included contemporaries Dwight Yoakam, Randy Travis and many more—forward with his 1986 debut, *Guitar Town*. To add to a spell of broken marriages, a downward spiraling addiction to heroin found Earle in jail in the early 1990s, but he returned to Nashville in the mid-1990s after a series of drug treatment programs to produce a string of critically-acclaimed (and many argue his strongest) albums, beginning with the acoustic-folky *Train a Comin'* (1995). These days the raw-voiced firebrand freely follows his muse into sharply subversive songwriting ("John Walker's Blues"), fictional prose (*Doghouse Roses*, a collection of short stories), barbed playwriting (*Karla*), and many other equally inspired ventures. His latest album was 2004's *The Revoltion Starts... Now*.

—JEWLY HIGHT

How does the album *The Revolution Starts... Now* exactly define the word "revolution"?

The revolution starts now in that it starts as soon as you wake up and realize that it's been going on with or without you, and that your input is needed. I'm not a believer in violent revolution, but only because a lot of people learned that for me... that came before me. I don't blame the shape the country's in on them; I blame it on us. I blame it on people that think like I do, that went to sleep, that became less involved. I think the part of it that people have a hard time getting through their heads is that there's never going to be a time when we can coast. Our brand of democracy just doesn't—and I'm not sure any brand of democracy—lend itself to that. Ours definitely doesn't. I don't really have a problem with conservatives. I don't agree with them, but these guys in power right now aren't conservatives, you know, they're neo-cons, which aren't conservatives. What scares me more than anything else right now is we've got liberals that are afraid to call themselves liberals and conservatives who won't say out loud that this guy isn't a conservative... and he's running the country into the ground because he's not [a conservative]. These are not conservative policies. I voted for Bill Clinton twice—the only Democrat that I ever voted for. And he was a lot more conservative than Bush ever thought about being, with most of the things conservatives are normally worried about.

In the liner notes, you used the word "immediate" to describe the atmosphere surrounding the recording of the new album. Is this an album just for these times, or is it meant to reverberate beyond that?

Some of it is just for this second, but some of it is not. I think "The Revolution Starts Now" is for all times. And I think "Rich Man's War" could be about any war. It's about three wars that are going on right now.

It takes an interesting turn with that last verse.

Yeah, well, the deal is the people who sit around and decide it's time for us to go to war very rarely get shot at, and I think that's part of the problem.

Is it harder for artists to speak out and be heard now than it was, say, during the Vietnam era?

Well, we're just living through this weird little pocket of time where somebody came up with this bizarre idea that it wasn't appropriate for artists to comment on the society that they live in. That's a new idea.

Mark Twain said artists are the true patriots.

That's it. That's what [John] Kerry meant when he was speaking before all those artists and said, "You are the heart and soul of America." It probably wasn't his best way to phrase it, but that's what he meant. We're people, you know, and a lot of us come from pretty humble backgrounds. And I come from a moderately humble background. My dad was an air-traffic controller and a GS-13 when he retired. We were comfortable but there were five kids.

You've started to write poetry and prose over the last few years, as well as paint and act. Has working in these mediums had any effect on your development as a songwriter?

Oh yeah, I think "Warrior" would have been completely impossible without my involvement in theater. It would never have occurred to me to write a spoken-word piece in iambic pentameter if I had not been heavily involved in theater for the last five years.

Who are you trying to reach with the new album? I think it's pretty safe to say that the people who bought your other albums will buy this one as well.

Yeah, they will. I'm trying to reach the people that have been quiet and aren't okay with what's going on. They know something's wrong, but haven't been comfortable with saying something about it. I think that's happening and that people are starting to look for something. The reaction to this record so far has been so overwhelmingly positive. It's very early but it's much different than when *Jerusalem* came out. I had the usual squawkers [with *Jerusalem*]—the people I was trying to piss off—and they responded the way that they normally do.

And that was mostly just because of "John Walker's Blues."

Yeah, and with this one I even got a four-star review in the *New York Post*, which kind of concerns me. My one-star review for *Jerusalem* [in the *New York Post*] is one of my prouder moments. It's been much easier to get [this album] on radio so far. It's the second day out, we're number five at Amazon.com, and that's a pretty good indicator for me. I'm an adult artist, so I sell records at Barnes & Noble and Amazon.com and Borders; those are my biggest retail outlets. I'm hoping to reach people that are not necessarily hard-core progressives but are starting to realize they got lied to. It's regular people that will go and die if we keep pursuing this policy we're pursuing. And it won't end in Iraq. It's not designed to end in Iraq. It's really insane. They're talking about us never having troops in harm's way. That's what they want, and it's not *their* kids.

In the mid-to-late nineties or so, you helped a lot of young bands and artists get their start with E-Squared Records. I'm thinking specifically of Marah and the V-Roys. Was that a way of doing the same kind of thing Townes Van Zandt and Guy Clark did for you?

Yeah, producing records and signing bands like that was a teaching process. I like to teach. I do sometimes. But I try to approach [producing] as a teacher. And some people are more teachable than others, and sometimes it's a better experience than others.

Any advice for aspiring young songwriters?

It's tough nowadays. Always be willing to do the work, but always be suspicious of anything any time anybody asks you to change the art itself… because probably the people that are asking you have never made art before. Especially if someone who has never made any art before tells you how to make art, you should definitely process that information very, very carefully.

Would this album have come out differently had you spent more time writing songs and recording in the studio, or do you like the sense of urgency it has?

It would have been different and it probably wouldn't have been as urgent. I think it was made exactly the way it needed to be made, and I'm pretty proud of it.

Shelly Fairchild

photo courtesy Shelly Fairchild

Shelly Fairchild is no stranger to the stage. She grew up in Clinton, Mississippi, and parlayed an early love for theater in starring roles in musicals and national tours of plays. Her family was highly musical and everybody sang.

Fairchild, whose debut album *Ride* (Columbia Records) hit stores in mid-2005 and was produced by Kenny Greenberg and longtime Kenny Chesney producer Buddy Cannon, was given her first guitar at age six. Soon, Fairchild entered talent competitions and started singing at state fairs, school events, and anywhere else her fellow Mississippians would listen.

Acting was another passion, as Fairchild received leads in area productions of *Always… Patsy Cline, Godspell,* and *Grease.* She even joined a national touring production of *Beehive* before finally moving to Nashville in 2001. Columbia signed her, and Fairchild's debut single, "You Don't Lie Here Anymore," impacted country radio in late 2004. "Tiny Town" came on its heels as her next single.

One of Fairchild's greatest strengths is her ability to fuse all the different musical influences she grew up with into her own powerful singing. "I realize I might be pushing the envelope," she says, "because I have a lot of blues feeling and rock energy in my voice. That's just how it comes out of me. I've always sung with a lot of passion and emotion." She's currently a staff writer at Big Tractor Music and is seeking a new label to release her second album.

—PHIL SWEETLAND

Interview by Kristi Singer

American Songwriter,
May/June 2005

What are some of the goals you've set with your songwriting?

I would really love to see my songs reach as many people in the world as possible. I love the songs that I write—of course, they're really close to home—and songs I record that I didn't write. There's so much time, so much thought, so much emotion that goes into picking those songs for my record. I'm really happy with what we came up with and I'm proud of the project. I'm proud of everybody's work on the project and really just want people to hear it. So, one of my goals for the next two years is just building, so people hear song after song. It's not necessarily about being a big star. It's about being able to make music, make a living, and have people hear it.

What are the challenges for songwriters these days?

In Nashville there are so many songwriters in town—from all over the country, all over the world—and a lot of the time, the only way songs get to live and be heard is by somebody who is a major artist getting out there and performing it. Like right now, Rascal Flatts has "Bless the Broken Road" [written by Jeff Hanna, Marcus Hummon, and Bobby Boyd] out, and that song's been around for years! It was cut [I think twice before], and then the guys come out with it, and they're a big act so now the whole world knows this song. I'll ramble on, but I feel really strongly about that—just being able to have the body and the heart of a song live out in the world for a lot of people to hear. It's so important.

Let's talk about the songs on your album. When did you start writing them? I know you co-wrote a lot. What were you focusing on for your inspiration?

I've written ideas and things since I was pretty young. When I was in high school, I had little journals of poetry. When I first moved to Nashville in 1997, I started sitting down with some people and figuring out how to write songs. I just

didn't feel like I was very good at it. So I would put my ideas down then put them away. I was like, "Nobody wants to hear this stuff." I just didn't get the whole songwriting thing. I felt really insecure about it.

So you got a record deal having been in Nashville for a little while?

[Yes]. I had written a handful of things, five or six songs, so I didn't have a lot of full songs under my belt. But the ones I did have I played for my management and for some publishing companies. There was some promise there because I was an artist, so they jumped right on it and I had a couple of offers. I decided I wanted to learn more and didn't want to sign a deal right away. I wanted to be able to write with all different kinds of writers, visit different publishing companies, and have an equal relationship with everybody.

So you started looking around for publishers and co-writers?

I decided to keep my publishing and do that exact thing—meet with different publishers about their songs and songwriters. I started getting together with songwriters in town, incredible songwriters, mainly because I had a record deal and there was some promise there. I would play some of my songs or whatever; I wanted to show them how I sing. I would do that and then they would say, "Okay, I see your style. Yeah, I'd like to write with you" or "No, I don't know if it fits." So I got to get right down to it with these songwriters. I had two appointments a day, five days a week when I first started, which was about two years ago.

So how did things work out, being something of a "new" songwriter?

I just started writing and it came out. I would try to be ultra-prepared for a meeting. I'd have titles, melody ideas, and I don't really play guitar great, but I'd play my guitar. For instance, "You Don't Lie Here Anymore," my first single, was the very first time I had written with Sonny LeMaire and Clay Mills. We got together, I had the title, a little of the melody idea, it was our first meeting together, and we automatically became really close. We had a great time and wrote what I think is a great song.

Tell me about "Tiny Town."

"Tiny Town" is my second single. The very first time I had written with Stephony Smith, we sit down [and] were talking about our families. I had just had a really hard conversation with my mom, saying I wasn't going to be able to come home and she's saying, "What do you do all day? Why can't you come home?" I'm trying to have this career and it's so important that I'm in town. It's so hard for her, my dad, and my sister to understand because they miss me. Out of that, we started talking about our families, got a little teary-eyed, and wrote the song.

What about "Kiss Me"?

I needed a love song, something that was a little sassy. So that birthed that song. Just writing, writing, and writing helps you learn more about who you are and helps develop a great songwriter. It helps develop that in you, doing it all the time.

You mentioned that at first you were insecure about songwriting. What helped you overcome that? Do you feel more secure now?

[It's] like if you are a kid and you start in junior high playing in the band. You don't know if you're that good, but you might have something that is natural, that you're born with inside of you. Your teacher is there to say, "That's great, let's work on that." That's where I was. About two years ago, I had a few things that I thought were good ideas; I just didn't know how to make them into great songs. So I had my managers, and I played my songs for them and they went, "Those

are great, you need to get with people who can help you develop that." That's when I started meeting with publishers. And they saw something promising. Every time that would happen, it would build my confidence. Somebody would say, "That's not a great song, but I bet you have it in you to be a really great songwriter. So I'm going to put you with somebody who's better than you so you can learn from them," and that's what I've done.

"You Don't Lie Here Anymore" is a really strong song, a very empowering song for a woman who's maybe been lied to or cheated on. Was that inspired by a real-life situation, fiction, or other people's stories?

I just think growing up you're always around people who have problems. Everyone's got their thing, big or small. My parents have been together for thirty-one years and they're completely happy. But there have been relationships around me, pretty much since I could understand the idea of a relationship, that have just fallen apart for whatever reason. Some have lied, some have cheated, some have just not been great for each other. And me personally… that has not happened to me. It's an empowering statement for me to come out with that song because others who listen to the song would come up to me after a show and go, "Oh girl, I love that song—the same thing happened to me." It's okay if they think it happened to me. It doesn't make any difference either way. It's just getting the point across that I, as a woman, am not going to stand for that.

So, which would you say is the most personal song for you on the album?

I've got two. "Tiny Town" is absolutely the closest to home because that's something I deal with all the time. I'm really close to my family and I've been away for a long time now. Most of my adult years I've lived away from Mississippi and

all my family's back in Clinton, and they all carry on with their lives. My mom turned fifty this year and I couldn't go to her birthday party. I'm so close to them that it's really hard for me. I've had to break away a little bit. And you know, any time you try to grow, there's going to be some pain.

The second one would be "Fear of Flying" [written by Hillary Lindsey and Gordie Sampson], the last track on the record. Speaking about relationships—I think sometimes there are relationships that aren't good for you. For whatever reason, one of you sees the "big picture" and the other one doesn't. So, you have to get them to that place. The song says, "I love you and I'm going to miss you, but I know that we're not good for each other and I'm going to be the bigger man [or woman] and say goodbye. I'm gonna kind of force you to say goodbye and on down the road, maybe you'll see [that things aren't right] and you'll make a change right away." Basically the hook says, "Maybe someday you'll get over your fear of flying." To me, I want to feel the freedom to soar through things in life. I don't want to feel tied down; I don't want to feel oppressed; I don't want to get down in the dumps—especially in a relationship—I just want to feel freedom. So that one hits pretty close to home.

What keeps you centered with this career move? Family, friends, faith?

Yeah. I love my God. I'm very… I wouldn't say religious or spiritual… but my faith is really number one. If you start spinning in a circle, if you just look up to God, you're like, "Please help me to settle down" or "Please help me to see why this is the way that it is, good or bad." That's really number one. Then next to that, my family. They're the people that love me and keep me grounded. My mom's always there, saying, "You're just Shelly. I saw you in that magazine, but you're just my Shelly." I'm like, "I know it, Momma." Every other hour she calls and something new is going on at home or with me, and she's reading about it and she's got ques-

tions. It reminds me that not everybody is on the same track that I'm on. I'm not saying I'm selfish by nature. I'm just saying that once you start with this, your brain is really focused on where you're going, so you've got to have people around you that care enough about you to say slow down.

What advice would you give to aspiring artists/songwriters? Maybe something you've learned so far?

I would say, find that thing that you do that's really unique and dynamic and work on it. Keep working on it. Work as hard as you can. I love to play guitar and I love instruments, but I don't discipline myself enough to sit down and play right now. Now I'm working on my brain in that area, but you know, I probably could be really good at it. But right now I'm working on being the best singer/songwriter that I can be. I just found that was my niche. I need to work on it and keep working on it. That's what I would say. Just whatever it is that you do—whether it's writing or whatever your passion is—find the people to put around you to make you better. Always have a coach of some sort. I have a vocal coach that I see every day when I'm in town. It's constantly learning about your own instrument and skills, whatever they are. If it's dance, art, drawing, whatever, keep working on it.

Jay Farrar
Uncle Tupelo, Son Volt

Alt.country pioneer Jay Farrar possesses one of rock's most distinctive voices—a rich, sonorous baritone that slides from note to note with the grace of a steel guitar. As a lyricist, he is capable of writing both straightforward everyman anthems and near-mystical poetry. Born December 26, 1967, in the industrial town of Bellesville, Illinois, Farrar started his first band, Uncle Tupelo, with his friend and fellow songwriter Jeff Tweedy, while still in high school. Their innovative blend of punk and country spawned a cult of devout followers. Tupelo would release four revered albums before tensions between the two songwriters caused Farrar to leave the band in 1993. Tweedy fashioned Wilco out of the remaining members, while Farrar started fresh with Son Volt. Their first album, 1995's *Trace*, was as strong a debut as one could wish for, an achingly beautiful country-rock masterpiece. Son Volt put out two solid follow-ups, *Straightaways* and *Wide Swing Tremolo*, before running out of steam. But there was no stopping Farrar's muse—his solo debut *Sebastopol* (2001) found the songwriter wielding experimental studio techniques and alternate tunings to craft his strongest material in years. *Terroir Blues* followed two years later, but as 2005 rolled around, Farrar, alarmed at the state of the world around him, felt it was once again time to rock. And so Son Volt rode again. Farrar reconstituted the band, drafting all new members to record the critically acclaimed *Okemah and the Melody of Riot*.

—EVAN SCHLANSKY

Interview by
Will Levith

American Songwriter,
September/October 2005

I did a little research on the name *Okemah*, and it seems to me that the reference to Woody Guthrie is a thread throughout the album. Give us an idea of what the title means. It seems to me that there's a bit more of a message than usual.

It's basically just a reference to the fact that Woody Guthrie showed up in the one song ["Bandages & Scars"], so it's basically a nod, a reference to the fact that my kids, the interest in Woody's music was kind of transferred to them, you know, the same way it was from my parents to me.

Was that one of the first memories of music that you had in your house?

It is, yeah. Both my parents were into Woody's music as well as other stuff, but that was always a common thread, definitely.

And that's probably affected your songwriting over the years.

It did. You can even see elements of it, I think, with the first Uncle Tupelo record, even [in] a song like "John Hardy." I think a lot of those guys did, from Leadbelly to Woody Guthrie, and we just gave our own attempt at it. [*laughs*]

So now to Jay Farrar the songwriter. I've noticed that, especially on the album [*Okemah and the Melody of Riot*], there is a new energy, but there's also a new darkness to it: shades of antiwar sentiment, calling out Bush on "Jet Pilot," I assume. Was that a conscious decision that you made… to make a "revolution" sort of album, or was it just how the times are right now?

I never thought about it, so far as consciously saying, "I'm gonna make a 'revolution' record," I was never thinking like that. It was the lead up to the election of 2004, when I was writing the songs, so it was just the climate of the time.

It's still the climate.

[*Chuckles*] Um, yeah, it was something I was feeling at the time, so I was writing about it; it's something that I hope to never have to write about again.

Do you think you might have to continue writing about stuff like this?

I'm sure I will whenever I'm feeling it or the inspiration is there, but right now I'm just kind of numb and cynical and I want to move onto other stuff—write about other things.

Now, I could ask you who "Who" is about, but…

I wouldn't tell you. I prefer to keep it open. I think it's great when people come up and tell me how this is what this particular song is about and that's what it means to them, and I find that more rewarding than just sort of having it be one-dimensional, saying absolutely, *this is what this song is about.*

I guess that's why I asked you originally about these war-themed songs, the Bush song ["Jet Pilot"]. Why attempt to write something like that?

There's a danger involved, it becomes kind of passé by the time you get it recorded, and it's already not totally politically relevant anymore. I tried to be oblique in a lot of ways, just so it's not immediately obsolete by the time it's recorded.

As the climate changes, views change, but it should stick around. In terms of the old songs you did with Son Volt on the first three albums, are you going out and playing those in your live shows, or are you sort of sticking to the new stuff?

Well, so far it's been a mixture; [I've] been kind of resurrecting some of the older songs.

Like what?

Like going back as far as "Loose String" and "Drown" from the first record. Songs like "Driving the View" and "Straight-face" from the last one.

Continuing on with this songwriting theme, what exactly is your routine for songwriting? I read that you pen stuff in the studio, but is there any sort of routine?

Solitary confinement.

So you stay away from the wife and kids?

And the rest of the world… it's usually finding some time, increasingly since I have a family, I'm usually getting up early in the morning or trying to stay up late at night to write and it's just doing a little bit every day, I think, has been the most productive, but yeah, it pretty much happens any time. There's this twilight period right before you go to sleep that usually a lot of ideas come to me, but I'm too tired to wake up. [*chuckles*]

And how do you work it?

I work in an old-school fashion, pretty much, just a cassette, tape recorder…

…and guitar?

Guitar, and a notepad, no digital extravagance just yet.

Do you deal with the slack-tunings when you start writing, or do you always write in the six-string, regular tuning?

The last couple of records I've written almost predominantly in alternate tunings. I just find that that kind of opens things up, and it kind of takes you back to a place where you're not sure where it's going, because if you're playing in standard tuning, you've sort of been all over the fret board hundreds of time, but with a different tuning, it adds a different voicing, different chord configurations—you're figuring that out, so it's kind of like revisiting when you first learned how to play guitar. There's an element of not knowing where it's headed.

Sort of a return to innocence. In terms of songwriting do you ever think, I've got a band behind me now? In the studio, did you ever think, I've written a bunch of songs for Jay Farrar solo, now I have to come up with new instrumentation? Or were you hopeful from the beginning that all these songs would transfer into a band mentality?

I knew that they were going to be written for a band context, so I hoped that they would sort of work with that configuration, and some of the songs are still more or less "solo."

Are your kids old enough to know that dad's a rocker?

They're old enough to know that I've recorded music, and they like to listen to it… usually they request it, and they get impatient with me because I don't want to hear it. [*laughs*]

Was "6 String Belief" always something you wanted to do as a Son Volt song?

I always felt like "6 String Belief" was meant to be a full-on rock arrangement, but with the *Stone, Steel & Bright Lights* [solo] record, it was a freshly written song, and that was just the way it got recorded—solo.

Why not "Doesn't Have to Be This Way"?

That was a song I wrote on the road with Canyon, and I felt like it should stay on that record. [*laughs*]

That tune had a very revolutionary-type theme to it. Is that something that you've found as you've matured, that you've become more conscious of writing songs that are about what's going on in the world—things that are going to affect your kids, things like that?

Yeah, there's some truth to that, I think. Once you have kids, you feel like you've become more of a stakeholder, and you definitely pay important attention to issues like that, but like I said before, there's a certain amount of cynicism, I think, that comes with thinking about that all the time and if you look at it in historical perspective, I think this country's always been kind of conservative, and you have to kind of have to come to terms with the fact that that's just the way it's going to be.

I guess that begs the question: Why do you live in the Midwest? It seems like a pretty big hotbed for conservatism.

It is and it isn't. I mean, there are definitely pockets that are open to new ideas, but...

Do you feel that that was one of the attractions you had to St. Louis, or was it just that you had grown up around there and you didn't want to leave?

It's the area that I grew up in, so I have that attachment to it. St. Louis is a progressive city, so I feel comfortable living there.

As a way of contrasting *Terroir Blues* to *Okemah*, right away I noticed that the first couple tracks on *Okemah* are straight rock songs. Is that the way you wanted your audience to perceive the record, or was it that you were over the acoustic stuff?

It was basically a certain type and spirit of songs that I wanted to get back to, that I hadn't done for awhile, and I think

a lot of that is represented on this record, and like *Terroir Blues*, I had a collection of songs that were more stark and not up-tempo, and I grouped them all together and they came out on that record.

Do you see this new Son Volt lineup as a permanent fixture for the next couple of years?

I'd like for it to keep going, yeah. I don't see any end in sight right now. We'll hopefully still do some solo recordings on the side, and maybe some other actual side projects with other musicians—I have done some of that, and some of that will be coming out soon.

Are you at liberty to tell me?

Yeah, there was this one record I did with Anders Parker [formerly of Varnaline], which we just have to figure out what to call.

As a side question to the fact that you have your own label now, that you have this "artistic freedom," do you see yourself continuing recording your own stuff, producing your own stuff?

I don't see myself in that role of producing other bands, but I will continue to produce my own stuff. I think it's pretty important. I feel like every musician or every songwriter should produce themselves; it's basically finding your own way, [and] I think it's best to learn it firsthand, how to get it done.

Ben Folds

photo courtesy Sony BMG

Taking the baton from pop balladeers like Billy Joel and Elton John, singer/songwriter/pianist Ben Folds employs humor, pathos, exquisite melodies, and his sweet falsetto to craft some of the most hummable music in alternative rock. The multi-talented Folds, born September 12, 1966 in Winston-Salem, North Carolina, started out as a bass player in the rock band Majosha before gravitating to Nashville, where he worked as a session drummer. On the strength of his songwriting, he was offered a publishing deal with Sony Music, and he returned to North Carolina in 1994 to start his own band, the Ben Folds Five, with drummer Darren Jessee and bassist Robert Sledge. Their self-titled debut, released on Caroline Records in 1995, generated a buzz with the scene-skewering "Underground." The band gained worldwide recognition with their sophomore album, *Whatever and Ever Amen*, which included their most famous song, "Brick," a plaintive ballad about abortion. They released one more album, 1999's *The Unauthorized Biography of Reinhold Messner*, before splitting up.

Folds was able to parlay his talents into a successful solo career, returning in 2001 with *Rockin' the Suburbs*, on which he played virtually all the instruments. In 2004 he released the critically acclaimed *Songs for Silverman*, which featured the single "Landed," as well as "Late," a touching tribute to late songwriter Elliott Smith.

—EVAN SCHLANSKY

Interview by
Brian T. Atkinson

American Songwriter,
July/August 2005

133

You recorded material last year for a solo album and scrapped it, right? How much of that made it onto *Songs for Silverman*?

Yeah, I made demos. I guess about five or six of them are on the new album. "Give Judy My Notice," "Time"… what else? I don't know. I don't have the list in front of me right now. But about five or six of them. The rest of them ended up on the EPs [*Speed Graphic, Sunny 16,* and *Super D*]. And it wasn't as dramatic, as I'd recorded the whole album and scrapped it. I was recording anyway. I was putting a lot of stuff out on EPs, and I had stuff left over. So, we considered making an album, but when I really looked at it, I realized that I was just recording to record.

Tell me about the new album's title.

It's called *Songs for Silverman*, and there's no Silverman.

Can you explain that?

No, not really, there's no story.

What's the story behind the first single, "Landed"?

"Landed" is about a friend of mine who was in a bad relationship. I just wrote a song about it.

You wrote "Late" about Elliott Smith. What were your experiences with him like?

We toured together for a few weeks… a good tour. He was a talented guy. Yeah, I mean, he was playing before me, then I played, then Beck played afterwards. We hung out a little bit, but not much. I didn't really know him that well, but I liked him. He was a great guy. You know, when you're on tour, you don't get that much of a chance to hang out. I was usually just traveling. But we got along well. I was really sad when he died.

I'd imagine that would be a hard song to write.

Actually, it wasn't a hard song to write. It may have been a little difficult to decide that it's okay to release it, but all in all, it was fairly easy writing. It was just a matter of cutting out anything unnecessary that wasn't absolutely true, if that makes any sense. It was about keeping the song really honest, and keeping it to what I know. I didn't try to make a big concept about it.

What inspired "Jesusland"?

"Jesusland" is sort of a walk across the country. You know, "There's a billboard, there's a McMansion, there's a couple nice houses"… just trying to put together a montage that recreates the playing field as you have it.

Did you write it on the road?

No, I never write on the road. Well, I wrote one album on the road that I had to scrap because it sounded too much like a Foghat record. That was real dramatic because it was a real big-budget record.

Is there any particular new song you'd like people to hear the most?

Nah, not really. I sequenced the album in the way I'd like it to be listened to. You also make every song individually so they stand on their own, so anything that someone listens to is fine with me. I mean, sometimes when you hear fifteen seconds of something taken out of context, it can be a little disconcerting. But I'm totally fine with it if people are listening.

I read that you said *Songs for Silverman* **is "spiritually tight." What exactly do you mean?**

I don't know. I mean, what I probably meant was if you spend a lot of time in the studio trying to tighten the living shit out of everything, you can loosen the overall emotional effect of the music. You can concentrate on the wrong thing. So what I probably meant was that we were spending time—instead of sliding drum tracks around trying to make things

You also make every song individually so they stand on their own, so anything that someone listens to is fine with me.

perfect—more concerned with the impact and the subtlety. That's more important. We did the takes very much live.

Now that you're back with a band, which do you prefer, playing solo or with others?

They're just different. It's hard to even really compare and contrast the two. It's all making music. I'll do both in the future. I might go out with eighty-seven people in the band next year.

That would be quite an undertaking.

It is, but you get a different eighty-seven people in each city to play. I played with the Western Australia Symphony Orchestra recently. The idea came up to do a tour [playing with orchestras] because we've been offered a show in every city in Australia by now.

Let's talk songwriting. You said that you don't write on the road. Do you have a typical writing process?

Usually, I come up with the music first. The way I think of it is that the music is some sort of abstract interpretation of the way I'm seeing things. I'm not usually all that aware of what the song's actually about. When I look into what's going on and think about what the song might be about [lyrically], I

realize that's what the music's about to begin with. So, they kind of collide, and you put the two together. I can take a long time on a song. I can do it quickly, too, but I've started to take a long time on each song. The music always comes first, but then there are the things I'm thinking about writing at the same time. The music is like an interpretive dance. It's what's going on in your life, and you take it in and process it.

Do you think a song has to have meaningful lyrics to be good?

Well, I don't think there's any rule. Shitty lyrics and shitty music can come together to make a great song. It's the way that they come together and the impact they have. I mean, if I were reaching into a stack of lyrics for a song to work on I wouldn't pick up "Wooly Bully." And if someone played me the tune and I heard it, I wouldn't give a shit. But it's a good song. It has its impact and it's certainly lasted a long time. It's not my favorite song, but there's something to it.

In what ways do you feel your songwriting has matured?

I think by the time I hit my stride, what I did was good enough to be on a record. I'm not so sure it's actually changed that much. The presentation has changed, but basically my style of writing songs has pretty much stayed the same. I try to be subtler about some things. I don't even know, though, I couldn't really say quite honestly.

Has being a parent changed things?

Yeah, but that hasn't changed my songwriting. I wrote a song for my son on one record and a song for my daughter [on *Songs for Silverman*], but to me that's not a change in writing style. I used to write about whatever was in front of me, and

that's what I still do. I think that's pretty normal. It's like if having kids made me decide what's really important in life is streamlining my chord progressions or being less dramatic or something like that… I wouldn't say that. I don't think it's changed my writing style.

Many readers of this magazine are aspiring song-writers and musicians, presumably looking for a record deal or publishing deal. How did you land your first one?

Well, if I was going to give solicited advice to an aspiring songwriter or musician, I would say don't make a demo tape. Concentrate on your music. Play live shows. I think the last thing someone should be going for is a record deal. I know that's easy to say because I've got a record deal, but there were certainly a lot of times in the last ten years when I wished I didn't have a deal. This is not the day and age to be concentrating on that. There's a whole other music business going on out there. I just have always thought that if some-one's music is there and that was their guide, they'd have their day in court. That's turned out true for almost every-one I know who stuck with it. It does take a lot of persistence,

and you do the whole handshake thing. You meet some pretty nice people, people who are good at what they do. I wouldn't say go for a record deal—I'd say go with the most money, because most of the people at the label are probably gonna change. Keep concentrating on music.

What are the challenges for indie artists these days?

The Internet has changed that a lot. It's really giving the labels a run for their money. I think as an up-and-coming band, a label would almost be like natural selection. Like if you sign with a major label, you have Darwin'd yourself. You kind of went to the gutter there. Why not self-release albums? Concentrate on your craft—that's what you should think about when you wake up and go to bed. Not the rec-ord deal. It's not about the charts, and it's not about the airplay. You have to keep that perspective, or you won't last. I think a lot of people have lasted and outlasted criticism because of that. Even Madonna. Because at the beginning of the day and the end of the day, she remembers that if she doesn't make a good record, she doesn't have a job. I wouldn't talk about it so much if I didn't think it was kill-ing music. I know a lot of really talented musicians who I wish weren't as obsessed with their record deal, because I think they would have made much more great music.

Concentrate on your music. Play live shows. I think the last thing someone should be going for is a record deal.

but a record deal is really overrated. It's just someone to put out your record. A record deal doesn't necessarily mean a *good* record deal. There are a lot of things to look at when it comes to distributing your record, and you're in busi-ness with [the labels]. That's about it. You get about twenty minutes with each of them, they come out to your shows,

Fountains of Wayne

Fountains of Wayne fun fact: The band took their name from a gift shop in New Jersey that sells lawn ornaments.

The genesis of the band goes back to Massachusetts' Williams College, where dual songwriters Adam Schlesinger and Chris Collingwood met in 1986. Together they recorded an album of demos under the name Pinwheel but abandoned the project to seek their fortunes elsewhere. Collingwood became a member of the Boston band Mercy Buckets, while Schlesinger found success as a member of the New York based indie-rock band Ivy, which he still plays with today. In 1996, Collingwood and Schlesinger gave partnership another try, recruiting guitarist Jody Porter and drummer Brian Young to form Fountains of Wayne.

Their self-titled Atlantic Records debut showed off their power-pop hooks and skewed humor, and the quirky single "Radiation Vibe" became an alternative rock hit. They returned in 1999 with *Utopia Parkway* which, though lauded by critics, failed to spawn any hits. But the world was reintroduced to their subtle pop pleasures with 2003's *Welcome Interstate Managers*, which featured the MTV surprise hit and rhapsody to older babes everywhere, "Stacy's Mom." Their most recent release, *Out-of-State Plates* (2005), gave fans a generous dose of B-sides and rarities.

—EVAN SCHLANSKY

Interview by
John D. Luerssen

American Songwriter,
July/August 2005

137

Was there a formative moment in the creation of Fountains of Wayne?

Schlesinger: When I got to [Williams] college, I started listening to all of the English new wave stuff. I was a big Aztec Camera fan when I was eighteen. Roddy Frame was the guy who made me feel like I could try to be a musician for real, because my voice kind of sounded like his. Some music you grow in and out of, but it hasn't happened to me yet with Aztec Camera. When I first met Chris at college, he used to sing their songs all of the time at open mic nights. He can actually sound uncannily like Roddy Frame when he wants to. When I was in middle school, I started to discover Steve Miller and The Cars.

Collingwood: Our story isn't that great. It might be more interesting if we met in the Chicago blues clubs or rehab or something. Unfortunately none of that applies. Williams is a really, really small school. Basically every musician on campus knew each other pretty quickly. We first got together and started doing covers and wound up living in the same dormitory.

Chris, who are some songwriters you emulate?

Collingwood: Tom Petty was my hero as a kid but, but like Adam, I was also really into The Cars. It's arguable that that was good songwriting, but it just felt a lot more fun than some of the other stuff. I was a crazy freak fan of it. Also Echo and the Bunnymen. I don't know if I would call that great songwriting either or just really good theater. Anyway, the Bunnymen are still amazing. We actually got a chance to open for them at this big outdoor show [sponsored by KROQ-FM] in L.A. with The Cure and Duran Duran. So I got to meet [Bunnymen singer] Ian McCulloch and he had a little bit of Keith Richards attitude going on. It's astonishing how good they sounded for a band whose heyday was, like, [twenty to twenty-five] years ago.

What was life like for FoW post-college? Didn't you guys get into some legal trouble with an indie label?

Collingwood: We were signed to a label called Pipeline and dropped before the album ever came out. I don't know if they ever put any records out. They started as a distribution company and we were their guinea pigs. God, it seems so long ago—like 1991 or something.

Schlesinger: Chris and I had a band that was the precursor to Fountains of Wayne [known as The Wallflowers until Jakob Dylan paid the duo a minute sum to stop using the name], although basically it was the same thing. But we signed with this little start-up indie label. We made this record for them and it's a long boring story, but we got in a fight with them. They put us with a producer we didn't like, we got in a fight with him, which turned into a fight with the label, and the whole thing kind of imploded. Then we ended up in this legal purgatory where we couldn't get off the label and they wouldn't let us do anything or release our record or let us go work for anybody else. It was kind of a nightmare for two years. We were so depressed at that point. We felt, "We're only twenty-four years old and we've totally fucked ourselves."

And after that, you were signed to Atlantic Records, right?

Schlesinger: "Seed [Records] was really Atlantic Records. This was at the time when it was super cool to be on an indie and super uncool to be on a major, so all the majors were starting "fake indies." And Seed was kind of the worst of both worlds because it didn't really have any credibility and it didn't really have any money.

How did the FoW offshoot band Ivy play into the mini-major formula? You hear so much about Ivy when people talk about the history of your band.

Schlesinger: Ivy kind of got in there first, and by the time Fountains of Wayne came along, I knew some people at Atlantic and they dug the music, so for a brief period, both bands were actually signed to Atlantic. And while neither band was a massive commercial success, we made some good relationships and the good thing I can say about Atlantic in hindsight is that they never meddled with us creatively. They left us to our own devices, which is far different from what I've heard about the Clive Davis school of thought, where they mold you and turn you into something else. We were what we were, for better or worse.

How do you manage your music publishing affairs? For the novice songwriter, how does self-publishing compare with being a part of a publishing company?

Schlesinger: I was signed as a writer and as part of both bands and actually that [publishing] deal just ended a couple of years ago, and now I don't have a publishing company—I just do it myself. But that was a great experience for me because I was really interested in trying to write, not just for the band, but for other stuff. If you're vocal about doing that kind of thing, a publishing company can be a great resource for hooking you up with these kinds of opportunities. Basically [with self-publishing], you get to keep all the money. That's really the bottom line. But the other benefit is when you get offers from people who want to do something with your song, you don't have to consult with a million people… you can kind of decide for yourself what you want to do.

You guys exercise the classic Lennon/McCartney setup of splitting publishing royalties 50/50 as a rule, though you write apart a lot. Does that ever cause any tension between you? Or are you guys pretty amicable when it comes to the split?

Collingwood: We decided early on, it's better to not have arguments that some bands have where someone might say, "I wrote 15 percent of that song," and try to figure out those numbers. It just seems ridiculous.

Schlesinger: We just agreed many years ago that if we were to have a band we'd just split the songwriting to avoid having a conversation every time we tried to finish a song. But we really haven't collaborated as writers in years. And that's kind of intentional, too, because we didn't want it to turn into a thing where people would say, "Adam's songs are like this…" We wanted the band to have an identity more than we wanted each of us to have an identity in the band. We like the anonymity in sharing the credit. A band doesn't need to be dissected that way. I could decide to write something that's really atypical of me and something that's really more typical of Chris, but if I could pull it off and he likes it, then we can just do it. When it comes down to writing songs for a new record, we just always say, "Write whatever you feel like writing." We try not to map it out or talk about it in advance at all, and that way, whatever mood you wake up in, you can write something.

Is there some sort of a symbiotic blueprint for each FoW song? You two seem to complement each other really well.

Schlesinger: That sort of happens by accident, to be honest. We don't sit down with a chalkboard and try to figure it all out. But what will happen is if we go in with a batch of twenty songs and fourteen of them thematically relate to each other, we might throw out the other six, partly because it feels like they don't fit. But we won't really plan it beforehand like that.

Collingwood: Sometimes if I get mealy mouthed on a lyric, I might change it on the spot. Or other stuff changes, too. Sometimes we change a chord, but the basic spirit of the song is retained.

Schlesinger: And I'd say, like, 95 percent of the time, we agree on which ones are good and which ones aren't. There have been a couple of cases where one of us has been fighting for our own songs and the other guy is like, "Dude, I'm not into it." But that's pretty rare. I think both of us look at songs as a crossword puzzle. If all the lines fit and the idea is clear and you execute it right, then it works.

Your lyrics are pretty satirical as far as modern pop purists are concerned. Are there ever any reservations about balancing witticisms with more serious lyrical content?

Schlesinger: It's a touchy subject as far as how much of a sense of humor you should have. We always get lumped in with comedians, you know? And that's not really the point. We're not trying to be Weird Al [Yankovic] or Ween. But I do think humor is part of real life, and part of reflecting who we are is sometimes writing songs that make you smile a little bit. At the same time, songs don't [necessarily] need meaningful lyrics. I think "Radiation Vibe," which Chris wrote and was our first single, is one of the best songs ever, and it doesn't make any fucking sense. That's part of what I love about it...that it is sort of anthemic, but when you stop to think about what you're saying, it's hilarious. We used to lie in interviews and say it was about Phoebe Cates and her struggle in Hollywood when she first got there and her big break with *Fast Times at Ridgemont High*, but it had nothing to do with that. [*laughs*]

Collingwood: Some songwriters just take themselves too seriously. That was definitely the trend in the early nineties with grunge, with all the Eddie Vedders of the world. I wouldn't even really call people like that songwriters. They consider themselves "artists." My favorite songwriters have never taken themselves too seriously. I'm a big fan of Paul Simon—he uses little jokes here and there. I'm also a fan of Neil Finn [from Crowded House]. Even though he can

be a bit of a wet towel… wet blanket… isn't that the word for it? He's good at doing it, too.

Is there a specific time of the day that you set aside for writing songs?

Schlesinger: I have a calendar on the fridge. I try to plan ahead a little bit. I probably write more often on guitar, but usually I need some kind of lyrical idea first and then I can figure out a way to make it work musically. Sometimes I'll just have a sort of stream-of-consciousness verse thing and I'll just try to keep writing what it's about. Other times I'll have a phrase that feels like a chorus and I'll work backwards. Most often I think the best stuff is written with no instrument. You just kind of have a melody in your head or you can just sort of imagine it all and you go to an instrument and figure out what you were hearing in your head after the fact.

Collingwood: I defer to Jules Shear, one of my favorite songwriters. Jules once said, "The best place to write a song is in your head." And I thought that was really brilliant.

What happens when you succumb to the much-dreaded writer's block? Is there a proven method that works in terms of beginning or finishing a song?

Schlesinger: I usually smoke a lot of weed and drive around. Seriously, there's no real rule about it. Things just pop into your head for no real reason and I'll write them down or put them into the computer until I decide what I want to do with them. Sometimes I will call my answering machine and sing a couple of lines in case I can't remember when I sober up the next day. There are some songs where you feel like something is there and then six months later it's still nothing. There are all kinds of stuff that just gets thrown out for that reason. A lot of times I just find it easier to start working on something else than to continue trying to force something that isn't working.

Collingwood: Some songs might take a little longer, but I don't think of songwriting in terms of ease or difficulty. There will be a thing where I'll have a song where I know what it's about and it's missing a few lines. I just have to be patient until I have those lines, but I don't think of it as hard. But forcing a song can make it feel terribly wrong.

Schlesinger: Sometimes you come up with a song and everyone you play it for is like, "That was great… that feels nice." But I try to stay away from that whole "writing the perfect song" mentality. All that does is make you sit under your bed in the fetal position. It keeps you from doing anything productive.

I've talked to a lot of bands who have mentioned the difficulties of juggling touring responsibilities with songwriting. How does one restart the songwriting muse, so to speak, after a particularly grueling tour?

Schlesinger: First of all, if you're doing it because you think you're going to get rich, go do something else, because there are a lot easier ways to make a lot of money in the world. You might get lucky, but if you want to be rich, go work in a bank. Most musicians that I know have done it for a long time and just do it because they can't imagine doing anything else. And no matter how bad things get, they haven't figured out what they'd rather be doing. And that's kind of how it is for us. We just like to play music. And it may be a cliché, but we'd be doing it anyway. I think you have to have that attitude, despite whatever stupidity you might be put through.

Collingwood: I think that people think if they hear your song on the radio all the time that you must be super rich. But it's very, very hard to squeeze out a living being a musician. I'm not complaining about it because at least I'm doing it and not I'm working in an office every day.

> *We try not to map it out or talk about it in advance at all, and that way, whatever mood you wake up in, you can write something.*

Collingwood: We get so tour weary. Neither Adam [nor] I has much luck writing on the road. You've got to get home and take a breather for a while.

Do you have any tried-and-true advice for anyone who is considering a career as a musician?

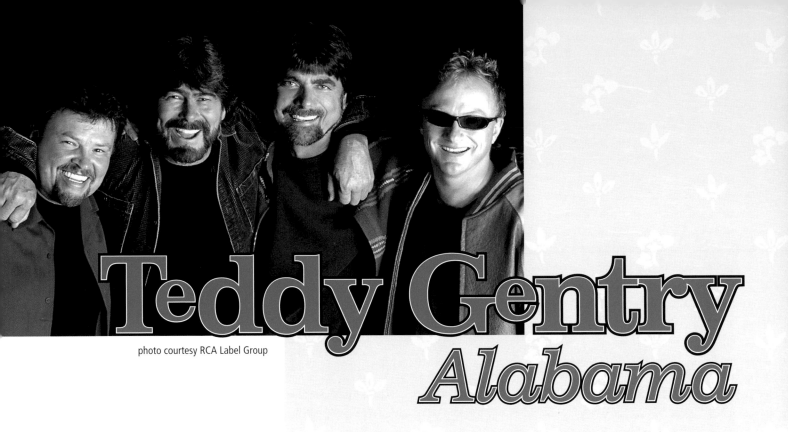

Teddy Gentry
Alabama

photo courtesy RCA Label Group

Interview by
Deborah Evans Price

American Songwriter,
March/April 1988

Country music giants Alabama formed in Fort Payne, Alabama, in 1969, the musical confluence of cousins Jeff Cook (guitar, fiddle, vocals), Randy Owens (guitar, vocals), and Teddy Gentry (bass, vocals). Their success was not immediate—at first they gigged mainly on weekends at local amusement parks. The trio soon moved to Myrtle Beach, South Carolina, where, with drummer Rich Scott, they began focusing on writing their own material. In 1979, they signed to MDJ Records and had modest hits with "I Wanna Come Over" and "My Home's in Alabama." After moving to RCA Records, their 1980 single "Tennessee River" hit number one, the first of forty-two country music chart-toppers for the band. In the eighties, Alabama sold more records than any other country group and were the first band in their genre to earn quintuple-platinum sales status. In 2002, the band announced their retirement and embarked on a wildly successful farewell tour. Only time will tell if country music's most successful group is *really* gone for good.

—EVAN SCHLANSKY

Where does songwriting fit into your highly successful musical career?

I guess writing songs and playing is what attracted me to music to start with. That's really my first love—songwriting. Becoming an artist, the first ten years before success started, you had a lot of time to write… a lot of time to hone your craft. But after things got to rockin' in 1980 with our first hit, the pace of our life went so fast that you didn't have time to write. So I went for probably five or six [years] without actually sitting down and just enjoying writing. But after that period of time, I just realized that songwriting is what I still loved to do the most. So I just started making time to write every month—at least once a month. That's what I continue to do now. Songwriting is… I hope I can do it until the good Lord lays me down.

How does the writing process work for you?

Writing is kinda like fishing; you never know when they are going to be biting. You never know when the good lines or song titles are going to come. Sometimes you can come across a great title that takes a while to develop. Sometimes you come across a melody. One of Alabama's number one songs was called "How Do You Fall in Love," and the song started with a melody I carried around. That melody was there for months before I ever came across the right words for it. Sometimes it comes fast… it's flowing and it comes very fast. Dean Dillon was an experience for me. You know, sometimes people can draw out songwriting for days, weeks, or months. But with Dean, two hours with him and the song was finished. Or maybe even less. I think that different people in writing influence you [to allow it to flow] sometimes. It's more important, you know, [rather] than trying to pick it to death. Then sometimes, it's more important to pick it to death. Sometimes it takes a long while to get a song like you want it.

What do you most enjoy about co-writing?

Well like I said… it flows from Dean. He's probably one of the most talented people I've ever written with as far as letting it flow out in a natural rhythm and natural flow when Dean gets into the groove. There are a lot of other great songwriters I enjoy writing with too. Ronnie Rogers is one of my favorite songwriters. I think for me, it's like fishing again. Make sure you enjoy spending time with somebody you like being with… and enjoy being with. So whether a hit song comes out of it or not, you haven't wasted your time. You've had a good time. That's kind of my philosophy on songwriting, too. Hang out with the writers you enjoy writing with. If you come up with a big song, fine. If you don't, you had a good time.

Is there someone you especially click with as far as a co-writer?

Greg Fowler. Greg was an old Myrtle Beach buddy who came in from radio. He was the program director in 1979. And in 1980, the station won an award for Greg's work. He was excellent at what he did, so when we went out on the road, Greg was hired to come out and do promotion for us. But later on, I found out that Greg was very creative and very good at lyrics. So we started writing songs together. There's nothing that gives me more satisfaction than when you finish a song and feel like it's finished. That's one of the best feelings in the world.

Give us an example of how you and Greg wrote a song.

Me and Greg were in Pennsylvania one night and he had this other song started. He had like a verse written on this song. In the middle of the verse, it said something about the fans. And as soon as I saw that title, I thought, "We gotta write a song for all the people out there who have made our lives great." We started writing that song ["The Fans"].

From an emotional standpoint, it was one of those songs that every word of it was meant. It was one of those things that as we went through it—our lives and our career—I think to all those people who have made it. It was kinda like writing a song for my kids. It was the closest thing to that rush of writing something that you really wanted to get out. Later on in our career, we got a chance to rewrite for the king of stock car racing, Richard Petty, and John Gerard was another songwriting buddy of mine [who contributed]. He helped us because he was a big racing fan and a big Richard Petty fan. That song was very important and had a special meaning. It was one of those songs that we got to do on our farewell tour. It really hit home. It's hard to keep from crying every night when we do it.

What songs are you most proud of and why?

All songs have a different meaning for different reasons. I think the songs about my kids are real personal. Maybe "Pass It on Down," [which talks about what] we are doing to our earth and what our kids and grandkids have to deal with. I think that's one song when it wasn't just me speaking. It's someone speaking through me saying… it's more like a message I guess… but still. "Give Me One More Shot" is another one of those songs about my relationship with God that I feel in my heart, "Thank you for letting me do what I do and give me one more day to enjoy it." So in any song that you write in one way or the other, if it's something that you create or you feel that's a piece of you and what you stand for, I think those songs probably mean the most to you—not the commercial success they have.

Is co-writing a source of camaraderie for you?

Well, songwriting is something that's a great way to meet people. That's one of the reasons I love it. I can say, "Hey, I want to sit with you and write a song." Some of the older [writers], you know, like Harlan Howard… I wish I could've gotten a chance to have written with Harlan. I'm such a big fan. But you know, I got to write with Bill Anderson, one of my heroes. Never gotten to write with Vince [Gill]. I would like to write with Vince. Don Henley, you know… I would like to write with Don Henley sometime. I would like to write with anybody. [*laughs*] Call me, we'll write.

Do you have any advice for writers who are just getting into this?

Songwriting is a hard business. It is a tough business. In fact, I had a gentleman that sent me a tape. He's married and had a little kid and he wrote some songs. And he said, "I'm thinking about quitting my job and moving to Nashville and becoming a songwriter full time." So I listened to the material and I said, "Don't take this as discouragement, but…" It took me a while to call him back because I didn't have the nerve. But you gotta be honest with people. That's the biggest thing. So I told him, "Don't give up your job now and put yourself at the mercy of your songwriting." From a business standpoint, I said, "Take some of your better songs there, and if you get somebody to offer you a concrete writing deal, then that's an option. But to go there and be at the mercy of the town…" I [told him] there are thousands and thousands of people who wanna get in the business and be songwriters. Most of the time, 95 percent of the hit songs come from hit writers that have written for years. It's like a brick mason, you know; if you lay brick for fifteen to twenty years, it looks easy to do. It looks like it all falls together [naturally] until you try it and realize how clumsily you feel trying to do it. So I think it's a matter of honing your craft no matter what it is until it's second nature. And if God gave you the talent, you keep digging for it. And eventually, you know, you'll get out something's that's great.

Dave Gibson

Anyone born in El Dorado, Arkansas, and raised in Odessa, Texas, is likely to love country music, and Dave Gibson is no exception. After moving from Arkansas to Texas with his mother, brother, and sister, Gibson was introduced to the music of Roy Orbison and Buddy Holly, who lived down the road in Lubbock, Texas. Elvis was his idol and his influence can still be heard in Dave's vocal performance.

After Texas, Gibson went from Chicago to Nashville and hit the streets looking for a record deal and people to listen to the songs he wrote. Early meetings with music legend Tony Brown and producer Norro Wilson led to his introduction to producer Doug Johnson and Blue Miller, guitar player for Bob Seger's Silver Bullet Band. Together, Gibson and Miller formed the Academy of Country Music Award-winning Gibson/Miller Band in the early nineties. Despite recording several top ten hits, including a Gibson/Miller remake of "Mamas Don't Let Your Babies Grow Up to Be Cowboys," which was featured in the movie *The Cowboy Way* with Keifer Sutherland and Woody Harrelson, Gibson was still looking forward. His efforts as a songwriter had skyrocketed with songs like Alabama's "Jukebox in My Mind," Tanya Tucker's "If It Don't Come Easy," Confederate Railroad's "Queen of Memphis" and "Daddy Never Was the Cadillac Kind," and Joe Diffie's poignant hit "Ships That Don't Come In."

—LISA WYSOCKY

photo courtesy Kris Kristoffersen

Interview by
Lisa Wysocky

HitWriters.com, 2005

145

How did you break into the Nashville music scene?

Well, I met Tony Brown when I first came into town in 1982, and he basically changed my whole life. I was working here at the clubs and doing everything I could to survive. I walked into his office one day and played him four songs. He said, I like two of those songs real well, and I want to [record them]. He and Norah Wilson were at RCA at the time. They took me in, and two weeks later, it all happened. I didn't get a record deal out of that recording session, but I met everybody in town. Tony said, "Write me a song for Steve Wariner, 'cause I'm producing him." And that's what happened. I had an idea called "Midnight Fire" that I had started. I got together with Louis Anderson, who I just met through Tony. We sat down one day, and in about two hours wrote that song. Within a month's time, it was recorded [by Wariner] and picked as the title of the album and first single. So I was off and running. I got a publishing deal with The Oak Ridge Boys through Silver Line Music. And that was the beginning of everything.

You had a string of successful hits with the band Confederate Railroad.

I was very lucky to have a couple of big hits with Confederate Railroad. Danny Shirley and all those guys were real good to me. Barry Beckett was their producer at the time.

> *I made my living as a songwriter for ten years and finally got a record deal.*

Barry loved a song of mine that I had written with Kathy Louvin. Kathy played it for him, and he said, "You know, I love that chorus. That chorus is a hit." But he said, "You gotta change that second verse." And we wrote that second verse about a boat. It really was about a guy that had just come off the farm—basically going through the rites of passage, learning about life. We finished writing the song and called it "Queen of Memphis," talking about an old riverboat.

So they were a good fit for your songs?

Those guys really liked my songs. I ended up with another song on the album called "Redneck Romeo," which I had written with Craig Wiseman… everybody knows ol' Craig now. He's pretty hot. It was great to be in with Danny and the band. They always listened to my songs, and Barry Beckett loved them. The next song I had was called "Daddy Was Never the Cadillac Kind," which I wrote with Bernie Nelson. It was a great time for me because everything sort of happened at that time. I got a record deal with the band and all. So, it was a good thing. It's nice to be in a clique like that.

What was it like having a record deal after years of writing for other artists?

Playing in concerts with the Gibson/Miller Band was awesome. I never really realized how powerful a song is, but when we go out and play our hits—"Texas Tattoo" "Big Heart," and "High Rollin'"—these people went nuts. They knew 'em because they heard them on the radio. It was the most satisfying feeling in the world to just rock 'n' roll with a great band. I met Blue Miller in 1991 through Doug Johnson, who ended up being our producer. It put a bunch of guys together who all worked well [together]. It was so much fun on the road. It was a totally different thing. I made my living as a songwriter for ten years and finally got a record deal. It wasn't the way I thought it was going to be, but it was even better because it was with a band.

You have to learn to edit yourself and learn that every song you're writing is not a hit. But you just keep on writing…You gotta keep on writing. It's like practicing an instrument or being an athlete. You gotta keep that muscle going. You need to be out there doing it every day.

So the band was very positive for you. How did it compare to the songwriting scene?

You got to share it with a bunch of other guys. Being out there on the road had its ups and downs, but for the most part, it was awesome. Playing songwriter nights and doing the little seminars we do, and going out and playing for people in the rounds across the country and here in Nashville, is a very satisfying thing, too. It's very personal and up close. People can sit there and talk and tell jokes. You can be a lot more yourself and play the songs that maybe will be a hit for somebody else, or had been a hit. And people can't believe it: "Man, you wrote that?" It's two different things but it's really satisfying. Both of them are.

Do you have any advice for upcoming songwriters?

For all you new songwriters out there, it's 90 percent emotion, 10 percent hard work—and it sort of ends up the other way. You have to learn to edit yourself and learn that every song you're writing is *not* a hit. But you just keep on writing. The whole key to it is—Norah Wilson told me one time—you gotta write volume. You gotta keep on writing. It's like practicing an instrument or being an athlete. You gotta keep that muscle going. You need to be out there doing it every day. Networking is the next biggest thing. You get out

there and write with everybody you can. You just get a lot more people involved in your life that can take you to different places. The more lines in the water, the more fish you are going to catch.

What is your favorite hit song that you've written?

In the last twenty-five years, the biggest song that I feel is the most important song to me… is a song called "Ships That Don't Come In" that Joe Diffie recorded… and Sony Music got it to number one, even though it had a couple of cuss words in it. That song has meant more to more people, it seems. John Berry told me he had to stop his car when he heard that song. He pulled over and cried and said, "I gotta do it."

John Hiatt

*Interview by
Paul Zollo*

American Songwriter,
January/February 2006

John Hiatt has been laboring away on witty, vibrant, blues-infused roots rock for quite a while, first testing the waters with *Hangin' Around the Observatory* in 1974 and finally arriving at his trademark unpretentious, stripped-down sonic milieu in 1987 with *Bring the Family*. A prolific and prodigiously talented songwriter, his compositions have often brought him the mixed blessing of partial obscurity beneath the shadows of higher profile artists' renditions of his songs. Case in point—Bonnie Raitt's solo career got a far bigger boost from "Thing Called Love" than his did. Still, every bit of critical acclaim and royalty check garnered by this wry, cerebral singer/songwriter has been deserved. The prolific Hiatt has released a string of critically acclaimed albums lately, including *The Bar Is Open* (2001), *Beneath This Gruff Exterior* (2003), *Master of Disaster* (2005), and *Live from Austin, TX* (2005).

—JEWLY HIGHT

When did you write your first song?

I was eleven. It was called "Beth Anne."

A love song?

It was indeed. She had breasts and was only eleven. She was an early bloomer.

Did songwriting come easily to you?

I guess it did. I picked up the guitar when I was eleven, and I immediately used it for that. I took lessons from a guy named Orlindo Masterpolo. The lessons were for a couple of weeks, and he started teaching me to read music and play notes. I wasn't interested in that. I didn't want to be a lead guitar player. I wanted to play chords. And they wanted me to buy a guitar, which was the scam. So I quit the lessons. And two weeks later I convinced my mother to buy me a Stella guitar for thirty-five dollars. Steel strings. And with the guitar I bought a Mel Bay chord book. And I just instinctively knew that I wanted to play chords so I could accompany myself. And as soon as I learned three chords, I wrote my first song.

What were those chords?

A, G, and D. Though the song actually only had two chords, A and G.

At that age, did you want to be a professional musician?

Yeah, I already knew. I knew from that first song. I kind of knew as I was going in to buy the Mel Bay book and the guitar. I knew it was my destiny.

Did your parents encourage you?

My mother, God bless her. You see, I had already lost interest in school, so she was balancing her encouragement for my music [*laughs*] with her uneasiness about my lack of interest in education [*laughs*]. So she was having a tough time.

But she never discouraged my music. And I'm very thankful for that. As crazy as our family was in other ways, I always got plenty of encouragement. Her love of my music really helped me to believe in myself.

Your songs have such great titles. Do you ever start a song with the title?

No, no. Words are the last thing I get to. Usually I come up with the chords first. Just like the Mel Bay book [*laughs*]. I go to the Mel Bay book first [*laughs*]. Pick up the guitar, and get the chord structure going, and then a melody, hopefully. I start singing nonsense, and out of all that, some kind of lyric gets knocked loose, inspired by all that music. It's all about the music to me. Then the lyrics, which are the inspiration springing forth from the music.

You're such a great lyricist, that's kind of surprising.

Well, thank you. But to me, the lyric is so connected to the music; I can't imagine starting the other way around myself. I have done that, but not all that often.

So is songwriting for you more a sense of following where a song goes, or leading it?

Following it, *totally*. It's like a *trip*. I don't ever know what it's going to be about. We make this shit up [*laughs*]. At least I do. It's as much a surprise to me as anybody else when I'm done with it. It's not like I have a strategy and have it mapped out. That's what keeps me coming back.

Yet your songs are not abstract. They're very specific, with great telling details, and a sense of place.

Yeah, I like that. I like a sense of place. I like it when it feels like the music goes somewhere.

Do you write more lyrics than you use for songs?

Not often. It's funny, I edit as I go. But I don't do much after. It may take me a couple days, or a week. Then the work is

done. I just try and leave it be. I don't think about it, I don't stew about it. I don't want to know. I just want to get back in, and take the trip again when I pick it up again. I don't want to be disturbed about it. It's not a puzzle. It's an adventure.

Do you make demos of your songs?

Usually just guitar [and] voice. I got out of making anything more elaborate than that.

Is it sometimes hard to re-create the magic of your demo when you make a record?

Well, that's the problem. I learned that a long time ago. No sense [*laughs*] setting yourself up for failure.

Does it feel that songs come from beyond you?

Yes, I'm just an antenna.

Do you finish every song that you start?

Can't say that I do. I'm sure there are bits and pieces lying around. I know there are; it is so pitiful how disorganized I am. When I croak, there are all kinds of shit nobody's ever going to find. [*laughs*]

Do you tape yourself while working?

Not so much anymore. If I'm writing something, I usually remember it.

Do you still write some of your songs on piano?

Not that much. I don't even have one set up anymore. I haven't written a piano song for quite a while.

Do your piano songs come out differently than guitar songs?

Yeah. I write ballads mostly, because I'm not that good on piano.

You're great at writing beautiful melodies. Any idea what makes a melody work?

No. It's a mystery to me. I know there's something about when I'm writing on acoustic guitar, something happens. There's a resonance about the chords and the way my voice resonates, rubbing up against the chords, and the way it sounds in my head. I also like the way the back of the acoustic guitar actually feels up against me. This is part of the reason I've never been good at overdubbing my vocals.

I love the song "Love's Not Where We Thought We Left It." It's got some great rhymes: "Love's unorthodox/it changes all of nature's clocks…"

Yeah. That's a good one. I like the fiddle on it. I was getting into a book I read. There's a theologian, Elaine Pagels, who has a short little book called *The Gnostic Gospels*. I read that and it got me thinking. I often do that. I'll read books and it gets the mind going.

Have you always been an avid reader of books?

Oh, no, I come from a family that has a stack of *People* magazines on the back of the toilet. [*laughs*]

There are also great rhymes in "Master of Disaster": "The master of disaster gets tangled in his Telecaster/He can't play it any faster, when he plays the blues/When he had the heart to ask her and every note just shook the plaster/Now he's just a mean old bastard when he plays the blues…"

[*Laughs*] I like it when rhymes keep going. That's a funny song, because that was one that got changed, which doesn't happen very often. I had a whole different chorus for that one. The chords were the same, but the lyrics and the melody were different. It wasn't really working for me. I had the verses, but I didn't like the song. So I changed it about a year ago. The song sat for maybe six months, and I wasn't digging it. Then I came up with that "master of disaster" idea, and that whole rhyme thing, and I said, "That's it. That's what I'm talking about." That's unusual. I don't change things very often.

I was curious about why with that song, which is about a guy playing electric guitar, you have a saxophone riff throughout it—

[*Much laughter*] You were expecting a solo on the Tele, weren't you? That's just the kind of fucked up people we are. You know?

Do you write all the songs for an album at the same time and then stop writing, or are you always writing?

Usually it's mostly new stuff, and then there are one or two things that have been lying around. Like "Old School," I've had that ten, fifteen years. But the other stuff is all new.

You write so much. You're so prolific.

Not really. People say that about me, but I think these craftsmen around here, in Nashville, my God, they make *dates*. These songwriters write three or four songs a day, these crazy people. I don't know how to do that.

But they're not songs like yours.

Well, it's a different kind of thing. But, no, over the years I've done a little bit of it all. I've tried every conceit to try to trap a song, you know? [*Laughs*] But I've quit doing all of that. I just write when it comes.

Do you always use the same guitar to write?

No. I move around. Sometimes I'll write on this little small box Gibson LG2, circa 1947. I love that. I've got a Gibson J-45 that's an '87. It's a good one, and that's one of my favorites. And I've started playing on an old Harmony archtop that Luther Dickinson found in a pawn shop and gave to me.

It's got a really cool sound, so I've been writing stuff on that. Sometimes I'll write on my Telecaster.

You write in so many styles—rock, blues, folk, country, and funk. How do you master so many different styles?

I wouldn't say I've mastered anything. I just like all that stuff. I sort of signed on early to the singer/songwriter thing, if you want to call it that. And the American singer/songwriter sort of has carte blanche. You get to do all that shit. [*Laughs*] It's legal in all fifty states.

You mentioned when radio was good, when it had a mix of things, and your albums are like that.

Yeah, it's a reflection of when I grew up. It's what I listened to and was influenced by. I love all that stuff. Before I even started digging on my own, it was pretty broad just on the radio. You had a pretty good choice. So if you followed just the idioms that were on the radio at the time, you could find the roots.

You've had a lot of covers of your songs. But when you write, do you write them for yourself?

Oh yeah. I'm just writing for the love of writing. It's just the thing I do.

I love the song "When My Love Crosses Over."

Thanks. Love songs are tough. I'd like to write a whole album of nothing but, but like I say, it is hard going. It's hard to say when you're in love, because it's hard to talk about it. It's hard to really say it.

You live out in the country now, after years of living in cities. How does that affect your songwriting?

Probably in a good way. Living out in the woods a little bit, it's peaceful. It's good. It's good for me. It's quiet.

Do you listen to a lot of music?

Yeah, I'm always listening. I must admit, I tend toward older stuff a lot of the time. But I try to pay attention to what's going on. There's just so much *stuff,* for God's sake. It's ridiculous. It's hard to tell when anybody even has anything out. It's like "Oh, by the way, Neil Young's got a new album out." Who knew? That's part of the trouble that the industry's in. It's just *flooded.* It's a glut of shit. You can't even tell when something good is out. You don't even *know* it. Unless Burger King's backing it up. It's a shame. But that's sort of the way things are. Course, I don't think you're going to see Neil Young hooking up with any of that shit anytime soon. Fortunately. But the problem is that you don't know he's got a record out.

Neil is an exception these days, as is Tom Waits and Springsteen. But Paul McCartney, the Stones, and even Dylan have allowed their songs to be used in commercials. Would you ever do that?

No. I had a little accident where BMG ran a little regional thing with "Have a Little Faith in Me" a few years ago, and it was a misunderstanding, and we got it stopped. But my intention was, and is, to not have my songs used. But I've always said, if somebody said, "Here's five million dollars," and we needed it, who's to say? But so far I haven't needed it. I'm not trying to be a saint here, but my gut says no. Do I have a price? I don't know. Nobody's ever come to me with a big hunk of money. I'm just being honest. But my stand is that I don't want my songs being used as promotions.

Because it cheapens them?

Well, yeah. It hurts my feelings when I hear Beatles songs being used to sell shit. They didn't want that to happen. But the Stones and Paul McCartney, they have to do that. They have to do that to let people know they have a record out. I don't hold that against them. But I also honor people like Neil Young who don't do it.

Unlike a lot of songwriters who never surpass their early work, you've continued to keep a high standard.

I don't really think about that. It's all about the work in front of me. I get really involved in the process, I get real excited about the making of a record, getting involved with that group of musicians and/or that producer, and seeing what happens with the songs, the interpretations that ensue. I love the total experience. And then going out touring with that record is the culmination, that's the cherry on top of the whole process, the final thrill. And then there is the end of that particular work. That's its own reward. So when that's done, it's like, "Next!" [*Laughs*] So that's kind of how it goes for me. It's all about, let's do another thing.

Byron Hill

Byron Hill is from Winston-Salem, North Carolina. Hill's parents exposed him to many types of music around the home, from his mother's old scratchy 78s of Perry Como, Tex Williams, and Gershwin's "Rhapsody in Blue," to his father's love for Tennessee Ernie Ford, Roger Miller, Johnny Cash, Merle Haggard, Flatt & Scruggs, and Ray Charles.

A few years after college in the late seventies, Hill chose to follow his musical calling to Nashville. The hits started happening for Hill as a writer in 1979 with Joe Sun's "Out of Your Mind," and in 1981 with Johnny Lee's "Pickin' Up Strangers," with many other cuts and several smaller singles along the way. Hill co-wrote George Strait's first number one, "Fool Hearted Memory" in 1982, and many other early cuts including recordings by artists such as Ray Charles, Juice Newton, Conway Twitty, Mel McDaniel, Ricky Skaggs, Margo Smith, and Reba McEntire.

An unprecedented number of placements followed steadily throughout the eighties and nineties. To date, Hill has had more than 493 recordings of his songs. His songs have earned sixty-nine Recording Industry Association of America (RIAA)-certified gold and platinum albums, eight ASCAP awards, and six number one singles in the United States and Canada.

—LISA WYSOCKY/DOUGLAS WATERMAN

Interview by
Lisa Wysocky

HitWriters.com, 2005

153

How did you get started in songwriting as a career?

Starting about 1975, I was contacting various publishers here in Nashville from my home in North Carolina. I made several trips to town about 1976 and got in touch with a publisher, Jonathan Stone, who was with Sony/ATV Music Publishing at the time. And he started listening to my songs and critiquing them, sort of tough-loving me through the song experience, learning how to write. About 1977, he contacted me and said he had a tape-copy job here in town, and he asked me if I wanted to fill in for another writer who just had a Charlie Rich single. So I stepped into his job in 1978. I moved here in 1978 and signed my first publishing deal in September. And on from there, I started getting songs recorded by various artists, and it all went pretty quickly from that point on. Conway Twitty, Mel McDaniel, Juice Newton, quite a few people…

What's your musical background?

When I was at Appalachian State University, I was hardly a good student. That really wasn't much of my focus, as I was playing guitar and writing songs and hanging out with some of the musician types. But I had a roommate [at school] who introduced me to Doc Watson. I got in with some of the bluegrass players around there, and I started a little duo with a Dobro player, Gene Wooten, who later moved to Nashville. So my education was more involved with hanging out with the musician types and playing in coffeehouses instead of going to class. So, I'm not an example of a good college student. I left there in 1973 and went back to my hometown. I started playing music in a little trio back there and writing songs and formulating my dreams to move to Nashville.

What was your first big break?

"Fool Hearted Memory" was a song that really put me on the map as a songwriter. I had been given the job of writing a song for a new guy who was on MCA Records at the time. And my publishing company, Sony/ATV Music, set me up with the producer, a guy named Blake Mevis. The mission of the day was to sit down and write a hit for this new artist, George Strait at MCA, for a movie. So it was not too short of an order there. It was a big task to come up with something that would be a hit for this new artist, and it was a lucky moment. We came up with a cool song and the rest is history. It was George's first number one and my first number one. The way it really affected my career, I didn't know much until later. I was on the road one time writing with Tracy Byrd, and I remember Tracy's guitar player said, "Hey, I love that song. I was twelve years old when it came out." And I kind of realized that, man, it's been a long time since that tune came out on George. But, I jokingly told him, "That's interesting. I was five years old when I wrote it." Anyway, the song has been a ticket for me to get in with a lot of other writers and artists. It really changed my life and put me on the map as a writer.

Tell me about "High-Tech Redneck," which George Jones recorded.

I wrote "High-Tech Redneck" with Zach Turner. Zach and I have a strange little common thing. We're both ham radio licensed operators. So we sat around one day, both trying to think of all that technical knowledge of ham radio and putting it into a song. We came up with this little high-tech redneck thing. I think we jokingly called ourselves high-tech rednecks that day. And that's where the idea came about. You know, we weren't the only ones in town who were ham radio operators. Chet Atkins was. Also, I think Ronnie Milsap is into that. We used a little bit of that, but we ended up covering all bases with that. Celluar phones… all kinds of stuff… anything high-tech we could [think of]. And I remember George Jones asked the song plugger who pitched the song whether we were drinking when we wrote the song. I remember that I thought that was pretty funny.

You co-write a lot. Do you prefer it?

I really enjoy it because co-writing is a learning process. Even now, for me, after twenty-five years in Nashville, I like to co-write a lot. And I always learn something from my co-writers, be they new writers or writers that have been around for awhile. And it sometimes is the quickest way between point *A* and point *C*. You know, you can really cover a lot of ground. You can get the song finished in a short amount of time, get it into the demo process quicker; there are a lot more people working to promote the song. It's a cool thing. I still like to write alone. One of my biggest hits I wrote alone. I still have to keep reminding myself of that. But co-writing has been good to me.

Do you have any advice for upcoming songwriters?

I always tell songwriters to stick with it. But you always have to have talent and some qualified people along the way who have told you that you can do it. I think that's real important. A lot of people go at it blindly and waste a lot of time trying this. I think that if you have been told that you have the talent to do it and you have gotten enough qualified feedback, you owe it to yourself to really stick with it and not give up. I've seen it happen too many times that writers come to town and it all eventually turns around for them. So I think that's my main advice: Hang in there and keep working.

Is finding a publisher the best first step in the business realm?

I think in the beginning you have to find a publisher, and I was fortunate to find a publisher early on. But these days, it's a crowded field and there's a lot of competition, so it is a little difficult to capture the attention of a good publisher. That, I think, is the problem facing a lot of writers these days. There are just so many writers here [in Nashville]. Here again, it comes down to making contacts and not giving up. I think that if you have what it takes, eventually someone will recognize that and open the door for you. I think making contacts and getting to know people is such an important part of it. It's a small campus in some ways, but it's a crowded campus. So I think Music Row will pan out for those who work it like a business and treat it like a business and get around and meet a lot of people and grow together. I think through the years, I've seen a lot of us grow with each other. And with every generation of songwriters, there's always gonna be someone who's tomorrow's producer, tomorrow's manager, tomorrow's artist. So get to know them before they are. And hopefully, you will grow with them.

And with every generation of songwriters, there's always gonna be someone who's tomorrow's producer, tomorrow's manager, tomorrow's artist. So get to know them before they are.

Byron Hill

Bruce Hornsby

*Interview by
Kristi Singer*

American Songwriter,
September/October 2004

Bruce Hornsby is one of the great American songwriters of our day. Recognized by other artists as such, he's collaborated on more than one hundred records with the likes of Bob Dylan, Don Henley, Bob Seger, and Willie Nelson, to name a few. His songs have been performed by stars of distinct genres, including Chaka Khan, Huey Lewis, Sara Evans, and even the late Tupac Shakur. Mr. Hornsby has been awarded three Grammys for his work and has sold over 10 million records since 1982. The No.1 smash "The Way It Is" (1986), set the stage for his prolific career. In 1990, after the break-up of his longtime band The Range, he became an honorary to The Grateful Dead. This led to touring and quite a few side-projects with the legendary folk-jam group. Hornsby continues to record and push his music to fan-pleasing and exciting new levels. His latest studio album, *Halcyon Days*, was released in 2004, and Sony/Legacy has recently released a career-spanning box set.

—JEWLY HIGHT

What do you feel makes a successful songwriter?

The lyrical aspect is very important to me. Songwriters I've always been drawn to are people who've dealt with something of depth in the lyric writing. Whether it was Bob Dylan—the icon of songwriters, or Robbie Robertson, who wrote all the great songs for The Band and his own solo work… Elton John, Bernie Taupin. I've always loved Bernie's lyrics, especially the first records where he was writing such great stories into the music. I've always been influenced by the folk song, the storytelling tradition in folk music. And so for years I wrote mostly story songs. I still do that, but as I've gone on, it's gotten a little more personal. I used to write mostly in the third person. I write a little more in the first person now.

Do you prefer one to the other, first- or third-person writing?

No, not really. I've never been very much of a "woe is me" songwriter. Not much of a confessional, "oh my life is so messed up." I've always thought it was a little pompous or pretentious to think that anyone would be interested in your own private "woe is me" tale unless you're telling it in a very artful manner.

You like to focus on happier things?

It's just not about confessional. No, not necessarily happier at all. It is not first-person wallowing in misery. I'll write and sing about someone else's misery in a story many times. A lot of times I write songs about interesting stories that I hear or stories from my past, events from my past—like the first interracial romance in my small southern town and all the consternation and freak-out that caused around the town. The song's called "Talk of the Town." Or "The Way It Is," of course, a song about racism inspired by my growing up in that same small town in Virginia. The song "White-Wheeled Limousine" is about a guy who gets caught in the bushes with another woman on the day of his wedding. Or there's the song about a playground basketball legend, "Rainbow's Cadillac." There are so many areas rich for writing that are not simply about "I love you." And I've tended to gravitate more toward those that I consider to be more interesting areas subject matter-wise rather than just another attempt at a relationship song.

What words of wisdom would you give to aspiring songwriters?

My words of wisdom would be this: Be your own toughest critic. Be a strong, self-critic… Try to have the same perspective about your own work, which is very difficult, believe me. I struggle with it all the time, as you do critiquing other people's work. Be your own toughest critic. I mean, not to the point of beating yourself up and flogging yourself into submission and into quitting. That's the fine line here. You have to be unswervingly tough on yourself, but at the same time not drive yourself into wanting to stop.

Be your own toughest critic.

Any final thoughts?

I hope that anyone who's reading this who loves songwriting will just pursue it and be very passionate about it and very intense about it. You have to do it all the time. If you don't, somebody else is, and they will probably get there before you.

Mason Jennings

*Interview by
Matt Fink*

American Songwriter,
May/June 2006

Mason Jennings has always been resolved to do things his own way. And, having sold over thirty thousand copies of his first two self-released albums, he's clearly onto something. Born in Honolulu in 1975 and raised in Pittsburgh, Pennsylvania, Jennings first began writing songs at the age of thirteen. By sixteen, he'd dropped out of school and headed to Minneapolis to pursue music full time. After three false starts, he completed his first album, the solo acoustic *Mason Jennings*, released in 1998. His second album, *Birds Flying Away*, was held up when Jennings contracted mono during the recording process, prompting him to throw out the tunes he was working on and begin all over again. 2002's inspired *Century Spring* found Jennings playing with a full band for the first time. In 2006, he became the first artist to sign to Modest Mouse front man Isaac Brock's Epic Records imprint Glacial Pace, and released the excellent *Boneclouds*.

—EVAN SCHLANSKY

What was it like to work with Noah Georgeson?

He was really great. He's really good to hang out with, just really mellow. My favorite record of the last year was Joanna Newsom's record, and that's why I contacted him, because it sounded so good. He can make acoustic records with an immediacy and intensity that doesn't sound like anything else.

So why the jump to a major label?

It was basically getting to be a lot of work for me, my manager, and Isaac was such a good dude to hang out with, and he'd had a lot of experience making that jump. It just made more sense to me. He was like, "We come from a lot of similar situations, and it would be cool for me to help you and cool for you to have this experience." Isaac being involved was a big factor for me.

How did you meet him?

He just gave me a call one day. He had heard my record and asked me if I wanted to tour with them.

> *I think it's only natural to be searching for a higher power or a connection.*

Had you been a Modest Mouse fan?

No, I hadn't heard them before, but I got their album when I went out on the road, and I really dig it. I don't think there's a big difference from my music. A lot of the lyrical content is pretty similar.

Did you find yourself returning to any particular themes as a writer when writing *Boneclouds*?

Just searching for meaning in life or the idea of, "What's it all for?" I've been traveling so much, and I started to get a little tripped out being in a different city every day for the last five years. I think it's only natural to be searching for a higher power or a connection.

Do you consider yourself a religious person?

Not really, but I've wrestled with a lot of religious issues. I've been searching for a long time.

The song "Jesus Are You Real" seems to really capture that sense of confusion and searching really clearly.

With this song, I wasn't trying to write something specific, but it just sort of popped out, and I was embarrassed by it at first. Then I'm like, "Well, if you're embarrassed by something, there's probably something true there." It wasn't really a Christian thing. It was just asking what was going on.

I don't think I've ever heard a song like "Where the Sun Had Been" on one of your albums before, with the synths and everything...

Right! I'm surprised that that's on there, actually. It has this simple patch on a keyboard. It just didn't sound like it would fit. We wrote that as a band. It was the first time that I've ever co-written with anybody, and I went into the studio with the intention of writing something that no one would ever hear. I just wanted to make something that had a weird feel and would be fun to play. And that just popped out and I loved it, probably because I didn't worry about the arrangement at all. Then Isaac heard it, and was like, "Man, you've got to use that on the record." And I was like, "Uh...alright." If I like it, maybe someone else will, too. That's what's so cool about him. He's just like, "If you dig it, use it."

What was it like opening up for Modest Mouse? I wouldn't necessarily think their fans would be receptive to your music.

They were actually great. I was definitely wondering what was going to happen, and we definitely played more of a rock set than we usually do, but they responded very positively. I think Isaac was impressed, too, that I was welcomed by his crowd. That's what he said, "Let's just give it a shot." He wasn't always there during the recording process, but during the editing process and picking the songs, he was always around to give feedback or if you had a question or anything. It's very rare to get somebody who is honest enough to say, "Man, I don't think this is working. I think you better change it."

ing. It was a time for a change. It's not the record I thought it was going to be, and I'm glad. I can actually sleep now.

It must have been a bit scary at first.

Yeah, for sure. I definitely had reservations. Isaac told me, "It's my label. I can do what I want to do. If I like it, I'm going to get it out there." And I said, "Okay. I trust you." But you're always doubtful, because every single label situation you've read about never goes well. I guess I shouldn't say that, since my record hasn't come out, but it usually doesn't work. But I trust Isaac.

> *It's very rare to get somebody who is honest enough to say, "Man, I don't think this is working. I think you better change it."*

Is it hard working with someone who is so blunt with his opinions?

No. We're similar people. We grew up in similar situations. We've both driven a van around the country trying to make a living playing music.

What was it like working with Epic?

I was surprised that I could make a record this honest and raw. I'm surprised that it's going to be released, that Epic would be cool with that. I'm actually excited that they're into that, that they're actually doing that kind of stuff. It's inspir-

Jewel

Sultry singer/songwriter Jewel's rise to fame is a modern-day Cinderella story. Raised in relative isolation in the wilderness of Homer, Alaska, Jewel Kilcher began her music career at age six, performing for the local Eskimos. As a teenager, she decided to try her luck as a songwriter and moved to San Diego, where she lived in her van. Performing in the local coffee houses, Jewel was soon discovered and signed by an Atlantic Records talent scout. After unsuccessfully shilling her debut album, *Pieces of You*, for fourteen months, Jewel finally scored a monster hit with "Who Will Save Your Soul" as well as the singles "You Were Meant for Me" and "Foolish Games." 1999's *Spirit*, 2000's *Chasing Down the Dawn*, and 2001's *This Way* expanded Jewel's musical range, and provided the hits "Hands" and "Standing Still." In 2003, Jewel reinvented herself as a modern diva, challenging dance-pop conventions with the built-for-pleasure *0304*. She also released an album in 2006, titled *Goodbye Alice in Wonderland*.

—EVAN SCHLANSKY

Interview by
Katie Dodd

American Songwriter,
July/August 2006

You tend to go about three years between albums. Do you find that that's the amount of time you need to create something that you want to put out there?

It kind of takes that long to recover and feel like doing another. If all I had to do was write a record, I'd put them out every three months, you know? I wish it wasn't always so serious, and every record's taken so seriously, and you have to tour it for two years! People don't realize that I toured on *0304* until 2005. So, finally getting a break, getting to be home and regroup and actually think about what I want to say, it didn't seem like that long to me.

So how long would you say it took to put *Goodbye Alice in Wonderland* together?

I kind of came and went. It was a bit of an odd process. I really, really cared about this record. I've never had a great relationship with being in the studio. I've always found it a bit forced. I've never felt like my songs came off as good as they do when I'm singing live. I just wanted to be sincere. I didn't want a producer to come in and take my six-minute songs and want to whittle them down. The songwriting is pretty different, it isn't mainstream pop, and I really wanted the songs to come off honestly and tell the stories they are.

I produced it myself, I brought in some players from Nashville, and I cut the whole record in its entirety, and played it for a friend. They were like, "You know, your fans are going to love it. But I hate to tell you this—I think I found a guy who's going to make it sound even better." And he mentioned Rob Cavallo, and I was like, "The rock guy? Have you not heard a word I'm saying?" And he said, "No, he's really going to get it, I promise." And we sat down with him and I knew pretty much instantly that he really understood songwriting, he really understood what was authentic for me and wanted to stick up for it. He also got the sort of tangible undercurrent of irony and anger

even and was able to really bring that out as well, than I think other producers … Dann came closest to it, on *This Way*. Other producers wanted to take me into lush, kind of like *Spirit*. So we recut every single track. I'd just do it in shifts. I'd do four days in the studio, then go home to Texas for two weeks. I'd come back, I'd record for five days, go home for three weeks. So if you added up all the days it didn't take me that long, but I really spread it out over a long period.

You've said songwriting comes really naturally to you. Has it always been that way, since you were young?

I started writing poems and short stories and essays. I never really wrote songs, 'cause I never played an instrument. But when I was sixteen, I wanted to hitchhike through Mexico for spring break, like most parents hope their children do one day. I didn't have any money. I was going to school in Michigan and I had enough money to get on the train and make it to Chicago. So I learned four chords, which were A minor, C, G, and D, in that order. I couldn't go out of order because I literally had just learned probably that day. I'd written my whole life, and I'd sung my whole life. I couldn't read music, so learning other people's songs was way too much work. It was just so much lazier and easier to make up lyrics about people who walked by as I street sang. The only point was to sing well, because nobody really paid attention to the lyrics anyway. I just started writing about stuff I saw around me as I street sang my way across the country as a sixteen-year-old, and I made it to San Diego across the border. Hitchhiked across Mexico and all the way back to school. That ended up being the first song I wrote, I just kept writing verses. There are like three hundred of them. I'd never write a bridge to the song because I couldn't switch chords. That ended up becoming my first single when I was eighteen. That was "Who Will Save Your Soul."

Do you have a favorite place to write?

Not really. I like being in Texas or just anywhere outdoors. I was raised outdoors. I always like to get outside and let my mind wander. I tend to write more relevantly about social issues if I'm away from society for some reason. If I'm out of the noise, I can hear the noise better.

Can you just write anywhere? Are you ever someplace really odd when inspiration strikes?

I write all the time, I write in my head. Yeah, there are billions of napkins. I used to be really good about carrying a book around and writing out longhand. But yeah, I pretty much just write all the time. My thought process is kind of a long, rambling dialogue. As you get busier, it's your job, you know your mind can't wander like it used to because you're always thinking about the business and a billion things keeping your life going in a million ways.

Do you ever have to make yourself sit down—like this song's been bouncing around in my head and I really have to sit down and get at it?

I can tell when a song's trying to happen. I can feel it percolating. Ty [Murray, Jewel's boyfriend] can even tell now when it's happening. He's like, "A song's starting to come to you, isn't it?" It's like they incubate for a couple days and then I can kind of tell when they're ready.

Do you usually finish them in one sitting or come back to them over a period of days or weeks?

Generally it takes a couple hours. Once they're ready to come out, they usually just come. Sometimes it's just as fast as I can write them—it's like reading a book in your head. I don't really always know what the song's about, it's like I'm turning a page in my head and I'm like, "I wonder what happens in the next chapter." Sometimes I don't even know what the song's about until it's over.

Were you surprised when you realized so many of the songs you were writing lately were so autobiographical?

Everything has a season. Sometimes I don't write at all, and I was an art major, so I'll draw instead. I'm thirty-one, I've been doing this a long time, and I've just learned that everything has its season. Sometimes I don't want to write songs for months, and all I'm writing is poetry. Sometimes I couldn't write a poem if you forced me because I really want to write a rambling, narrative-style prose piece, and sometimes I can't write words at all, I can only use color. It sort of has its season, and I've just really learned to kind of trust it. It has its own kind of rhythm, which is why I never really worry about it.

So when you hear songs in your head, it's always the words and the music together?

Yeah. When I used to write songs a long time ago, I think my songs used to take longer to write. You know I think just over the years you get a little more homed in on the skill of it.

Do you know right away when you write something whether it's the best thing you've written in a while?

Everything's different. A song like "Words Get in the Way" isn't an earth-shattering song, a single, or tremendously clever. It just is what it is. They each have their own little flavor and their own little place in the world. If you do your job, hopefully it serves its purpose perfectly. They don't always serve the same purpose—they're not always earth shattering or hooky. Songs that aren't good, I just quit writing

halfway through. I don't even like finishing them, because they feel unfocused and fuzzy.

Do you ever go back to those?

Not usually. Sometimes you'll have what I call the song junkyard, you might take a door off one, the hood off another.

Actually, there's "The New Wild West" on *This Way*. I started writing that when I went to the Democratic Convention way back in 1996 or so. And I came up with that idea of the new Wild West and that guitar part, but I never could finish the song. It always got fuzzy, it always got preachy or something. And it wasn't until years later when I was working on *This Way*, and I was out in the yard, and then the whole thing just came out in an hour.

Do you ever go back to your older albums and see songs that could have gone in a different direction, or things you could have done differently?

The studio has been a really big learning curve for me. When I got signed at eighteen, I was fairly good at singing and writing, but I was just really unprepared for the studio. Everything changes in there. How you record it changes, and you have to sing it ten times, and I just hated it. It took me until this record to where I felt like I could control what was happening. I think production-wise this is my favorite record. I sang live on the record, those are all my scratch vocals. We cut live with the band, so it isn't like this pieced together record, where you sing it ten times and take the best pieces out of all ten takes. I didn't Frankenstein the record together. I felt like the layering of the songwriting—the humor, the sincerity, the earnestness, the irony—all comes out in the production, so it's as fully dimensional as I could get it so far. The point being, I do look at my old records and there are things I could have done differently on the production, but I had to rely so heavily on a producer at that point.

Who are some of your songwriting influences?

A lot of my biggest influences have been authors. The thing that really got me into writing in the first place was Plato's *Symposium*. I was really into the classics, then I got into poetry, which was really good for me, and it really changed my writing from a dry kind of intellectual drivel to more emotional-based writing. A lot of Latin poets are my favorite, like Pablo Neruda, Octavio Paz. And then I kind of got into poets like Bukowski. I liked Anaïs Nin's diary writing a lot.

I guess I read way more than I listened to music. It wasn't until I was eighteen that my friend Steve made me listen to the Beatles, the Rolling Stones, Big Star, John Prine, Tom Waits. He kind of gave me a music education.

You know, I think one of the best educations I had as a songwriter were my parents. My dad and I became a duet when I was eight and we did bar singing with bands, and he played guitar. We did all the American classics. I never heard Elvis sing "Heartbreak Hotel," but I grew up singing it. And I think it taught me a really instinctual, innate sense of song structure and lyric, and I was so into words and writing that I was always analyzing, "Ooh, I like the way that lyric fits, I like the way that melody goes up," and I think that was kind of a great education, even though I never got to hear the artists sing it themselves.

Do you do any co-writing these days, or do you mostly write by yourself?

I love to write, I've been in Nashville a lot, writing for other people. I wrote a duet with a new country artist named Jason Michael Carroll. I tend to co-write when I write for other people.

What is that like when you're so used to your own process?

It's really fun because I love all music styles. I like writing rock songs, or country songs. I get to write stuff that I wouldn't necessarily get to do myself. Because when you write for your own records it's all taken so seriously and it says something about you. When you write it for someone else, it's just an exercise in writing, for the pure skill, love, and art of it.

When I write for myself there is no plan, no title, no word, just a feeling, and I follow it. When you write with other people, it's much more structured. You have an appointment at 10 A.M. and you know that by 5 P.M. you'll have a song written. It is much more concrete and pretty technical.

What's it like to collaborate with someone else? Does it bring out something different in your songwriting?

A lot of songwriters are really prideful—they don't want to admit they write with other people. To me, it's awesome, I learn about the way their brain works, they way they string together chords, the way they'll do a passage into a chorus. Everyone's mind works so differently, and I feel like it's something that makes my own writing better on my own.

Do you prepare for those sessions? Do you ever go in like, "I've got nothing"?

Some writers really hate the unknown. They'll sit down with a song started. They want to sit down with something solid. Which is fine, I can totally go with that. But I know that if I start with nothing I'll end up with something. I'm fine sitting down with a perfect stranger and just finding it, following that invisible thread. So I don't find it nerve-wracking, but like I said, I've been writing for so long, I'm really comfortable with the unknown aspect of songwriting. In the beginning it's nerve-wracking, and you think, how will I ever write again? But as you get used to the process, that empty space doesn't bother you anymore. You know that it won't be there one minute and the next moment it will.

Do newer songwriters ever ask for your advice?

Most everybody I've written with has really good chops. Most of them have more hits covered than I do. This kid Jason that I wrote with is a little greener, but he has all the right instincts. He has a really good heart and he writes more from his heart than some of the staff writers do. I was able to help him with that process of finding something out of nothing and following that nebulous feeling. We also had a third co-writer on that, Shaye Smith, who's had a lot of country hits.

Are you planning to do more of that kind of co-writing in the future?

Yeah, I always looked at songwriting as my retirement plan. I won't always want to work as hard promoting records, you know, the big push it takes just isn't that fun. Hopefully, I'll have a family one day and just concentrate on writing songs, and have the studio there in Texas.

You were very young when you signed your record deal. Did you feel like you had time to think it through, or was it an overwhelming experience?

No, I had a bunch of labels, it was like a little bidding war, and I called the whole thing off and went back to Alaska and spent a lot of time thinking about it. I didn't know where my life was supposed to go. I didn't know if I was supposed to be a ranch wife in Alaska. I kind of liked law, but I didn't know. I was pretty cautious about fame.

I felt like I was in a really great negotiating position, because I lived in a car. Nobody could take anything away from me. It was going to be my way or no way. And then my first record was so successful; I sold eleven or twelve million copies so I was in another great position because I didn't need to do shit the rest of my life. It was like, I didn't need to be successful, I never wanted to be famous, so I didn't care if

I dropped off the map after that. So it was like, "Wow, I just get to make records and follow my muse and challenge myself musically, and push myself in the studio, explore music, and get a kick out of it."

I almost got signed at sixteen, though, and that would have been the worst thing for me, because I was so full of ghosts and just half-cooked, especially as a writer.

Part of the thing that's made me feel really competitive in my job is the writing. I think it's really easy to write a really bad pop song that's going to be a hit, and I think it's easy to write a really cool credible song that the press is going to love but is never going to see the light of day. You'll just play it in your room when you're depressed. To combine the two—it's really hard to write a smart pop song. Something that you feel lyrically has integrity, and that you feel like you pushed yourself melodically, that you're proud of. That's really the Holy Grail, and it's really kept me turned on.

Is it hard when you write a song like "Goodbye Alice in Wonderland" that you feel is an important statement, but it takes six minutes to say, so it won't ever be a single?

Some songs, it's just not their job. "Goodbye Alice in Wonderland"'s job was not to be a single, it was just to say something I needed to say, and it took that long to say it. It took three verses before the chorus, and it works. It's hard to write a six-minute song that holds people's attention, because you have to keep changing it up musically and lyrically to keep people hearing it because your ears turn off. Hopefully it's like a movie, you get caught up in the world and it passes quickly.

It doesn't seem like there's as much overtly political songwriting on this album as there's been in the past. Was that just part of the shift to a more personal feel?

There are usually only ever one or two political songs. I tend to do it more within each song. It's like the trinity, I call it: me, the immediate world around me, and the social view. Even "Goodbye Alice in Wonderland" says a lot about society, and to me that song talks about myself in a really personal way. "Satellite" is probably more of a social statement.

That's true—there are a lot of pointed one-liners in your songs that kind of sneak up on you. Is that intentional, to take people by surprise?

You know, it's funny what I've gotten away with. I think I called Hitler gay on my second record, and I thought I was going to get murdered. In the song "Innocence Maintained" I talked about the Midwest and how it makes people "spread their legs for ignorance." It was really lyrically brutal, but I guess the production was so pretty and I sang it so sweetly that everyone was kind of like, "Aw, we love her. That sweet girl." I was really shocked.

My only rule with writing social or political songs is to never be didactic. I hate preachniess. I hate when people tell you what to think. I just love to raise questions. I love to do it with a wink and a smile. I don't ever like to answer a question. I just like to take snapshots of the world around me. I'm pretty equal opportunity about it. I find hypocrisy within new age, Christianity, hippie, Republican, conservative—I find it all to be equally ridiculous.

Jack Johnson

photo courtesy Brushfire Records

Few people get to be as good at so many things as Jack Johnson. The good-natured native Hawaiian (born 1975 on the North Shore of Oahu) was already a champion surfer and award-winning filmmaker before attracting a cult audience with his relaxed folk and blues-based music. After studying film at USC Santa Barbara, Johnson began making surf documentaries like *Thicker Than Water* and *The September Sessions*, using his own musical compositions to fill out much of the soundtracks. Surfers and other admirers took notice, and soon he was befriending and jamming with musicians like G. Love, who included a cover of Johnson's song "Rodeo Clowns" on his 1999 album *Philadelphonic*, and Ben Harper (one of Johnson's idols). Harper's producer, J.P. Plunier, helmed Johnson's debut album, *Brushfire Fairytales*, which Johnson released on his own Enjoy Records in 2001. While he expected to entertain a few friends and family members, the record took off to become one of the runaway success stories of that year, and Johnson's smiling mug was plastered in music magazines everywhere. He further spread the love by embarking on a tour with Harper and releasing his second album, *On and On* (2003), featuring the single "The Horizon Has Been Defeated." It reached the number three slot on the *Billboard* album charts and gave fans more of the trademark easygoing jams they had grown to love. Johnson released his third album, *In Between Dreams*, in early 2005.

—EVAN SCHLANSKY

Interview by
Bill Locey

American Songwriter,
May/June 2005

So you've had an interesting life—surfer, film-maker, musician—how'd you pull all that off?

I don't know. It's pretty funny. I got real lucky and it seemed like all three of them sort of had their own path. But to me, it's just what I spend a lot of time doing. Lately, I've been surfing a lot and just been getting caught up on home time. But on those surf trips, I had the camera out in the morning when the light was good, then put the camera away and got out the surfboard in the afternoon, then got on the boat and had dinner and pulled out the guitar. That was a perfect day for me when we were making movies on those trips. It was music and film and surfing everyday.

And you get paid for that?

Well, I was breaking even. We paid our expenses and traveled the world, so that was great. And the music has been really great because I get to travel and play live… and I can make a living doing that, so I'm happy.

UCSB is a notorious party school, but you actually did work there?

Well, more or less. That's where I got into film, but it didn't really feel like work—I was just kinda making these student films, so that was a lot of fun.

Did you go there originally to study film?

I started out with statistics, focusing on math, but it was a nice switch after the first year in film.

Statistics was fun?

Statistics was kinda fun, but I started falling behind a little bit. I remember p equals q, but q does not necessarily equal p, or something like that—that's all I can remember. I kind of lost it, but then I did the film thing, which I actually pulled off in four years. I think I'm the only person to ever do that, and then I started making the surf films right out of school.

As a film student, what's the greatest movie ever made?

Greatest surf film or film? One of my favorite movies is *The Royal Tenenbaums*, and the greatest surf film? I'll go with *Endless Summer* probably. It's what everything else is based on.

So these surf movies are obviously a hit with all the finheads that live near the beach, but do they play in Kansas and places like that where the surf isn't so hot?

That's funny because we play them before our shows sometimes and they're nice background. People drink a beer or do whatever and watch them while my roadies are working. Sometimes we'll play them during set changes and instead of watching the guy setting up the drums, they can watch the waves. So they play pretty well and I've had good responses in middle America. And yeah, we play pretty much all across the States, but I do like playing along the coast because I can surf. I also like these little adventures to Europe or Japan, and it's cool just getting away from my normal life sometimes.

So did Dick Dale invent surf music?

Well, I don't know. I don't know that much about the history of it, but he plays the quintessential surf music.

His music invokes the wild power of the angry ocean and those gnarly board and body-busting waves, but now a lot of surf films use all these crazy punk bands. Does it have to be like that?

Not necessarily. There are other sides to it. I was super into punk music when I was in high school and even when I'd watch the surf films, that was my soundtrack of choice. When we started making films, we wanted to show the other side—sort of the feeling you get when you're riding your bike home after a long day of surfing, and it feels like slow motion. That's kind of why we use the mellower music.

So how'd *Thicker Than Water* come about?

There was a phone call from [surfer] Chris Malloy. I was just coming home from Europe and I was out of money. I went over there with my wife and we bummed around for four months until we ran out of money, and Chris called at the right time. He was getting a budget together to do a surf film and he needed someone to shoot it, so I was the guy. We started traveling—just breaking even and traveling the world—not getting in debt, at least.

How does that work? Is there an itinerary or do you guys just drive around aimlessly praying for surf?

More or less aimless, but a few months ahead of time he'd give me a call and say we were going to these islands off the coast of India or Australia. We went to the Andaman Islands in the Indian Ocean; we were at Port Blair, which later got wiped out by the tsunami.

So you met Malloy surfing?

Yeah, but we've known each other since we were kids. He'd come over to Hawaii and sleep on our floor for a week, then he'd sleep at my friend's house down the street for a week.

***Surfer Magazine* named *Thicker Than Water* film of the year. How did that help you?**

That was really nice and very flattering, and it definitely brought some attention to the film. That was a pretty big deal for us since it was the first film we had tried to make.

How do you score a film? Do you watch the footage first?

Yeah, basically I'll put on a lot of music while I'm watching the footage playback and deciding which waves to use. Something really upbeat, something acoustic—I'll just try all kinds of music. Sometimes, I'll find something perfect by another band and I'll use that. Other times, when I'm just not finding something I like, I'll just sit there and try to work out something that seems to go with the image and re-edit it. I'll lay down the music, and when it's pretty close, then I'll try to bring up the intensity a little bit for certain parts. Then I'll go back and move the images around so they hit the beats just right.

How does a band end up being part of the soundtrack to one of your films? So you're watching the footage and all of a sudden you think, "Wow, man, I want to hear Bowling for Soup," is that how it works?

Yeah, pretty much. A lot of times, I'll just want to watch it twenty times before I'm even able to pick the waves I want to use. Sometimes, you remember shooting a wave that was really good and those are the obvious ones. And other times, there are waves you didn't think would be so great on film, but then I watch it twenty times and it's whatever's on my CD player. If G. Love and Special Sauce works but the song is not quite there, I'll start listening to other music in that genre and kind of narrow it down.

How many different bands have you used besides your own?

Quite a few. We put out two soundtracks for the films and there's probably eight or ten bands on each of those. On soundtracks I've worked on from start to finish, there's probably twenty different bands.

How many of them are punk bands?

None of them are punk bands, actually. It's pretty mellow stuff like Ozomatli, G. Love and Special Sauce, and a lot of obscure stuff that I forget the names of right now.

How is it different doing a studio album as opposed to a soundtrack?

The soundtrack is different because it's all about the image, so you don't focus on the audio quite as much. If it feels right, then it's there; it doesn't have to be sonically perfect or anything. For the movie *Thicker Than Water*, I did all the music on a four-track that was sitting on the desk of the editing bay while I was just watching the images. I only had one microphone and we always thought we'd go in and record it better in a studio, but we never did. We ended up using the four-track version in the movie.

So when is your next surf movie?

Maybe when this music thing slows down, but right now, I don't know. I'm having too much fun with the music right now, and the films take a little effort, you know? So I'll have to decide to take some time from making records, touring, and all that stuff, but I am about to do the soundtrack for *Curious George*. I've already written the songs for it and I've been working with the composer and getting ready to go in and record. They're doing all the drawings by hand—not computer style. Will Ferrell is doing the voice for the Man in the Yellow Hat and in a way, I'm Curious George's voice because he doesn't speak, so the songs sort of tell what's in his mind.

How'd you get that gig?

They just called me up and asked me if I wanted to do it and I was real excited about it. There will probably be a record that'll come out with it; so far, there are about five or six songs from the movie, and we'll probably put together more kids' songs and make a record of it.

How is this similar to making a surf film?

Well, they send me the black and white sketches of what the scenes will be like and more or less the timing, so I write the songs lyrically with what's going on. Then they take my song and go back and actually change the amount of frames so it lines up perfectly with the beat. So, I've done rough versions of all the songs so they can edit and get a final picture. Then I'll go back and spend more time and solidify all the songs—just kind of add strings and things like that over the top of it.

So making a studio album like your latest, *In Between Dreams*, is quicker than making a film, I'm assuming?

It doesn't take very long to record it, about a month. I'm always writing songs whether I'm on a surf trip or touring—just putzing around with a guitar. After a year or two, then I have enough songs to record.

Where does *In Between Dreams* fit in with what came before?

It's pretty similar—it's just a new group of songs. We don't get very sophisticated. I play acoustic guitar, a friend plays bass, and another friend plays the drums, then we do a little layering with voice and add a second guitar sometimes. It's pretty much in the same genre… barbeque music.

What's the coolest thing about your night job?

The best thing about it is the party itself—playing music and all the energy that comes back toward you. The worst thing is going to bed so late. I like to go to bed early because I'm a morning person. Trying to stay up late is hard for me. It's hard to be a rock 'n' roll guy with the daddy morning hours.

Rickie Lee Jones

*Interview by
Dave Steinfeld*

previously unpublished interview, 2005

Rickie Lee Jones burst onto the pop music scene, seemingly out of nowhere, in 1979. Her self-titled debut album was esoteric and eclectic—but also accessible enough to earn her two top forty hits (including the smash "Chuck E's in Love") and a Grammy for Best New Artist. In a little over a quarter-century since then, Jones has followed her muse through nine more studio outings and two live recordings. Though she hasn't again scaled the commercial heights of her debut, she has proven herself to be one of the most talented, albeit unpredictable, artists in popular music. Jones's diverse catalog includes *Pirates,* her landmark sophomore effort, which featured lengthy story songs about urban life; 1991's *Pop Pop,* an intimate set of mostly standards with an old-time jazz feel; *Ghostyhead,* a 1997 excursion into trip-hop; and her most recent album, *The Evening of My Best Day,* from 2003. Last summer, Jones finally compiled her first anthology. *Duchess of Coolsville,* released by Rhino Records, contains two discs of material from her ten studio albums and a third disc that features assorted demos, duets, live tracks, and other rarities.

—DAVE STEINFELD

171

Duchess of Coolsville **provides the first true overview of your career, and it comes more than twenty-five years after your debut album. Why did you choose this point in your career to release an anthology?**

This has actually been some time in the making. I first started the conversation with Rhino about three or four years ago. The original guy I was talking to left and then I decided to put out *The Evening of My Best Day* before I thought about a collection of work. Then the conversation began again last year, and [co-producer] Karen Ahmed stepped up to the plate about four, five months ago, and really she made it happen. It was her perseverance, her feedback. She listened to every song [and] found the tracks I wanted. Her very casual and real attitude made me feel like the collection was actually a record. The process of culling the herd, that actually made me contemplate what at the end of the day made the best record, was the most representative… or was simply the best song. That's not easy, because I think we tend to love our songs, all of them; leaving out songs that seemed to be important was really like shedding a lot of weight. [The final three records] I think are very satisfying.

You have worked with many artists throughout your career, from Paul Buchanan to Joe Jackson to Dr. John. Who haven't you worked with that you would like to?

I have not sung with Van Morrison, and much of my style is uniquely suited to sing a little harmony with [him]. I can match his tone, be comfortable with his phrasing and with his message. I would like to have that happen to me. Sing "Into the Mystic" or something. I would like to play more with Bill Frisell and his band. I would [also] like to play with some of the great old guys. I played once with Joe Henderson and a couple of the most famous old jazz cats about ten

years ago, and it was like physically being lifted and carried upon the top of the notes they were playing. They knew how to play music that suspended the physical world—supported my intention. Man, I would give a lot to sing with jazz cats, or any people that adept.

I'd like to ask your thoughts about some specific songs from throughout your career. Tell me whatever you would like about any or all of them. "Altar Boy."

I guess abstinence, celibacy, colors of sublime longing… whether the subjects are gay clergy, or me, my imagination—and the object of my desire.

"Chuck E's in Love."

What a good song.

"Company."

I wrote that for Sinatra. [Warner Bros. executives] Lenny [Waronker] and Mo Ostin actually flew to Palm Springs and played it for him back in the day. Ah well, he couldn't have hit those notes anyway. But man, that woulda been something.

"The Horses."

I always thought more people would record that song. I had a nice moment this week. My daughter sang ["The Horses"] to me sitting out by the front door. That was pretty incredible. Write a song about a baby, the baby grows up and sings it.

Throughout your career, you have periodically released albums consisting mainly of cover versions. The songs you've chosen to interpret have been nearly as diverse as your originals. How do you select what songs to cover?

Mostly I just like singing them… then I [gauge whether or not I] have a rendition that is worthy of offering up. I have pretty diverse taste and like to do rock as much as "The Streets of Laredo." So I guess I just pick what I am thinking of at the moment, for the most part. [It] has to do with history, honoring my family, the song, what it stands for, my career, my voice at the time… all that stuff.

> *It's in my nature to do something quite different every time I step up to work. I just seem to exhaust myself of one kind of thing and then am free to go on to some other thing.*

One thing I have always admired about you is that from day one, you have never repeated yourself. After scoring a top five hit with their debut single, many artists would have written "Chuck E's *Still* in Love" and followed the same formula over and over. You didn't. *Pirates* was a great album, but quite a departure from your debut. Was this a conscious choice or just the way things worked out?

Well I think initially, that is with the second record, it was conscious. But of course to be conscious of what one is doing, one still has to be inspired, inclined, and able to pull it off. As it turned out, it's in my nature to do something quite different every time I step up to work. I just seem to exhaust myself of one kind of thing and then am free to go on to

some other thing. [But] sometimes I have wondered what I could have written that would have sustained the Chuck E. phenomenon on radio.

What is your ultimate goal in writing songs?

In the end, I want a song people are going to sing, at least in their hearts, that is going to bring them solace, sex, hope, laughter… some kind of bridge between their reality and the great place they could be.

Alex Kapranos

Franz Ferdinand

*Interview by
Matt Fink*

American Songwriter,
January/February 2006

Lots of British bands hope to make the same impact that Franz Ferdinand have made on American shores, but few can claim to have been so lucky. Taking their name from the Austrian Archduke whose assassination set off World War I, Franz Ferdinand have declared war on the dance floor, with their high-octane art tunes that marry punk and disco as their weapons. The band was founded by singer/guitarist Alex Kapranos, bassist Bob Hardy, guitarist Nick McCarthy, and drummer Paul Thomson in Glasgow in 2001. There they operated out of an abandoned warehouse, dubbed the Chateau, where they rehearsed and threw parties. Their debut EP, *Darts of Pleasure*, was released by Domino Records in 2003 and was followed by the infectious, breakthrough single "Take Me Out" in 2004. That single would spark a fire in American audiences, storming the Modern Rock charts and inspiring a number of copycat bands in its wake. Their acclaimed self-titled debut album was quickly followed in 2005 with *You Could Have It So Much Better*.

—EVAN SCHLANSKY

Was there anything you learned the first time around that you applied to making later records?

I wouldn't say there's anything in particular that we learned while we were making the first record, but I'd say thinking about what we did with the first record did influence what we wanted to do with the second. So, for example, the first record is very fun and pop and immediate, but we wanted to make the second record have a little more depth to it and for it to have a dynamic range and come up and down a little more. I suppose that's why there are songs like "Eleanor Put Your Boots On" and "Fade Together," which are a little more sensitive than anything we've done before. Then songs like "The Fallen" and "You Could Have It So Much Better" are a little more full-on than anything on the first record.

Did you think much about how to maintain the momentum from the first album to the second?

No, because the momentum was there anyway. I think to artificially maintain momentum would be a bit weird. We went into the studio because we were desperate to. We'd been on the road for a while, and we had a lot of ideas kicking around for songs and felt incredibly enthusiastic and wanted to get writing new songs. There was a momentum there anyway. We wanted to continue it.

Was the recording process very different?

It was. It was a different environment, though similar in some ways. The recording was similar to how we started the band, how we recorded our first demos. We started off by playing in our flats in Glasgow, in the old warehouse and stuff—places that were our own spaces and that we'd made our own. This time around we went around to my house and set up a desk and some microphones and recorded the majority of things there, whereas with the first album we recorded in Sweden. We recorded with a different producer this time around as well, and you get a different dynamic when you work with different people. Tore Johansson, who recorded the first album, is a good producer; he has a fine set of ears, but he has a distance between him and the band. And we prefer to almost collaborate with the producer, where you bounce ideas back and forth. I think that's where you get the best ideas, and Rich Costey is much more of a collaborator. He's someone that we could sit around and have a glass of wine with and talk about why we love music. It was a great thing to be able to do.

Did you have a pretty good idea of what you wanted to capture before you went into the studio?

I can't imagine a band being contrived enough to know what their album is going to sound like when they go into the studio. You have ideas of where you want it to go, but part of the excitement of recording a record is that you don't quite know how it's going to turn out. Songs like "Eleanor Put Your Boots On" and "You Could Have It So Much Better" and "The Fallen" were all written while we were recording the other songs. And songs like "Turn It On" and "Your Diary," which we thought were going to be main parts of the album, ended up being discarded from the recording sessions. So, no, I couldn't say whether it was how I expected it to turn out, because I didn't really have any expectations. I had things that I wanted to do. I don't think you should ever be satisfied with anything that you do, because if you are then you'll never want to do anything again, will you? [*Laughs*] So, no, I'm never satisfied with anything that we've done. With our record, yeah, I think it sounds great. But there's so much more we can do with the next one!

The video for "Do You Want To" has such a distinct look. Where did the idea for that come from?

We wanted to re-create things that we'd seen at parties. The song's about some things that people were saying to me at a party in Glasgow, and there were things that we'd seen at

art openings and things like that, parties where we'd go to get free drinks. At the same time, it's a slightly satirical approach to the art world in general. I wouldn't say a mocking approach but satirical, like Nick (McCarthy, guitarist) peeing on Duchamp's urinal, and Bob (Hardy, bassist) with his Yoko Ono magnifying glass and dragging the naked girls through the paint. That's just a bit of fun. It was great doing that video because we did it with Diane Martel, who is an amazing woman, just fantastic. And usually when we do videos we

> *I don't think you should ever be satisfied with anything that you do, because if you are then you'll never want to do anything again, will you?*

make a big list of things we'd like to do, just stupid things that we'd like to do in the video, and then we find a director that we get on with, and then the director says, "Right. We can do these two things, but we can't do anything else." Diane turned around and said, "Let's do them all! Let's put everything in there!" And she got it together, and my God, it was fantastic what we managed to do with it. She's a very cool woman.

Do you think most listeners are picking up on the irony and musical references in your music?

Occasionally people do get it. Quite often, actually. I couldn't tell you what it is, because I don't play too close attention to what people write. If I do see an article, I scan through it just to get the general gist of it, but I don't pay too close attention, I'm afraid. Because I think if you start doing that when you're in a band that has a lot of things written about you, you could spend the whole day reading stuff that has been written, and I don't think that would be healthy for anybody. I'd much rather read a book or watch a film or talk with my friends or have a drink than read about myself. It's bad enough that I have to talk about myself all day, let alone having to read it back again. [*laughs*]

With Franz Ferdinand, it seems that listeners hear a lot of different things, with some people simply seeing it as immediate dance music and others enjoying it as sophisticated pop music.

I really like that. I think it's a wonderful thing, because you can never dictate to people who listen to your music how they should listen to it. You can never say to them, "Oh, there's a great depth to what I'm doing here. You have to pay attention to what I've done." And sometimes you see singers and songwriters trying to do that, and you can't. If all people get from our music is some catchy riff that they like to dance to occasionally or that makes them look up from their job while they're working, that's fair enough. Because there's going to be just as many people who do get what you're about and who do get the subtle references and who get the more delicate emotion that you were trying to convey in the first place. Often you find the best music does both anyway. If you think of the best classical music, it's music which is both direct and complex at the same time. I was listening to New World Symphony the other day because it has this tremendous riff, and I was noticing because it was ripped off by Serge Gainsbourg for the song "Initials B.B." Do you know that song?

I don't.

You should check it out. It's a brilliant song, and he ripped off one of the refrains from New World Symphony, and it's a wonderfully complex piece of music, but it has this wonderful riff, and if that's all you hear from it, fair enough. But there is more, if you want it, and you can never dictate how people should listen to it.

How do you feel about Kanye West saying Franz Ferdinand is his favorite rock band?

That's amazing. That was very touching, as well, because I do feel that there is too much distance between R&B and hip-hop and white indie rock music. There's not as much inspiration taken from other genres as there should be. It's great to know that there are a wide variety of people who get things from our music, and I think that's related to the idea that you should never have an idea of who your audience is. You should never try to dictate who they are or who you want to play to. Once you write something and put it in the public domain, you have no control over how people interpret it or enjoy it.

How do you measure success for the band?

Oh… you know, I've never sat back and thought, oh, I'm a success now. I don't know if that means I don't think I've had success. No, I don't feel particularly successful, which probably sounds stupid, because we've obviously sold quite a few records and got all these prizes and things. In a way, I'm afraid of the idea of feeling successful, because it's related to that idea of losing your sense of dissatisfaction, because often your sense of dissatisfaction is what drives you on to do something greater than what you've done already. And I certainly don't want to stop now. I don't want to feel successful.

At the same time, it must be gratifying to win awards and sell records…

It is great, and don't get me wrong, I love it. I absolutely *adore* traveling around the world and being able to write music and play it for millions of people. God, it's amazing. I totally love it.

Do you have any specific goals for the future of the band?

Writing more songs, writing a different type of music, writing a type of music that I haven't heard before. Also, going to places like Southeast Asia and South America, that's quite thrilling. But also I look forward to little things like going back to see friends in Glasgow. One of my closest friends there had a son last year, and I've not seen him since he was three weeks old, and he's going to be a year old the next time I see him. It probably sounds really daft, but that's the thing that I'm looking forward to as much as a South American tour.

Do your old friends treat you the same now?

Yeah, the real friends do, definitely. It's funny, because with a little hint of success you can tell the difference between the people who are your actual friends and the people who are your acquaintances. The people who are acquaintances drool all over you in a slightly embarrassing way and your friends talk to you in exactly the same way they did before. And it's great to go out for a drink with your real friends and talk about… anything. To just be yourself and be very comfortable and be very much at ease. It's fantastic.

Robert Lamm

Chicago

*Interview by
Vernell Hackett*

American Songwriter,
March/April 1997

One of the most successful American rock bands of all time, Chicago has sold over one hundred million records worldwide, due in part to rock radio staples like "Hard to Say I'm Sorry" and "You're the Inspiration." The band formed in 1967 in Chicago, Illinois. Their debut album, 1969's *Chicago Transit Authority*, laid the groundwork for their trademark fusion of jazz and rock. Chicago recorded a number of chart-topping singles for Columbia Records in the early seventies and, after a move to Warner Bros. in the early eighties, produced a second string of memorable top five hits. In 2006, the band returned with their first studio album in a decade, *Chicago XXX* (minus vocalist Peter Cetera).

Keyboardist and vocalist Robert Lamm has written or co-written dozens of songs for the band, among them "Dialogue Part II," "Does Anybody Really Know What Time It Is?," and "Another Rainy Day in New York City."

—EVAN SCHLANSKY

Did your growing up in a major metropolitan center influence your musical style?

Being a city kid, stylistically I am drawn to urban music. So, while some of the tracks are more organic sounding and were tracked with live musicians, the bulk of it I'm using loops and samples combined with live musicians. I suppose it's my nature to be a little jazzy—at least other people would call it that—but to me, it's not. I think there's an urban hip-hoppy thing about it.

What musical concepts drive your writing approach?

One is, of course, my harmonic approach, which I think is unique. It certainly has been formed and molded by my very early years listening to everybody from Antonio Carlos Jobim to Thelonius Monk to Burt Bacharach. I grew up in the years of Motown and the Beatles so all of that is in there, too. I start from playing or inventing chord changes. For me the rhythm element is real important, either as the element that drives and suggests how the melody goes, or even suggesting the mood or motif that I place the song in. Usually this all comes before the lyrics.

So how do you approach songwriting from a lyrical standpoint?

I keep a working file of lyric ideas, and sometimes the lyrics are fairly complete even though I don't have any music to go with them. Sometimes I don't know what it is going to be about lyrically until I'm four lines into it. You start with one line and you add a second line that relates to the first line and by the end of four lines, it should be fairly connected. Maybe some of that is the subconscious waiting to shake the conscious.

Do you set aside time for writing specifically?

I have a very active life and I'm blessed with a great relationship with my kids and wife, and I'm very busy with Chicago. So I'll say to myself at the beginning of the week, "I know I've got Monday, Tuesday, and Friday where I don't have to be anywhere." At some point, I'll sit down and just start where I left off the last time. I tend to work pretty slowly. I just finished something in New York last week that I was co-writing with Walter Parks, who is part of a band called the Nudes, kind of an alternative folk duo who had asked me to produce their next album and write with them. I'd say about three months ago we got together and started something, and whenever I had time I whittled away at it because it was a cumbersome musical idea and I had to shape it into something that could be a song. I'm not saying that I worked every day for three months, but I lived every day nibbling at it, and when I was finished I was happy with it.

So do you like co-writing?

For a long time, I didn't write with anyone and then it seemed like, starting in the mid-eighties, it was something many people were doing. I started collaborating with people, made some great friendships, and have written a number of songs that are very interesting. I've just now started to not do that and see if I can remember how to write by myself. Most of my biggest hits were written alone and now that I've started doing it again, it's very satisfying. But I'm very much open to writing with others, especially writers I admire. There are a ton of guys I'd be honored to sit down and write with. I'd like to see what writing with Dave Matthews would be like, or somebody like Peter Gabriel. I would like to see what working with Babyface would be like. I like so much of the work that they've done. I think that would be a challenge, an interesting fit.

Most of your recent album addresses strife in foreign countries. Was it difficult to write these kinds of observations?

I don't find it too difficult to write those kinds of lyrics. I find it almost unavoidable to write those kinds of lyrics. If we're talking lyrically, I think when I talk about how I really feel about the people around me in my life, whether it's positive or not, then that's what I'm gonna write about. If I'm concerned about a friend of mine's lifestyle and I feel like he's heading down a dead-end street, then I'm going to write about that. I'm not holding back. I'll show it to him and take my lumps.

What are the best selling points for songwriting as a craft?

For me, the biggest thrill has always been discovering that you can write a song. It's a major sell for your friends, and that hasn't changed. I've always felt that what happens to the song after it's written, after it's recorded… is kind of out of one's hands after it's written. Anything that hap-

> *Sometimes I don't know what it is going to be about lyrically until I'm four lines into it.*

pens, whether they are huge hits or not, is accidental or incidental. So I think for me, the songs that I've written that are very popular, I'm very grateful for, but it doesn't put any additional pressure on me for what I write now. The enjoyment and thrill of discovering a new group of chord changes is what really motivates me. I enjoy having a top ten song as much as the next man, but that's not what drives me.

Would you write another song if you never had the chance of getting it cut?

Yes, that's really what I've been doing for awhile. There have always been a few of my songs on most of the Chicago albums, but it's been awhile since one of my songs has been a single, and that's just the way it is. But then having said that, I have to say [I've become] disappointed in the last five years, especially that, given the opportunity that the success of the band has afforded us, we're not taking any more chances. That's why I'm doing my solo work.

What advice can you give rising songwriters?

The best songs are songs that ring true to people. I remember a long time ago Chicago was doing an album with producer Tom Dowd and I had written a song called "Doing Business," and in the lyrics, I was whining about how tough it is to be a rock star. Tom looked at me and said, "These are good lyrics, but only twenty people in the world will be able to relate to this and the rest of us won't. Rewrite them." I think people on some level have to relate to what you are writing about. But you definitely must write something you know, even if it's something horrible as your own pain. You must do that rather than total fiction, because it won't ring true otherwise.

John Legend

photo courtesy Debbie VanStory

When you give yourself a name like John Legend, you create a lot of expectations, and the twenty-seven-year-old neo-soul sensation has worked hard to live up to his moniker. Legend was born John Stevens in 1978 in Springfield, Ohio. He began playing the piano and listening to gospel at the age of four, and served as a choir conductor while attending the University of Pennsylvania. Post-college, Legend toiled for years playing club gigs around New York City, Washington, D.C., and Philadelphia. After being introduced to hip-hop producer Kanye West, the two formed a creative partnership. West signed Legend to his G.O.O.D. Music label and served as executive producer for his debut album, *Get Lifted*. That album reached number one on *Billboard*'s Hip-Hop and R&B charts and spawned the hits "Used to Love U," "So High," and the Grammy-winning single "Ordinary People." *Get Lifted* was awarded the Grammy for Best R&B Album in 2005.

—EVAN SCHLANSKY

Interview by
James Kendall

American Songwriter,
November/December 2005

Do you think that back when you were nineteen you could have made this album?

No. I wasn't ready for it yet. It would have been decent, but it wouldn't have been this good.

Last year, a music magazine said you were arrogant like Kanye [West]. Why?

I don't think I am. I told [the reporter] that I thought my record was going to do really well. He challenged me. He said, "How do you know you're not going to be another artist that has a lot of critical credibility but doesn't sell any records?" I said, "I'm just not. I'm going to sell two or three million records." I was kind of defending my project. I was so used to being in the position of—I have to sell this project—because I had been trying to get signed for five years. So that's the stance I was still in. I was defending myself, and to him I was arrogant.

You've described music as "natural" for you, not easy. What's natural?

I just try to go with what feels right musically and melodically. I'll sometimes establish the musical format of the song and the melody of the song within the first ten minutes of the original idea coming to me. That's the natural part of it. Once I have that, I know what the song sounds like. Then I come up with a couple lyrics that feel like they fit with that original melody.

Is that how you tend to progress through a song? Music first, lyrics second?

Always. I think music should dictate the lyrics—*always*.

How long do you keep the music in your head? Are you rushing to get to a piano or to get it down on paper?

No. I keep it in my head for a long time. The lyrics always take a long time for me.

The lyrics do?

They usually do. Very seldom will artists sit down and come up with that original in ten minutes and then finish the lyrics in the same day.

Some of the lyrics on your album have different feels from song to song. Does a lot of that depend on whom you're writing with? With Kanye? Or someone else?

Yes it does, and also it just depends on the song. I try to get in the mood and the character of that song.

You'll have a song with a strong beat and you'll follow with something like "Let's Get Lifted Again," which is pretty heavy falsetto.

It's all falsetto.

The style of music ebbs and flows.

Those songs were written separately. I wrote the songs over four years, so it wasn't a conscious choice that I wanted to have different moods or different vibes as a writer. "Alright" is a song about me getting drunk at a club and hitting on someone else's girl and so for that song, I sing it like I'm drunk. And the vibe is like I'm drunk. I'm saying things that I normally wouldn't say because I'm drunk. I wouldn't go up to [another guy's] girl in a club and try to holler at her. I don't want to start any fights in a club, but [in the song] it's like I'm empowered by the liquor.

I read that Prince said to you, "You write songs. Nobody does that anymore."

He said that specifically about the song "Ordinary People," that it's a real song and you don't hear people making real songs nowadays.

Do you agree that that's the trend?

I think it's harder to find really good songs these days. But people make them. There are plenty of good songwriters out there. But I think in R&B particularly, songwriting is very weak.

There seems to be a lot of concentrating on the hook and not so much on the verse.

I agree. I think the verse is thought of as just filler to get people to the hook these days. And the hook is what people use to get on the radio. So, as long as they think they have a good hook and a good beat, they're happy with the song.

I just try to go with what feels right musically and melodically.

[Then they] just throw in whatever for the verse. I feel like what ends up happening is a lot of boring lines—a lot of corny lines.

Is it because there's a rush to get the music out?

People rush in the studio more now, and the standards are lower. Hip-hop has had a certain influence because rappers usually are quicker than singers at writing songs, and that has kind of changed the process.

Do songwriters need more revision in their music?

Oh man, definitely! The thing is, some people don't realize that it needs to be edited. They think it's good the way it is.

And that's just a matter of taste. Some people think they're done with a song when I think they should go back and revise it. Even sometimes I'll think a song's done, but I have friends I work with who will tell me to revise.

That's how you make the decision? You rely on other people?

I can rely on myself a lot of times, but I work with people like Kanye and other producers that will make comments and I'll make changes based on them. They're smart people and they have good taste, too.

When do you think revision should stop?

I want the melody and the music to feel like it flows in absolutely the most natural way it could have been written. It doesn't feel like I've forced any chord changes and the melody just feels like it brings out the right singular voice in me. So that's music to me. It should feel like it flows. It's natural. It's easy. It doesn't feel overly monotonous. I feel like there's enough growth and movement in it. It's the way it's supposed to sound even though I didn't know in advance how it was going to sound.

Lyrically?

Lyrically it needs to tell a story that people can feel and that makes sense to them. I want the lyrics to have coherence throughout. Some artists are very abstract and metaphorical. They write songs that you don't completely understand—which is fine. It's just not me. I think in R&B and hip-hop, [metaphor] doesn't tend to be the tradition. It's not what I'm used to anyway, so it's not how I write. When I write I try to tell stories that are entertaining. I want to say something that's familiar and that feels real to people, but I want to say it in as clever a way as possible so people will actually remember lines from it. It'll feel fresh and familiar at the same time.

Are you always conscious of what your audience wants to hear?

I think of what I would want to hear first. No, actually I don't even think that. I think, what would make this song perfect? Which is a very subjective judgment but that's what I'm thinking when I'm writing a song. What would make this song the best it could possibly be?

So we're back to standards.

It's the whole "standards" thing. Some people's standards are really low and part of it has to do with whom you work with. If you look at the records I've been on, just by the nature of my catalog my standards are high because I work with so many great people making great records. So, I feel I have to measure up to that every time I go in [the studio].

I promise that the next album will be better songwriting, actually. I haven't even done most of it yet, but I know I'm in a better place as a songwriter now than I was before. And I know what I want more of, so… I'm telling you that.

I don't really think that's arrogance, either.

I'm comparing myself to myself.

I want to say something that's familiar and that feels real to people, but I want to say it in as clever a way as possible so people will actually remember lines from it.

There's always been the tendency to write verse, chorus, and throw a bridge in there somewhere. Do you ever have the urge to write extremely complex music? Or maybe throw in a 7/4 rhythm?

[*Laughs*] No, no. I stay pretty formatted and classic. I haven't done anything revolutionary with song structure. Pretty much I stick to the formulas. In other words, it feels good to me—structure. I want the songs to feel like they have that.

You've gotten an amazing amount of critical acclaim for this album.

Little Barrie

Little Barrie is a London-based trio who meld influences like Marc Bolan, James Brown, Captain Beefheart, and Cream to create a potent blend of modern rock with retro leanings. The group formed in Nottingham, England, in 2000, coalescing around the impressive fretwork of guitarist, singer, and band namesake Barrie Cadogan. Cadogan hooked up with singing drummer Wayne Fulwood and bassist Lewis Wharton. The trio released a series of infectious singles like "Shrug Off Love," "Don't Call It the Truth," and "Memories Well" on small boutique labels. After a chance meeting with eighties pop singer Edwyn Collins in the guitar shop where Cadogan worked, Collins offered to produce the band's debut album. Dubbed *We Are Little Barrie*, it was released in the United States on Artemis Records in 2005. A British jam band with an ear for tight, classic-sounding songs and unfettered six-string magic, Little Barrie is clearly going places.

—EVAN SCHLANSKY

*Interview by
Josh Baron*

American Songwriter,
July/August 2005

Obviously your sound is rooted in tradition, but why are people suddenly thinking it's so fresh?

Cadogan: I think we're obviously influenced by certain things but we wanted to put it across our own way. We are influenced by a lot of black music. Because we're English and we're born in the seventies, it's going to be different anyway. I think music has gotten sort of treated and sort of overproduced. And when you look back to performers like James Brown at the Apollo [Theater], and things like that, there are no whistles and bells. The sound you're hearing is being made by people. It's not like nowadays where you go into the studio where they can take your voice and make it sound great. I think we kind of wanted to get back to the days where people could do it themselves without any extra help. It's kind of a harder, longer way to do it, but it's a lot more rewarding.

Fulwood: Part of it is the whole soul thing. It seems like every generation of music, something else is taken out and it gets more and more watered down. It always seems like the real soul elements or the gut that's in music… that kind of suffered, and we wanted to put that back.

Your sound when playing live and on the album are remarkably similar. There's clearly not a lot of studio trickery.

Fulwood: Like Barrie says, analog is great if you use it right. You don't have to use it on everything. We're not out to just use tape because it's retro and we want to be retro. We use it because we like the sound of it. It's a warmer sound.

Do you record all analog?

Fulwood: A lot of it, yeah. It does make a difference. But we really didn't set out just to say, "Oh, we want to re-create something happening forty years ago." We just like those records. A lot of those sounds are timeless. We wanted to make something that would stand up in thirty years' time and people could still listen to it without saying, "Oh, that sounds really dated now." So we started working with Edwyn Collins because we liked the sound of his records. We met him through a mutual friend and we went to his studio just to say hello. He had heard the record and while we were up there, he said, "Oh, do you want to record your next single here?" And we said, "Yeah, that'd be great." We were really excited about it. We did the single and that went well. And he said, "Well, now [that] you started, might as well do an album if you want." So we did the whole album there. It was one day a week for… about twenty-six weeks. One Wednesday every week.

Why was it just one Wednesday?

Fulwood: Because it was free studio time. Downtime in the studio, that was all he had. But it was kind of good because when we went in, we had tons of time from the following week, get like three backing tracks down, a couple of lead vocals, we were really productive. And it kept it really fresh.

Wharton: And then it was mixing once we actually recorded it… it was good to work like that, though.

How long have you been doing this particular project, this sound?

Cadogan: We've just been sort of playing together for straight on four years. We've always put records out.

Fulwood: The sound kind of came from all of us. The first single was kind of Barrie's project although we had just met. That's got sort of a very individual sound and the next two singles were when Lewis just joined the band. But then we started recording with Edwyn and it's just gone to the next level. Just the sort of stuff that you've been hearing now that's going to be on the album. But all in all… this lineup is about three and a half years, isn't it? Something like that.

Did each of you play something else besides what you're playing now?

Wharton: Yeah, I used to play guitar in other bands. I started playing bass just before I met Barrie and Wayne, and I was playing in about three bands. I had just joined two where I was playing guitar and one where I was playing bass. But I'd literally just picked one up and just swapped it for this. What I'd heard, [Little Barrie's] first single, was without a doubt the best band I've ever heard in cotemporary music…

We just kept doing what we were doing and people said, "This thing isn't going away."

Fulwood: I'd played guitar in bands before. I had always sung in bands and played bass in one band… that was kind of funny. But I'd always played guitar in the bands I'd been in. The first band I was in was like a blues band, playing Howlin' Wolf, Muddy Waters songs, Albert King, things like that. And a bit of our own tunes. I was about eighteen then and I was doing that all the way through college. It was kind of a professional band for one of the members but for everybody else it was like semi-professional; [we were] still in college. I came back to Nottingham and I met Barrie in a bar, and we just started chatting and stuff. We ended up living about two minutes 'round the corner from each other. Just up the street. So that was our start.

Cadogan: We used to just lend each other records.

Fulwood: You socialize. You have a drink, you watch videos. We're into the Stones and we're watching Stones videos and we're doing the usual Keith Richards impressions and Mick Jagger impressions. You just do daft things when you're drunk. I'd never played drums before. And Barrie said, "You know, we should really be doing something together. I kind of want to sing and play guitar, I want to get that thing going. We got Jim on bass… can you play drums?" I can't. I never really tried. And he said, "Well, I know someone selling a kit for 150 quid and I was like, "Well, okay…" At first it was a bit of a joke, "Okay, I'll play drums—ha ha" for about a week, and then we went and bought the kit and we jammed loads and it just kind of happened. We were recording demos after two weeks.

Cadogan: We hadn't known each other that long but I just knew he could do it. I just knew.

Fulwood: We stumbled into London. We had met Lewis because we had sold him records in the shop and we knew he was well into it. And then we asked, "Can you play bass?"

Were you nervous about coming stateside for the first time?

Fulwood: We've all said we believe in what we do and we all felt like we could do it here. People would appreciate what we did. It's just getting the opportunity to come over, really. We were nervous…

Wharton: There are bands in England that are really successful and don't get a chance because people in America haven't taken to it or aren't interested. [We thought], we've got interest already, so let's just go and do it.

Cadogan: The way that we felt like it might work here wasn't a blasé kind of way because we work really hard. We just had a feeling that people might tune into it.

Fulwood: The music in the U.K. can be a little fashion-oriented. In America, it seems to be a lot more about music.

Would Little Barrie have been as accepted five or ten years ago?

Wharton: Even when we started years ago, we were playing venues a lot of bands weren't playing, staying out of the circuit of all the bands… there are just so many bands doing the same thing, same night… that's what worked in our favor. It took us a while to get people to take a chance on us because it wasn't by numbers as most things are now. We just kept doing what we were doing and people said, "This thing isn't going away."

> *We're interested in music that's current, but we're not chained to it. We don't live our lives by it. We just do what we do.*

Cadogan: Punk didn't actually start until 1976, and it's exactly the same attitude. This whole post-punk thing where a lot of journalists think that everything that came before punk was shit and everything that came after was great. Actually, the punk attitude was exactly the same attitude that stands out in 1963, or with people like Elvis and Johnny Burnett in the mid-fifties; it's the exact same attitude as what Muddy Waters had in the forties. It just morphs itself into a new thing. It always shocks the generation it comes to.

Wharton: It's kind of that aggression/frustration thing. We're not saying we're fighting against the system or anything. But we are shaking things up musically. We're creating a whole new thing, we just hope it's something as vital…

Fulwood: The attitude is within the music, rather than the attitude of the person.

Wharton: There are lots of bands that were influenced by these things and try and re-create exactly, whereas we're just trying to get in the mindset of [our influences]… James Brown didn't want to make another James Brown record like his last one. So hopefully we can take those things and take them a step further. And that's definitely where we're coming from in that respect. It's easy to call it retro because of this or that. The Strokes wear their influences on their sleeve as much as anyone else.

Cadogan: I think with what we do, we have sometimes felt like outsiders because we haven't particularly cared whether what we do is fashionable or not. We're interested in music that's current, but we're not chained to it. We don't live our lives by it. We just do what we do. Whether people like us or hate us, they can't say we don't put 100 percent into it.

Wharton: We're being taken and shown around, doing these gigs and people are into it and stuff, but when you get the doorman of the venues saying, "That's fucking great, man," you don't have to say a word…

Cadogan: We just want to really get down to it, get down to the feeling, get down to the rawness.

Fulwood: We're just a cool little band that hopefully plays good songs. That's all we ever wanted to be.

Kenny Loggins

Kenny Loggins's first experience as a hit songwriter dates back to 1970, when the Nitty Gritty
Dirt Band scored a hit with Loggins's "House
at Pooh Corner." Joining forces with former
Poco member Jim Messina, the duo of Loggins
and Messina produced seven albums and the
well-known singles "Thinking of You" and "Your
Mama Don't Dance" before their dissolution in 1976. As a solo artist, Loggins's
popularity skyrocketed, in part due to his memorable contributions to the
soundtracks of several iconic eighties films, including *Footloose* ("Footloose"),
Caddyshack ("I'm Alright"), and *Top Gun* ("Danger Zone"). In addition to releasing a string of introspective solo albums in the 1990s (*Leap of Faith*, *Unimaginable
Life*, and *December*), Loggins has also written several children's songs, compiled
on *Return to Pooh Corner* in 1994 and *More Songs From Pooh Corner* in 2000. Loggins and Messina reunited as a touring force in 2005, to the delight of many.

—EVAN SCHLANSKY

*Interview by
Robyn Flans*

American Songwriter,
November/December 1987

Why did you start playing guitar?

It's hard for some people to really understand the impact of what it's like to have buck teeth and finally get the courage up to ask a girl out for a date and have her cringe when you get up close because you look like Goofy. The continuous rejection is very difficult, and after a while you just stop trying because you know there is a 50 percent chance that she is going to say "Eww!" You just want to say, "Excuse me, I didn't mean to be ugly." So my main compensation was learning to play the guitar and sing. I found that in order to get to meet the girls in the girls' wing of the school, I would form folk groups and help form them as well.

When does your best songwriting happen?

The best musical statements are usually the ones that aren't calculated and the ones that come out in the largest chunks. Michael McDonald and I must have written "This Is It" four times. The first three times it was a love song, "Baby I this, baby I that…" and we both said, "Eh! This is boring. This song is not working as a love song." Then I had a fight with my dad when he was going into the hospital because he gave me the feeling that he was ready to check out. He'd given up, he wasn't thinking in terms of the future, and I was so pissed at him. It was real emotional. That afternoon, I was meeting with Michael to work on new tunes and I walked in and said, "Man, I got it. It's 'This Is It.'" And Michael said, "This is it?" and I said, "Trust me. This is it." But that one took a while. And then one reviewer said that it was your average boy-girl song and the writer didn't understand why people were making such a big deal out of it. The fact of the matter was, he didn't understand the song and it didn't move him because he wasn't in a situation to be moved. But immediately after that, I got a letter from a girl who had recently gotten out of the hospital from a life-and-death situation and that was her anthem. She was holding onto it. That means so much more to me.

She hadn't read the press about my father or anything. All she knew was that the song was on the nose for her, exactly what Michael and I intended. That makes you feel like you are doing something important.

How do you respond to those in the press who interpret your themes of love and hope in a negative way?

I've been painted as a cockeyed, optimist-type character, and the reason why I think people perceive me as that is because I refuse to give in to the darker side and say, "Okay, everything is screwed," but things can be so great, and you have to remember that. I wrote "Brighter Days" when I was coming down with hepatitis. I didn't know what was wrong with me. All I knew was that I had felt a lot better at other times. So, the statement is, "Sure things might be bad now, but remember, things have been okay, so they can be again in the future." I don't subscribe to that lifestyle of despair. It doesn't work for me. I would be unable to create. A number of artists I have known feel they derive their creativity from darkness, and I was fortunate in that when I learned to write, things that made me happy moved me to write. A friend of mine who is an excellent songwriter, Jimmy Webb, is moved by sadness and never moved by happiness, so he strives at putting himself in the situations that make him unhappy in order to stay creative. A lot of people find the derivation of new and avant-garde creativity is on the blue edge, and I have found it there too, but I prefer not to live there and I think I'm fortunate that I can also be creative from the other side. I'm not invalidating the dark side. I think it works for creativity, but it's not the only reality. Some people seem to think that sadness is true and happiness is the perversion of sadness. [*Laughs*] But they're both just as valid and you're allowed to have either. It's okay to be happy.

Lyle Lovett

photo courtesy Michael Wilson

Lyle Lovett has forged a healthy career out of defying categorization. The Texas-born singer-songwriter is sometimes photographed sporting a ten-gallon hat, but his eclectic sonic palette directs a nose-thumbing gesture at the pure country moniker. His second album, 1987's *Pontiac*, as well as 1992's gold-certified, R&B-heavy *Joshua Judges Ruth* and 1996's high-charting return to country form, *The Road to Ensenada*, rank among his biggest successes, though the rest of his ten-album catalog, including his most recent release, 2003's *My Baby Don't Tolerate*, have maintained his healthy, genre-transgressing following. Lovett eases his buttery tenor through vignettes rife with quirky, literate wit, and has been known to employ a hefty backing ensemble—his "Large Band," no less—possessing the power to barrel ahead through light-hearted, two-step romps and the nimbleness to dredge up gospel fervor or slow to a simple, drawling ballad. Before music became central, Lovett sharpened his keen eye for detail by studying German and journalism at Texas A&M, during which time he shared a house with fellow aspiring songwriter Robert Earl Keen.

—JEWLY HIGHT

Interview by
Kelly Delaney

American Songwriter,
July/August 1989

How did you come to write "I Married Her Just Because She Looks Like You"? That's such a complete title.

I really ran into somebody who looked like an old girlfriend. It's basically a cheap shot, you know; this person is exactly like you, only she's nice. I was on my way from Austin to Nashville and I made it on the airplane. It was a flight attendant. She was nice. Flight attendants are always nice.

So it didn't involve much rewriting?

No, just years of painful research were all behind it.

You make it sound so easy.

Writing has never been easy for me, but some things work easier than others. It is hard and you do have to edit somewhat. Playing songs for a while you can figure out things that work and things you need to change.

You kind of put them to the acid test then?

A lot of my older songs I played acoustically for years and that gave me a lot of time to think about them—what sort of band arrangements would be nice. Then when I met the guys from Phoenix, it seemed possible to do all that stuff. But songs always change a bit.

Do you come up with fresh ideas for your songs by letting your imagination take over?

Yeah, sure. But you don't always have to let your imagination take over. The most important thing about writing is insight. You don't always have to take off with your imagination. You can just write about what's there.

Should songwriters try to get beyond the mere commerciality of an idea and try to get more out of it than that?

It just depends on what somebody wants to do. It's really an individual thing. You always have to make a choice. If you're

a staff songwriter, you've still got a choice. The choice might be between writing a certain way and having a job—that may be the choice. I'm not going to say anything bad about the way something works. It's what you consider your job to be and what you're after in your writing. I don't get any outside cuts and sometimes I think, well, if I'm such a good writer, how come nobody is calling me up to do my songs? But I can write more for myself because I get to do them. If I weren't able to do that and I was looking at this as more of a job and concentrating on getting cuts, I might think about things differently as well.

Do you approach an idea lyrically or musically first?

For me it's always the lyric first. I have the idea and think about how to express it. Certain words suggest certain melodies and the whole style.

The lines in "If You Were to Wake Up"—"If you were to wake up/time reaches to you/ just like a willow/ that bends to the water/ and clings to shore"—are such tight, expressive lines.

Thanks. I made that up and thought maybe I was being a little too poetical. It was just a picture I got of a creek and trees covering up the whole creek.

How do you apply the test to determine if it is too poetic?

Well, not genuinely poetic. There's a difference between something poetic and something trying to be poetic. You know what I mean? I'm always aware of this. The real test is how comfortable I am singing this? How comfortable am I doing that on stage?

That's a good test. In a broader sense, songwriters might apply that same test when pitching songs to recording artists.

It really does work because some songs I feel more comfortable singing than others. If there's any doubt at all in your mind, try it and then see how stupid you feel.

What are you hoping to achieve with the songs after you record them?

What I'm after really is this: I enjoy records from the standpoint of background music, a record I don't really have to listen to. But then if I stopped and paid attention, there would be something to pay attention to. That's really what I'm after.

Have you ever looked back over something you're working on and noticed that it sounds like some other song?

Yeah, and I think I need to change that or I just go with it. Like "If You Were to Wake Up" is melodically close to "Farther Along" so I gave it credit on the album. I just couldn't get away from [the melody]. I think a lot of times ideas can be coincidental, but I wouldn't intentionally write a song because another song gave me the idea.

"If I Had a Boat"—now, that tune is really imaginative.

It's almost like somebody else wrote it. That's the way songs sometimes feel to me. I don't really think of myself as having a great imagination. I consider myself a pretty good liar. Writing is hard for me and it's even tougher being out on the road and having so much to keep up with.

Do you trust the memory or do you write it down?

I really do trust a lot of things to memory and then write it down when I've got it shaped up. I don't take notes much. When I was a kid, I saw an interview with Buck Owens and he said that if it were good enough, by golly, you'd remember it. I've never forgotten that.

Do songs spin out songs?

No, but I do go in patterns where I write songs that are similar. I'll write the same song three different times. I mean, it's a different song, but…

Is that a way of refining an idea?

Well, the three new songs on the new album [*Lyle Lovett and His Large Band*, 1989] I wrote in the space of a couple of weeks and musically they're all similar. "Good Intentions," "I Know You Know," and "What Do You Do." It was the same on the *Pontiac* album with "M-O-N-E-Y," "Pontiac," and "L.A. County."

Has your background in journalism related in any way to songwriting?

I feel like I am a naturally curious person, curious about human nature, which a lot of the time would have nothing to do with journalism. But I really try to represent things that are real, that in an emotional sense are things that people really experience. Things that are common for people. I stick close to things that really happen as opposed to taking off on something imaginary. That's what makes me country—the words.

Have the great song ideas been used up?

Ideas are universal; it's what you do with them.

photo courtesy Jim Marshall

Shelby Lynne

*Interview by
Lacey Galbraith*

American Songwriter,
July/August 2005

In the six years since Shelby Lynne released her seminal statement of self-determination, *I Am Shelby Lynne*—for which she received a Best New Artist Grammy—she has been headed in a wonderfully irreverent and eclectic direction, and seems a great deal more comfortable in her own skin. The "new artist" moniker was deceiving. Lynne had already endured more bumps and bruises by that point than most people do in a lifetime, from a troubled and violent home life to five albums and thirteen years of having a disingenuous image superimposed on her. After finding her earlier pristine country-pop excursions (*Sunrise, Tough All Over, Soft Talk, Temptation* and *Restless*, all released between 1989 and 1995) to be exceedingly chafing, Lynne burst forth with her heady, Grammy-winning synthesis of vintage southern-tinged soul, bluesy country, and formidable rock energy. It proved to be a fruitful and liberating exercise. The Alabama-reared artist, whose sister is fellow alt.country songstress Allison Moorer, has followed her own muse ever since, turning out three more decidedly non-Nashville albums. Lynne released *Love, Shelby*, a straightforward rock album, featuring the hooky single "Killin' Kind," in 2001, and most recently recorded a pair of raw, stripped-down efforts, *Identity Crisis* in 2003 and *Suit Yourself* in 2005.

—JEWLY HIGHT

194

Growing up, what kinds of music were you drawn to?

Mainly country music. My father liked Bob Dylan and my mother liked pop, the Bee Gees, and that kind of stuff. Bobbie Gentry. Beatles. Elvis.

What about these days?

Nothing really in particular. Some days I go without listening to anything. Yesterday I was listening to T. Rex. I drag out everything. I'm really an LP person; I listen to my albums. I drag out Charlie Rich, old Les Paul stuff, Black Sabbath.

Your latest album [*Suit Yourself*] was done partly in your home studio and partly in Nashville, correct?

Another friend of mine's studio here in Nashville, yes.

So what was your reasoning for coming back to Nashville?

The reason I recorded there this time is because it just happened that way. A friend of mine has a home studio there but he's not in the scene by any means. There are a lot of people in Nashville who aren't in the scene, and it's a part of Nashville that people don't even know about. There are a lot of great musicians and a lot of great things going on. I guess you'd call it underground cool Nashville. It's not the mainstream country Christian Coalition thing.

Were most of the songs done in one or two takes? It really feels that way. There's a sense that the fourth wall has been removed—that the listener is right there in the studio.

Yeah, I wrote a lot of them at that moment and recorded them at that moment. About half of the songs were recorded the day and moment I wrote them. The other half were written on the spot and I recorded them with the fellas.

You didn't go back and do a lot to them after that?

The things I recorded at home that were basically me and [an] acoustic [guitar]; I had the fellows add on some flava.

Tony Joe White makes a strong presence on this album. It's great how you reinterpreted his "Rainy Night in Georgia."

Well, thank you. You can't go wrong with a standard. When I got together with him I couldn't let him get out of the studio without saying, "Tony Joe, please cut 'Rainy Night' with me. I don't know if it'll be on the record, but please let's cut it." And he said [*Lynne slows her voice to a deep drawl*], "Well, let's slow it down and do it a little bit different." So we did. It's edited on the record. It is seven minutes long, because I think originally it was twenty minutes long.

Looking over your career, it seems you could divide it into two eras: There's the Nashville one where you come across as more of a contemporary country, and the post-Nashville one sees you more as more of a songwriter/producer. Does what you are doing now fit you best?

Yeah, I think so. I have to realize sometimes that I've grown up in this business. I've been making records since I was eighteen, which is half my life. This is my ninth record, so I guess I should have a handle on it by now.

What was the catalyst for such a change?

I started writing on my fourth album in Nashville before I left. But they were collaborations. I left Nashville after my fifth album and decided, fuck that. I don't want to do that anymore. I want to write my own songs and get into more production and explore what I can do on my own. It started happening around the *I Am* time.

Was it a change in your thinking, or was there something specific that happened?

It was mainly about making records that I wanted to listen to and writing songs that turned me on, writing songs with a content that I know about. There's nothing wrong with cutting somebody else's song if you love it, because that's the beauty of songwriting. But if you have something to say, you should be able to say it.

What made you decide you had something to say?

I just started doing it. I just felt like, hell, I'm not finding any songs that really turn me on, so I might as well write them myself. I have a lot of things to say and hopefully [I] don't repeat myself when I do it.

Who are some other people you've looked to for inspiration when you're writing? Is there anyone specific from whom you've learned?

Oh yeah, yeah. I admire great songwriters all the way back to Johnny Mercer. It's about saying what you want to say as simply as you can. Make a point and make people feel. I'm a huge Kris Kristofferson fan. A huge Willie Nelson fan. I'm talking songwriting here. It's all in hitting that part of the heart. I think there are serious songs. I think there are

guitar and said, "Oh, okay, I'll throw down some words," and it wound up being on the record. It's probably one of the most unserious songs I've ever written, but it's fun. I've also realized everything doesn't have to be so deep and mind-fucking. You can just have fun sometimes.

How about production? Was the same reasoning that's behind your writing your own songs behind your decision to go solo in terms of producing your own stuff?

I just know what I want, and it's easier for me to just say, "Okay, this is what I want," instead of dealing with somebody else. It's easier for me to find a good balance with a great engineer. I have it in my head and I can do it the way I want and I don't have to waste a lot of time that way. I'm not saying I won't work with someone again, but it really has to turn me on. It's almost like a marriage.

Have you felt resistance from the business in terms of understanding what you're doing?

You know, I think they're pretty accepting if they hear it. It's just a matter of how or if they hear it. It's hard to get records like I make out there because it's something you might have to turn up the volume on.

> *It's about saying what you want to say as simply as you can. Make a point and make people feel.*

deep songs. I think there are kind of fun, throwaway songs. I think "Go With It," which is the opening track of the record, is a fun, throwaway number. I found a quarter on the

Richard Marx

Nicknamed the "King of Ballads," Richard Marx has written some of the most enduring, heart-tugging love songs of his generation, and no wedding or high school dance can be considered complete without his "Right Here Waiting" being played at least once. Born in Chicago in 1963 to jingle-writer parents, Marx began singing in commercials at age five. As a teenager, Marx recorded a demo that found its way to Lionel Richie, who recruited him to sing backup on hits like "All Night Long" and "Running With the Night." Marx also had his songs recorded by Kenny Rogers and Chicago. His 1987 self-titled debut included the power ballad "Hold on to the Nights," among the album's four top ten hits and sold four million copies. 1989's *Repeat Offender* was bolstered by the number one hits "Satisfied" and "Right Here Waiting" and helped turn Marx into a superstar. The ambitious *Rush Street* followed in 1991, and in 1994 he scored another top ten single with "Now and Forever." Around this time, Marx was beginning a second career behind the scenes as an in-demand songwriter and producer. In recent years, he's written hits for artists as diverse as N'Sync, Keith Urban, Barbra Streisand, and Josh Groban. Marx was the co-writer for Luther Vandross's moving "Dance With My Father," which earned them a Grammy for Song of the Year in 2004. A recent album of new Marx material, *My Own Best Enemy*, was released that same year.

—EVAN SCHLANSKY

Interview by
Deborah Evans Price

American Songwriter,
November/December 1990

Your first break came when Lionel Richie heard some of your songs. What impressed him most?

He really loved the fact that I knew how to write a chorus and I knew how to structure songs properly. He called me up after I had just graduated from high school and said, "Hey, I'm Lionel Richie, and I think you're really talented and you should move to L.A. 'cause this is where it's at. If you're gonna be discovered it's gonna be here." I was pretty blown away, even to this day every time I see him I remind him it was very cool on his part, being the megastar that he was, to pick up the phone and call some kid in Chicago he didn't even know. So I moved to L.A. about three or four months later and I didn't get any breaks as a songwriter, but Lionel used me as a background singer.

When did you get your first cut?

Lionel recommended me as a background singer to Kenny Rogers and so I got hired for the Kenny Rogers album *What About Me?* At the time they were making the album I overheard Kenny say he really needed a song like this or he really needed a song like that. So I went home and wrote songs just like that and came back the next day and handed him a cassette. I ended up getting three songs on that album. I think the first song they actually said yes to was a song called "Crazy" that went to number one on the country charts. Kenny's got his name on it, but he'll even tell you he didn't write any of it. It's just one of those details where it's, "Hey, give me half the song and I'll put it on the album" kind of thing. But it was a great opportunity. And then the doors sorta opened for me because "What About Me?" was a song that he did with James Ingram and Kim Carnes that was a top twenty hit on the pop charts… The other song was never released as a single by Rogers, but it's a song that 'til this day I still really like. I wrote it with a guy named David Pomeranz. It's called "Somebody Took My Love." It was recorded a few years later by a black artist named Durrell Coleman and

it went top twenty on the black charts. So all three of those first covers saw the light of day in one way or another.

After that, did you start getting a lot of cuts?

No, the opposite happened to me. After the Kenny Rogers album was done nothing happened to me for two years. I was doing a lot of background vocal work for a lot of good people and I was trying really hard to write my own songs. I wasn't writing "Right Here Waiting" or "Hold on to the Nights" back then. I was predominantly writing up-tempo rock 'n' roll songs. The songs I was writing for other people were so different and they were tailor-made for those artists, so it was a confusing time for me as a songwriter. I had to switch hats every day, and I went though a period of a year and a half, two years, where I just wasn't getting covers. I was just barely paying my rent by singing on other people's records. Then the next break came when I hooked up with David Foster, the producer, and we worked together on a lot of different records. I co-wrote with him on certain projects like the *St. Elmo's Fire* soundtrack. And I hooked up with Philip Bailey from Earth, Wind & Fire and wrote a song with him for a soundtrack.

Were you offered any publishing deals?

Yeah, I had offers. Lionel offered me a publishing deal when I first moved to L.A. and I said no. Then, when I had the songs with Kenny that became hits, Kenny offered me a very lucrative publishing deal, a lot of money, and I said no. It's not like anybody told me, "Hold onto your publishing." I just felt like as a songwriter, all I had was my publishing. It felt wrong for me to sell my publishing, so I never have made a publishing deal. When my first album came out I made a sub-publishing deal, but it excludes the United States and Canada. It's just mainly a small percentage deal for that company to look out for my royalties around the world.

Did you always believe you were doing the right thing by holding on to your publishing?

No, I went through many thoughts of, "Maybe I'm really blowing it." Here was Kenny Rogers offering me a lot of money for five years just to write ten songs a year and it just felt wrong 'cause he would own my publishing for however long and all the songs I'd written up to that point. I did have a lot of sleepless nights thinking, "Gee, I need the money really badly," but it just felt wrong. It just felt like a common sense decision over a desperation situation.

How did you get your deal with EMI Records?

Every record company rejected me over those five years, and no one was encouraging. I tell kids around the country that are being rejected by record companies, "If you get rejected long enough it probably means you're going to be a big star." I'd become friends with a guy named Bobby Colomby, who used to be a drummer for Blood, Sweat & Tears and had been an A&R guy at Capitol Records. He always believed in me, and he set up a meeting between me and a guy named Bruce Lundvall [president of EMI]. He listened to the same songs everyone else rejected and said, "I think you're great. I think we should make a record."

Some singer/songwriters have trouble finding time to write once their careers take off and they spend a lot of time on the road. I understand you don't have that problem.

I was out for fifteen months with this tour, and the boredom factor of touring can be excruciating. I don't do drugs and I don't go to clubs and I don't really have a lot of hobbies. So I just spend time sitting around a hotel room or on a bus, and I'm always having ideas. I'm always hearing a note in my head or hearing rhythm arrangements or guitar riffs. Instead of ignoring them until I get home, I work on them.

I don't really write complete songs on the road, but I come up with so many pieces of songs that when I got home, the album *Repeat Offender* was pretty much ready to go.

Do you write on the piano or guitar?

I do little of both. I used to write solely on the piano, but actually 90 percent of the time I don't write on anything. I stopped using an instrument to write songs because I felt limited. No matter how good a piano or guitar player you are, you're limited to write what you're about to play. So I figured as a singer my possibilities were a lot greater… It's made my melodies a lot stronger. Every song on the *Repeat Offender* album was written without an instrument except "Right Here Waiting," which I wrote on the piano.

I've heard if you don't have a cassette player you sometimes call and sing songs into your answering machine.

Anything to put it on tape, 'cause I don't have a good memory for ideas. Some people say if an idea is good you'll remember it. If you don't remember it, it wasn't good. I think that's bullshit. I think a second of inspiration should be put down some place so you don't forget it.

Do you co-write?

Yeah. About 80 percent of what I write by myself, but I've always enjoyed co-writing. Co-writing is like a marriage. You've got to be comfortable with the person that you write with in order for it to be productive. Over the years I've tried writing with a large number of people. One of those is the first guy I ever wrote a song with back in Chicago, Bruce Gaitsch.

When we interviewed songwriter/screenwriter Dean Pitchford, he mentioned that you almost didn't put "Right Here Waiting" on the album.

Do you think sometimes you can be too close to a song to see its potential?

Yeah. That song was written for my wife before we were married. My wife's an actress from Nashville, Cynthia Rhodes [*Dirty Dancing, Flashdance, Staying Alive*]. She was doing a film in Africa and there was a period of about three months where we couldn't see each other, and "Right Here Waiting" came out of that separation, came out of the most honest place any song could come from. It wasn't written to get on the radio. It wasn't written to be put on an album. It was written from one person to another to say something. It's obviously the most personal song I've ever written and I demoed it only to send to her. I had already written another ballad for the album. So I recorded the other song and mixed it. Then there was this little song, "Right Here Waiting," and everybody that heard it would go, "That song is great." And I would say, "But I don't want to put that on my album. It's too personal. It'd be like me writing Cynthia a love letter then putting it in *The New York Times*." It just felt strange. Then I realized that one of my responsibilities as a songwriter is to communicate with as many people as I can. And I started to get the idea that people were more connected to that song than any other I'd written. When I played him [Dean] the song, I was wandering around the studio eating an apple and the song ends and I look at Dean, and Dean is crying. He looks at me and says, "That is quite absolutely the best song you've ever written." I was blown away. I had no idea it would affect people the way it did... It's now become the second most-requested song for all the soldiers in the Middle East, behind "God Bless America." What started out as a little message between me and my girlfriend turned out to be a song a lot of people have adapted to their own lives, and that's what songwriting is all about. That's the greatest reward.

How do you determine what songs you'll record and what you'll pitch to other artists?

I write such a large number of songs, and I can only record ten every two years. I don't want to see the other songs sit around and waste. When I write a song I know immediately if it's something I want to record... I love writing for other people. The only problem is that I'm in a situation where if I write a song for somebody I'm probably going to try to do my best to produce it because I really want to see it through. There have been certain songs that I've written for other people that I've not produced and I've almost never been happy with the result, not because it's a bad production job. It's just not what I would have done. I think if you're a song-writer who can produce, an artist is getting a great package and an artist should take advantage of it.

You've co-produced your albums with David Cole and you've also produced other artists like Vixen and Poco. Is it easier to produce others than yourself?

No, actually it's easier for me to produce myself. I'm less ob-jective with myself and that's why I have a co-producer. The main reason I used David as a co-producer was for my vo-cals... when it comes to lead vocals it's tough to be objective. I'd probably be in there for two years on one song 'cause I'd never be satisfied with it.

You've done work on several soundtracks. Do you enjoy writing for films?

I think that my ultimate feeling about it is I don't like doing it anymore because 99 percent of the time the songs end up having nothing to do with the film. You write a song for a scene in a film and then the film people change the film, but they want to keep the song because all the film people are interested in is selling soundtracks and helping sell their film. It's a big corporate decision rather than a musical decision.

You wrote a song for the *Tequila Sunrise* soundtrack that the movie people wanted to release as a single, but you didn't want another single at that time. What happened?

I ended up recording and using the song that I wrote for the film, "Wait for the Sunrise," on the *Repeat Offender* album. When I walked away from the project they called and said, "We can use the song of yours that we found called 'Surrender to Me,'" which I had written with a friend of mine, Ross Vannelli, and I said, "Yeah, sure." They got Richie Zito to produce Ann Wilson and Robin Zander from Cheap Trick and it went top ten. I wrote the song but I felt really detached from it, and I felt that the song had nothing to do with the film. So therefore I don't look at that as a big triumph even though the record went top ten.

Have you had positive experiences working on soundtracks?

The only movie I remember writing a song for that fit the film completely was the song for *Sing*. Unfortunately, the whole project for *Sing* didn't really take off the way people had hoped. Dean Pitchford wrote the lyrics to the song that I wrote and also wrote the script for the film. Dean is a guy who has a lot of integrity. Even though the movie and soundtrack were not commercial successes, I feel like that was probably the most successful soundtrack experience I've had 'cause it really served its purpose in the film.

Would you ever consider doing another soundtrack?

It would have to be a situation where the songs served a purpose in the film. I've been asked to write songs for films at least a dozen times in the last six months and either I didn't get a feel for the film or the timing wasn't right... It's not something I'm excited about. Although I would love to score a film because then I could really take my time and every note of music will be to enhance the film rather than sell records.

What advice would you give novice songwriters regarding publishing companies?

I've always avoided them like the plague. I've seen them do good things and I've also seen them do nothing. I say if you want to be a recording artist, don't go to publishing companies. Do whatever you have to do to pay the rent, but don't sign a publishing deal. As an artist and songwriter, if you have no outlet and no way of getting your songs to people, then maybe a publishing company is the way to go. Always try to find short-term deals. Always try to find half-and-half deals where you're not giving 100 percent of your publishing. And beyond that, just watch out for the sharks.

How important is your songwriting to your overall success?

I'd place it first and foremost. In my own personal list of what I do best, I consider myself a songwriter first and foremost because that's what I work hardest at. I don't know if that's what I'm best at, but it's what I'm proudest of; then producing, second; singing, third; and musician, fourth. I think people really consider me more of a songwriter than a singer. That's fine with me. That's the way I want it.

John Mayer

*Interview by
Kristi Singer*

American Songwriter,
November/December 2004

Armed with an acoustic guitar, smoky-smooth vocals, and cleverly written original tunes blending elements of rock, folk, and jazz into mass-appealing gems, a young John Mayer popped onto the top of the pop charts before anyone could say, "Move over, boy bands."

With 2001's *Room for Squares*, the singer/songwriter filled the airwaves with pop/rock hits "No Such Thing," "Why Georgia," and "Your Body Is a Wonderland," which earned him a Grammy Award for Best Male Pop Vocal Performance. His sophomore album (*Room for Squares* follows Mayer's 1999 debut EP, *Inside Wants Out*) made John Mayer a household name, setting precedence for artists like Jason Mraz and Gavin DeGraw. Since then, he has gone on to release *Heavier Things* (2003), *Try! The John Mayer Trio Live in Concert* (2005), and a new solo album, *Continuum*, was released in 2006.

—KRISTI SINGER

With this tour almost coming to an end, are you excited? Sad?

I'm excited. There's no love lost for me getting off the road for a little while. The more you go around, the more you figure stuff out, so that when you go around next time you can get closer to what it is you want to do. I think this is the closest I've ever been to the set image of who I want to be or what I want to sound like.

What is that "set image?" Can you describe it?

It's just control. It's an instrument control thing. Being on stage as the front guy, singing and playing guitar—there's so many tasks involved in it. If you can find a way to do all of those at the same time, but also not really exert a lot of energy, I think that's really the place to get to.

Is that difficult to do?

Yeah, because what you want to do is knock people over with the power of the song. So, for the first two years of my touring, I was really throwing the songs at people. Now I feel like, you know, we've done that. And if you come to my show right now, you're there for a different reason than you used to be. Because when you have a first record out, and you have hits and stuff, people come out and they want to check you out. And now I think the fact that people are there means something different than it used to. I take my time a lot more now.

There's not a rush anymore to prove something?

I feel like I must have had to prove something to people for them to come and check out the show. So I'm learning to not rely so much on big balls of energy.

It sounds like you're becoming more comfortable with yourself as an artist and performer.

I think I'm becoming so comfortable on the road, and playing, that it doesn't really jostle me anymore. Like, "Wow, I'm on stage in front of fifteen thousand people." It's like, "No man, that's what you do."

Are you working on any new songs? Or still enjoying *Heavier Things*?

I'm working on new songs. When you're an artist/songwriter and you put records out, they're your records for a couple months and then they're everybody else's records and you go back to make another one of "your" records. I'm at the point now where I'm waiting to go home and start writing another record. It's frustrating sometimes because—like last night in my hotel room—sitting down and wanting to write a song but really not being able to, knowing full well that it's because I'm on the road. It's really frustrating.

Why was it difficult for you to write?

It's just a different mindset to be on the road. I just can't write songs on the road because I know they would only be better if I had written them at home, so I don't even finish songs.

Do you write down your ideas?

Yeah, I write them down in a book, sometimes I record them.

How often do you write? Every day?

When I'm home, I'm usually digging every day. It's a variable as to how much, but I definitely wake up, pick up a guitar, and listen to what I did the night before. Nine times out of ten it's total crap. But if it's something good then I keep stacking on it.

What do you find inspiration in when writing your songs?

I don't know. Myself. I don't know. I don't really know when I'm inspired. I'm not like "Oh my God, that book was incredible, I've got to write." I think it all kinda seeps in and at some point, it comes out.

You're not a relationship, political, or social writer?

I write songs about stuff that I've had an opinion on or had some sort of hold on in terms of having the ability to observe the goings-on.

What has surprised you the most about your career so far?

That it's still going.

Really? Why?

A lot of people put records out and they do really well, then they don't after that. When I look out at the crowd now and see *that* many people—they're still there, they're still just as excited as if it was my first record—I appreciate that more now than I ever have. Because it's such a true thing to see people showing up and supporting it. It's almost like the way you would feel if your family came to see you. There's a little shred of that because you know there's a real genuine kind of affection from the crowd. I just feel like I've eked out another summer and "Oh my God, they're all still here."

From an outsider's point of view, I think you've contributed a lot to mainstream pop/rock and to singer/songwriters coming back. Do you acknowledge or realize it?

I realize that the success of it has sparked the signing of a lot of other artists. I would never make the assumption that people who weren't writing songs are *now*. I haven't made more singer/songwriters, but I've probably made more singer/songwriters a little bit of money.

What has been the most difficult adjustment for you in entering this world of pop stardom? Are you more comfortable with it now?

It's a difficult adjustment. I think the difficult adjustment is always going to be tempering your own evolution with what people still want to hear from you and who you still really should be. Evolution is addictive and if you do it for the sake of it, I think that you'll end up losing everybody. I think it's always going to be the most difficult thing to go home, come up with a new record that's going to surprise people, but still hit them in the same place they always were hit by you. I think that's always the difficult part. I think I risk every record putting something out that people listen to and go, "We've lost him."

How do you stay grounded?

Having a bunch of people around me who can fully tell me I'm an asshole at any time. I think if you have people around you who can't, or who won't, then you'll never know it. And months will go by and years will go by and you'll wake up someone that you shouldn't be. So at any moment, I've got someone going, "That's not that cool, take that shirt off."

Have you been called an asshole at all?

No, no. People will very slightly give me the elbow, like, "Hey, that's not that cool." But that's what friends do for each other.

What advice would you give to aspiring artists?

I'd have to meet them. I'd have to meet each and every artist to give them one specific, customized piece of advice for their personality. I don't think it's that cut and dry. Don't die. I guess my first piece of advice is don't die. You want to be alive to see this happen.

Ian McCulloch
Echo & the Bunnymen

As the leader of Echo & the Bunnymen and on his own as a solo artist, Ian McCulloch's songs have inspired a devoted legion of fans. The Bunnymen were one of the eighties' seminal alternative rock acts, and modern bands like Coldplay continue to list them as a major influence. Formed in 1978 in Liverpool, England, the band's profile increased over the course of six lyrically dark, heavily atmospheric albums. In 1987, their eponymous fifth album, featuring the single "The Game," became their biggest hit in the United States, reaching number fifty-one on the pop charts. McCulloch left the band in 1988 to concentrate on a solo career, resulting in the albums *Candleland* (1989) and *Mysterio* (1992). In 1997, the Bunnymen reformed, recording a string of well-received albums: *Evergreen* (1997), *What Are You Going to Do With Your Life?* (1999), *Flowers* (2001), and *Siberia* (2005). McCulloch's most recent solo album, *Slideling*, came out in 2003.

—EVAN SCHLANSKY

Interview by
Evan Rytlewski

American Songwriter,
January/February 2006

How did you decide to have Hugh Jones produce *Siberia*?

Well, we used Hugh Jones because we liked him a lot and he produced, as you know, [Echo & the Bunnymen's] *Crocodiles* and *Heaven Up Here*. We decided that we wanted a producer for this record, and I ran into him last year in a studio in Liverpool where he was recording with a band. Will had mentioned his name a few times in the last five or so years, [asking], "Is it possible to use him?" And I kind of thought that [would be] looking nostalgically backwards, which I try not to do—because I can't remember anything. And I'd always thought that maybe we should be looking somewhere else.

But I ran into Hugh in Liverpool, and we got on great. We had a few drinks together, and it was lovely, especially hearing Hugh's anecdotes about the things we've done together. There's no punch line to any of his anecdotes! See, an anecdote to me is kind of a historical joke. There's no point for me in anecdotalizing something serious. So he'd say [*raspy imitation*], "Remember that time when we were doing *Heaven Up Here*… and you had a pint of beer?" And that was it! I was like, "Yeah… I probably had nine more pints and lots of rum, so what's your point, chief?" But he still had the same crappy way of regaling anyone who was around him. I just found that he had the same charm he's always had.

To be honest, my love of music has really narrowed itself down over the last twenty-odd years into things I've always loved. I've always loved Bowie, Lou Reed, Iggy Pop, quite a smattering of Dylan, Neil Young, Rolling Stones, a bit of Beatles, lots of Elvis Presley, lots of Frank Sinatra… you know, the things I've always liked. But Hugh told me everything he'd heard in the last month, and I thought, "I haven't heard anything in the last month! Because I don't listen to anything!" Expect for Rufus Wainwright, the *Want One* album, which is just one of the greatest things of all time.

He also told me some stuff that he quite liked at the time, and I thought that if he likes that, then he's going to shit himself when he hears "What If We Are?" or "In the Margins" or "Stormy Weather"—basically every track on the album. I realized that he was the bloke to produce it. Usually, I always want the decisions to be mine, because I easily have the highest IQ of anyone I know, combined. And because we all know intelligence isn't how high your IQ is, it's how intelligent you are, I'm also the most intelligent person ever. That's why I make decisions. But by and large I like songs that are played on acoustic guitar and then become something else. You know, Neil Diamond is one of the greatest, one of the schmaltziest [performers]. It's amazing how he can schmaltz it up! I saw him play Wembley [Stadium] five years ago, and he wore this all-in-one trouser combination. It was amazing. Whoever did the clothes for *Star Wars* couldn't have made this thing. It was a completely generated stage costume.

You're into Neil Diamond? When did you first get into Neil Diamond?

It was probably when I first heard him sing, "I am, I said, to no one there—not even the chair…" and I thought, "That fella was totally fucked up, he's got no friends! But he's presumably got a chair." Also, when I heard that track "Sweet Caroline," and I suppose before that, without me even knowing it was Neil, when I heard "I'm a Believer," which is completely brilliant.

Neil Diamond has a flashy rock star persona. Is that something you looked up to?

Flashy rockstarism? I think not! [*Laughs*] No, I look down on flashy rockstarism, boy! Seriously, though, I looked up to people like Lou Reed and David Bowie… people with some obvious charisma but also some enigmatic mysteriousness-nessnessosity—which is one of my favorite words that I made up. I like things that are a little bit, not outer spacey, but, certainly, out of my normal… well, sort of an etherealority.

So if you were attracted to performers with this mysterious, um, mysteriousness—

Mysteriousnessnessnessocity!

I can't pronounce that, so I won't try.

[*Laughs*] Well, so long as you can write it. Mysteriousnessnessnessocity… it's got three "nesses" and one "ocity."

Did you try to give yourself that kind of aura when you were establishing yourself as a performer?

Some things need to be tried and some things are already packed in the bag. I came out of the womb with charisma a-go-go. And also, humility, hand in hand.

Humility aside, how do you balance that? You've got this charisma and this myster—Mysteriousnessnessnessocity! Are you getting it?

Mysteriousnessnessnessocity! I'm starting to get it—I'm trying at least. But how do you maintain that aura, since your songs are very open now, almost heart-on-sleeve? Can you sustain that image when you're revealing yourself?

That is one of the realities. I think with the Bunnymen when we started out, I hid behind a veil of crypticisityisisnosity—as I like to call it—but then as I've gotten, well, not older, because I don't feel any older, but as I got more affected by what I need to write… and what I need to hear from other people when they sing to me on the radio or on the TV or whatever… that's why I basically only listen to Rufus Wainwright's *Want One* from the last few years or so—I always feel like musicians are pretending. I don't hear anything. I don't care about these new bands with this sort of playground songwriting, and songs that aren't about anything because maybe they haven't been through anything. It just sounds like everything's invented.

For instance, I was in Paris yesterday and I listened to this tape that the hotel people had on, and I was sitting there and I was listening to this country musician with such obnoxiousnessnosity or whatever… and it was just the most cliché, banal, trite piece of crap I'd ever heard, but then again, this girl was singing along, so maybe that's the way to go. Maybe my next album should be country-western, banal shit. Every time I hear things like that, I wonder, why can't people see through the pretense of it all?

Going back to the question of mysteriousnessnessnessocity, and the fact that now I seem to be leaving myself wide open—part confessional, part guilty until proven innocent, in a sense—for me, the most serious thing in our lives is how we all find, well, for me anyways, I always find the truth really difficult to pin down. In the early days of the Bunnymen, there were songs like "Rescue," which was an obvious cry for help, or at least attention. But now when I look at what I've done lately, I find that now I'm picking up the pace and now I can say things like "Everything Kills You" and I can say "What If We Are?" On basically all the songs on this album, I tried to pin down and simplify everything and really connect with someone.

I never thought that the Bunnymen were mass material because we're too mysteriousnessnessnessousnestic, and I never wanted to appeal to everyone. I wanted to appeal to whoever it was a week ago who came up to me and said, "'Nothing Lasts Forever' saved my life." I've heard that a few times from people who have been suicidal.

I always aimed for people who were like me when I got into Lou Reed and Bowie. [But when] our appeal broadened, it felt like maybe the temptation was to try and appeal to a mass audience, and it's real difficult to do that when you don't know what the fuck is going on in your own life. I mean, you can't write a real heartbreaking song if you're thinking about someone else. To write a heartbreaking song, your heart needs to be in pieces.

John McCrea

Cake

photo courtesy Sony Records

Interview by
Kristi Singer

American Songwriter,
November/December 2005

If you think you have to choose between smart songwriting and tunes that make you blissfully bob your head, this band proves you can have your Cake and eat it, too. A funky, horn-laden party vibe plus quirky arrangements and distinctively twisted wordplay make Cake one of the most consistently entertaining bands around.

Vocalist and songwriter John McCrea formed Cake in 1992 in Sacramento, California. The band produced and released their debut album themselves, 1993's *Motorcade of Generosity*, and its early success earned them a slot on the roster of Capricorn Records. But it was their second album, 1996's platinum-selling *Fashion Nugget*, that thrust them into the limelight and gave them their first hit record. The driving lead single "The Distance" gave radio a major shot of adrenaline—and it's still heard at sporting events around the country.

Despite major personnel changes and a move to Columbia Records, Cake returned in 2000 with *Prolonging the Magic* to prove they were still firing on all cylinders. The album had an alternative radio hit, "Never There." Cake proceeded to prolong the magic even further in 2001, when their fourth album, the offbeat *Comfort Eagle*, debuted at number thirteen on the *Billboard* charts—the highest chart debut of the band's career. In 2004, they released their fifth album, *Pressure Chief*.

—EVAN SCHLANSKY

Are you working on songs today?

Today I'm not writing any songs because, well, what happens when you release an album is a lot of other stuff gets scheduled. This is like the traveling circus part of my life. The songwriting part is hopefully when I'm through with this. I'm actually working on our record cover. I'm designing our record cover and I am going into the studio later to work on a song, an old B-side for a vinyl single we're releasing.

Tell me about the cover. What are you designing? What's the image?

It's an old Roman graphic, literally from Roman times, that I stole from those Roman urns, those vases, where they have beautiful artwork on them. So I took that and made it into a black-and-white graphic, and then I'm imposing a face on top of it, in the middle of it… sort of an exasperated-looking face. It's for the single "Carbon Monoxide," and it's sort of an exasperated song that I wrote when I was a kid.

That's interesting that you wrote it when you were a kid.

Yeah. I started writing when I was a teenager and there are a couple of songs that I wrote back then that don't completely suck, and that's one of them.

Can you tell me a bit about what "Carbon Monoxide" is about?

I was sitting on a bus bench in Los Angeles, California, a place that I hated at the time, and the cars just kept going by and going by and going by. The air was just so foul and polluted that I wrote this song of protest to all these cars that were driving by me. It sounds pretty hippie, but the song has a sense of humor.

Do you remember how old you were?

I think I was fifteen or sixteen. So yeah, I think when you first start writing songs, you have to have a certain suspen-sion of disbelief, and I think teenagers are sometimes able to believe in themselves just because of hormones.

A more innocent perspective on life, I guess?

Yeah, if it gets you started then it's a good thing. You can't really get started with anything unless you believe you can do it. If it's hormones, it's hormones.

Did any of your other teenage-written songs make it on the album?

Not on this album, but they've surfaced on some of the other albums. I just wrote songs for so long that I had literally hundreds and I never needed to write again. And this is actually the first album in a long time where I needed to write anything. There were so many years of I think prolific frustration that I ended up doing a lot of my work before the band was even formed.

What do you mean by prolific frustration?

I was so frustrated that I expressed that frustration prolifically. The music business isn't the easiest business to make a living at—and I thought that I could. But I didn't realize what a drag it would be having to jump through all the hoops, so there were a lot of years where I didn't have to tour in a band and I stockpiled songs, I just wrote and wrote and wrote. I wrote a song every day, practically. A lot of them I've thrown away, but a lot of them still sound pretty okay to me.

One thing I want to talk about is your lyrics. They're so eccentric and unique. How do you come up with some of your sayings and mis-matched lyrics? Do you have a process?

My process is that I have to write continually. I have to always have a pen and paper with me and I'll observe something in everyday life that seems either sad or very strange or a combination of those things, or it's maybe inspiring, and once in awhile I'll write something that's happy. But for

the most part it's just something that strikes me as interesting and I'll jot it down and then revisit it at a later date and hopefully flush it out and write a melody to it. But there are also songs where I'm walking down the street and a melody comes to my head and it sounds good and I have no lyrics for it. It happens both ways. But I think it will only happen, for me at least, if I'm constantly involved in it… in the process of writing. It's something that's hard to turn off. It's hard to turn on and it's hard to turn off.

What inspired you when writing the songs for *Pressure Chief?* Were there any particular thoughts or ideas that really inspired your songwriting?

I think a lot of the songs on this album are inadvertently about being at war with oneself. Not so much being at war with oneself, but being one's own worst enemy. And how one person can house two diametrically imposed imperatives. I like that because it creates a balance. Opposites are great because they complete each other. And so, thinking about this album after the fact, which is probably not a good thing to do, I see that sort of thread running through it, that it's sort of about needing things and hating them at the same time. About being a hypocrite, about feeling the pressure from the inside, the pressure of cognitive dissonance. When two things are in opposition but also both true. That's a lot of talk, and I think I wrote about the way I felt the last two years living in the United States.

Do you feel like there's a building pressure?

I definitely feel there's a lot of change. There's a lot of authority and pressure. People don't know what to believe or who to believe in anymore. People are in different tribes and its one tribe against another tribe. Sometimes it's not so much about the issues as it is about being a part of something greater than yourself. If you're a Republican or Democrat or Communist or whatever, it's important to take everything on an issue-to-issue basis. And to me, it's about corruption and pork barrel politics right now; it's not really about Democrat vs. Republican. It's about honesty vs. dishonesty. At any rate, this album is a sad and hopeful album. I don't know how else to describe it. It's kind of a downer, but there's also a glimmer of hope in it.

It's funny to me that you're writing about things that you're feeling down about because the music comes across as upbeat and happy. Is that a dichotomy that you create on purpose?

I think a lot of people are not comfortable with one song housing opposites inside of it. I think a lot of baby boomers are uncomfortable with comedy being mixed in with the tragedy and immediately they'll say, "Oh, that's just a joke and I think that's a product of being raised in a time where they had the luxury of pure cultural gestures." In the sixties, things were simpler, and now I think things are more mixed together. In the sixties there was pure earnest striving and belief, and now I think successive generations have come to realize that that's a luxury, that's an indulgence. There's no such thing as pure, idealistic struggle. There's a lot of… there can be idealistic pragmatism, or pragmatism that's informed by ideals, but there's no purity. And to answer your question, which I'm doing in a roundabout way, I think our music houses both humor and sadness and levity and depression. And I think a lot of people that aren't used to that sort of write us off as all for fun and games and all sort of a joke and I think that that's not the way anybody but baby boomers interpret us. Baby boomers are the ones that, I think, were really raised on pure, muscular striving and everything was in its concentrated form and I think that the next generation and the one after have had to realize that there's nothing that's really pure or concentrated in the world; it's all polluted, and that's a good thing. These are such… I'm talking about ideas that are too big, let's talk about songwriting.

I read that you learned as you went and made mistakes that you kept on the record. What advice would you give to artists in regard to recording this way? Do you recommend going in like, "We're going to figure it out."

No. Well, I don't think you should go in and say, "We're going to figure it out." I think you should go in and say, "We're going to figure out what sounds good to us and what doesn't sound good to us, and there's no right or wrong." There are bands right now, a lot of bands that are making albums that sound exactly like August of 1972 or June of 1967, these sort of immaculately designed replicas of precise moments in music. And they're doing that not by making perfectly recorded music, but they're doing it by doing just the opposite. What is perfection? Perfection, I think, would be more about not exactitude, but more about appropriateness.

And honesty.

Yeah, and honesty. And clear communication, of course. But sometimes production values communicate one thing and your song communicates one thing and the production values communicate just the opposite. Let me make it very drastic. If you're a blues artist and the producer comes in and records the drums really huge like Led Zeppelin-sounding drums, but the song is about being down and out, sitting on the street corner… somehow mighty Viking drum tones, although they may be appropriate for one kind of music, are maybe completely inappropriate for something that's about being down on your luck. You don't want drums that sound like Mighty Zor unless you're trying to create some cognitive dissonance in people. You have to be careful about that.

What general advice would you give to aspiring songwriters, if there was one major point you could make?

The best advice I got was from a novelist who told me that she really liked a certain song that I had written and she told me why: I used concrete imagery, using viscerally satisfying examples rather than saying something to describe something… you can say it through description better and more emotionally than if you just go ahead and say it. In other words, describe the smell of oranges, concoct a combination of sensory inputs that actually state your point or your emotional status. Rather than saying I'm sad, describe the rotten oranges and dog shit. You know what I mean? I think that's the best advice I could give to other songwriters. It's like your English professor used to tell you, describe it, don't say it. Describe it.

> *Sometimes it's not so much about the issues as it is about being a part of something greater than yourself.*

Bob McDill

Interview by
Kelly Delaney

American Songwriter,
January/February 1988

Bob McDill has authored thirty number one country hits, a feat made all the more impressive by the fact that the songwriter came to country music late in life. Born 1944 in Beaumont, Texas, McDill befriended Allen Reynolds, who ran a publishing company in Memphis. While serving in the Navy, McDill began sending songs to Reynolds, who got Perry Como to cut what would become McDill's first hit, 1967's "Happy Man." When Reynolds moved to Nashville in the late sixties, McDill came with him. It was there he stopped writing tunes for the rock and pop market and focused his energies on country and western music. His first major country hits came in 1973, with "Catfish John," and "Rednecks, White Socks and Blue Ribbon Beer," recorded by Johnny Russell, and "Amanda," a hit for Don Williams and later Waylon Jennings. In 1977, Bobby Bare recorded an entire album of his songs, dubbed *Me and McDill*. Most recently, McDill's songs have been covered by Pam Tillis and Alan Jackson.

—DOUGLAS WATERMAN

Do you consider songwriting an art form?

I think songwriting can be art; most of it isn't. I certainly know the difference when I hear one whether or not it's commerciality or art. [Joni Mitchell's] "Both Sides Now" is art. [Janis Ian's] "At Seventeen" is art… things that are more reflective or philosophical or generally have a point of view.

The definition is somewhat subjective, though, isn't it?

You can argue with people about what art is. Some people will tell you that any product of a creative thought is art. Well, I think that's bull. If you do that, then a campaign for selling Big Macs is art. "Baby's Got Her Blue Jeans On" is not art. It has no purpose other than to entertain. "Song of the South" is art. Whether or not it's good art is subject to opinion, but at least it's an attempt to say something.

Is that a mistake many young writers make— being too arty?

When I came to town, everybody was too arty, too introspective. Songs were esoteric. That was usually the mistake young

> *You can argue with people about what art is. Some people will tell you that any product of a creative thought is art. Well, I think that's bull.*

writers made. I think now the mistake young writers make is that things are too flippant, too puffy. There's nothing of the writer in there. Young writers could probably benefit by reaching for a line that's a little more unique and memorable.

Is it easier for a young writer starting out today than when you began?

It's not easier to get good, which is the final question. Are you really good? It's easier, I think, to have some success because of co-writing, and the fact that publishing companies are bigger and have more writers and everybody co-writes. It's easier to be a part of a hit, but it's not easier to get good. It's no easier than to be confronted with that empty page and be able to make something out of nothing.

You've always had a reputation as a serious nine-to-five writer. Does that still hold true?

I used to be a classic workaholic; now it's fashionable to be one, and now that it is I can truthfully say I'm not one. The only reason I could take a vacation was so that I could rest my head long enough so that I could get back to work. It wasn't to enjoy myself. But you get to be about forty and you think, "Is this all I'm ever going to do… accumulate copyrights and money? There's got to be more to life than this." So, a few years ago, I started duck hunting again, and fishing, and camping out. I'm also starting to collect books and gardening. I'm trying to reflect and make life more fun before I look up one day and I've missed it all.

Why do you try to keep regular writing hours?

I think the most important thing is to organize your time so that you put in a day. I've said this many times; you look at people who have long careers creatively, who didn't burn out or go crazy or become alcoholics, and they all have one thing in common. They get up early every morning and do it and quit at the same hour. They try all day and then

the monkey's off their back and they've done the best they could for that day.

So there has to be more than inspiration?

If you write whenever inspiration hits you, or when you felt like writing, it's insanity. That's what happens to people; they come home at night and they haven't done anything and they should have done something. They can't sit down because they feel guilty. The thing to do is organize your time.

What if you get inspired after hours, so to speak?

If you get an idea and you feel like playing with it, and you feel great about it, go do it. That part's gravy; you don't have to do it.

Do you do much rewriting?

More than most people, I guess. I hate to let them go if I know they're just mediocre, because you have to admit to yourself that you wasted all that time. It's so competitive now that you really have to be good. If the songs aren't good, you're just playing games with yourself.

What makes a song a hit?

I don't know what it is. So much of it is by luck and accident. I'm not one for predestination.

What turned you toward writing country music, given that you came to Nashville to write rock songs?

When I heard George Jones sing "A Good Year for the Roses," I suddenly understood, hearing that song, what was going on. You've got to like it to write it, you know?

Do you have an identifiable writing style?

I don't know what my style is. You look at anybody who's had a long run and they certainly have more than one trick.

Your song "Amanda" is filled with ironies. Is that one of your tricks?

Anytime you can take a little couplet and make something happen aside from the overall song, then it's really a strength. Sometimes you don't have anything to say and you're just reduced to alliteration or word plays. But every line ought to be interesting by itself, ideally. But you can't always do that so you use any trick or method to keep it interesting.

How did you come to write "Amanda"?

To be truthful, I was sort of inspired. I think I wrote it in about thirty minutes. It's the last easy one I had.

What approach do you take to find an idea worth writing?

A lot of times I brainstorm everything that comes to mind. I'll write down everything. When you're flowing, get it all. A big mistake is to get a great idea and you feel yourself flow and you think you've got to get that first line. By the time you get that first line, all the rest of it is gone.

So it all boils down to love and hard work, doesn't it?

James Dickey once said something like art doesn't come out of a bunch of little old ladies patting you on the back at a tea or luncheon and bragging on your poem. It comes from the courage to face the awesome empty page. It does get grueling year after year by yourself and that empty page. But then, you can always go to lunch!

John Mellencamp

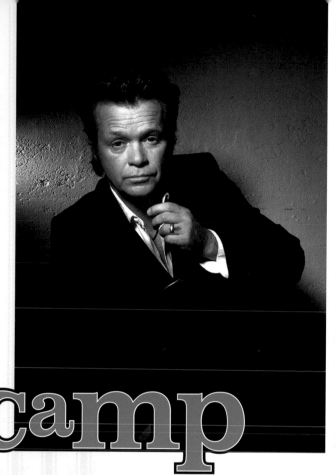

photo courtesy Mark Cornelison

Perhaps more than any other rock artist, John Mellencamp's music cuts straight to the heart of the American Dream. The Seymour, Indiana, native moved to New York City at twenty-four, where he was given the name John Cougar by David Bowie manager Tony DeFries. DeFries signed Mellencamp on the strength of his voice and helped him release his 1976 debut, *Chestnut Street Incident*, which featured no original songs. The nation would not fully recognize Mellencamp's songwriting talents until his fifth LP, 1982's *American Fool*, featuring the Grammy-winning "Hurts So Good" and the Americana staple "Jack and Diane." Mellencamp then hit a golden streak with 1982's *Uh-huh*, (featuring the hit "Pink Houses"), 1985's *Scarecrow* ("Small Town," "R.O.C.K. in the U.S.A.") and 1987's *The Lonesome Jubilee* ("Paper in Fire"). In the mid-nineties, Mellencamp began experimenting with dance rhythms, as on 1996's *Mr. Happy Go Lucky*. His latest album, 2003's *Trouble No More*, is a collection of blues standards.

—EVAN SCHLANSKY

*Interview by
Paul Zollo*

American Songwriter,
January/February 2005

215

Did you grow up in a musical home?

Yes. My grandmother could play piano, string instruments, and she could sing. It was all Appalachian-type stuff. And I had an older brother who played guitar and was in the choir. I was exposed to a lot of music. My dad is only twenty years older than me. When I was a kid, he was into folk music. We had Odetta records around the house. I loved folk music— from Peter, Paul & Mary to Woody Guthrie.

When you started writing songs, you already had a record deal?

Yeah. Isn't that wild? That's why my first songs are so crummy. [*Laughs*]

You were John Cougar then.

That was put on me by some manager. I went to New York and everybody said, "You sound like a *hillbilly*." And I said, "Well, I am." So that's where he came up with that name. I was totally unaware of it until it showed up on the album jacket. When I objected it to it, he said, "Well, either you're going to go for it, or we're not going to put the record out." So that was what I had to do… but I thought the name was pretty silly.

When you started writing your own songs, were your managers okay with that idea?

Yeah, I think so. There were always managers wanting to put their two cents in. But after the Johnny Cougar debacle, I pretty much rejected just about everything they ever said. You know, I've always been an outsider. I've never really been part of any New York-hip or L.A.-cool scene. I've always been from the Midwest. I've stayed here and done things the way I've wanted to do them. I listened to people when I had to sometimes, but generally I just did things the way I wanted to do them. I wrote a song called "Minutes to

Memories" a few years ago that says, "I do things my way and I pay an awfully high price." And I still feel that way.

When you started writing songs, did it come easily to you?

No. Listen to my earlier records. You know, it takes a person a long time to find his voice. I always marvel at guys whose first records are so well written and so well done. Take Elvis Costello's first record. How did he do that?

Yes. Or John Prine.

Yeah, John Prine's first record. How did that happen? So, for me, I was singing in bars. I was fourteen years old, playing at college fraternities. I was singing Sam & Dave. I was the singer in the band.

Once you started writing songs, did you write a lot?

I had to, because I had a record deal. I was in a band and playing in bars when I first got a record deal, so my experience of the world in my mid-twenties was being in bars all the time. We played 365 days a year.

Did you learn a lot about songwriting from playing all those covers?

I didn't at the *time*. But looking back at it, I see that I did.

How did you learn to write? Was it trial and error?

Trial by fire [*laughs*]. Once I started writing songs, and once I found my voice, I knew what I had to do. I saw myself as an American songwriter in the troubadour fashion; it's just that I happened to have a rock band behind me. But if you'd heard my songs when they were originally written, they were just fragile folk songs.

Do you write words and music together?

Yes. Generally. I write the melody and the lyrics and the rhythm all at the same time. It just happens. And then sometimes I'll go back and rewrite. Sometimes I don't.

So often you will get an entire song all at once?

Sure. Not often. Most of the time.

Are those the best songs—the ones that come all at once?

Generally speaking. But there are holes in those songs. I'll hear a song I wrote many years ago called "Pink Houses" on the radio, and I'll think, "Man, I wish I would have spent a little more time on the last verse." I never really view my songs as *done*. I just think they're *abandoned*. You think, "Okay, well, I'm in the studio now, and now it's time to think about what the guitar player is going to do, and what the bass player is going to do, and what the drummer's going to do." So once you get to that point, the song is pretty much abandoned. You've got to be able to roll with what these musicians try to do with the song.

Nowadays, do you write songs all the time?

Once you start writing songs, you write all the time. Everything's a song now. It's just a matter of looking out my window. I won't even want to write, but I'll think of a good idea, and I better get that down. And all of a sudden, I'll have two or three verses in my head, and I'll think I have to put these down on paper… because if I don't, I'll forget them pretty soon. I have to say that I have to write ten songs to get one good one. I'll write ten, fifteen songs, and there won't be a good one in the bunch.

Do you finish those, even if you don't think they're good ones?

I get to a point where I can see if they're going to work or not.

How much do you have to write to make that judgment?

A verse and a chorus. The first verse and the first chorus always come easy to me. But then it's where the song goes from there that I always start to make missteps. I take it in the wrong direction or get too literal about something. So it's hard to write in a vague manner but still be poignant. It's very hard to do.

Why vague?

I've never really enjoyed getting too specific about topics. I always feel you have to be a really great songwriter to get specific and captivate the imagination of the listener. That's an impossible task. There are only a couple of guys who can do that. It's important for me to keep it vague, so that when people hear it they are able to put themselves inside the song. I try to make my songs not about me as much as possible.

You've written some powerfully specific, narrative story songs like "Jack and Diane."

Well, they're not story songs as much as vignette songs. I'll go from vignette to vignette in a song and then tie it together with a chorus. But a lot of times my songs come out on the angry side, or the pessimistic side, or the craggily side, until you get to the end of them… and then I'll try to write something, in the end, that gives hope to the situation. Never try to answer any questions—only ask questions.

In "Jack and Diane" you sing, "Here's a little ditty…" But it's more than a ditty.

From the perspective of a young man in his late twenties, when I wrote that song, it was such a small story. It wasn't as much about the song. It was the characters. They were just so average. So the word "ditty" just seemed appropriate. Even as you said it, it still does to me.

That song became a big hit, as have so many of your songs. Does it change your feeling about a song if it becomes a hit?

No, not really. Sometimes I'm disappointed that some songs [that I thought were better than hits], people weren't able to lock on to. But I don't really have feelings about songs the way some people do. You know, I paint. And I do the same things with the paintings. I enjoy creating them, and I enjoy working on them, and I enjoy the problems that they create for me to solve. But once I've done that, and abandoned it, then I'm done with it. It's on to the next painting. Or it's on to the next song. It's on to the next thing to try to create. It makes things bearable… doing that. Hanging on to a song like "Jack and Diane," I really don't take a smidgen of pride in that I've written that. I don't take pride in the fact that one song was able to climb the charts and one song wasn't. I take pride in the fact that I was able to create these songs. That seems to be more important than the fact that this song was a hit or that song was a hit.

Do you think of a title before writing a song?

Very rarely. Generally, the title comes after the song has been written, and sometimes even after the song has been recorded. I don't hang much importance in a name.

It seems that sometimes a song is based around the title, such as "Paper in Fire."

A song like "Paper in Fire"… I didn't really have to title the song, it titled itself. That was the only logical, creative choice. There's nothing else to call that song.

When you say that a song titles itself, is songwriting more a method of following a song than leading it?

Oh yeah. I *never* try to lead a song in a specific direction. Because then you start editing yourself. And I *do* do that, and I think every songwriter probably does that. But, that makes

life a lot harder… when you start editing yourself. The best creation is when you're free with it and it becomes what it becomes. I know in my paintings, if I labor over it too much, it gets ugly.

But with painting, you can create it without any literal ideas. Is that a different process than creating songs, where you have to deal with verbal thoughts?

You're still dealing with reality. There are certain things that have to happen in a painting. It's like a language. If you don't use that language on the canvas, it won't work… it won't look right. Then you realize you tried to sidestep that part of the painting process and tried to take a shortcut that didn't work. And you have to deal with it.

Does music come easily to you?

Melodies are very simple for me. I, for some reason, have an unlimited amount of melodies in my head. I very rarely feel that I am repeating myself. A lot of the instrumental lines on my records are lines I've given the musicians to play. Making up melodies is the simplest thing for me to do.

Do you come up with melodies in your head, or on a guitar?

In my head. Then I have musicians figure them out. That's when I throw the guitar away. I don't like being confined to an instrument. I'll sing a melody—and the violinist or the guitar player or the piano player, or all of them—will figure out that line and help each other.

Many songwriters write melodies generated by chord progressions they play on guitar or piano…

Well, you have to follow a melody inside the chord progression, so the chord progression can dictate which direction the melody goes. But there are *so* many notes that can go into a D chord. It's limitless how many notes will work inside that chord. I never think about that. I never think about the math of it.

The math?

Yes, the math. Music is math. There are so many beats in a measure. It's all math when you get right down to it. Music is a mathematical problem. And I never, never try to look at the math of a song until the song is over. And then I decide if the math is correct. In many of my songs, I have crammed so many lyrics into a melody and into a measure that mathematically it doesn't work. Ah, but it *does* work if the next line doesn't follow that cadence. There are so many things you can do. And I try to do it more from feel than from the mathematical point.

What kind of feel are you going for?

That depends on each song. Each song has a different cadence and a different rhyme and a different message, so each song dictates that feel. If you take a song like "Walk Tall," when I play it acoustically, it's a folk song—in the tradition of Woody Guthrie. But I knew right away that I wanted to have an R&B feel for that song. I played it for Kenny "Babyface" Edmonds, who's a real R&B guy. I said, "Listen to this song, and see what kind of R&B feel you can put to it." I think I played one verse and one chorus and he had already come up with the feel. And that happened within, no exaggeration, *thirty seconds* of him hearing the song. He hadn't even heard me play the song once, and he was already playing that rhythm against my folk rhythm. So I looked at him at that point and said, "I'll see you in Indiana in a few weeks."

Where do you think your ideas for songs come from?

I just look out the window and they come to me. I see myself in the old tradition of the troubadour. I read the papers.

I watch the news. I talk to people. I'm inspired by those things. There are *so* many things to write about. Anyone could be a songwriter. I could start writing today, and write two or three songs a day for the rest of my life, and still never run out of material.

Can a song contain any content?

Sure. If it's any *good* is questionable. That's the problem most people have when they start writing songs. They expect to write at the level of songs that they've heard on the radio. But that's all magic. When I started writing, I didn't know how magical [Bob Dylan's] "Highway 61 Revisited" was. How do you compete with that when you're twenty-two years old and trying to write songs? You *can't*. There's just so much that you can't even compete with. It's like putting a grade-school football team against the NFL champions. It's not going to work. There's no level playing field for the songwriter.

How does a songwriter reach that magic?

He has to find his own voice. And that takes a long time. I admire guys like Elvis Costello, who found his own voice [early in his career]. Some songwriters stop at a certain point and don't keep going forward. Elvis Costello was able to keep moving forward. He might be the best songwriter of all of us guys who started out in the seventies. But when you put someone up against Bob Dylan, he is the *only* singer/songwriter. With Bob, it's God's mind to Bob's fingers. There's just nobody else. You know, I asked Bob how he did it. And he just looked at me and said, "I write the same four songs every time I write." [*Laughs*]

I love your song "Human Wheels."

That song was co-written with George Green. That was the eulogy from his grandfather's funeral. He didn't intend for me to use those lyrics as a song. He read them to me, and I said, "George, send those over to me… I'm going to put mu-

sic to those... those are so beautiful." I wrote that song without a guitar or anything. I just sang that melody. I figured out the cadence in my head, and then I went to my guitar to figure out the chords.

Where do good melodies come from?

With me, and I don't mean to appear smug, it's innate. I'm just able to do it. It's something I've never struggled with. The whole point is writing simple melodies that people can sing along with. That's what Lennon and McCartney were able to do. That's what Hank Williams was able to do. That's what John Fogerty was able to do. That's what Bob Dylan was able to do. I mean, "Stuck Inside of Mobile With the Memphis Blues Again"... how hard is that to sing? It's not. It has just enough movement that it creates this beautiful melody. Or "Knockin' on Heaven's Door." His melodies are so beautiful.

Is the melody more important than the words?

I would say probably... to the general public... it is. It's not to me. I think to your casual music listener, they have to relate to the melody or they're never going to get the words.

You've talked about writing vague songs, yet you're written many specific songs, such as "Jackie Brown."

When I'm writing songs like that, the melody really has to be beautiful. I think that is a specific story. But if you get into the details of it, you're back into the song being vague again. It paints a picture, but you depend on the listener to fill in. I'm proud of that song.

"Small Town" is specific.

I disagree. That's a vague song. "I was born in a small town." How many small towns can you apply to that situation? Is that La Crosse, Wisconsin, or is that Bloomington, Indiana, or is that Collins, Texas? "I had myself a ball in a small town." I mean, doing what?

It's open-ended.

It's *so* open-ended... it's *so* vague. But I think that's what made the song work. And plus, I think I use the words "small town" 975 times in the song.

Do you remember writing it?

I wrote that song in the laundry room of my old house [*laughs*]. We had company, and I had to go write the song. And the people upstairs could hear me writing and they were all laughing when I came up. They said, "You've got to be kidding." What else can you say about it?

Do you remember writing "Hurts So Good"?

George Green and I wrote that together. We exchanged lines back and forth between each other and laughed about it at the time. Then I went and picked up the guitar, and within seconds, I had those chords.

What is your favorite song that you've written?

I haven't written that song yet.

Dan Messe
Hem

photo courtesy Hem

Hem has cornered the market on beautifully rendered, serene country-pop songs. The New York City band formed in the spring of 1999 when songwriter Dan Messe and producer/engineer Gary Mauer (who'd worked with alternative bands like Luna and Fountains of Wayne) hooked up with guitarist/mandolin player Steve Curtis. Fed up with the rampant irony and aggression dominating the popular rock music of the time, the band turned instead to the fertile stomping grounds of old-time Americana music. An ad in *The Village Voice* netted them their singer, Sally Ellyson, whose understated soprano serves as Hem's secret weapon. Though she claimed she wasn't really a singer, Messe was transfixed by her demo, a tape of traditional a cappella lullabies. Snippets of the demo ended up making it on their debut album, the self-released and produced *Rabbit Songs*.

Messe sold most of his belongings to help finance the record, and the band took their time with the recording, forgoing digital technology but splurging on their own eighteen-piece orchestra. The extra care paid off, and *Rabbit Songs* received rave reviews from critics at NPR, *Rolling Stone,* and *The New York Times.* In 2003, having swelled to an octet, Hem released their second album, *Eveningland,* on Rounder Records. Since then, they have released a collection of covers, *No Word from Tom* (2006), and *Funnel Cloud* (2006).

—EVAN SCHLANSKY

*Interview by
Caine O'Rear*

American Songwriter,
January/February 2005

You've described the sound on this album as "countrypolitan." Can you elaborate on that term?

What I think of is what took place in the late sixties and early seventies, ranging from Ray Charles to some of the stuff Glen Campbell was doing—that weird crossover that brought country into other directions, usually with an orchestra… some of the stuff done at Muscle Shoals. It's sort of like country, but *arranged* country.

Are you writing consciously with Sally's voice in mind, or do you just give it to her and let her take it to her own level?

Always with her voice in mind. As a songwriter, that is one of the most singular muses I have ever found. You have that voice in your head and you know what it can do and what it sounds like doing certain things. It opens up a whole new world. I think most songwriters tend to write in their own voice. They think of their own voice singing it even if they're not singer/songwriters.

Do you do most of your writing on piano?

I do, but like I said, your hands get into a certain habit, and they tend to repeat themselves. Sometimes it's a great exercise to write on a different instrument. I'll pick up a mandolin or guitar or something that I play badly and it definitely tends to open up a different direction that I wouldn't have otherwise gone in.

How large of a role does Brooklyn play in your songwriting?

I think it plays a huge role. I don't think this band could have taken place in any other city but Brooklyn. I don't think that group of people could have found each other in any other place but Brooklyn. And also that it's an urban place, but it's full of this natural wonder and these secret gardens and these courtyards that will have like one beautiful tree in it. To me, that speaks to what the music is trying to accomplish. A lot of the imagery and lyrics are taken from my childhood in Michigan, which was very rural. That to me is just a metaphor for home, which for me is Brooklyn.

When you write with Steve or Gary, do you approach those collaborations any differently? How do you work together as a team?

Each collaboration is very different. It's been great the last five years, growing up together as songwriters. We definitely bounce off one another. But when I collaborate with Gary, he'll usually just have this really great guitar lick and I'll be like, "Whoa, I love that," and I'll take it away and turn it into a song. And with Steve, it's much more back and forth, being in the same room.

So you are more on the same level, so to speak.

In terms of our sensibilities. I think Steve is a very different writer than I am in terms of topics. Steve can write these really happy songs without sounding trite, whereas I tend to write these very dark songs. Lyrically, it's hard to incorporate our voices together, but musically it's fun to sit together and work on songs. On "A-Hunting We Will Go," for example, we worked on the music together and then the lyric was basically mine.

Was recording with the Slovak Radio Orchestra something the band had planned for a while? Did you write the songs thinking that you were going to record with them?

It's funny. I didn't actually write with that in mind. We knew we wanted the sound of this album to have an orchestral palette, in much the same way as those artists I talked about do and some of the other seventies artists we love, like the Carpenters and some of those Tin Pan Alley songwriters… and the way those songs got produced. We knew we wanted to incorporate that sound, but I didn't write it with the orchestra in mind. It was an afterthought. How are we going to take this simple folk song and then take this palette of orchestral instruments and use that? Once the songs were written, we put on our production hats and attacked it that way.

How did you get hooked up with the Slovak Radio Orchestra?

We knew we wanted that sound, and they just don't make rooms like that anymore in the U.S. And even if we could afford it in the U.S., there just are no rooms like that right now. We were asking around and Greg Calbi, who does all of our mastering, had just gotten done doing a project where they use this orchestra. He played us some of it, and it sounded like some of those Ray Charles arrangements. And we were like, "That's it," and we just got in touch with the liaison over there and somehow we made it happen.

Are there any poets who have a direct influence on your work? I think of Robert Frost and Woody Guthrie.

Thank you. I do read poetry. Most lyrics I love tend not to sound great when I read them—they do need to be married to music. Robert Frost is obviously a huge influence, and a lot of the transcendentalist writers. Emerson is a huge influence, although more in philosophy than actual style. Robert Frost is a perfect example of someone who can use an image to convey an emotion. To me that is what I always want to do in my lyrics. I love songs that are like, "I love you baby, why'd you leave me," but to me they're not nearly as interesting as an image that encompasses that.

The tone and mood of your music seems to be almost out of place with what's going on in the world now. Is it meant to be an escapist kind of music?

I guess escapist is one way to look at it. I always look at it as I'm trying to find comfort. Certainly in this world today, the need for comfort is great, to say the least. For myself, the reason I'm making these albums is because I figure if I can write a beautiful enough song and have Sally sing it, maybe I can listen to it someday and feel better about things, and just feel comforted.

Do you have any advice for aspiring young songwriters?

When I was in my twenties, my philosophy was: "Be so good that people won't ignore you." And I thought that was a really clever motto until I realized that people's capacity for ignoring you is pretty endless. So to me you just have to stick with it; it's an endurance thing. You do have to be so good that people can't ignore you… but then you just have to last so that, when they ultimately do take notice, you're still around.

When did you start writing songs?

I've been doing it my whole life. I don't think I found my voice as songwriter until 1999. That's sort of the year that I gave up trying to write cool songs, and just wrote like myself for the first time. I was in all these other bands where every song was like tongue firmly in cheek and there was no honest emotion and everything was ironic and it was all posture, and it was stifling in the end. And I did Hem as a side project to get away from that, to have one project where I was totally not worried about irony or being cool. And that was so liberating to just let go of all the postures that I felt like the world wanted. And then all the sudden I found my voice as a songwriter.

Rhett Miller
Old 97's

Whether fronting his band or making solo records, Rhett Miller has proven himself to be alt.country's most creative voice. His best songs read like good fiction, and his boozy, deftly woven tales of heartbreak and bravado keep fans anxiously awaiting his next batch of songs. Born in Dallas, Texas, Miller displayed a flair for wordplay early on. He briefly attended Sarah Lawrence College on a creative writing scholarship, but his love of music compelled him to drop out and return to Texas. In 1993, he formed the Old 97's in Dallas. They released two independent records, 1994's *Hitchhike to Rhome* and 1995's *Wreck Your Life*, that saw them attracting a growing cult following. Signing with Elektra Records, the band began dialing down the twang and released the critically lauded *Too Far to Care* (1997), *Fight Songs* (1999), and *Satellite Rides* (2001). In 2002, Miller released his major label solo debut, *The Instigator*, on Elektra (his first solo album, a collection of acoustic folk songs named *Mythologies*, appeared in 1989). Working with producer/multi-instrumentalist Jon Brion, Miller proved that his tales could be told just as effectively inside a lush pop framework. In 2004, the Old 97's reunited to release the masterful *Drag It Up*, which became their highest charting album. *Alive & Wired*, their first live disc, followed in 2005. His solo album, *The Believer*, came out in 2006.

—EVAN SCHLANSKY

Interview by
Bill Locey

American Songwriter,
September/October 2004

224

So where does *Drag It Up* fit in with what came before?

I have a hard time getting a perspective on any of our albums. The earliest ones are just now coming into focus for me. *Drag It Up* is the sound of a band that's been together for a long time and has found the way that the machine works for us, you know? I think every decent band is a machine, and we've sort of figured out what we do, each of our respective responsibilities or functions within that context. I think it's a really strong record and I think part of that is that we had a couple of years worth of songs, you know, backlog—some of the songs are old and date back to the early days of the band and sort of got reworked. We really had time to pick out the best songs, which is the most important thing in any album.

It seems that the folks at New West Records at least chose the right songs for singles, unlike your previous labels. "The New Kid," and especially "Won't Be Home," are rockers.

I know. Leave it to an indie to figure out what the best songs are on the record. And yeah, "Won't Be Home," that's a good one. That's what we call a fastball in Old 97's parlance. That one and "Timebomb" [from *Too Far to Care*] are songs we can open or close a set with.

So now you've got a bunch of closer songs— "Timebomb," "Won't Be Home," and "Our Love."

Yeah, but the band doesn't do "Our Love." The band doesn't perform songs off *The Instigator*; that's like the other woman.

Tell me about "Borrowed Bride." That song is a mindbender.

Well, thanks. I just had this one crazy night in a motel. My wife Erica, who was very pregnant, and I were driving from Atlanta to New York so we could move into our new home—anyway, I ended up writing three songs. It was just one of those nights. I was a conduit for something and "Borrowed Bride" was the best thing that came out of that night. There was a black-and-white short film from the forties called *Borrowed Bride*. It was a short, surreal film and for some reason this story just came into my mind about a guy who was married who didn't really know his wife. There may be something going on that he doesn't understand and he's starting to suspect things. It's not autobiographical by any means.

To me, it's about a greedy chick who's working some fool but woke up to temporarily survey the emptiness and went, "Uh-oh."

Yeah—that's good. I have a hard time explaining what my songs are about. My mom does a much better job of explaining my songs than I do.

Maybe you should have your mom write the liner notes.

I really should, actually.

That was a funny quote by your Uncle Ed after your solo album came out: "Rhett's married now, so I guess that's the end of the good songs." So where do all these sad songs come from? People definitely seem to relate to them.

For some reason, I think I'm better at writing that kind of a song than the happy love song—but some of those come out of me, and most of them have a dark lining. I don't know where they come from. Every songwriter I know has some element of manic depression or anxiety disorder. I am not immune to that occupational hazard.

Does bad love make for good songs?

Yeah, yeah, absolutely. Although I'm writing less right now, but I think that has more to do with 7 A.M. feedings.

So do writers need cats?

I think everyone needs a cat, but when you go on tour, the cat hates your guts. I can't have cats anymore. Erica is allergic. I'd love to and I used to write about the cat, but no more. Erica won't allow it. She'll sneeze all day long.

What comes first, music or lyrics?

Usually there's a phrase that suggests a melody and then that melody suggests a larger melody. Sometimes you hear writers say that they're just a vessel or a conduit or a cable box through which God sends his programming. I see it very much as a craft but I do let the song dictate what comes next. Whatever pops into my head may seem like a verse, but then I might write something more meandering, and that has to be the verse; so then the first thing becomes the chorus, which demands a middle break, which needs to go up or down, or something to take the song wherever it needs to go. It's the way novelists talk about their characters writing themselves and being excited as they watch a character unfold because it has a life of its own. It's similar to that—I try to let the song lead me along as opposed to vice versa.

Write. Write. Write as much as you can, because your first hundred songs are going to suck, then they'll get better and better as they go.

So there's no formula?

The worst songs I've ever written are the songs where I had something in mind ahead of time, as in, "I've got to write a rocker with the word 'love' three times in the chorus." Invariably, that's a nightmare because it's not real. If it's not real, the audience on some level knows it. You can't get away with it. Actually, people do get away with it all the time and make shitloads of money, writing these phony-baloney songs.

Who moves you as a writer?

As for young people, I like Ben Kweller, but my old-school favorites are David Bowie, Bob Dylan, the Beatles, Ray Davies, and Hank Williams. And what I love about Hank Williams—people think he's as real as they come—but he used to just buy romance novels and take the plot line and lift phrases from the romance novels and turn it into a song, like "Your Cheatin' Heart." It's not rocket science, and all it has to be is something that can touch somebody and make them feel for three minutes that they're not alone in the world or in their feelings.

What would you tell an aspiring songwriter?

Write. Write. Write as much as you can, because your first hundred songs are going to suck, then they'll get better and better as they go. There are people who have proved that wrong—Neil Young writing "Sugar Mountain" at seventeen. I'm never going to allow my high school record to be re-released.

Roger Miller

Texas-born and Oklahoma-raised, Roger Miller earned enough money picking cotton to buy a guitar at age eleven. He also learned to play fiddle, piano, banjo, and drums. Miller joined the Army during the Korean War and was stationed in South Carolina, and a friend there who had a connection with the country music industry helped set him up with RCA Records A&R boss Chet Atkins.

However, Miller's career really began to take shape on the songwriting end; Buddy Killen signed him to Tree Music Publishing in late 1957, and his songs were cut by Ray Price, Faron Young, Ernest Tubb, Jim Reeves, and many others. By 1965, Roger Miller the recording artist was in full swing—and at the top of the country industry. "King of the Road" was a runaway hit, and songs like "Engine Engine Number Nine," "One Dying and a Buryin'," "England Swings," and "Kansas City Star" were all top ten hits.

In 1985, Miller cracked his way into Broadway with *Big River*, an adaptation of Mark Twain's *Huckleberry Finn* and *Tom Sawyer*. The musical won him two Oscars for Best Musical and Outstanding Score. He passed on in 1991—the result of throat cancer—but he left a strong songwriting legacy for generations to come.

—DOUGLAS WATERMAN

Interview by
Vernell Hackett

American Songwriter,
September/October 1988

How did you get into songwriting?

I grew up not wanting to pull cotton or milk cows; I wanted to write songs and be in the music business. There was something magic about the music business. Sheb Wooley was my brother-in-law and he used to sit around the house and play songs and talk about going to Hollywood and all of that. So I learned to play the fiddle for Minnie Pearl. The first job I had was playing fiddle for Minnie Pearl. Then George Jones started recording my songs… and Ray Price, Jim Reeves, and Ernest Tubb. Then I started writing songs nobody would record, sort of offbeat, and I started recording them myself.

Is there a certain songwriting regimen that you stick to?

I just wrote when the thought hit me, and I tried to have as many songs as I could in a short amount of time. I never was one who could go into an office and sit down and write. I can if I have to, but I don't get the quality of work that I do when I wait for inspiration to hit.

Talk about when Broadway producer Rocco Landesman approached you about turning *Huckleberry Finn* into a Broadway musical. Were you honored that someone would consider you for such an overwhelming project?

Of course I was honored, but I was reluctant to do it. The first thing that caught my attention about him was that he knew every lyric I'd ever written. He would sit around and recite lyrics I had forgotten myself! I'd think about it and he'd write me letters, and it took him about six or eight months to talk me into doing it. What really got me into doing it was that I realized I would regret it the rest of my life [if I didn't]. The script was good, the story was good, and I knew I could pull stuff from it, so I went for it. And in doing

it, I found pieces of myself that I could put into it. It was a great adventure for a year and a half.

Where did the song "River in the Rain" come from?

I had never lived on a river, but it's not hard to close your eyes and imagine sitting on a bank. And I would do that and think about a boy growing up on a river and wondering what he would think… probably the same things I would think as a boy growing up on a concrete river, which was Highway 66 going west in California. I used to see cars on that highway and wonder where they were going and want to go with them, so that's where "River in the Rain" came from, I guess.

Was the structure of writing Broadway music numbers vastly different from how you approach songs regularly?

The structure is different because in a play, you have the framework of the script to work within. As I got into it, I could see and feel the music. I found that I could look at the story and write music like I did for the Walt Disney movie *Robin Hood*. I also had a setup where they would say they needed a song here or there, and we'd reprise a little bit of it in another place. I didn't just write the songs for where they had song suggestions; I couldn't go by those, I had to go on my own. And the directors and producers… all of us would sit down after I'd write songs, and they would place them in the script at certain places. It was all very interesting.

Is there a difference between a good song and a great song?

A good song is well crafted and singable and nice, but a great song blows your hair. A great song comes at you. Someone can sing you something and you know it's a good song, but you hear something else and you just know it's great. Great songs usually have less words. They just say, "Your cheatin' heart will make you weep, you cry and cry and try to sleep…" That's a great song because it doesn't say what you're doing now is going to cause you anguish in the future.

You've said in the past that you can measure a good song by how well children respond to it.

I noticed in the early sixties that little children liked my music more than the grown-ups did. I really looked hard at that because I knew that they were going to live longer than their parents. I have a silliness about me that allows me to be flippant with music. I think good writers are the ones that can really look at life and laugh and really know where a song comes from.

you imagine what he thought the first time he heard them as marches?

Do you like it when an artist who records your songs puts a different take on it?

When I started writing, the first thing I noticed was that they always came out different when somebody recorded it. I thought, "Wow," or "That's great," because George Jones [had recorded a song]. I'd think, "Wow, I didn't know I wrote that." 'Cause you know, a guy puts his artistry into a song and it becomes a different song. So I always like to leave room so an artist can put their mark on the song.

A good song is well crafted and singable and nice, but a great song blows your hair. A great song comes at you.

Is there such a thing as being born a songwriter?

I've seen people learn the craft from ground one like Hank Cochran. He was just dabbling with songwriting when he came to town, and he learned. I've seen guys who never thought about songwriting get interested in it and start learning and then go to the top of the game with it. I don't know what makes a songwriter except a good heart and a little intelligence.

Did you teach yourself to write by studying your heroes?

I was always interested in Hank Williams, Sr., Stephen Foster, John Philip Sousa, and what caused those guys to write. Rumor has it that Sousa wrote all his songs as ballads. Can

Stuart Murdoch

Belle and Sebastian

Interview by
William T. Wallace

American Songwriter,
March/April 2006

Scottish pop outfit Belle and Sebastian first formed in 1996 for a school project, under the false assumption that they would release two albums and break up. A decade later, the band is still going strong, having earned a steady cult following and the undying love of both the United Kingdom and United States's music press. The seven-piece band was founded in Glasgow by singer/songwriter Stuart Murdoch, who was asked to produce an album for a university-sponsored music business course. The result, the sonically and lyrically striking *Tigermilk*, became a highly coveted purchase upon its release in 1996. Belle and Sebastian's second full-length album, *If You're Feeling Sinister*, followed at the end of that year. A deal with U.S. label Matador Records resulted in 1998's *The Boy With the Arab Strap*, one of the most highly regarded albums in alternative rock. 2003 found them teaming with eighties record producer Trevor Horn for *Dear Catastrophe Waitress*, and in 2006, they garnered some of their strongest reviews to date with the imaginative *The Life Pursuit*.

—EVAN SCHLANSKY

In the past, you have made assertions that you would retire if your albums didn't sell, or, as you put it, "go gold in the States." Where your music can be described as "pop," it is nonetheless not the archetypal sort of accessible pop you hear on the radio. Do you think your music could achieve mainstream appeal in the United States?

The thing that has been proven again and again is that I don't know shit. It's a mystery to me. The thing is, perhaps our music would have been acceptable to the mainstream in the late sixties, early seventies, but perhaps now it's a little bit strange.

Dear Catastrophe Waitress sort of dispelled the myth that you were, in essence, a lo-fi band. *The Life Pursuit* appears to take it to the next level—further beyond the rustic buzz and accidental distortion, if you will. Were you attempting to form a more sophisticated, hi-fi sound?

Yeah, that would be fair. I think it's the production. It has nothing to do with whether we have an orchestra on the album or a harp or dancing girls. It sounds chunky. It sounds right. It sounds permanent. You get a good performance out of the band. It just sounds like a record that could be on the radio and just play and play.

I want to reference your online diary for a moment. You referred to the band as being "late bloomers." I am curious what you meant by that—as songwriters? As performers?

Well, perhaps it is a little bit misleading. Some groups, by the time they actually put a record out, their image is already formed and the record company knows what to do with them and they know each other well. But Belle and Sebastian, we sort of fell together in 1996 and three months later, we had our debut LP. And so, it took a long time to get to know each other. I think it feels like we finally have got the best out of each other.

Your sound is thicker, with more elements of buoyancy than previous recordings. How much did Tony Hoffer, your producer, help shape this new Belle and Sebastian sound?

A lot. You have to give acknowledgment where you should, to the production. We were in a good place and playing well together and Tony was exactly right. He would tell me to drop a couple verses out of this song and maybe forget about this song… and the group would kind of snicker because they were too afraid to tell me themselves. It is quite a risk and we could have sent him back to Los Angeles. But he was right and he proved it. He knew what the hell he was doing.

As I have come to understand, you are the primary songwriter.

There is collaboration in the writings of these songs, but I did write quite a lot of the stuff.

Is that collaboration developing more and more?

It specifically came around when two of the original band members left. Then we became a really confident group and we could help each other when we needed help. It has stayed at that level for the last four years.

The new album seems to have a menagerie of influences, from an atmospheric Bowie to the funky, laid-back blues of George Clinton, a late-seventies vibe. As you wrote the various songs that ultimately ended up on *The Life Pursuit*, what artists helped inform such songwriting?

I wasn't listening to anything when I wrote the stuff. I was just listening to the sound in my head. It sounds arrogant, but I need silence to write. I don't want to hear anything. It's the group that brings the influences. It's the players that bring influences to the table.

Religious sentiments abound in this, your seventh release, from images of the good book to "Act of the Apostle," parts one and two. What was the impetus for these images and this sort of focus?

That's just something that interests me. I just like it. I like thinking about it. I don't know why particularly this time there is a quite a lot of references to the Bible and spirituality. But it does. I think there is something common with songwriting. It inhabits a similar air. To me, songwriting comes from somewhere else. You go to bed at night and say your prayers then you wake up and you've got a song. It's an elliptical process.

How much of you, Stuart Murdoch the person, goes into the characters and personas you create through your lyrics?

Perhaps some of the older songs and characters, there was more of me that went into them. But as I've gotten older, matured in some sort of way, I have achieved more separation from the characters. I do see them as slightly more cin-

ematic. I feel that I could make a little film about each one of those characters if anybody was interested.

What does the title of your album, *The Life Pursuit,* **come from?**

It's a bit of a funny one. It was the name of one of the songs we recorded. It was always the key song and it was going to be on the record. I liked the feeling you got from it. It had a comforting message. But then in the end it didn't go on the record. We kept the title.

To me, songwriting comes from somewhere else. You go to bed at night and say your prayers then you wake up and you've got a song. It's an elliptical process.

Michael Martin Murphey

Oak Cliff, Texas, native Michael Martin Murphey said recently that he didn't really feel he knew what the lyrics of his most famous song, 1975's "Wildfire," really meant until decades after he had penned it during a long, sleepless night in Los Angeles. Given his upbringing and early life, this sense of mystery and wonder make perfect sense. Murphey grew up in Dallas with dreams of becoming a Baptist minister. To that end, he went to the University of North Texas in nearby Denton and majored in Greek.

In 1965 he left Texas for Hollywood, where he landed a gig writing songs for Screen Gems. He penned "What Am I Doin' Hangin' 'Round?" for the Monkees; hung out with Jackson Browne, the Eagles, and Linda Ronstadt; and eventually teamed with Boomer Castleman and had a minor hit with "I Feel Good (I Feel Bad)" under the stage name The Lewis & Clarke Expedition in 1967.

But it was a 1971 move to Austin that really changed Murphey's life. It was there he became part of a remarkable alternative country scene, and his writing flourished as A&M Records signed him to a deal. The song "Cosmic Cowboy" came in this period, but by 1974, Murphey had left Austin for Colorado. In 1979 he relocated again—this time to New Mexico. In 1982, his ballad "What's Forever For" gave Murphey a long overdue number one single as an artist.

—PHIL SWEETLAND

Interview by
Kelly Delaney

American Songwriter,
July/August 1987

233

Someone once told me they remember you used to spend a lot of time in your high school library researching song ideas. Do you still do that?

Everybody's got a different method. Some people sit down and turn personal experience, but I also do a lot of research and reading on my songs. I always want to make sure that the language in the song is as rich as I can possibly make it.

Can you elaborate on your methodology a bit?

Once I start a song, I may have a general idea and a sketchy sort of direction I'm going with it. When I've got a concept, then I'll buy some books or go to the library and read those books that I feel are connected with the same general idea. I'll try to pick up just the general feeling of language that surrounds the same kind of concept. It really helps me finish the song, particularly since a lot of my songs are graphic in image.

Would you cite an example of a song you wrote through doing some heavy research?

I wrote a song, which was never a hit, called "Natural Bridges." It was on my album called *Swans Against The Sun*. The whole song came out of an article in *National Geographic* about the countryside surrounding Arches National Monument and Natural Bridges [National Monument]. I was trying to make "Natural Bridges" into an image of natural bridges between two people, things that connect us that we would never think of. In it, I used a lot of imagery from nature that I got from this article in *National Geographic*. Although I'd been to those places before, there's a separation between language and direct experience. Sometimes you don't pick up the words from an experience that maybe somebody else has.

How much does this contribute to your songwriting?

I think that's where I pick up at least half of the ideas I have for songs. Believe it or not—and I'm probably gonna catch some flack for this—but a great source of ideas for songs is watching soap operas on television, if you can manage to sit through them. Once in a while I'll watch a whole day's worth of soap operas and reflect directly on the vernacular of what's happening right now in the social structure of our society. Most of them are about interpersonal relationships, and most songs are also. I'd say that has value in the direction of the more commercial songs.

That's one way to get over writer's block.

I used to experiment when I was a staff songwriter at Screen Gems years ago. You talk about writer's block; we devised a lot of experiments to try to unblock ourselves. One thing we would do… two of three of us would sit down on a Monday afternoon and turn on the soap operas, but turn off the sound, and try to make up the dialogue to what they were saying. Sometimes we'd laugh so much we wouldn't take too many notes. But we would tape it and then we'd go back a week later and listen to the dialogue we'd made up while we were watching these images. The dialogue often led to good ideas for songs—catchphrases or at least good lines in songs.

A good line can be as valuable as a hook.

I think a lot of songwriters tend to collect titles—ideas for titles of songs. What they don't often do, and what I've learned I have to do, is collect good ideas for lines in songs also. Movies and books are just a tremendous source for that. Often, I'll think of what the hook should be just from collecting good lines.

Another experiment we used to do was we'd go to the library and check out twenty books at random. It would almost be like a game. We would get four or five people together and each pick up a book and round-robin, and we'd try to string phrases together out of these books.

Sometimes it would come out total garble, but it was a focus on the fun of expression. Sometimes if you're not inspired, there are other things you can do until the inspiration comes.

Ideas are everywhere if you're open to them.

I'll go out as a songwriter and interview people. If I meet an interesting old man or woman who's had a lot of experience, or an interesting character like a truck driver, I'll sit down and say, "Hey, I'm a songwriter, could you just tell me what it's like to be a truck driver?" or a waitress, or a cowboy, or whatever.

Have you done that recently?

I was on a train going out west about six months ago, and I met two hobos, nineteen and twenty years old. I started talking with them and asked what it was like to be a hobo in our modern times. I ended up missing the train and taking another. The point I'm getting at is that there is no experience in life, no place you can go that there's not a song hiding in there somewhere.

Sometimes if you're not inspired, there are other things you can do until the inspiration comes.

Tom T. Hall is known for going out in the real world to find song ideas.

When you talk to other songwriters or other people in the business all the time, or just to your peers, their vernacular is limited to what we talk about. Those interesting words and phrases, the jargon of other kinds of work, are not gonna pop out at you on Music Row. A book is a way of having a vicarious experience of somebody else's life, but it's also really good to directly meet those characters.

"Desert Rat" is a song about one of those characters you once met, isn't it?

I used to go out and make tapes of things he said. He's the one who said, "Success is survival." He was a miner until he retired and lived out in the desert all of his life with no electricity. Somebody who's done that for fifty years has got a lot of interesting things to say. The song is part something he said, part a tribute to him, and part a tribute to his wife, who put him up with him all those years out there in the desert.

So the song came from direct experience and your interpretation of it.

I never would have come up with the images in the song if I hadn't actually been there. Like the lines, "She waits on the front porch of the old house that stands scorched, her old man fillin' the sun with rattlesnakes and keepsakes, boxes of cornflakes, old beat up door frames, bleached bones and rocks in the sun." That kind of imagery comes from going there and seeing what those old desert rats had around their house. Being able to string those together gives you something you can hold onto to give the listener a way to get into the song.

In a way, some songs are like mini-novels.

The difference between what we do and what a novelist does is… we don't have as much time, so we have to look for that one little phrase that capitalizes or crystallizes the whole thing—a word, a phrase, or an image we can hang the whole experience around that sort of tells us everything about it. You can't know the whole life of the guy in "Mr. Bojangles," so the images of the guy—his pants, the way he walks and

talks—become the story of his life. That's probably my favorite song ever written, just because the description of a few images gives you a sense of the guy's whole life.

Do you rewrite your songs very much?

Yeah, I do. In my position, being a recording artist—if I'm writing for myself—I wait until the last possible minute. I

> *The difference between what we do and what a novelist does is… we don't have as much time, so we have to look for that one little phrase that capitalizes or crystallizes the whole thing…*

don't consider it finished until I've laid the final vocal and we know we have to mix and turn it in by such and such a date so it can be released. I'm always rewriting and re-editing. What can end up happening is that years later you may say, "This song would have really been better if I'd done this." What you have to think is that a really good first verse [could] end up being a better last verse.

You did that with "Geronimo's Cadillac," didn't you?

Yeah, just thinking it through, the way it flows on stage, I found after singing it for ten years that it made more sense if I reversed a few lines. I think that an important trick in songwriting is to get a lot of verses down and interchange them. Often, what you think is a really good first verse ends up being a better last verse.

Songwriters need to be flexible for their own best interests.

The thing that annoys me most about songwriters, and I've had to learn this lesson the hard way, is that the more successful songwriters—particularly ones who are pitching songs to artists—are unwilling to change, to work with you. I've seen people blow a really good chance at an album cut or a single just because they were unwilling to change a line or something. You have to make a decision as a songwriter: depending on what it's being used for, [should I go ahead and change this]? That's the way I look at a song; I look at a song as a child that grows.

How did "Geronimo's Cadillac" come about?

It really started with a photograph I saw of Geronimo sitting in a Cadillac, which came out of his autobiography, *Geronimo: His Own Story.*

It's such a vivid title.

The two images together—Geronimo and a Cadillac—just struck me as a song title. It was every irony I could ever think of about our culture in two words—their attempt to make of him what we would define as a civilized person. That was the reason they put him in a Cadillac in the first place. He was actually in jail at the time.

It makes a valid case study of history.

I think studying history is really valuable for songwriters. It has been for me. A lot of my songs are really nothing more than comments on something that happened a long time ago. I may be a fool for assuming that people care, but I think they generally do, especially when you're talking about somebody as well known as Geronimo. If we worried about not talking about anything that didn't happen today, then there would be no gospel songs, either; Jesus lived two thousand years ago.

photo courtesy Greg Kessler

My Morning Jacket

The Louisville, Kentucky, band My Morning Jacket has earned critical accolades and a rabid fan following due to their ongoing sonic adventurism and attention to songcraft. With a sound reminiscent of Neil Young played through an echo chamber, the band, led by singer/songwriter Jim James, debuted in 1999 with *The Tennessee Fire*. Their second album, 2001's *At Dawn,* saw them refining and expanding their high-lonesome sound, and garnered strong reviews. In 2003, after touring with the Foo Fighters and Guided by Voices, they signed to Dave Matthews's ATO Records and released the sprawling *It Still Moves.* My Morning Jacket underwent a lineup change in 2004 that saw the departure of James's cousin Johnny Quaid and keyboardist Danny Cash, who were replaced by Bo Koster and Carl Broemel. The new Jacket—now consisting of singer-guitarist-songwriter James, keyboardist Koster, guitarist Broemel, bassist Two-Tone Tommy, and drummer Patrick Hallahan—proved a potent combo and scored their best reviews to date with 2005's adventurous Z. A double live album, *Okonokos*, was released in 2006.

—EVAN SCHLANSKY

Interview by
Benjy Eisen

American Songwriter,
November/December 2005

Was the songwriting process for *Z* different from any of your previous albums?

James: Not really any different. It just started off with me coming up with stuff and then bringing it to the guys.

So you write stuff by yourself first—you mean with an acoustic guitar?

James: Yeah, I have an acoustic guitar, keyboards, drum machine—it's really everything—electric guitars. The four-track is really my main songwriting tool.

Do you come up with a full demo?

James: It's a shitty demo, yeah. Sometimes I do a quality demo but most of the time I just lay all the ideas out, like the first set of lyrics and my attempt at rhythm and whatever ideas I have going on. And then I just kind of show that to the guys and they make it "real."

Do they add to the songwriting process? Can they modify or change things?

James: It depends on the song, because some songs I have a real strict vision of what I want to happen and other songs I don't and they add their thing to it.

So you even write the bass line?

James: It just depends on the song, but most of the time I have a pretty clear picture of what I want to happen. I don't always write the bass lines, though. That's one thing that [Two-Tone Tommy, MMJ's bassist] usually does.

Do you write on the road or…

James: Off the road.

Are you the type of songwriter who schedules songwriting sessions? I know some songwriters

will, for example, go to the beach or a cabin for a few days just to work up songs.

James: No, I can't do that because a song just comes when it's going to come, you know? I've been on vacation in some of the most beautiful places and never got a song. Or I've had the worst day and I'm just running around doing errands and a song will just pop in my head and I'll just have to write it down.

John Leckie produced *Z*. How much control did you give him in terms of the songwriting? Do you let him tinker with the arrangements?

James: No, not at all. He was more the quality control guy—you know, he made sure it sounded good, made sure we gave good performances. But he really didn't give any input on the song structure itself. He could've, but he said we did fine with that.

The band's lineup changed last year. Did that affect your songwriting at all? Did you write differently to account for the personal styles of a new keyboardist and guitarist?

James: It didn't really affect my songwriting, because I kind of just started off with the songs the same way I always would—that always starts off as a process just by myself. But then the execution of it was different. Bo and Carl are just different people thinking different ways. I feel like they really brought a lot to the table because they were thinking about the whole picture, not just their parts, and we would all talk about what everybody was doing. And that was the coolest thing. Most of the time, in the past, John [Quaid, previous guitarist] and I would talk about the whole thing as a picture more than the band would. But now I feel like all of us discuss everybody's parts. We try to come to the best thing we can do, where everybody's happy.

When you came up with the name "My Morning Jacket," you wrote it down in a notebook of songs that, you said, you knew weren't going to be for the band that you were in at the time. How did you know they were for your next band? Were they different stylistically or were you just saving the best stuff for a better band?

James: Well, My Morning Jacket was more than just a thought process. It was never a band in the beginning. I was in a band and I had songs that didn't work with that band, so I just started making them on my four-track and playing the drums myself, as shittily as I could, and playing keyboard drums, or using drum machines, or using no drums and just doing it acoustic—My Morning Jacket started out, for me, more as recordings, and playing open mic nights and acoustic shows and stuff like that. So it started more as a project than a band. Eventually my cousin started helping me and he played a couple open mic nights with me and then we were like, "Well, let's get a drummer and a bass player." And it just kind of snowballed into a band.

What was the hardest song for you to nail in the studio this time?

James: We only had one song out of this batch that didn't work and that never got recorded. They all have varying degrees of difficulty. "Lay Low" took a long time because we had a lot of drum machine issues that we were trying to work out. We finally made our own loop, a different loop, and then once we did that we nailed it on the first take. It's just a matter of working with something until we get it right.

Hallahan: "Gideon" was another one that took a lot of hammering out and figuring out where we were going to put stuff. Just trying to nail that and trying to put down something that's going to last forever, you want to make it right.

On some songs on Z— "Off the Record" would be one, "Dondante" would be another—there are lush instrumental parts that emerge out of the tail. How much of that was prewritten as opposed to opening it up on the spot?

James: I'd say somewhere in between. The end of "Off the Record" is pretty planned out; we always kind of stay within that structure. And then "Dondante" kind of just evolved itself over a series of jams.

Hallahan: Wouldn't you say that for both of those, we had ideas? We knew there was going to be something there. In that sense, it was planned out. But what was there just kind of grew over a period of time.

Many bands, when they jam, tend to go back into the song, like bring it back to the head or close it with a chorus. I think it's really interesting how you ride the jam out to the end. Do you play around with that at all?

James: I was thinking about that the other day because, most of the time, I hear a song that starts with a jam and then it goes through like seven or eight minutes before the song comes in. A lot of those songs I don't really like. I think there's only a few times where I've heard that work. We've never really done that. I think it's cool when a song comes back in sometimes, after a jam, but I don't know, it usually just kind of happens that way. In my mind, the jam has always been at the end.

Hallahan: Because of the crescendo. I think this album has lots of songs that start at a certain point and then crescendo and then kind of taper off at the end, and that's kind of the way we were moving musically on this album.

I think it also, for me as a listener, avoids the clichés that bands can step into when recording

jams. With some tracks on Z, it seems more like the songs end but the music keeps going.

Koster: Yeah, the other way almost comes from the jazz school, where you play the head of a song and then you improvise on the chords of the song structure and then you go back into the head. That's kind of the classic way to do it. [*To James*] I kind of like the way we do it better. Because the jam comes after you've said what you have to say and it's like, why go back and say that whole song over again?

James: It's been established.

Koster: The song takes you somewhere and then that's what gives you the inspiration to improvise and play with it.

Reverb is so central to your sound. Do you remember when you first discovered it as an effect?

James: I don't think I even thought of it consciously, but when I listen to my favorite music, most of it has reverb all over it. Like Marvin Gaye. I was just listening to Leonard Cohen last night and realized I never paid attention to the fact that there's tons of reverb on his voice.

Do you remember when you first experimented with reverb in your own music?

James: Just being a kid, I think somebody left the reverb on on the amp I was getting ready to sing through, and I turned it up all the way and sang through it and it sounded amazing. I couldn't believe it. It was like a key was unlocked. And ever since then I hated singing without reverb. Reverb *is* singing to me. I don't ever sing without reverb, even if I'm at home. I hate it whenever I have to sing without it—it's torture.

You famously used a silo to record reverb in the past. Did you continue to use that method on Z?

James: No, because we don't have that studio anymore.

How important are your lyrical meanings to you in relation to the songs?

James: Lyrics are really important because if you have stupid lyrics you can ruin a song. But some songs are really great to have stupid lyrics. Like, I don't know, a good love song with lyrics that you've heard somebody say a million times. Depending on how it's produced and how it's arranged, it can still be amazing. I'm just into the whole package. Everything means everything to me—the rhythm, the production, how everything sounds. All of that stuff is equally important and just as important as the lyrics. And nothing is really more important, so I don't know. I just think lyrics are another fun way of trying to be weird, trying to say something. But I try to say something with the melody first.

Do you ever write the lyrics before the music?

James: No, it's always the melody and the song structure. I'll get a line or two of the lyrics and then I'll just start singing subconsciously and I won't even think about it and then I'll go back to the four-track and play back the tape and try to guess what I was saying. Sometimes I'll write it down and it'll turn into a neat thing.

Patrick and Bo, when Jim brings you a song, do you go over the lyrics and think about the meaning? Or does that come later?

Hallahan: I feel like it probably depends on the song. Sometimes the melody or the parts are so driven and so overwhelming that trying to figure out how you're going to capture that and accentuate it becomes more of an issue than figuring out what he's saying. Sometimes, for me personally, I don't figure out what he's saying until much, much later on.

Do you ever discuss the lyrics or the meanings? I've interviewed bands before where they each

think a song means a different thing, and I always thought that was great because a good song should be able to mean different things, even to its creators.

Hallorhan: Exactly.

James: Well, yeah, that's the thing about lyrics—I always try to make my lyrics kind of vague so it doesn't matter. You don't just have to be me to listen to them. I like to think that they could all be playing it and one of them will think it's about a candy store or one of them will think it's about a drug or whatever, because it's all about what you get out of it. It doesn't really matter what I want you to get out of it—that's just my interpretation. Those are definitely my favorite lyrics, the ones that are less specific and more abstract. Music is abstract.

power—whether you're reading a good book or listening to a great record or seeing a great movie or having a great conversation with a friend—that makes the great moments in life amazing. There are so many moments in life and so many of them are mediocre, you know? If you have a string of relationships, some of your girlfriends you just like and think they're nice, and some of them you are madly in love with. It's like putting on your favorite record and *loving* it vs. just listening to a record that is kind of okay. And I think whatever that *love* is, whatever that amazing power is, is God to me. It's life and it's what it's all about. It's all I'm ever searching for, just that feeling again and again. And I want it again and again and again.

> *I'm just into the whole package. Everything means everything to me—the rhythm, the production, how everything sounds. All of that stuff is equally important and just as important as the lyrics.*

You were brought up with a religious upbringing, but I've heard you say before that you get your spirituality through music. How do you think the two converge?

James: I think there's some force that powers everything and I don't have a name for it and I don't know what it is, but I think there's some force that powers everybody and everything and there's that goodness. And there's some magic

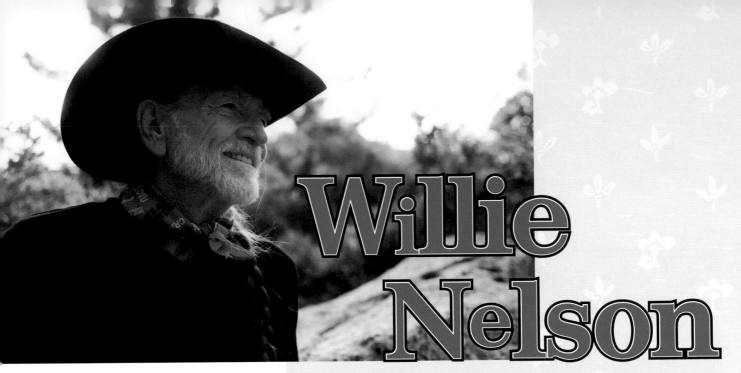

photo courtesy Jim Herrington

Willie Nelson

Interview by
Vernell Hackett

American Songwriter,
September/October 1984

Willie Nelson is a national treasure and one of the most influential songwriters of the twentieth century. He grew up in central Texas, hearing the music of the Grand Ole Opry on the radio and from Texas superstars like Ernest Tubb and Bob Wills at local appearances.

Ever since he was a little kid, Nelson had written songs. By the fifties, he wrote full-fledged gems like "Night Life"—a song so popular that even Frank Sinatra cut it—and "Family Bible." He moved to Nashville in 1960, met songwriter Hank Cochran and others including Patsy Cline, Billy Walker, and Faron Young, and two years later signed his first major recording contract with Liberty Records. Nelson's jazz-flavored pop song "Crazy," popularized by Patsy Cline, remains one of the most famous songs and performances in country history.

Among countless highlights of his remarkable career are albums *Red Headed Stranger, Wanted! The Outlaws* (the first record in country history to sell a million albums), and his collection of jazz standards, *Stardust*.

Nelson has also played terrific movie roles in *The Electric Horseman* and *Wag the Dog*. He remains a vital force, touring with Bob Dylan in 2005 at minor league ballparks, releasing a reggae album, and recording chart-topping duets with singers such as Toby Keith ("Beer for My Horses"). His most recent releases include 2005's *Songs* and 2006's *You Don't Know Me: The Songs of Cindy Walker*.

—PHIL SWEETLAND

What do you think about the new Kris Kristofferson movie [*Trouble in Mind*]? Is it a typical blown-out-of-proportion Hollywood production?

I think probably *Songwriter* [the 1984 movie that Nelson starred in with Kristofferson] may be a little more honest. The fact that Kris is there adds a little more authenticity to the movie, since I think he's probably one of the greatest. But other than that, it's a real story. We tell a lot of jokes with the music, but it's a real story. We tell a lot of jokes with the music we play, but the songs written in there are real songs. Most of the songs are new ones that either Kris or I wrote. I wrote "The Songwriter" and "Who'll Buy My Memories?" and "Write Your Own Songs."

So you contributed a good amount of material?

Then he made up some of his own. Between the two of us, we put it together. It's not really supposed to be accurate, but it just turns out it's pretty autobiographical.

What do you look for in good songs to cut, aside from your own?

I have to really like a song to cut it. Most of the time, I look to see if I have anything of my own to record, and if I'm not too lazy, I'll write something. A lot of time you get too lazy if there's nothing there, so you start looking for other songs. Instinctively I start looking for songs that I like already, songs I've known for a while, and that's why the standards are always coming up. It seems like whenever I didn't write a song, I could go find a good standard somewhere. It's worked so far; I hope it continues.

Do you feel like people are writing "standards" these days?

There are a lot of good songs coming along, like "Wind Beneath My Wings." There are a lot of them being written by songwriters like Rodney Crowell, Billy Joe Shaver… and Kris is writing. There are just a lot of great new songs being written now. But whenever it's time for me to go in the studio and I need something quickly, I don't have time to run to Nashville and get all the songwriters together and hear all the new tunes. So, I either have to have heard them before on the radio or at a party, or else I'll do a standard.

> *I have to really like a song to cut it. Most of the time, I look to see if I have anything of my own to record, and if I'm not too lazy, I'll write something.*

Does it bother you that you don't have time to listen to new material and discover new writers?

No, it doesn't bother me, because I'm a songwriter myself and I've tried to get my songs recorded all my life and I am still. Any time I hear of a guy in town looking for a song, I'll pitch him one. But if I've got something of my own when I'm recording, I'll do that first. I think everybody should. If you've got something good, you ought to do it because it's a new song, and if there's another song you like by a new writer, do it. I wouldn't refuse to do it because it's a new song, for sure. Any time I hear a good new song like "Always on My Mind," I want to do it.

Is it important to know what's going on commercially and on the radio?

A songwriter can listen to the radio and find out what's being played and what's commercially good. If you need to pay the rent, you've got to be commercial, and there's nothing shameful about that. A guy shouldn't run from the word "commercial" too fast… people who think they know what's commercial sometimes get bogged down in their own daily business and bookkeeping and they forget—or just don't take the time—to go out and see what the people are really wanting to hear. I think what you hear on the radio is what people want, eventually. I think mostly what you hear is what

Do you remember the first thing you ever wrote?

It was a poem, and I don't really remember why I wrote it. I just thought everybody wrote poems. I wrote a lot of poems until I learned to play the guitar, and then I started putting melodies to them. I really have no idea what the motivation was… it was just something I wanted to do. I loved the music and I always thought I could write songs. I wrote about things I couldn't have known anything about. What do you know about when you're four or five years old?

> *I wrote a lot of poems until I learned to play the guitar, and then I started putting melodies to them.*

is demanded. There's a lot of hype, too, where the record company hypes you into thinking it's a hit when it ain't. But you can't fool the people, not too often. They'll buy it once but they won't buy it again.

Do you have any advice for aspiring songwriters?

Go home [*smiles*]. It doesn't matter what I tell them; they're going to do it, and if they've got it, they'll make it.

What's your take on the current songwriting scene?

There are young writers out there and they're still learning. There are some young Kris Kristoffersons out there, but I don't think they're any better or worse than when I started out. The competition is rougher today. I had it much easier than a songwriter has it today. There are more of us around today. I've never been given any advice about songwriting. There ain't nobody to go ask about that.

Randy Newman

Randy Newman, a keen social critic known for his wry, caustic wit, is virtually an American institution. He got his start at seventeen, as a staff writer for a Los Angeles music publishing house. His first album, 1968's *Randy Newman*, initially sold poorly but created a buzz in industry circles, and soon his songs were being covered by artists like Ray Charles, Peggy Lee, and Wilson Pickett. 1977's *Little Criminals* featured Newman's first big chart hit, "Short People." The eighties saw Newman move into composing film scores, earning him a Grammy for his score for *The Natural*. In the nineties, Newman branched into animated films, providing memorable music for movies like *A Bug's Life, Toy Story 2,* and *Monsters, Inc.* But Newman never stopped making pop records, garnering critical acclaim with albums like 1988's *Land of Dreams* and 1999's *Bad Love*. In 2003, he released *The Randy Newman Songbook Vol. 1,* on which he revisited many of his favorites, including "Sail Away," "I Think It's Going to Rain Today," and "You Can Leave Your Hat On." Newman also wrote the score for the soundtrack for Pixar's film *Cars* in 2006.

—EVAN SCHLANSKY

Interview by
Paul Zollo

American Songwriter,
May/June 2006

You've been writing songs now for decades. Do you find it ever gets easier?

It's always easy for me when I have an assignment, a movie assignment. Everything I've ever written for a movie has come relatively easy. And once you get started on something, for yourself, sometimes that will go quickly. But starting can be difficult. I haven't *learned* anything that I didn't know before. The real secret to that, like so much else, is stamina. Hanging in there. And showing up every day. With a movie deadline, you have no choice. And what it does is—for motion picture composers, a lot of them—when you don't *have* to do anything, after having to do something *every day, every day, every day*—James Newton Howard just did *King Kong* in four weeks—so when you don't *have* to do anything, you don't want to do *anything*.

So you haven't been working on any songs for yourself?

I got a few. But it's coming funny. Usually I write a really simple kind of country song to start with, and I have done that. But I'm leaving them. I'm not a good finisher anymore. I'm not finishing off the three or four that I have. I'm *hoping* that I'll have a better idea.

But it takes stamina to stick with it?

It takes stamina to go in there and sit, and work at it, unless you're optimistic about a final result. I'll start and it will sound *terrible* to me, absolutely *terrible*. I never think I'm gonna get anywhere with what I'm playing, where things are taking me. No plan. So it makes you want to quit and do something else. Particularly when you don't exactly *have* to do it. The world isn't waiting for the next Newman record—like, you've *got* to have this record. Those days are gone for the whole record business.

I saw Paul Simon play at some special memorial kind of thing, and I also heard James Taylor—on the last picture

I did, he sang a song—and both those guys—Simon did "Bridge Over Troubled Water" but he was playing different kind of chords with it—when I get a song, I don't mess with it, I leave it alone, but I admire him, both those guys, for looking for chords other than I-IV-V-I. It's not easy. They're trying to find something *better,* not just taking what comes. Sometimes you just take what comes, and that's the best thing to do. Not revise.

You write fully orchestral scores for motion pictures. Is that because you think an orchestra is the best medium for a movie?

For the ones I've been given. There are some movies for which straight rock 'n' roll would be best—a movie about young people or modern life, urban-style stuff. I love an orchestra in what I've done; I've thought it was the right thing.

With animated films such as *Monsters, Inc.* and *Toy Story 2*, your music brings a human warmth to movies that have no humans on the screen.

That's *exactly* what they wanted. And *exactly* what they were worried about. That's what you *always* try to do. The characters in those pictures are adults. *Toy Story 2* is a kid's movie, but their emotions… you take them seriously.

Do you start a score by writing melodic motifs for certain characters? In *Monsters, Inc.*, for example, you have a beautiful motif whenever the little girl Boo is onscreen.

Yeah, but she's late in the picture. In *Monsters* nothing really good happens for a long time. There isn't a consonant, straight-out chord for a long time. There is for some establishing stuff, but then it's in danger for a long time. But I might be able to unify things more if I did do something like that. Sometimes I'll write themes that are related, but it isn't motific development. Sometimes it will be a sound more than a melodic motif. Like, the pizzicato on *Desperate Housewives* [by Steve Jablonsky] is a sound, irrespective of the notes they're playing. I've done that for pictures. If you can [add warmth], you've done what you're supposed to do. I don't want [the audience] listening to me instead of looking at the movie, *ever*. But you want to *count* for something. When they're running down the hallway, write something that runs them down the hallway and increases the heartbeat of someone in the audience.

In many of your scores, certain melodies are prominent but they don't take away from the image.

Yeah, I don't think that takes away from the image. It's such a miniscule part of the whole… the music. They turn it down to a level where you can't hear it anyway. Like in *A Bug's Life*, the dragonfly sounds like a B-29. I can't hear what I did. So you might as well write a melody. Sometimes you don't want it. But in most cases, like the scenes with Boo, she's got a little tune for her that isn't just aimless wandering.

That "melodicism" might be why people come to you.

Yeah, but I've been offered mostly comedies. I've been typecast. What I do best, probably, would *be* a movie like *Pride & Prejudice* or *Brokeback Mountain* or *Cinderella Man*— something where if they want that kind of stuff, I can do it. But this other action-comedy stuff is goddamn hard, these Pixar movies. *Cars* wasn't quite so hard, because they didn't have feet. My cousin Tommy [Newman] lucked out in that [*Finding Nemo*] was underwater. *Monsters* was really hard because they're running around. And *A Bug's Life* was like *three times* the size of the average score, because they're *really* moving. And it doesn't look right if you don't move *with* them. There's a school of thought that says, no, you don't

have to [move with them]. But in an animated picture, you *do*. I don't think there's any way around it. You don't *always* have to move when a grasshopper is flying after an ant, but it doesn't look right to me if you don't.

Do you always compose on piano?

No. I used to, before the synths were around. But I'll write on a synth and then put it down on paper. If it's an action scene, nothing's gonna make enough noise for you, usually, but brass. It just won't. There just isn't anything else besides brass and percussion. Woodwinds are just not gonna do it. So you play a brass figure [on synth]. I come from a background and a family that would have *hated* that. You get used to any modality. I was always scared when I'd write an oboe solo, and I'd worry about a million different things. With a synth, it isn't particularly accurate, especially in my versions. I'm not good at using a synth, but I'll listen to it, and I'll still put it on paper so I can see it.

Do you score while watching the images?

It varies. Sometimes you'll have it broken down in certain scenes. It used to be that you couldn't look at it. You couldn't get the video; you'd just work from a cue sheet. Now you can look at it and lock in the place you're gonna start, and the place you're gonna end, and fiddle about. So, yeah, you look at it. There's a little silent movie type stuff you'll do, where you're playing along with it, but you don't do the real writing when it's on.

Your Uncle Alfred wrote three hundred movie scores.

He did. He worked all the time, every day.

And you sometimes watched him work?

I did, since the time I was five years old.

Did you watch him compose or conduct?

I would go visit him when he was working, and he'd ask me what I thought. I might have inherited some of my attitude about composing from my uncle… because here was this guy who was the best movie composer there *was*, and he was asking *me*, when I was eight years old, "What do you think of this?" And he looked *worried*. And if he was worried, maybe I thought, subconsciously—because I didn't want this to happen to me—"Oh God, maybe I should be worried, too… maybe I should suffer, and live in a garret." I've yet to be able to stride confidently into the room where I'm gonna be working. If it's going well, sometimes you know where you're going the next day. But then the next cue will come up, and you've got that empty page stuff. I don't even like to hear myself say it. But it's not unique to me. John Williams feels the same way, accomplished as he is. James Newton Howard feels the same way when he starts a picture, as many as he's done, and as fast as he can do them. I was talking to him once, and I said, "I really hope that I get hit by a car, or something, and get out of this. I don't want to die, or anything… I know that's hard to believe." And he said, "No, I feel the same way."

It's really ridiculous and *laughable* to look at things that way, and harmful to yourself, and harmful to anyone who has heard you, who aspires to be something like you, and thinks you're great, and wonders why you wouldn't have confidence in what you're doing after *all* you've done in the past. Wouldn't you just figure that the numbers would just *favor* you? What's the worst that could happen to you in there? But you can't always change, though it's stupid and nonproductive.

You once said that Alfred would drink every night.

He did drink every night… at five o'clock. I saw him in funny instances. There are other people who knew him differently.

Did Alfred offer any advice on scoring?

He said, "Never be afraid of melody." But nowadays I think you have to be wary of [melody] because [directors] might not want it. He said not to worry about things going too slow musically, but I do. He said, "Don't work at night." But mainly, [it was] because he was loaded at night. I try not to [work at night].

You mentioned that James Newton Howard had only four weeks to write the score for *King Kong*. Is that uncommon?

No, it's not uncommon, but I wouldn't do it. I would *never* do it for anyone I didn't *really* love [*laughs*]. Cause it's just not enough time. The first thing that I try and get is as much time as I can—to do the job right. You're working all the time, anyway, but it's nice to get eight weeks. It used to be more… ten… or whatever you could get. But now it's more common that someone would get four weeks or three weeks.

Is eight weeks sufficient?

It's a sufficient amount of time to hope for if you've got forty minutes to write music for. I think James must have had an hour and forty-five minutes or more to do. It's a three-hour movie. He plays *very* well. And he can do synth stuff with real facility and write five to seven minutes a day. I can't write five minutes a day. I have written two minutes a day.

Do you work on a film score all day long?

Yeah. I can't do that with songs. But film scores, from morning 'til night, and usually seven days a week. Sometimes, if things are going really well, I'll take Sundays off. It usually gets down to a scramble, where you're writing specific scenes. You have to. You've got to do a certain amount every day. You can't have too many bad days. You can't have two in a row, so you just don't. Maybe what you end up with is not the best thing that you could have thought of. Maybe you're never satisfied with it completely. But most of the time it turns out okay. It isn't like, "Oh no, I'll throw that out."

Do you have any say about where music goes in a film?

Yeah. Starts and stops... not like what composers used to have, where you'd decide yourself. The director often wasn't there when you spotted a film. I don't think [Milos] Forman was there when I did *Ragtime*. When [my uncle] Al used to do a picture, sometimes the director didn't even show up, and now they come from rock 'n' roll. They've listened to it all their lives, and they know what they like. The problem with that is that it's a very arcane business. I'm not saying it's *exalted*. It's not like small particle physics, but it's odd. I once saw a scene from a Cary Grant movie without music. He was moving around, and there he was. Then they put the music in, and they would have music for little things that he did—not like a cartoon, it didn't catch everything—and it made him look graceful. It did something for him. You can give somebody more intelligence than they might be indicating they've got. And you can do lots of stuff for action.

Director Martin Scorsese edits to the rhythms of songs. Do you try to match editing or rhythms in the movie?

Oh yeah. Cuts. Not ostentatiously, but you try. It's movement... or the end of lines... the end of dialogue. It's changed a bit, in that a lot of times in action movies, they'll just dial you down. It used to be that you'd get down and then people would say stuff, and you'd come up again. Yeah, there are a hundred little things you *can* do for a picture. That makes the picture better. It's all supposed to do that. That's all that music is for in a movie. *Pride & Prejudice*, if it's supposed to make you tear up a little bit, music can help do it. Or make someone look smoother than they are, or cooler than they are, or just as cool as you possibly can. You can't make a bad movie look like a good movie, but you can make a good movie look like a really classy, great movie.

Do you write to match a character, or are you thinking more of action and emotion?

All of it. Often it's movement rather than words—little things, little stops, little starts. There's no way that a director's gonna know that kind of odd stuff. He shouldn't have to. You hire someone who's sort of an expert, who's watching for that his whole life, and you kind of let him do it. You can tell what they want from what their temp track is. It's their medium; it's their picture. If I write something that the director doesn't like, I change it.

Does that happen a lot?

Not a lot, but it happens, yeah. Stuff gets thrown out, moved around. The odds are that the music guy will be right more often than the director will be right. But [the director] is right because it's their picture, so they know presumably exactly what they want it to be like.

Do you choose your projects based on scripts?

[Based on] who I'm gonna be working with. I think of what kind of musical opportunity it is... like *Seabiscuit*, which looked like a big opportunity for music to really help something out. Certainly *Avalon* did. The things I've been doing lately, the Pixar things. *A Bug's Life* needed things. *Monsters*, too. And maybe I helped them all, but doing comedy—*Meet the Parents*, *Meet the Fockers*—maybe I made them $320 extra [*laughs*]. I don't know what I did for them. The second thing I look for is who I'm gonna be working for, to see if I can deal with the guy. Lot of composers can't be that fussy about it, and if they're offered something, they take it. But I don't want to work for someone who's gonna make me write things four different times and not know why.

I understand that you weren't happy with *Seabiscuit* because you weren't allowed to do what you wanted.

No. I wasn't, but I'm not sure what [Gary Ross, the director] wanted. I did what I thought was right. He ended up changing a lot of what I did, and that hurt my feelings, and I think it hurt the picture. Horses are racing. You don't necessarily *do* the horse race, but you do the *doubt* about the horse race. He felt that everyone knew what was gonna happen, but it isn't like everyone knows the history of Seabiscuit. Even if they had, you play fair with them. You don't give away surprises with music. I *hate* it when that happens. When you know that, oh Jesus Christ, this is gonna happen now.

Like when you suddenly hear spooky music.

Yeah. You know, *those* are the kind of movies that get helped most by music. Think of some of that stuff *without* the spooky music. Music's *really* important in films [*laughs*]; it's amazing.

Is it difficult for you to write a score?

Very difficult, because it's writing for an orchestra and being in the right place at the right time and doing the right thing. It's very different from songwriting. You just *have* to do it. There's no way *out*.

Do you always use the same size orchestra?

No. Smaller one for smaller films. If it's a big outdoor thing like *Maverick*, or an action picture where you need a big brass section, then you need a lot of strings to soak it up. Less on *Meet the Fockers*. *Cars* is pretty big. It also has electric guitars, acoustic guitars, mandolin, and some bluegrass stuff that I recorded separately.

Do you compose a score from the beginning of a film to the end?

No. I *wish*. You get different parts of it. They're finished with *this*, and then you get it. They're never finished, exactly. It used to be that they'd finish a picture and then give it to you. Sound and music was the last thing done, but with an animated picture, it comes in different parts. It makes it difficult somewhat because you don't get to *set* anything. You can write something you can use all right. Like in *Cars*, I did the last race better than I did the first, in my opinion. It's really little, boring stuff like that that you end up thinking about. You realize that you're talking about taking enormously seriously an ant and a grasshopper. It's because the studio succeeds in doing it, so you have to figure out what music would look good with an evil grasshopper. I really like writing music for movies. I like it because I *love* working with the orchestra. I love the sound an orchestra makes, and I love the guys and the women in the orchestra. I feel very comfortable doing it and it makes it worth it... almost... the process.

Ben Nichols
Lucero

photo courtesy Adam Smith

Lucero is a southern rock outfit that blends spunk and country influences with the same élan as their musical forbearers Uncle Tupelo, Whiskeytown, and the Replacements. Vocalist/guitarist Ben Nichols and guitarist Brian Venable formed the band in the late nineties in Memphis, Tennessee, taking their name from the Spanish word for "bright star." Persevering through personnel changes and label switches, the band continued to grow their audience with a string of excellent albums, from 2001's *Lucero* and 2002's *Tennessee* to 2003's *That Much Further West* (which earned them a valued spot on *Rolling Stone*'s Hot List.) In 2005, they teamed with famed Memphis producer Jim Dickinson to produce the gritty, hardrocking *Nobody's Darlings*. In 2005, they were the subject of Aaron Goldman's documentary *Dreaming in America*, which chronicled the making of *Nobody's Darlings* and the group's slow rise to fame. Lucero released *The Attic Tapes*, a collection of rare early recordings, in 2006, in addition to a new studio album, *Rebels, Rogues & Sworn Brothers*.

—EVAN SCHLANSKY

Interview by
Brian T. Atkinson

American Songwriter,
September/October 2005

251

At what age did you start writing songs?

When I was fourteen. I guess since I picked up an instrument I've been writing songs on it. I wrote songs on the bass guitar until I started Lucero. Then I wrote songs on the guitar. I started playing with Brian Venable, and he'd never played guitar in a band either, and the two of us had poor guitar-playing skills. But the two of us, I thought, would make one good guitar player.

When you write songs, do lyrics or music come first?

It usually works out that you come up with one guitar part that fits with another guitar part pretty well. Most times I write a vocal pattern and find a vocal melody that goes with those guitar parts—before I write the lyrics. I struggle for months and months writing the lyrics. You just stumble across stuff. The guitar parts… I don't know that they come easier… well, they *do* come easier. But it's a lot easier to write stupid lyrics than to write stupid guitar parts.

> *Most times I write a vocal pattern and find a vocal melody that goes with those guitar parts—before I write the lyrics. I struggle for months and months writing the lyrics.*

How did you develop your singing style?

It just happened. I have no good answer for that. I have been singing since I was young. I was a really poor singer from about fourteen to nineteen but once I got to be nineteen, it's been that way ever since. I'm thirty now. That's a boring-ass answer, sorry.

Tell me about the title of your latest album, *Nobody's Darlings* [released in 2005 on Lucero's Liberty & Lament Records].

The songs develop out of one phrase or one idea, and I kind of structure the song around that one idea or phrase. That was a phrase that just popped into my head, and it kind of summed up the band pretty well. That was the last song that Brian and I worked on before he quit the band. He was on hiatus for about a year. But then he rejoined the band, and it just made sense to call it *Nobody's Darlings*. I think it might be the way we feel.

Is that because of the kind of music you play or your view of your part in the music industry?

It's a general pessimism [about] the world.

I read somewhere that you said being from the South is important to how you write music. Tell me about that.

I think the Pogues wouldn't be the Pogues if they weren't from Ireland, and Springsteen wouldn't be Springsteen if he wasn't from Jersey. I was born and raised in Arkansas, and we started the band as an experiment to write country songs. There was a lot of roots influence. Everybody in the band is from the South, and we each grew up with different musical influences. I don't think that any of us were raised on old-time country music exclusively. I think we've all come back to those roots, though, after playing and listening to a bunch of different kinds of music. I know I, for one, wanted to be from anywhere other than Arkansas when I was growing up. I wanted to be from New

When I was in my early twenties, I just really grew to appreciate where I was from, and the certain character and soul and history it has.

and the next I want to write like the Pogues. Another day I want to write songs like Johnny Cash, then the next I want to write like Modest Mouse, then the next Godspeed You Black Emperor. We don't sound like any of those bands, but in the songwriting in my head, they're all in there somewhere. We're different.

Speaking of being different, why did you record "The War" acoustically on *Nobody's Darlings*? It's the only acoustic track and is dramatically different from the other eleven songs.

Well, it just seemed to lend itself to that. The entire record is very straightforward, very bare-bones, and [producer] Jim Dickinson's idea on that one was to just make it as raw and as straightforward as possible. It has fairly serious lyrical content, and I think adding anything that's unnecessary—at least in Jim's mind—is taking away from those lyrics.

York or California, but then you get older. When I was in my early twenties, I just really grew to appreciate where I was from, and the certain character and soul and history it has. I moved to Memphis about nine years ago and you're just surrounded by history there. There's a real soulful quality to the city. I mean, it's a shithole, but it has a certain character to it. I'd like to think that comes through in our music.

You said you wanted to write country music. Related to that, how do you categorize Lucero's music—or do you prefer not to label it?

I think labeling music has its place. There's country music and there's rock and roll. I guess I don't know if it's important to label stuff. I don't mind it because it's part of the music business. We started the band in 1998 and I'd never written a standard country song before, so I wanted to give it a shot. I didn't think we'd ever become a real band or do anything real with the music. But we did. We started playing shows and going on tour, and it kind of evolved into its own thing. It went beyond that experiment to just write a country song, and the band had a character of its own that evolved over time. The songwriting went from trying to write country songs to trying to write *good* songs, and allowing a number of influences to come through. I didn't want to get pegged as any one style. Labels exist and they exist for a reason, but one day I want to write songs like "Thin Lizzy"

John Oates
Hall & Oates

Interview by
Kristi Singer

Singer Magazine, *2003*

With six number one singles and an equal number of platinum albums under their belts, the classic eighties vocal duo Hall & Oates has become a smooth rock institution. The two met back in 1967 as students at Philadelphia's Temple University. Daryl Hall (born October 11, 1949, in Pottstown, Pennsylvania) was already doing session work as a singer with an early incarnation of Gamble and Huff, while John Oates (born April 7, 1949, in New York, New York) was fronting his own soul band. After competing against one another in a local battle of the bands contest, they forged a brief musical partnership, playing together in various projects. When nothing came of it, they went their separate ways.

But after a fateful re-teaming in 1969, they caught the attention of future music mogul Tommy Mottola, who became their manager and landed them a deal with Atlantic Records. Their early seventies albums showed a band struggling to define their sound and failed to yield any significant hits. But by 1975, they had found their distinctive groove, and after a move to RCA, released *Daryl Hall & John Oates*, which featured the top ten single "Sara Smile." The eighties proved to be their era, as they cranked out such instant ear candy as "Kiss on My List," "Private Eyes," "I Can't Go for That," "Maneater," and "One on One." The duo released *Our Kind of Soul*, an album of R&B standards, in 2004.

—Evan Schlansky

You're going on tour soon with Michael McDonald and the Average White Band. You recently received a big songwriting award. No early retirement, huh?

Last week, we were inducted into the Songwriters Hall of Fame, and Michael was there and he was inducting [Barrett] Strong—who wrote the song "I Heard It Through the Grapevine." So we're always just running into each other. Michael worked with Kenny Loggins, who did our last summer's tour with us.

I think there's a lot of mutual respect within all the groups. Daryl [Hall] and I are fans of the Average White Band and Michael McDonald. And I think on the same token, they are fans of ours. They like our music; we like their music. It's not like "Let's put three groups together and see if we can go out and make some money." We really feel like the music we're all doing has a connection. We're all soulful—it's the kind of music that works together.

You're working on a new album titled *Our Kind of Soul*. How far along are you with it?

The album is finished. It will be out in the Fall [2005].

Where did you record?

It was recorded in the Bahamas, at a little studio that was built in Daryl's garage. It's a collection of soul classics, but we took the songs that we really liked and we approached them as if they were just written recently, like a brand-new song, and recorded them like we would any brand-new song. There are some originals on it as well.

Tell me about the original songs on the album. What's your favorite and what is it about?

"Let Love Take Control." What's cool about it is that during the making of this album—doing all these incredible soul and R&B classics—we wanted a song that was modern and new but still had the spirit of those old classic songs. And I think as a songwriter, as a craftsman, being able to actually achieve that... it's one thing to *want* to do something, it's another thing to be able to *do* it. We really nailed it. I mean it's totally Hall & Oates as soon as you hear it, but at the same time it's got the spirit of some of the older songs—without sounding like we're trying.

Speaking of the album title, what is *your* kind of soul?

It's soul that's not about trying to re-create or copy black music. It's music that comes from the heart and soul. Soul, to me, is anything that moves you, anything that can be felt on a very emotional level. If it gets right to the heart of the matter—that's soul. It doesn't matter if it's country music, Irish music, African-American music; it doesn't matter. What matters is that the music is all about truth and it's all about heart and that's what soul is.

What are some of the "classics" you re-created?

"Ooh Child," "Fading Away" (a B-side of a Temptations hit), a Marvin Gaye song called "After the Dance," Barry White's "Can't Get Enough of Your Love," "Standing in the Shadows of Love" [by] Four Tops...

Will you perform any of these on tour?

We'll probably throw one or two in there. I've got so much stuff going on. I've got a solo DVD that's out. It's my first solo DVD. I'm really excited about it. It came out really amazing. The fact that I don't tour as a solo artist... this is a chance for people to see what I do. It's called *Live at the Historic Wheeler Opera House*. We were at the Opera House in Aspen, Colorado. There's a lot of extra stuff, like a documentary of making my solo album, a video with Paris Hilton, and all this stuff.

photo courtesy Robert Clement

Conor Oberst
Bright Eyes

*Interview by
Rich Sullivan*

American Songwriter,
May/June 2005

Bright Eyes' Conor Oberst is a singing poet with the ability to effortlessly spin life into verse—a wandering troubadour of teenage philosophy. Born February 15, 1970, in Omaha, Nebraska, Oberst began recording his own songs at age thirteen, when he began fronting the indie rock band Commander Venus. They started their own record label, Saddle Creek, and released three albums together before splitting up in the mid-nineties.

Oberst continued to record with a variety of musical friends under the name Bright Eyes. In 1997, he released *A Collection of Songs*, followed by *Letting Off the Happiness*, featuring members of Neutral Milk Hotel and Of Montreal, in 1998. After 2000's *Fever and Mirrors*, the secret was out, and Oberst was dubbed "rock's boy genius" by the music press. His breakthrough album came in 2002 with *Lifted or the Story Is in the Soil, Keep Your Ear to the Ground*, a sprawling, loosely autobiographical epic.

In 2005, he released two separate albums on the same day. The brilliant *I'm Wide Awake, It's Morning* featured two duets with Emmylou Harris and contained his first bona fide classic, "First Day of My Life." *Digital Ash in a Digital Urn* found Oberst exploring electronic music, with the aid of Yeah Yeah Yeahs guitarist Nick Zinner, to equally strong results. A compilation of B-sides and rarities, Noise Floor: Rarities 1998–2005, was released in 2006.

—EVAN SCHLANSKY

How's New York treating you?

It's been really great. I haven't been there for a while. I was there recently for a few nights, but haven't been there in a while. I really like it there. I got a place there in—I guess—the spring of 2003.

There have definitely been some allusions to metropolitan life in your latest work. How has the city impacted the way you write?

I guess it infects the things you think about. My songs come from whatever occupies my thoughts. Obviously, your environment contributes a lot to the way you think. And I think [in New York] you're forced to be running at a little higher speed to deal with the business of everything—so I think it just kind of leads to more synapses firing.

The pace of life is different.

Yeah, yeah. And it's kind of hard to articulate, but I try to absorb wherever I am. Try to absorb it, and sometimes it comes back out through the music. Obviously, it's a very intoxicating place.

> *My songs come from whatever occupies my thoughts. Obviously, your environment contributes a lot to the way you think.*

One thing that I found interesting is that Omaha has become a Mecca of sorts for songwriters, and you're certainly instrumental in creating that atmosphere. Do you feel like you left it in its prime? Or did you have mixed emotions about leaving Omaha?

I still kind of have one foot in, one foot out. Because I've got a house [in Omaha], friends and family and all that. I go back frequently so I don't feel like I completely left. It's kind of strange how many talented songwriters have come out of [Omaha].

Your two new releases are very different, stylistically. Why two albums at once?

Well, it was actually, this sounds strange, more of a practical thing. We finished the *I'm Wide Awake* record first. This was in February, I guess, of last year. It was basically all done and ready to go. And we could've released it in the summer, but I simultaneously had ideas and sketches for the *Digital Ash* record and both myself and Mike Mogus—who's the producer and friend that I basically make the records with—were really excited about working on this other batch of songs. So it was kind of like a [timing] thing, where if we wanted to finish this other record, then we kind of had to put the release of *I'm Wide Awake* on hold. So that's what we ended up doing, and then they were both done and we were like, "Well, should we put them out a few months apart?" But I guess at that point…

I think they work well together, even though they aren't a double album. I think they complement each other in some ways.

Nice.

On *I'm Wide Awake*, there's definitely more of a political slant to some of your lyrics. "Road to Joy" stands out in this regard. Other than current events and politics, what subjects drive your creativity? What are your sources of inspiration?

I guess just life in general. Everything's kind of been written about before, you know? Love gained, love lost. All that. But it's one of those things you can't [burn out]; there will never be enough written about that subject. I guess the human condition—the strangeness of being alive. It seems like that's enough material to last a songwriter forever.

As far as politics goes, that's something I guess you pick up reading the newspaper. It really hasn't been in your past work. Is that a sign of becoming more mature as a writer, or is it just something you felt so strongly about that you had to cover it?

I never really saw myself, or I never thought about writing about politics or anything like that until it, sort of, infiltrated my life and made me afraid and kept me up at night. It was really at that point that it started entering into the songs. And I'm sure part of that is getting older—becoming more aware of things in the world. But yeah, it really was more of a conscious decision that started occupying my thoughts and therefore entering into the songs. I don't really sit down and think, "I'm going to write a love song" or a protest song or whatever. It's more like I let the songs come out however they come out. Let other people categorize them.

What are you currently listening to? Saddle Creek artists are disqualified...

[*Laughs*] Okay. Let's see, actually I just bought this cool record a few days ago when I was up in Canada. It's [by] Feist. It's kind of like vaguely connected to Broken Social Scene and all those bands in Toronto and Montreal, but it's really cool. It reminds me of—I don't know—I've always liked Suzanne Vega and her weird kind of production aesthetics and cool take on everything. Yeah, that was one record that I got recently that I have been digging on. Um, I can tell you, though, I think the best record—I may be proven wrong—

but I think the best record that'll come out [in 2005] is my friend Matt Ward's, M. Ward. He has probably three records out already. But he's got one... I have a copy of it... that's coming out in February on Merge Records, and it's just amazing. It's like if you could somehow imagine John Fahey and Louis Armstrong combined with some kind of more indie aesthetic. It's such a beautiful record.

On your latest stuff, Emmylou Harris contributes to a few tracks. Name a few artists you'd like to collaborate with in the future. A wish list, anybody in the world.

Anybody? I'd say Björk. That'd be amazing. Boy, I don't know. Paul Simon. That'd be pretty great. [*Long pause*] I'm trying to think. That's a hard question.

How about this—from any time period.

Well, you just made it a harder question [*laughs*]. I don't know. I would have loved to have had Nina Simone in one of my songs. That would've been a dream. She's one of my favorite vocalists.

So no Ashlee Simpson?

[*Laughs*] No. I don't know about sweet, sweet Ashlee.

Does it frustrate you that corporate radio, or the marketing machine behind corporate radio, forces what seems to be canned musical products on the masses?

Yeah, absolutely. It's really a tragedy I think because it homogenizes everything and encourages people to copy each other. And, you know, the idea that the public wants to hear a slightly different version of the single that they've already embraced is really detrimental to creativity. It leads to everything sounding the same and kind of sucking.

You said David Bowie is a pretty big influence. Have you seen *The Life Aquatic With Steve Zissou*?

I haven't, actually.

All of the music in the movie—80 percent of it—is Bowie rendered in Portuguese.

Aw, nice. David Bowie is amazing. Obviously a great singer, songwriter, and performer, but the way he constantly re-invents himself… he seems to always be a few steps ahead. That's cool.

doesn't really work that way. Just keep going and keep going. That's all I can say. Never stop, never be discouraged.

What's next for Conor Oberst?

Well, the next six months are pretty much locked down with playing shows. The tour we're on will end in mid-April, and then we've got a tour for *Digital Ash* that starts in May. After that, I don't know, I'll probably lay in bed for a long time. I'll write more songs, record more. I don't know. The future's pretty wide open at this point.

> *I don't think there's any substitute for live performance, and performing your songs in front of real, live human beings.*

You're a great example of DIY success. You built from scratch what you're doing now, and with obvious talent and some exposure, you're enjoying some success. Is there a formula to breaking through?

I would say, truly, persistence. And doing it because you love it and for no other reason. I think that's the most important thing, and then just play. Play everywhere you can. I don't think there's any substitute for live performance, and performing your songs in front of real, live human beings. That's the way we always did it—just tour, tour, tour. If no one comes to the shows, come back again because the five people that came to that show will bring ten more friends the next time. And that's really the only way to do it. The dream of sending your demo off, having some DJ play it, and having it sweep the nation is kind of dead. It

Paul Overstreet

When he was nine, a young Paul Overstreet watched a film that changed his life: *Your Cheatin' Heart*, a biopic about Hank Williams. By age seventeen, Overstreet had moved to Nashville, cut sides for an indie Arkansas label, and had been encouraged by members of Dolly Parton's family to pursue a music career.

Overstreet married Frieda Parton, Dolly's younger sister, in 1975—but it was hardly a match made in heaven, as they divorced the following fall. By the early eighties, Overstreet was becoming a hit factory as a songwriter. "Same Ole Me" went top five for George Jones in 1982; four years later, after conquering alcohol in 1985, Overstreet and Don Schlitz (who had written Kenny Rogers's smash "The Gambler") began co-writing. Two big results were "On the Other Hand" and "Forever and Ever, Amen"—back-to-back Country Music Association Songs of the Year in 1986 and 1987 for a new traditional country (at the time) artist who doubled as a shrimp cook: Randy Travis.

Overstreet was also a major label recording artist from 1982–1996 (he still releases records on his own Scarlet Moon label), with number one singles "I Won't Take Less Than Your Love" (1987) and "Daddy's Come Around" (1990). Other smash Overstreet songs are "When You Say Nothing at All" (number one for Keith Whitley in 1988, number three for Alison Krauss & Union Station in 1995) and Blake Shelton's "Some Beach" (number one, 2004).

—PHIL SWEETLAND

Interview by
Vernell Hackett

American Songwriter,
July/August 1988

260

How did you get interested in songwriting?

I don't really know. As a kid I just had the ability to write a song.

Who were some of your influences?

I guess Hank [Williams] Sr. was one of the influences as far as writing, and Marty Robbins. I listened to a lot of different ones. As a teenager I liked the Doobie Brothers and Jim Croce and Elvis. I was exposed to those through my family; my sister had Elvis records and I just listened to the radio.

How old were you when you got serious about becoming a songwriter?

Probably, I realized that was what I wanted to do for a living when I was eight years old. I did it all through school. I had little bands and stuff and played at proms. I cut a record when I was a junior in high school. The first thing was a song I wrote called "The Old Blind Man."

What do you think of those early songs today?

I don't know. "Wanderer" is a pretty good song. "The Blind Man" had a lot of heart in it and a lot of neat phrases and all, but it's not real tight. I've looked at it, but I don't really think I can tighten it up. I don't know if it has all the things it needs.

How long did it take you to get to the point where you knew you were writing good songs?

I still don't know that. I don't ever know that. I just write and try to make the song good, and usually I'm the first one to know when it's finished. Maybe at the same time, you just don't ever know how to judge what's good. Is it because of the success that it rises to? Is it a song that may never be cut but still says something that moves people and may be the best song you'll ever write—yet it'll never be recorded? It's hard to judge what's good.

Do you write every day or just when an idea hits you?

Well, a lot of times, I'll write without an idea but I'll be seeking an idea when I go write. And usually I'll come up with something. But if an idea does hit me, then I'll go write it, but I don't try to sit down every day and write because I don't know that I have that much to say.

Some people say that, for a new writer, the hardest thing to learn is when a song is finished. How would you explain that to a new writer?

Usually when it's cut and it's out on a record, you've finished it. 'Til then, you can usually, a lot of times, make them better and better and better. It's just something you don't know until after years of work; it's not something you can acquire within a week. It's like saying, "How do you know how to be the person that you are?" It's all the things that you go through that make you that. It's just gonna take time, it's gonna take experience, and the more songs you write, the better you get at it. You can rewrite anything, but that's not it. It's when you're satisfied with it and [you're at the point where] you're ready to let it ride.

Do you enjoy co-writing more than writing by yourself?

Co-writing is fun, you know, and that's the thing about it. After you've written a lot of songs, then you kinda like to have fun as much as you do sitting down and working hard. I like co-writing because of that, but there are some ideas that come that I just go, "You know, I just need to write that by myself," because I don't know that anybody has that

exact feeling in their heart that I do. Some songs are not co-writing songs; you just have to sit down and drill them out yourself.

How do you determine what kind of demo to do on a song?

I very seldom do full-blown demos because they are expensive and I have mostly all the equipment in my studio to do what I need. I have drum machines and synthesizers and keyboards. My songs are real simple... a lot of them are guitar/vocal songs. In other words, the song stands on its own and doesn't need that full-blown demo because the demo is not what sells the song. In country music, I think the song stands on its own. So the song kinda dictates what goes on it.

Is it hard to go back to work on a song that's basically finished, rather than start a new one?

It all depends on the song and the period of time. I realize the more you are away from a song the better perspective you have on it when you come back to rewrite. You get too close to it if you're stuck, and it's better to go on to other things and write some songs that aren't so hard... and then look back later at the hard one. Sometimes it will be right there—what you are supposed to do—and be real clear to you.

You've worked for some different publishing companies, and now you have your own. Do you have any recommendations to other writers about this?

I worked for people for a long time, and I came to the place where I just had different views on some things I thought should be done with a publishing company. At this point, we have a lot of doors open for our songs, so that helps in the pitching process. Five years ago, or even three, I still needed to be with a company that was pitching songs... opening doors for me. I don't necessarily think that being with a large company helps you; you just need to be with a company that believes in you.

Do you feel like you have a message to give to people through your songs?

I think there is a message in every song. I think your heart comes out in verse. You don't write those songs for money. You write them because that's where your heart is, and when you're successful, you just thank God and go on.

When you sit down to write, do you write with a particular artist in mind?

I tried that years ago, and I never had those songs cut by the artist I tried to write them for. The publisher would call and say so-and-so needs you to write them a song and I'd sit down and try to write and they never recorded the song. When you do that, the nucleus of the idea is not the song; the nucleus is the artist, and I think that's wrong. I think the song has to say what it is trying to say, and then if it fits an artist, if they feel like they can say what the song says, then at that point you have a relationship. But if you sit down just to write a song for the artist, then the artist is the center of attention and the song is just like a sugar coating.

Dolly Parton

People too easily forget what a phenomenal song-writer Dolly Parton is. It's not just her fluent, lilting, twang-inflected soprano, coiffed blond tresses, and girlish good looks that are immediately recognizable to anyone anywhere on the globe—it's also her time-less songs, such as "Joshua," which became her first number one hit in 1970, "Coat of Many Colors," or the often-reprised "Jolene" and "I Will Always Love You." From the time of her 1963 recording debut, to her late 1960s and early 1970s collaborations with Porter Wagoner, to her crossover success with pop songs like "Here You Come Again" in 1977 and dual-Grammy-winning movie theme "9 to 5" in 1980, to recent back-to-roots albums *The Grass Is Blue* (also a Grammy winner), *Little Sparrow* and *Halos and Horns*, Parton's songwriting has always possessed pal-pable warmth and effervescence. Considering her wealth of business sense—after all, this is a woman who has successfully juggled film acting, writing books, and running a theme park in addition to her music career—it becomes obvious that Parton is not simply a compelling performer but also a woman of great all-around ingenuity. She released an album of cover songs, *Those Were the Days*, in 2005, which contained such classics as John Lennon's "Imagine," Cat Stevens' "Where Do the Children Play," and Tim Hardin's "If I Were a Carpenter."

—JEWLY HIGHT

Interview by
Deborah Evans Price

American Songwriter,
March/April 1990

You're a woman of many talents. You act, head up your own theme park, and have a keen business sense. With all of this, how do you find the time to write songs?

Songwriting is number one. I've always prided myself as a songwriter more than anything else. That's my personal feeling. That's not to say that's what I do best. That's my way of speaking for myself and speaking for life the way I see it. It's an ability that I have and I've always loved being able to express myself.

What drew you to songwriting?

It's therapy. It's fun. It's creative. I love getting on a big writing binge and staying up a couple or three days working on songs and knowing at the end of those two or three days that I've created something that was never in the world before. It's like a feeling of creating, not that the same story ain't been told before, but it ain't been told through my point of view. And it's a way of relaxing. Songwriting is a hobby to me and it's therapy. It's a joy. It's a thrill. It's like mind exercises or something.

What was the first song you ever wrote?

My first song I wrote before I could write. My mama wrote it down. I would just always write songs about things that I understood and I could always rhyme things. I always had a gift for rhyme. I wrote a song called "Little Tiny Tassel Top" about a little corn cob doll I had, because we didn't have store-bought toys. I had this little doll that Daddy had burnt poker holes for eyes in, and mama put the corn silk back on it and made a dress. I was five years old. Then I started playing guitar and writing seriously when I was about seven, and I started singing on radio and TV when I was ten. And I've been writing ever since.

Your songs have certainly matured over the years. How have your experiences aided in this maturing process?

I've improved just by growing older and living. Also, I think that my writing gets better because my life gets more involved. I can still write country better than anything and that's something that's never left me. That's why some of my songs on this album [2005's *White Limozeen*] are a little special. It was so easy for me to write those. I just write whatever I'm feeling at the time or whatever I'm going through.

What factors do you consider in recording outside material?

I look for a song that I can sing… that the chorus structure is something I can sing, not being a trained singer. I look for subjects that I understand and make sense to me, things that are real rather than just a bunch of hokey stuff, something that triggers something in me or something I think I could do a great performance on. Usually it's stuff that I should have written myself but didn't have the talent to say it exactly that way. Usually I say, "Why didn't I think of that? I should've written that. I could've written that." So I guess it just means things that move me and places that I've been… just songs I never got to write, I guess.

Do you prefer simple guitar/vocal demos or full-fledged demos?

It doesn't matter to me if I hear a song I love. If I hear a good song I'll know it. I can always picture what music would do it. I always try to demo my songs before I send them places because I know some people don't have the imagination, but I am an arranger in my head so I can hear a song where maybe some artist might not be able to.

Who would you like to record one of your songs?

Everybody, anybody. I'll take anybody. I'm always flattered that anybody would record my songs, even if they change them. Certain songs… I'll hear somebody do it and I've had mixed emotions. I think either "Wow, that's great" or "I never thought of hearing it like that" or "Oh Lord, they've ruined the song." But you're still glad as a writer that they did it, no matter how it turns out. But you do have your favorites. I guess the ones I'd like for them to record right now are the ones having hits or making money.

unless you were just the luckiest person in the world to have somebody knocking at your door and say, "Hey, I've got an opportunity…." But to be realistic, you just have to stick with it. If you really believe [there's] true talent and that's all you know and want to do, you'll find a way to do it. Just don't give up if that's where you think your true talent is. That's not to say you can't work on a job where you can make some money; we all have to do that, but you still have to get out there and pretty much put yourself into it.

> *I love getting on a big writing binge and staying up a couple or three days working on songs and knowing at the end of those two or three days that I've created something that was never in the world before.*

Is there any advice you'd like to give to aspiring songwriters?

There's no such thing as a set pattern. Like somebody was asking me yesterday about somebody else that they really believed in, saying this person was such a great writer and great singer and that they were thinking about trying to do something for that person—they themselves being a writer and singer. I said, "You've got to be crazy. This person has been in the business that many years and they're still working on another job and expecting somebody else to get out there and do it for them? You need to pay attention to your own music and if that person is sincere, they'll find a way." You have to be willing to sacrifice. You have to be willing to pay those prices. And I've never seen it done any differently

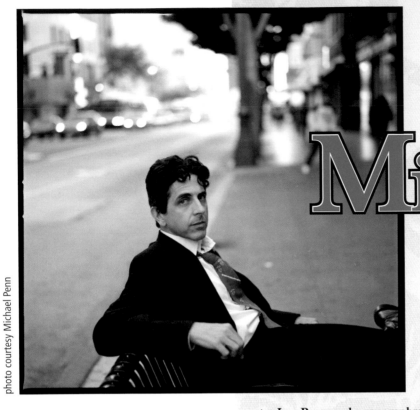

Michael Penn

Michael Penn was born August 1, 1959, in New York's Greenwich Village, the eldest son in the prestigious Penn acting family (his father is actor/director Leo Penn, and a younger brother is actor Sean). A self-described black sheep, Penn avoided going into the family business, choosing instead to lose himself in the music of the Beatles and craft songs in his bedroom.

After high school, he moved to Los Angeles, where he fronted the short-lived band Doll Congress. He caught his big break performing his song, "This and That," on a 1987 episode of *Saturday Night Live* that his brother Sean was hosting (the other musical guest was LL Cool J). That song would end up on his debut album, *March*, released in 1989. That album also marked the renewal of his partnership with former Doll Congress keyboardist Patrick Warren, who would add a variety of textures and musical quirks to each of Penn's subsequent albums.

The excellent *Free-for-All* followed in 1992, but record label apathy and legal hang-ups slowed Penn's momentum. Over the next ten years, he released only two albums, the underrated *Resigned* (1997) and *MP4: Days Since a Lost Time Accident* (2004). In the interim, Penn married fellow singer-songwriter Aimee Mann and scored films for director Paul Thomas Anderson. Penn made a welcomed return in 2005, with the glorious post-World War II song-cycle, *Mr. Hollywood Jr., 1947*.

—EVAN SCHLANSKY

Interview by
Evan Schlansky

American Songwriter,
September/October 2005

Is this a concept album? Who is Mr. Hollywood, Jr., and what is the album about?

It's a concept album of *sorts*. I think the operative phrase is "of sorts." I kind of look at it as an *album*. It's kind of a drag what has happened to music, post-CD. Once upon a time, albums started out as a collection of singles, really, not singles so much as collections of 78 discs, and as pop music evolved, they became these things unto themselves—where people made albums and they thought of their music in terms of making albums and stuff. One of the things that happened after records stopped being vinyl and started to be on CD was that you had forty minutes of music in one fell swoop. I think that's just too much music for most people. And one of the great things about vinyl albums is the music—the album is separated into two distinct tracks. So I have memories from my childhood about loving side two of this record, or side one of this record, and they were these manageable little twenty-minute sides, and then there was the interactive part of it, which is if you wanted to listen to more, you actually had to get up off your ass and flip the record over. With CDs, all of that sort of went out the window when a lot people stopped making albums in the way that I think of albums… As far as [*Mr. Hollywood*] being a concept, it's no more of a concept than any of my other albums have ever been. I was writing a bunch of songs and I was finding that, for a variety of reasons, I was placing myself and all the things I was writing about in L.A.… but in L.A. in another time, in L.A. in this sort of post-World War II world, and I think why is because there are so many things that are going on politically that have strings that are tied back to that year. That year has been an obsession of mine for a long time. It's a year that, I think, the world kind of changed. We won World War II, and all of a sudden America became this incredibly beloved nation who was in the position, if it wanted to, to take over the whole world. But it didn't, you know? Except it really did. There was this switch that happened, where all of a sudden there were all these things going on politically that were leading to what I think is going on in the world now, and it's the year that the National Security Act was passed, which meant the insertion of the national security state, which in turn lead to the creation of the CIA. It was the year that the UN partitioned Palestine into the countries that now exist there. The end of the old British empire and the beginning of the American empire. And also there was all this technological stuff going on; it's the year that the transistor was invented, which leads directly to computers, the year that television finally reached the west coast of North America. [Pilot Chuck] Yeager broke the sound barrier. It's just an amazing year, a watershed year. My obsession with that year and everything that was going on politically… I'm trying to figure it all out in hindsight, but I'm fairly confident that's why I was seeing all these songs in that period of time.

Are there any thematic albums you remember?

There are a lot of records that are sort of themed that aren't considered concept albums, like Randy Newman's *Good Old Boys* or something, that just by the mere fact of them being divided up into two acts, you start to appreciate the sequencing of a record more, because you understand they're sequencing an experience that starts and ends with the first and last song on a given side, and it makes for a good record; it makes for two great listening experiences.

Are you a big history buff?

Well, I am a big history buff, of certain aspects of history.

Who is "Walter Reed" about?

If America has a hospital, it's Walter Reed. Walter Reed is the hospital in Washington, D.C., where soldiers coming back from war would go, and it's one of the first hospitals to

really deal with what we would now call post-traumatic stress syndrome. At the time they would call it shell shock.

Can you talk a bit about the last song, the "Millionaire Song"?

I had written "Millionare," and it [didn't] really fit in with the album, because it doesn't take place in 1947. But it was inspired by a couple of things. It was inspired by, again, the politics of the day, and thinking about how there is sort of a class war going on. And how people in power can easily sort of get into a mindset where they feel that to question them is unjust in their view... because just the fact that they've reached this position of power means that they deserve it. I have an instrument I use a lot that's called a Marxophone, and it's basically like an autoharp. But it has a little keyboard on it, and when you hit a key, this little rubber hammer comes down and bounces on the string and it sounds sort of like a hammered dulcimer. There are these cool little instruments that were built by this company in the twenties, and they used to sell them door to door, and I was thinking about how there would be these guys going around in this little company selling these Marxophones and trying to make a living. I was kind of feeling like, now that I'm out of the corporate record companies, that's kind of what I'm doing, I'm going around selling stuff door to door. And you don't have to really pay for it anymore, 'cause people just steal it and download it from the Internet. It kind of started with that idea.

How do you know when you've written a great song?

That's a tough one, I don't really know. It's really whether or not it matches a mood, if it matches what I'm trying to write about, and if it evokes what the initial spark of [the inspiration]... then I feel like it's worked. But that's such a subjective moment in time, whether or not that really translates, and I don't know. I don't know that there's any rule of thumb about that for me. I just try to be honest and get whatever I'm thinking about and feeling in some kind of form and hope that I don't get bored with it, because my biggest problem in writing is just getting bored with stuff too quickly.

When you're in your teens or twenties, it can be easier to write lyrics because you have this wounded-by-the-world perspective. Is it more difficult to write when you're older and wiser and you're married?

Well... it depends on how good your memory is [*laughs*]. For me, I think I have enough... I have a trunk full of stuff that I can certainly tap into and remember how I felt. I can be in a relationship that feels good and has helped me and still remember when I wasn't. Or I can look around me and see friends of mine who are in pain, and I can sort of see what's going on and relate to, because I'd been through it or whatever. Most of the time I can put myself there.

How soon after you write a song do you play it for your wife?

I don't actually... that's not the way we really work. If Aimee's writing something, and she's not sure about something, she'll maybe play it for me, and I'll do the same, but once it's done, I kind of know it's done. And at that point I might stick it in a live set at Largo [a club in Los Angeles] and try playing it. I play there every month.

What makes a great song?

I hate modern country music. Just like I hate most pop. It's just pop; it doesn't even really have the identity of country music to it; it's just the same glossy slick crap you hear everywhere, but every once in a while something gets past them and there's this LeAnn Rimes song called "Nothin' 'Bout Love Makes Sense," which I think is a real unusual and cool track. The melody's beautiful.

Was the record before this—*MP4: Days Since a Lost Time Accident*—historical, too?

Those songs aren't set in the past. It's about relationships. All my records are ultimately about the same thing, which is me trying to figure shit out about the way people work, and *MP4* is about the kinds of issues I was thinking about at the time… trying to think about things I had done in my past and things that were going on with friends of mine in their relationships. "Perfect Candidate" is about the phenomenon of people projecting their own issues onto other people, even to the point where, in love and relationships, they can actually blind themselves to the reality of the person in front of them—if the person in front of them for some reason triggers off issues they have. And the best people for that phenomenon to occur are people whose personalities can be sort of blank slates. So the blanker the slate, the easier it is to project onto them. And a lot of my stuff is about this

All my records are ultimately about the same thing, which is me trying to figure shit out about the way people work…

phenomenon of limerance, which I find really interesting. It is what a lot of people think of as love [and] isn't love at all… limerance is essentially these very heightened feelings people feel for other people in a romantic way that combines lust with sort of a belief that this other person completes them, and that feeling, that need, doesn't really have anything to do with love, it has to do, *always*, with parental

issues and childhood issues. And the pain and the need, and all of these horrible things that can happen in relationships, almost by their very definition, make it clear that this isn't love… because love isn't painful; love isn't needy; love is choice; love is affection; love is friendship, taken to another level. So that distinction is something that I write about a lot.

It sounds like limerance can account for most rock lyrics.

Absolutely. And it's funny, because people used to be more aware of it than they are now. And even with "No Myth," which was me without actually being aware of the term limerance; I wasn't even aware of the term at the time, but I was writing about it from that standpoint and writing about it from the standpoint of, well, for example… when Shakespeare wrote *Romeo and Juliet*, which a lot of people now think of as this incredibly romantic saga, and that's not what he intended. What he intended was a tragedy. They weren't in love! That was his point! They were drawn to each other because they were rebelling against their families and they were able to project on each other all kinds of stuff from their own issues, and they wind up, you know, killing themselves! But now people think about it… "Oh, it's so romantic." But no, it wasn't romantic at all… it was horrifying! It's a horrible, sad tale.

Gretchen Peters

Interview by
Kandy Crosby

American Songwriter,
May/June 2000

If the only song Gretchen Peters ever wrote had been Martina McBride's 1994 hit "Independence Day," Peters (born in Bronxville, New York, in 1962 and raised in the college town of Boulder, Colorado) would nonetheless be a very important country songwriter. But that song and its accompanying music video—testaments to Peters's wonderfully crafted and brutally frank treatment of child and spousal abuse—were in some ways just the appetizer for what would become an entire decade of powerful tunes.

In just about every way, Peters is different from most Nashville writers. She's not from the South, for one thing, and she just about never co-writes—except when she works with the Canadian rock icon Bryan Adams. Adams and Peters often write together during Adams's rock star-styled tours, meaning Peters may hit the road for Hong Kong or London at any moment.

Solo compositions include Trisha Yearwood's "On a Bus to St. Cloud," whose title town Peters discovered on a map of Minnesota; George Strait's "The Chill of an Early Fall," a 1991 number one hit; and Andy Griggs's "If Heaven," released as a single in 2005.

—PHIL SWEETLAND

When did you first discover your musical gifts?

I found that I was *pretty* good at a lot of things. I was pretty good in school. I was good at writing. But music, in some ways, was the most challenging thing—the thing that I wasn't really sure I was that good at. In that sense, it was much more intriguing for me, because I think you're always intrigued by things that you're not sure you can master. I guess I never really looked at myself as being particularly musically talented. I'd been writing short stories and poems and things my whole life, since before I could really write. I finally made that connection in my teenage years… that there was such a thing as writing songs… that there was a way of writing words with my total involvement in music. That's when I started to realize that maybe music was something I could use all those abilities in: the words, the music, and everything. That is, I think, when the bug really bit me.

You mentioned that you were a teenager when you first started writing songs. Do you remember what your first song was?

I do, actually. It was my first really serious attempt at a song. I'd been fooling around with writing a little bit. Some friends of mine that were in a band had started writing their own stuff. It made me realize somebody had to write these songs. So I just started fooling around with it a little bit. I was a convert to country music. I hadn't been raised on it. I went to see Dolly Parton one night at a club in Denver. I saw her do her show, and I was completely knocked out by the fact that she was, quite obviously, the only person that could have written those songs. They hadn't been manufactured for her. They were so much a part of her identity and her personality. That night, I went home and wrote my first really serious song.

When you write a song, how does it make you feel? Do you know when it's right—how it's supposed to be?

Yeah, I think you have an inner compass that says, "This is right," when it is right. I really am a big, big believer in trusting your instincts. This has happened to me a lot of times. You have a line in a song that doesn't quite make literal sense, and you think, "Well, maybe people won't understand what I mean there; I'm not even sure I understand what I mean." That kind of thing. But when your instinct says that it's right, you listen to that and then you go with that. I've never gone wrong relying on that. I don't think you can go wrong. And being done with a song… *relieved* is really the best word I can think of to describe it. I'm always mystified when I hear people say writing songs is fun. I've heard people say, "Oh, it's so much fun. I like it." Fun is not the way I would describe it. I mean, it's sort of, to me, like breathing. Breathing is not fun, but you have to do it in order to stay alive. That's kind of how I feel about writing. Oftentimes, it's not fun and it's really frustrating. You tend to wonder, "Will I ever write anything worthwhile again?" You have all kinds of scary thoughts. But it's a necessary thing. And when I finally get something out that I feel really proud of, it's an immense sense of relief. Unfortunately, that relief only lasts for a few days, and then I have to turn around and do it again.

You have written many songs that have become big country hits. One of your most famous is "Independence Day." How did it come about?

That was really a gift. I don't, to this day, know exactly where it came from or why I really wrote it. The words of the chorus just kind of came out. I was literally just fooling around with my guitar, and the words came out. It took me a very long time to finish the song, partly because I couldn't understand what the chorus was really saying. I mean, if you listen to just the chorus of the song, it doesn't tell much of a story or give much of an indication of what's going on in the song. So I had to wait a long time for the rest of the song to come, to try and figure out what it was trying to be, if you

will. And when I finally hit on the whole story line, with the woman in the house and the daughter and everything, I was really kind of scared of it. I really thought, "This is a little too dark. Maybe I shouldn't go this way." But, again, instinct won out. I kept going back to that same story. I found it pretty compelling. In the end, I just said, "Well, you know, maybe it's dark, but this is the way this song goes. This is the way this song is meant to go. And whether anybody records it or not, I'm going to finish writing it this way, because it's right." And, lo and behold, the first artist that heard it, Martina McBride, is the one that cut it. She was very adamant about recording it. She knew that she wanted it and knew that she wanted to sing it. I think it took a lot of guts for her to do that, because it was not an obvious radio song.

How does the songwriting process usually go for you?

It can vary immensely. I mean, "Independence Day" took me a year and a half to write. Not that I was working on it all that time, but it took me a year and a half to get all the pieces together and figure out where the song was going. Sometimes I have written a song in an afternoon. "You Don't Even Know Who I Am" was written in an afternoon. Those are really rare for me. More often, it takes me several months to finish something. I always have eight or nine or ten things going at one time. I usually sort of slide around from one thing to the next, depending on what captures my mood or what I'm feeling determined to finish. For me—and I really stress that, because I think it's different for every writer—it just seems to work better if I don't force it, if I wait around until the powers that tell me it's alright to finish the song. I think a lot of the work that you do when you're writing is very subconscious. It's very hard to remember that when you're staring at the walls, not getting an idea, not knowing whether you're writing or wanting to take a nap, the fact is, you're still working internally.

What advice would you give to someone who wants to pursue a career in songwriting?

Well, I guess there's a lot of practical advice out there. I'd say it's very good to follow all that—advice about business and so forth. But I would say the one thing that maybe new writers and new artists don't hear enough is to stick to your guns and be true to yourself. I think that people, in their anxiousness to get into the business and get a record deal or get a publishing deal, think, "If I can just write like what I hear on the radio, if I can just become more like Artist A who's successful, then maybe I'll be successful, too." I think that not only is that not really healthy in terms of your work, but it's also probably not a very successful strategy. I think the only way that you can really be unique—stick out from the crowd—is to be yourself and listen to your own instincts. Take advice for what it's worth, but internalize it, and in the end, make your own decisions and go with what feels right to you. I really think, at least in my experience, that's the thing that's always brought me success. I've never really had success trying to conform to what radio's playing or anything else like that. It has never worked for me.

Michael Peterson

photo courtesy Michael Peterson

Michael Peterson was raised along the Columbia River in eastern Washington state. After excelling in football in high school and college, he spent some time songwriting on the L.A. music scene, with cuts by pop star Deniece Williams and gospel mainstays The Imperials. Peterson made his living as a motivational speaker for schools and youth groups, but he became enthralled with the music of Keith Whitley, Kris Kristofferson, Willie Nelson, and other country stars. Country songs began pouring out of him.

Peterson moved to Nashville in 1995 and signed with Warner Bros. Records a year later. In 1997, the lighthearted "Drink, Swear, Steal and Lie" became his first country smash. He followed it with the chart-topping wedding vow "From Here to Eternity." Travis Tritt sang a duet with him and recorded "No More Looking Over My Shoulder" as the title tune to a 1998 CD.

Peterson was named Top New Artist of 1997 by both *Billboard* and *Radio & Records*. "Too Good to Be True" became his third straight top ten hit in early 1998. *Michael Peterson,* his debut country disc, went gold. He was named *Country Weekly*'s Male Newcomer and the *Gavin Report*'s Artist to Watch in 1998. *Being Human,* his second country album, contained a sizzling duet with Bekka Bramlett called "Two of the Lucky Ones." Peterson has continued on as a recording artist with subsequent acclaimed albums, and he remains an influential fixture on Nashville's songwriting scene.

—LISA WYSOCKY

Interview by Lisa Wysocky

HitWriters.com, 2005

273

What made you come to Nashville to pursue music?

I spent [about] fifteen years speaking to people all over the world, predominantly teenagers, from 1983 to 1995 before I came to Nashville. I gave that up to come to Tennessee to write songs and make hit records. After ten years of being in Tennessee and accomplishing some of those things, I began to feel in my heart a real desire to speak again. I felt in my heart a real desire to be with people, sharing their dreams in what I call "the great exchange." And it all started with walking into a Ramada Inn in 1993 when I first started coming here on a serious level. I used to sit there and dream that I would have a song in the karaoke book. Lo and behold, in several years, I had one or more. I had several songs in the karaoke book. When you have a hit record and your face is on TV, you find out you have a lot of friends you never knew you had. You inevitably end up some night at karaoke bar and you have people come up to you and say, "Hey, aren't you the guy with the hit record? Why don't you get up and sing your song on karaoke?"—which I would never do. I thought that was totally cheesy. But you know, one night I got talked into it. And wouldn't you know it. I knew it was a big mistake when I got done. This guy walks up to me and says, "You know, you're really good, but you're no Michael Peterson." As funny as that was, it started me thinking. I mean, life is a lot like karaoke. Don't most of us know other people who go through life singing somebody else's song? That's a message I've been sharing now over the last year to a lot of different audiences. I've been really encouraging people to identify the things they are passionate about instead of just living and working for a paycheck. Find your song, you know? Sing your song. So the new speaking that I'm doing is born out of the heartfelt desire to connect people with their passion, whether it's music, math, dogs, hunting, or culture. But to connect with your passion, 'cause I believe that the desires of your heart are there for a reason. When you connect those things to what you are doing with your time, you find a lot of fulfillment and joy.

How did your passion for songwriting develop?

When I was in college, I had to make a decision between playing sports and playing music. I had a scholarship and you know, being in my late teens and early twenties, I was very interested in being a part of the prestige that comes along with being in a successful college football program. But I thought that I could also go back to music. So I made a decision to veer away from the path of music. And it actually, ironically, is the decision that led me right into the music business. My quarterback was a guy named Brad Westonering, and when I got out of college and wanted to make a record, I didn't know of anybody in the music business except him. He ended up marrying a pop star by the name of Deniece Williams, who had a lot of huge hits like "Let's Hear It for the Boy," "Too Much, Too Little, Too Late"… a lot of big hits. They signed me to my first publishing deal and first record deal. Sometimes a left turn becomes a right turn. You just have to follow what's in your heart. And that path led me into getting into the music business. I was ready to buy a new boat and new house and had a bunch of songs that Deniece recorded on Columbia Records. And you know, it ended up inevitably having its run and I had to end up making a decision as that started to dry up about whether I should stay in the business or not. I knew a lot of friends who were going broke trying to play clubs. I knew that there had to be another way for me, so I started speaking to people, speaking to kids. And through those contacts, I got to do a lot of music. So twelve years went by… I wrote a lot of songs. I had a few hits for other artists. But I pretty much lived in obscurity out in Seattle. I, of course, traveled around the country speaking to people.

What was your first big cut?

I had my first number one song in 1993 for a group called The Imperials. They were a gospel—what do you call it—contemporary Christian group. And I thought, "Okay, I've got one number one song, so maybe I can go to Nashville and maybe someone will give me some time." So I came to Nashville and was standing in the salad bar line down at Shoney's on Demonbreun Street, and a guy walks up to me, hands me his card and says, "Who are you?" I said, "Who are you?" He said, "I am Michael Perrier. I'm vice president of music publishing at BMG in the gospel division. Come see me." So I went to see him. He encouraged me after hearing a couple of songs to be here on a regular basis. So I came for a week a month for two years all the way from Seattle and invested in relationships and learning. That led to standing, again, waiting for dinner. There's something about food and success with me. I was waiting for dinner with a guy who

---

Don't most of us know other people who go through life singing somebody else's song?

---

was an engineer at EMI and a guy walked by me. He literally stopped five steps past me, turned around, looked, and said, "Who are you?" I introduced myself and he handed me his card. I said, "Who are you?" He said, "I'm Pat Finch, vice president of A&R at EMI Publishing. Come see me." He offered me my first publishing deal. So I packed up my family, cancelled all my speaking bookings 'cause this was my dream, so I came. And within seven months, I had a major publishing deal. Not with EMI, but with Warner/Chappell. Within six months, I had a record deal. Within a year, I had hit songs on the radio. So you know, it seemed like a long journey looking ahead. But looking back, it seemed just like a blink of an eye. It's been a lot of fun. I'm really looking forward to what's next.

You continue to write and record songs these days.

I've often been asked over the last few years which do I enjoy more: being a songwriter or being an artist? And that's a difficult question to answer because I really enjoy them both. The satisfaction to me of writing a song is more of an intimate satisfaction—when you sit and come up with something… and it moves you… and you feel like it's really great. Then you take that, and you take it out of the public and you watch it fall like a duck that's been shot. You say, "Well, um, maybe there's still some things to learn. The beauty of being a performer is that you get a chance to get out and see what works and learn from that process. Boy, I performed for audiences as big as seventy thousand people down to the toughest audience I ever had, which was three kids in detention. They were in middle school and they were mad at me for trying to make them laugh and there they were in detention. That was the toughest audience I ever had. I enjoy them both. I really do. The thing about being an artist is that it can really eat into your songwriting time. It truly can. I have people tell me, man, you should just write songs. Let those guys go on the road and live a crazy life. And I guess there's some sensibility behind that.

Where do you find inspiration, and what writing habits have you picked up over the years?

I believe that there are some habits. I mean, if you were interested in photography, everywhere that the word "photography" showed up, whether it was in a newspaper or on television or in a conservation, your ears would perk up because it's something you were interested in. I think that if you are a songwriter, you have the same kind of attention to things that pop around you that are re-

lated to songs. And if you are like me, you don't have time to write them [down]. So you collect ideas in a bag, so to speak. You collect ideas in a database or in a book. Then, when it's time to sit down and write, you open up your bag and you say, "What's in here today?" You pull out stuff that you are interested in. I mean, I probably have five hundred ideas sitting in a database that, in any given moment, I can go back to… and begin to cultivate something real out of it. I was writing a song today with a guy that I started twenty-two years ago… a melody I just had. I think what keeps it fresh is that these ideas you collected that you thought were interesting are somehow intersecting with something that's happening right now with your life. And that's a part of what keeps it fresh and interesting. I was listening this weekend to a song by Billy Joel called "Leningrad." It's so different from the type of music we create in Nashville. I found inspiration in that. It's this great story about history. It's not up-tempo, not positive, but brilliant. So I mean, if you look for inspiration, you'll find it. And I do. I look for inspiration.

Is there a secret to your success?

Sometimes people ask you, "What did you do to become successful? How did you make it?" And that's always a dicey question because I can tell you how *I* did it, but I can't tell you how *you* are going to do it. You know, we all end up at the end of the day with our own story. The one thing I do think that is consistent with people who capture the desire of their heart in a livelihood, whether it's songwriting or becoming a doctor, is a consistent commitment to going after it. I mean, I was driven to learn everything I could about songs, songwriting, publishers… I never took my focus off of it for twenty years. I mean, it takes a commitment that's complete. And then someday when somebody asks you how you made it, you can tell them, "I know how I made it, but I can't tell you how you are going to make it." I think it's that

kind of commitment that leads you down the path you are supposed to be on.

Are you most proud of any song in particular?

It's hard to say what songs make you the proudest, 'cause the songs you are most excited about are the songs you just created, 'cause they are the most fresh to you. But there is this one song that I wrote this last year for one of my heroes—Dan Fogelberg. I heard that he had been critically ill. I remembered being seventeen right after my dad died and finding the [Fogelberg] album *Netherlands* and how it changed my life… how it made me say, "If I could do this for other people, that's why I wanna be a songwriter." So when I heard he was ill, I wondered, "Did he even know what an impact he had on other creative people's lives?" So, I guess that's the song currently I'm most proud of. It's a song called "His Way With Words." It's just really a tribute to Dan Fogelberg.

What's in store for Michael Peterson in the next ten years?

You know, as I look ahead to the future, ten years from now and try to work backwards, I see that in ten years I will have several books published. I see that in ten years I will have written more songs that have moved people. I see that in ten years I'll maybe have a daughter that will be getting married… and one that's just about getting ready to get out of college. I'll see in ten years that I will have a real handle on how not to have my wife be so mad at me all the time. I see that in ten years I will be healthier than I am now. Man, I just see so many things when I look ahead. What I really see in ten years I can boil down to this: great friends, great music, great work, great family, great faith, and a great life.

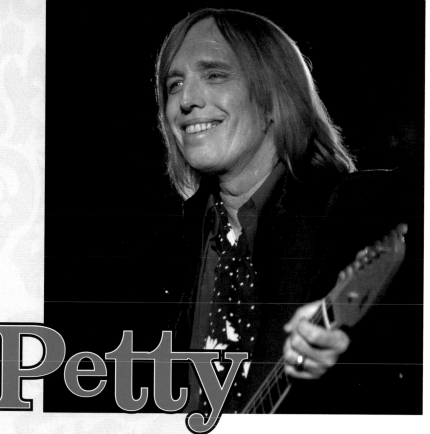

Tom Petty

Tom Petty is one of America's most beloved songwriters. On both his solo albums and those cut with his band, the Heartbreakers, Petty has delivered three decades worth of radio hits, thanks to his affinity for jangly, crowd-pleasing roots rock laced with undeniable hooks. Tom Petty and the Heartbreakers's 1979 debut, *Damn the Torpedoes*, introduced the band with early hits like "Don't Do Me Like That" and "Refugee." 1985's *Southern Accents* featured the MTV staple "Don't Come Around Here No More." In 1989, Petty's career reached new heights, thanks to the popularity of his first solo album, *Full Moon Fever*, which spawned the contemporary classics "Free Fallin'" and "I Won't Back Down." *Wildflowers*, his top-selling studio album, featured the good-time rock of "You Don't Know How It Feels" and "You Wreck Me." In 2002, Petty and the Heartbreakers tackled a corrupt music industry with *The Last DJ*. In 2006, Petty released his newest solo album, entitled *Highway Companion*.

—Evan Schlansky

*Interview by
Paul Zollo*

American Songwriter,
November/December 2005

Where does *Highway Companion* rank among your previous work?

I think it might be *one* of the best things I've ever done.

What was your father like? I hear he was very in touch with his machismo.

My dad was pretty wild. He used to always be going to get his car out of a ditch somewhere. I thought it was *completely* normal to run your car into a ditch. Now I realize… wow. And he was quite a gambler, and my mother hated it. It was quite a turbulent household, really. Very turbulent. He was quite a drinker… just as wild as the wind, really. I never liked it. My dad was a *hard* man—to be around. He wanted me to be a lot more macho than I was. I was this real sort of tender, emotional kid, more inclined to the arts. I didn't want to be trapped in a boat all day.

What was it like hunting with him?

It was *awful*. It was sitting in fields, really cold, to shoot a bird. I remember birds stuffed in bags, and cleaning the birds, picking all the feathers off. It was *gross*. I hated it. One day this small alligator came up by the boat, and I actually saw my dad take his forefinger and his thumb and punch the eyes in on the alligator… to show me that he could knock the alligator out… and the gator rolled over in the water. He was just *nuts*. But he wasn't afraid of anything. I once saw my dad grab a rattlesnake by the tail, swing it round his head, and pop his neck. That's pretty wild, you know? So I was kind of scared of him.

But it was your father who bought your first guitar. How did you begin playing?

Lessons were too formal. I met a kid who actually knew how to play, and he showed me chords, and we sat and played guitar; you learn really quickly that way. The first key I learned

was C, so you had to have F, and F is a tough one. I remember playing "Wooly Bully." It was the first one I mastered, and I was on my way. From there it just went on. "Baby, I'm Leaving," a twelve-bar blues kind of thing, it was in C. [My father] was really proud of it. When he would have a friend over, he'd say, "Bring your guitar out and play a song for this guy.'" [My mother] was amazed that I could do it. She'd say, "I can't understand how you can do it if you didn't have any lessons, and you don't know how to write music. How do you do it?" And I said, "I don't know, I just learned it from other kids."

What impact did the Beatles have on you?

The minute I saw the Beatles on the *The Ed Sullivan Show*, *there* was the way out. *There* was the way to do it. You get your friends and you're a self-contained unit. And you make the music. And it looked like so much fun. *This* really spoke to me. I had been a big fan of Elvis, but I really saw in the Beatles that… here's something I could do.

What was your first experience playing in band like?

We got together one afternoon in my front room and played. It was the biggest rush in my life, the minute it all happened. We learned four songs, all instrumentals, including "House of the Rising Sun" and "Walk, Don't Run." We all wore blue shirts and jeans, so we looked like a band.

Your first gig was during intermission at a school dance. How did it go over with the crowd?

We were such a hit that we were invited to play during the next intermission, and we repeated the same four songs. At the end of the night, as we were packing up our instruments and amps, an "older kid" came up to us and asked, "Do you guys ever play fraternity parties?" I answered, "No, we've never played anywhere but here." The guy said he could get us some bookings. This was a Friday night, and the following Saturday, we were in Dennis Lee's garage, trying to learn more songs. And it never stopped from that moment. We were called The Sundowners.

You were only fourteen at the time. What did your parents think of you playing gigs and making money?

My mom was like, "Where did you get this money?" and I told her I got it for the show. She said, "*Really*, where did you get this money? If you took this money, you're gonna have to own up to it." I said, "I swear to God, Mom, they paid me this for playing." She didn't believe me. So she called the Moose Club, and the guy said, "Yeah, they get the door, and that's what they made."

How many shows were you playing?

We worked constantly; Gainesville had so many opportunities to play. There was a fraternity row where they had parties every Friday and Saturday night and they had socials that you could play in the afternoon. They were only hour gigs, so if we were really lucky, we'd have a social in the afternoon and then we'd do the show that night and maybe a dance. We were working guys. We were obsessed with it. *Completely*.

Tell me about joining The Epics.

It was kind of mind-blowing [to join The Epics]. They worked all up and down Florida. That's when we first started to go on overnight gigs. You'd go and stay in a motel room, and these guys were… *crazy*. They were *really* into girls—and into bringing them back to the room. That's where I kind of grew up, in The Epics, watching these guys. They were just completely bonko, wild, partying, drunk… but they had a really good drummer. The guy just played the most *solid* beat. I loved playing with him.

After leaving The Epics, how did you and Tom Leadon meet Randall Marsh and Mike Campbell?

Randall responded to the ad in Lipham's music store, and we went out to his place. I told Randall it was a shame that they didn't have a rhythm guitarist, and Randall said, "My roommate plays guitar." In came Mike Campbell, carrying a Japanese guitar. He kicked off "Johnny B. Goode," and when the song ended, we said, "You're in the band, man." He had to be in the band, and he didn't necessarily even want to be in the band. Somehow we convinced him to stay in the band, and that became the Mudcrutch that people know. Mudcrutch got to be *very* popular in Gainesville. That band really worked.

Lipham's seemed to be the place for musicians to hang and listen to each other play. Who else did you meet in there?

It was also at Lipham's music store, a few years earlier, that I had met keyboardist extraordinaire Benmont Tench, who was only thirteen at the time. Benmont came into the store, sat down at the Farfisa organ, and proceeded to play all of *Sgt. Pepper*, adjusting the stops to get various sounds. Everybody there was astounded at the kid's virtuosity. But I never saw him again until, God, about 1970, and my roommate came in the door one night with this guy, and he was all bearded and had really long hair. Slowly I realized it was Benmont. It was like, "You're the kid!" And he said, "Yeah, I have a band in New Orleans." I said, "We have a gig tomorrow night. Do you want to play with us?' He said, "All I have is my Farfisa organ." I said, "Okay, you're in." Ben made it to the show with organ in tow and winningly played five sets with the band, all with no previous rehearsal. I knew Benmont was ideal for the band.

Was it at this point you decided to get the band a record deal?

I wrote a song. "Up in Mississippi"—you have to be pretty far south to go *up* to Mississippi—which we recorded and made into a 45. The record received a lot of airplay on Gainesville

radio stations because we bribed our friends into calling the request line. It led to more gigs, and Mudcrutch became one of Gainesville's foremost bands. We fell in love with it. *Totally.* We just fell in love with the whole idea of being in the studio and hearing it come back on those great big speakers. And it sounded so *good.* [But it took] all the dough we had to pay for one session.

What was it like hearing the song on the radio?

Oh man, it was such a gas. *Such* a gas.

After that, didn't you guys throw some mini-rock festivals in a field behind Randall and Mike's place?

That was the key to our success. We became really famous around town, and when we played, a lot of people came. Before that, we used to play at Dub's [a Gainesville club]. We would play there six nights a week. Five sets a night. Got a hundred bucks apiece a week. But at Dub's, the crowd wanted covers, so to get around this problem, I would say, "Here's one by Santana," and play an original.

Gainesville was a small town. How many other places could you play?

That's when California came into the picture. We were constantly just trying to keep enough gigs to pay the rent and keep working. But we could see it wasn't going anywhere. How big can you get in Gainesville? We had certainly hit the top of the ladder there. We were probably even then the most famous band in Gainesville. I *still* meet people who tell me they saw Mudcrutch. But we knew we had to break out of there.

So you drove out to California with no contacts or gigs?

The only addresses we had we'd written down from record ads in *Rolling Stone.* I was trying to find some more, so I went into Ben Frank's diner on Sunset, and I went to a phone booth to look up record companies. On the floor of the phone booth there was a piece of paper, and it was a list of twenty record companies—with their phone numbers and addresses. I kind of went… "There are a lot of people doing this." But I swear to God it was there. On that very first day, the band hit pay dirt at MGM, where they were invited to record a single. The next day, London Records also expressed interest in the band, wanting to sign them right away. Following that, Capitol Records also got on the Mudcrutch bandwagon: [They] wanted to book demo time in their studio. We were so silly and indignant that we didn't want to do a demo, and we didn't know there was a difference between record companies. We were really green. We just felt that if they put out records… that was fine with us. We didn't know there'd be any difference between Shelter Records or Capitol Records. They all put out records nationally, or internationally. That's all we were interested in.

We stayed for a few more days, and on the last day we were here, we went by Shelter Records and gave the tape to this girl named Andrea Starr. She opened the door, and she thought we were cute… she told me later. She took the tape to Simon Miller Mundy, who was their A&R guy. We went home [to Florida] and sold everything we owned and got ready to come to California. And literally, in a rehearsal, the phone rang and I answered it; it was Denny Cordell. I thought he was calling about a car we had for sale. And he said, "I really want to sign your group. I think you guys are really great. I think you guys are like the next Rolling Stones." I was like… "What is this?" But we knew who Denny Cordell was. We knew he had done "A Whiter Shade of Pale" and the Joe Cocker stuff. We knew that he was a real guy we were talking to on the phone. But I had to say, "Well, I'm really sorry, but we already promised London Records we would sign with them." And he said, "I'll tell you what. If you're going to drive out here, I've got a studio in Tulsa,

Oklahoma. And that's going to be not far out of your way. Why don't you stop in Tulsa and meet with me, and then you can see if you like us."

What happened in Tulsa?

We met Cordell in the middle of a windstorm on the street. He brought us to Shelter's studio, which was built in a church… it was called the Church Studio. It was a really nice studio. [Cordell] said, "Spend the night, and tomorrow we'll go in and do a session. We'll see how you like it." We were like, "Wow, we get to do a session in a studio! Hell, yeah, we'll spend the night." We spent the next day recording, and he went, "That's it. I'm sold. I want to sign your band." And we liked him a lot, much better than the guy at London, who was an executive type. So we said, "Okay, we'll go with you." We recorded an album, with the song "Depot Street" released as a single.

After that the band split, right? What did each of you do?

I was offered a solo deal from Shelter Records. I cut some tracks with a phenomenal lineup of musicians, including Al Kooper, "Duck" Dunn, and Jim Gordon, but I didn't relish the idea of being a solo artist, preferring the camaraderie

> *It's important to give them something in a show that they didn't expect, and to take them somewhere that they didn't really plan on going.*

of a band. At the same time, Benmont organized a group to record his own songs and invited me to play harmonica.

(The band consisted of Mike Campbell on guitar, Ron Blair on bass, Stan Lynch on drums, Randall Marsh also on drums, Jeff Jourard on guitar, and Benmont on keys.) And it *instantly* hit me… that *man*, you know, this is home. This is where I should be. And I quickly did my pitch about talking them into going in with me. I wanted Lynch, Blair, Campbell, and Tench to be in my group and convinced them to join by saying I already had a record deal. They accepted, and the Heartbreakers were born.

Let's skip ahead a few decades. Now Tom Petty and the Heartbreakers are one of America's most beloved and enduring rock 'n' roll bands. How do you keep from "not becoming a jukebox" when you tour?

We've got a lot of material, but we're not stuck with the same fifteen songs. It's a big temptation sometimes just to play the really huge songs, because the crowd loves it, and if you let them have their way, they'll demand that. It's important to give them something in a show that they didn't expect, and to take them somewhere that they didn't really plan on going.

Sometimes I feel like I don't want to play "American Girl" anymore. We've been playing it for thirty years. But then…maybe you'll get two hours into the show, and the place is frenzied, and the vibe is so great, and the first couple chords of that song come on, and there's *such* a rush of adrenaline throughout the building… that the next thing you know, you're *really* digging playing "American Girl." [And I'll feel like], I can't believe I'm digging this again, but I am.

It's important to us that we don't turn into an oldies act. We don't want to turn into that great nostalgia machine. We've seen many of the people who we

came up with turn into that. I think you always have to have something new. That's what keeps us going.

Where do you see rock 'n' roll changing? How do you cope with new sounds and the colliding of genres?

I think rock 'n' roll is going to go the way of blues and jazz. It's not the predominant music anymore. But I think we can keep going on as long as we're honest. The music makes you feel young. It's a good way to stay in touch with that feeling. I think we can do it for a long time as long as we remain honest in what we're doing and we don't try to be some-

---

It's got to boil inside of you and then burst out.

---

thing we're not. Our audience is a rock 'n' roll audience. It hasn't turned into one of those passive, sit-in-the-seat kind of audiences. I'm *so* grateful for that, but maybe the reason for that is that we've never tried to pander to a young crowd. We never tried to pretend we were something we weren't, and so they always took us at face value. We're not trying to be teen idols. We had our days of doing that, and we're trying to grow up with the music. We tried to grow up, and as time went by, the music had to grow with us.

What can you do to explore new sounds and areas of your music?

I think there will always be new places to go, musically. And I think that's true because I've got a unit that can go any-where I want to point them. The frustrating part for me is having songs for them to play. If you ever hear this band warm up, it's *scary*! They play so effortlessly and so unbridled and so great. But I get frustrated because I want to harness

that and get it into a song, and it's hard to keep supplying them with material that will showcase that. It's hard to write a great blues or a great rock 'n' roll song, because there's purity there you can't fake. Try writing "Long Tall Sally." It isn't easy. It's a difficult thing to write because it has to be done with certain spontaneity. It's not something you can overwork. Those kinds of things just aren't handed to you every day. It has to just burst out of your heart. Those aren't things you can plan. You can't say, "I'm gonna sit down today and write 'Long Tall Sally.'" It's got to boil inside of you and then burst out. They're hard songs to write… it's a constant education. As you get older, you get more perspective on your body of work. I can see things that I'm better at than other things. So I'm trying to find the things that I'm good at and improve [on them]—rather than go all over the map and try everything. I'm still looking. I'm still search-ing. I try to be optimistic. The thing now is to keep refining, keep growing, keep finding things in us that we didn't know about ourselves. I think as long as we enjoy doing it, we'll keep doing it.

Grant-Lee Phillips

photo courtesy Denise Siegel

Grant-Lee Phillips is best known as the voice and vision behind the critically acclaimed nineties alternative rock band Grant Lee Buffalo. Phillips started Buffalo from the ashes of his first band, Shiva Burlesque, and they signed to Slash Records in 1992. After winning over fans in Europe on the strength of their 1993 debut, *Fuzzy*, the band toured America relentlessly, supporting bands like R.E.M., Pearl Jam, and the Smashing Pumpkins. During their tenure, they released four excellent albums, and Phillips was honored as Best Male Vocalist by *Rolling Stone*. In 1999, Grant Lee Buffalo dissolved and Phillips pursued a solo career, playing every instrument himself for the intimate, acoustic-based *Ladies' Love Oracle*. His celebrated second album, *Mobilize*, followed in 2001, and 2004 saw the release of the stark and lean *Virginia Creeper*. In between albums, Phillips continues to hone his increasingly experimental songs in performance at the popular Los Angeles songwriter's venue, Largo. Phillips put out an album of covers in 2006, *Nineteen Eighties*, which is a tribute to songwriters and artists who inspired him.

—Evan Schlansky

Interview by
Bill Locey

American Songwriter,
July/August 2004

So Grant, did *Virginia Creeper* make you a rich rock star?

Um, no—neither rich nor rockin'. "Enough is a banquet," as it says on the fortune cookie.

Where does it fit in with what came before?

I think *Mobilize* was more the black sheep of my family, and I'm certainly proud of that album, but it represents more of a departure from what I was most associated with—the typical acoustic approach, you know? In many ways *Virginia Creeper* feels like coming home to a very familiar terrain, and yet I feel as if I haven't hit this stride on an album before.

There are a lot of girls' names in the song titles— are all these girls your exes?

It's one of those things that stands out so glaringly after the fact—long after the album has been mastered and shrink-wrapped—I never put too much mind to it. Depending on the song, it can be deciphered any number of ways. "Sussana Little"' is about my great grandmother, and "Calamity Jane" is about an idea—using a Wild West hero to sort of identify that gun-totin' attitude that is in keeping with our current administration, more so than with an old girlfriend.

So, "Always Friends"—is that possible with an ex?

I wouldn't say so. We have a way of demanding an autobiographical connection to all we pen and listen to, but songs for me come from a deeper place, from a very internal place. And it just happens to be the case that when you access a certain character—addressing one or speaking through one—I'm able to enter into a dialogue that would be a lot less interesting for me if I were to rely on my experience alone.

Does bad love make for good songs?

I couldn't say because I feel I've been blessed by good love.

When you write a song, do the lyrics come first or does the music come first… or is every song different?

I don't know that there is a certain formula. The music tends to dominate, which is an odd thing. The words are really your ambassadors as a songwriter, but the words are bound to rhythm, rhyme, and all the basic tenets that you come up against as a songwriter. I guess, at some point in time, the two emerge as one idea. It's a process I continue to be dumbfounded by, frustrated by, and yet it keeps me coming back for more.

Is songwriting an art or a craft or something in between?

I think it's probably any and all of the above. There are certain songs that we've all heard that are all craft and nothing else. The songs that I tend to play over and over again are the ones I can't put my finger on and say, "Well, this song is about this." I'm not a mathematical kind of person. My favorite songs—those of my own and those I continue to listen to—are the ones that have a mysterious quality to them.

So who blows your mind as a writer?

These days, I'm always intrigued to hear from Gillian Welch. I like the band Wilco quite a bit, and I'm a big fan of Elliott Smith. Then, having said that, I forever return to people like Johnny Cash, Neil Young, and Van Morrison—all Mount Rushmore-like heads that loom over all of us. I go back there time and time again and find new meaning. It confirms my belief when I see young generations stumble onto [Bob Dylan's] *Highway 61 Revisited*. And they get it, and maybe, they find something other people might've missed.

So when people say, "Oh, Grant—he's that Americana dude," is that cool or does it even matter what people say?

I'm just glad they're saying something. Now and then I'm accepted to the Americana parties, the alt.country parties, or the alternative rock parties. I have to believe it's a little difficult to put me in a box, but I would imagine it's the same with a lot of the people I listen to. As I was saying, where do you file Gillian Welch?

Exactly. The Blasters and the Old 97's cannot be homeless, can they?

That's right. They may not have a home on commercial radio, but you'll find those records in homes across the world.

The words are really your ambassadors as a songwriter, but the words are bound to rhythm, rhyme, and all the basic tenets that you come up against as a songwriter.

It moves you in ways that nothing else can.

Exactly, yeah. It's at once passive—you can pop on the radio, drive in traffic, and talk on the cell phone and enjoy the new Norah Jones album. Or you can shut out the world and put on the headphones and hear the new Norah Jones album. There are many different ways to appreciate it.

What's the best and worst thing about your job?

I suppose there's a common thread that runs through the best and worst aspects of this, but it's just such an intoxicating, excessive medium. It's kind of a crazy ride when you're offered the opportunity to do something like playing music—to tour, for instance. To get up and play for people, to sweat and play the songs you've been playing for years over and over—that's a challenge as well as an opportunity. It's a strange thing to find yourself in a club environment where every night is Friday night. That has a way of taking its toll on your psyche. I'm not sure this always brings out the best in musicians—it forces you to rise to a new level. Not all of us are built of the same stuff as Willie Nelson and Iggy Pop.

What would you say to an aspiring musician?

I guess the best advice I can offer is to follow your muse. Allow the songwriting and that process to guide you. So much of this industry is built on sand, but the one bedrock you can always return to is your love of songs and your urge to create them. Music is that kind of thing that you can't really explain away too easily. It just sort of is.

photo courtesy Hugh Prestwood

Hugh Prestwood

Interview by
Vernell Hackett

American Songwriter,
May/June 1992

Based in Long Island, New York, Hugh Prestwood has been writing hit songs for the last couple of decades. He was born and raised in El Paso, Texas, and attended the University of Texas at El Paso for his collegiate experience. Unlike many songwriters who enjoy success in the country music industry, Prestwood *doesn't* call Nashville home and *doesn't* co-write. Sounds crazy, but it's true. He is a staff writer for BMG Songs, and his résumé is chock full of number one hits that are truly unique and inspirational: "Hard Rock Bottom of Your Heart" (Randy Travis), "The Song Remembers When" (Trisha Yearwood), "Ghost in This House" (Shenandoah, Alison Krauss), and "The Sound of Goodbye" (Crystal Gayle), among many others. Prestwood teaches advanced songwriting at The New School in Manhattan—which he has done since 1982—and he is also active with Nashville Songwriters Association International (NSAI) and its workshops and song camps.

—DOUGLAS WATERMAN

Your big break came very late in your career. How did an unknown and aging songwriter from Texas attract the attention of a legend like Judy Collins?

I was doing a showcase at [New York City's] Bottom Line and Tom Paxton was there. He came up to me and was very complimentary of my writing. I knew he knew Judy Collins, and I had some songs that I felt would be good for her, so I didn't say anything to him then, but I got his address and sent him some songs. At least a year went by, and I was working this day job because I had to have money coming in… I got this call one day and they said it was Judy Collins. I thought they were kidding me, but it turned out that she had really flipped over this song I'd written called "Dorothy," and that was the beginning of how I got in the big league.

After you had gotten a song cut by Crystal Gayle and you started coming to Nashville, did your writing take on a new direction?

I wasn't doing anything real different; it was more like there were probably certain songs I wasn't writing and certain songs that I was writing more of. And country was just getting more interesting. Believe it or not, country music was the first music I ever remember listening to. The first song I remember was "Humpty Dumpty Heart" by Hank Thompson. So when I left El Paso, I was totally into the folk thing, so I sort of came around full circle back into country.

When you write, is it spontaneous, rather than sitting down to write from nine to five?

Yeah, I mean, I don't even leave the house for days at a time sometimes. I get up and try to write very day, and I take my time. I don't want to be in a hurry. Some people work real good with the deadline, but I'd rather not have the deadline.

Do you co-write very much?

Practically not at all. I've given it a go a few times, and usually the first thing that happens is that we get together and about fifteen minutes later I'm thinking, "Oh God, I've got to be here another hour and a half." It's like suddenly I'm blocked into doing this thing, and it's just terrible. It has nothing to do with who I'm with. It just has to do with the whole situation. It's like a long time ago, when I got out of my straight job and Judy Collins got me a staff writing job. I had been writing at night and thought, "I'm going to have all day to write songs, so I'm going to get up and write six hours tomorrow." Well, about a week into it, I realized that the minute I said I was going to write six hours, I started looking at my watch, going, "Five-and-a-half hours to…" So eventually, I came around to the idea that all I was going to do is just get up and try to write. It might be five minutes, it might be fifteen minutes, but I was not going to go on longer than I wanted to go. Then, it's not like it's a burden to me. I can just do it and enjoy it.

How do you know when a song is finished? Do you have a method of determining this?

That's a real tough thing 'cause with a few exceptions, there are always some lines in a song that I wish I could make better. But what usually happens is that I just keep hammering on it until I really think that's the best I can do. I can spend a month on a song, even though I might get the majority of it written in two days. And by the time I've finished, I hate the song. I even wonder why I spent time to write it. But I think there's just this gut feeling that it's okay; it's time to move on. There is really no easy answer, but there is a point where you do need to stop. There needs to be a few really good lines in a song, but every line does not have to be great. But you have to make sure the key things are in there where they need to be.

You teach at The New School in New York City. What is it that you teach there?

I teach Advanced Songwriting. It's a very famous school; it was founded in the 1920s and it's basically an adult education format. The people who have taught there are unbelievable—Robert Frost, Aaron Copland, Norman Mailer… The first fifteen people who sign up for the course get in, so it's a great place to be. The class is made up of every kind of person who thinks they would like to write some songs.

What is the most important thing that you teach your students?

The thing I stress the most is to understand about the *formula* of writing… that it's not something bad. You always hear a lot of students in there who say, "Oh, don't burden me with these rules. I want my song to be eight minutes long." I try to really get them to understand that you can write a great song and still stay within the hurdles. A song has to have certain things and certain elements. Then I talk a lot about attitude. I'm a great believer that you have to take a long-term attitude. Everybody who gets into songwriting thinks it's going to be so easy. You write a song in two days and get it recorded. I'm telling you to think about songwriting just like medical school. It's going to take seven years of busting your butt. That's what it's going to take. It's much more difficult than you think to write a good song. The worst thing that can happen is to get lucky and write a hit which you can't follow up.

What is the market like in New York for songwriters?

New York is a tough place. I'm amazed anyone would go there. It's just so expensive to live, and it's pretty closed as far as publishing and so forth. I dread talking to receptionists at those places. The clubs in New York seem to be run by people who don't really care about music. Their attitude has always been, "We're not gonna pay you anything because you're getting exposed here in New York." If you are going to write country music, you need to come to Nashville. Nashville has some great clubs to showcase original music. And right now, a guy can come to Nashville and walk into a publishing company, and maybe they'll give him a break. Maybe they won't… but they might. I hope that doesn't change, but I see where it might.

What advice would you offer to new writers?

If you want to be a songwriter, you have to realize that it's really a competitive field. I keep telling my class… you wouldn't just dream of trying out for the New York Mets having just gotten into baseball. You'd be terrified that they would kill you. And yet, you go out and write a few songs and think that you're ready for the major leagues without paying any dues. You're crazy. You've got to think about this thing in terms of years, in terms of trying to write the best songs that you can. And you've got to love the process.

It's going to take at least five years to have any success, even if you have a lot of talent. You've got to love it or you are never going to go that long without success. What will keep you writing for five years without success? You have to write things that turn you on. Know the formulas and employ them when you can. But write songs that you love.

To me, the magic in songwriting is that when I was a kid, once or twice a year I'd hear a song and it would just kill me. I would go out and buy the record and play it over and over again. And six months later, something else would come out that would do me the same way. And to me, the magic of songwriting—instead of having to wait for that song to come along—is that I can sit down and write that song myself. I don't have to wait six months. I can have it this week. That's the great thing about writing a song that you love. That's the joy of it. If you write that song that really knocks you out, that's what it's all about.

John Prine

photo courtesy John Chiasson

The writer of "Angel From Montgomery" wasn't from Alabama but from Maywood, Illinois, where John Prine was born in 1936. Prine's parents were Kentuckians who lived near Chicago when he was young, but their love for country and bluegrass music would always influence his writing. When he was thirty-five, in 1971, Prine was working as a mailman and occasionally working clubs at night. Steve Goodman, who the following year hit pay dirt when Arlo Guthrie recorded his "City of New Orleans," had become a Prine fan by then and invited Kris Kristofferson to come listen.

He did, and Kristofferson invited Prine to open for him in New York at The Bitter End, where famed producer Jerry Wexler caught Prine's act and signed him the next day. His self-titled album yielded some classic tunes, including "Hello in There" (which Bette Midler soon covered), "Angel From Montgomery," and "Paradise."

Prine moved to Nashville in the late seventies, where he founded Oh Boy Records in partnership with his manager, Al Bunetta. By 2005, the label roster also included Kristofferson and the notable young songsmith Todd Snider. The advantage Prine obtained by running the show himself was that he could take the time he wanted on his recordings, and the result was just four albums between 1981 and 1995, but each was filled with strong songs. *Fair & Square* (2005) is Prine's latest release and arguably one of his best.

—PHIL SWEETLAND

*Interview by
Paul V. Griffith*

American Songwriter,
May/June 2005

At one point you worked as a mailman; if it weren't your job, would you still write songs?

Good question. I don't know. Increasingly during the last ten years or so, it's become more of a job to get the writing done—whereas in the early years it was an escape. When I was still a mailman, it was total escape. The best way to get away from the world was to go write a song. And then after I started making records, the first three or four records, I would just write 'em while walking down the street—just throw 'em over my shoulder.

I try and to do everything I can to make it fun—to make it a fun situation—especially when I'm co-writing. I guess that's why there's more co-writing on this record than usual, because I got with buddies like Pat McLaughlin, Roger Cook, and Keith Sykes, and it was a fun day to spend together. Pat and I got on a roll where every Tuesday we wrote… We'd start writing at ten in the morning, finish the song somewhere between two and three, demo it, and by six o'clock you'd have thought we'd just cut an album. It was just one song, but we'd both go home to our families with our CD in our pocket and play it forty-five times and think it was the greatest song in the world. Sometimes it turned out to be a really good song, and sometimes it just turned out to be okay; whatever we wanted out of it we got out of it that day. We had fun, and I try and keep that in the writing because if I don't, then it might become increasingly hard to write… if I have to look at it as work. I think it would show up in the song if I totally looked at it as work. That's the deal. It's the job I've had the most success at. What would I have gone on to?

Where do you start? Do ideas come to you as you're walking down the street, or is there a fully formed song out there that you have to carve away everything that's not it?

Both. The ones that I write on my own… I wait for those. I can't make myself, on my own, go write. So I wait and I wait and I wait, and when they do come along, they're a big block. The song is in there. All you've got to do is pull away the stuff that's not supposed to be there. I wish they could all be like that, but it takes a long time [these days]. I wait and wait and wait, trying to be very patient, but there comes a time, after I've got a handful of songs that I want to try to put together as a record. The difference with songs I co-write is that one of us will come to a meeting with an idea or one line and see if it sparks anything with the other one. With Pat it's like really… there's no subject matter… there's no story line. He's got a line and I say, "Great, will it go from there?" So I go into something… sometimes I'll just go wild and just write a verse all at once. And Pat or I will go, "Yeah, that's it," or "No, that's a whole other song." But we can go back and forth like that, and we never stop to discuss what the song's about. So in the end the song might really mean two different things to us. But as far as what the story is, what the song means, it's always been like the song is the dog and it's waggin' me. I just follow the song around the room or around the block and finally get the song to sit down… only when the dog is tired.

Is that true, too, for your stream-of-consciousness songs like "She Is My Everything": "From Muhammad Ali to teachin' Bruce Lee how to do karate"? Where do lines like that come from?

I finally have a subject area and I decide to sit down and write, and I just got to the point that, because of a couple of inter-rhymes in the beginning of the song, I wanted to keep building it like a house of cards, keep stacking them on top of one another and make 'em look like they're gonna fall and they don't, you know? I love it when it works like that.

Has the process changed over the years? Are you more receptive to those moments at this point in your career?

Once I get into it, it's pretty much the same as it's always been. Once I get the song going downhill and the engine kicks in, it's all those other resources that kick in when I want them to. When I'm writing on my own it's pretty unselfconscious. It just rolls along and it becomes more a decision on what not to use rather that what to use.

How many songs don't we get to hear?

Not many. I don't take the time to write that many that I'm not going to use. From those sessions, there was one in particular that—no matter what we did—to me it never sounded as good as the demo. And the demo wasn't good enough to build into a track. So I just finally had to set the song to the side; we had too many songs anyway when it finally came down to it. When we mixed, we had to eliminate a few.

But most of the ones you start, you finish?

Yeah. That song I was just talking about is mixed and sitting on a shelf. Somebody, for a movie or something, might ask me for something that hasn't been released. It might be used like that, or recut. But it's not like I've got a whole sack full of songs sitting around. I've maybe started something that I haven't used, but I've got a whole lot of other things I'd rather be doing. I rather go get a hot dog any day, or a donut, than write a song.

There's a lot of debate about suffering and art. Does suffering play a role in your writing?

No, but it's easier to write a really good sad song than it is a really good uplifting song. It's easier to want to put those emotions that are really pulling at you into words. Steve Goodman used to say, "When you're lucky enough that things are going really good, who wants to stop and write a song about it." But when somebody leaves you or something, you've got all the time in the world. But that's about as far as I would take it. I don't think I would want to put myself in the situation to suffer just so I could write a good song. I would rather have a nice, happy, balanced life and go, "Sorry I don't have any good songs this year; I'm livin' instead."

You mentioned Steve Goodman. I'd like to go back and get a sense of what it was like when you were both coming up in the Chicago folk scene. Does that scene still inform what you do?

First of all, going through that, it was a really great existing scene going on in Chicago at the time. And Goodman and I and Bobby (Bonnie) Pollock became the three that got record contracts. There were a lot of really, really great and very good musicians in Chicago at the time, playing clubs… the big thing was there were some Chicago labels where everybody said you had to leave town to get a contract. Of course you've heard that in other towns, too. But the fact is that we all got contracts within a couple months of each other and still lived in Chicago, and they were all well-received. In the folk world we were kind of like conquering heroes—if they could have given us a tickertape parade they would have. So that was really good, and Steve Goodman on many occasions was the most supportive friend/fan I could have had. He used to corner people before I ever had a record deal and sing one or two of my songs and one of his. He was always pushing me. That's how Kristofferson got to come over and see me because Steve wouldn't just sit by and let the light shine on him. He said, "You've got to come and see my buddy. You have to." How that carries on to today. It's a great memory to have—because that scene is no longer there. It all kind of left town. That folk scene left at the end of the seventies. By 1980, all of us had gone in differ-

ent directions. I'd come down [to Nashville]; Steve had gone to California; Bonnie had moved to New York City. But at the time, it was great to be a part of it.

You write honest, sentimental songs that don't sound corny. Not every writer can do that. How are you able to write about subjects that might sound trite in the hands of lesser songwriters?

I don't know. It's just that I'm trying to be true to myself. There are certain things about real, everyday life that are very corny, to me. Life isn't a Hallmark card, but there are certain things that happen in life that are hard to relate without being corny. But I try sometimes because there are places and certain feelings that I want to talk about and describe them, and when they're described well, I've just got to go with it. And it is a fine line, I guess, when you're dealing with something sentimental—to keep an edge on it—but at the same time I think anger in songwriting and music is highly overrated.

Your personality really comes across in your songs. People have been fans of yours for a long time because they see you in your songs.

Well, also they see a lot of themselves in the songs. If I thought I was writing to appeal to a certain kind of person, I'd be a terrible failure at that. So instead I try not to guess. I go with what I know, now matter how limited or whatever, it's still what I know to be true… my feelings. I hate giving advice, but I would say for songwriters starting out that you can't go wrong if you stick to what you know. No matter how limited it is, stick to your world. Make that your square that you write inside of. That's your foundation.

Who are some of your favorite songwriters and what influence have they had on you?

Well, the ones that were influential when I started, and remain so, are Bob Dylan and Hank Williams, Sr.—even though he existed entirely upon what catalog he left behind. The guy was twenty-seven. Still, it's amazing that all those songs are really, really great and they all came of that short a period of time. I really like Van Morrison; he's been a mainstay for me over the years. I love that he still makes as many records as he makes, and he sticks by his guns. It's not always what everybody would want him to be, but he's definitely chasing something, and he catches it every once in a while and takes everybody right along with it. I really like Nick Lowe and Elvis Costello. Ron Sexsmith kills me. I love his words, but it totally slays me that somebody can come up with new, exciting melodies like he does. He's got his head turned a certain way and he's saying this one thing, but he's saying it differently in all these songs.

Do you write on the road?

I don't normally try to write on the road but I stay open to it. Every once in a while an idea will come in the strangest place. I've learned to be receptive to it and to write it down, even if it's just another napkin that'll be around for ten years.… And I try to keep my antennas up and my gear clean. You never know when they're going to come along. I still don't know where they come from after all these years. Sometimes that's the only thing I appreciate about the guys that do it strictly as a job. They're craftsmen, and they're really good at what they do. Sometimes they write a real winner. But I can't do that; I've got to wait. The road's not conducive to it. Goodman and I were on the road, and he never shut down. We could have gone to two or three parties and played a gig, ate a fabulous dinner, and it'd be the wee hours of the morning, and Goodman would go, "Wait, wait," and he'd run to his room and get his guitar and go, "Listen to this." He just would not quit, and sometimes it was a really good idea that was going somewhere.

?uestlove
The Roots

Since rising from the underground in the early nineties, The Roots have earned the reputation for having not only one of the hottest live hip-hop shows, but one of the hottest live shows, period. The Roots stretch back to 1987 and the Philadelphia High School for Creative and Performing Arts, where rapper Black Thought (born Tarik Trotter, October 3, 1973) and drummer ?uestlove (born Ahmir Thompson, January 20, 1971) were both students. Too broke to afford the requisite two turntables and a microphone, the duo began improvising raps with just Black Thought's voice and ?uestlove's drum kit. After winning audiences over on street corners and at talent shows, they added bassist Hub and rapper Malik B and dubbed themselves The Roots.

By 1993, they had formed an airtight musical bond and evolved into live concert phenoms. In 1995, they signed to Geffen Records and released *Do You Want More?!!!??!* It was one of the first hip-hop albums to forgo prerecorded samples for live instrumentation. That year, they finalized their lineup by adding the talents of keyboardist Scott Storch and Rahzel, the world's dopest human beatbox. They gained national fame with 1999's *Things Fall Apart*, featuring the haunting Erykah Badu-aided hit "You Got Me." In 2004, the band founded their own record label/promotional company, OkayPlayer. Their latest release, *Game Theory*, came out on Def Jam in 2006.

—EVAN SCHLANSKY

Interview by
James Kendall

American Songwriter,
March/April 2005

Do you keep in mind to play to the audience or what the audience expects or doesn't expect?

I'm conscious of it only because twelve years into my survival level really depends on what I deliver. And it's weird because I can't seem too eager and just go for it. We're perfectly capable of doing the mainstream pop records that would have us on the Fugees level or the Outkast level but we kind of know that's our survival... I don't know... it's kind of weird. Have you ever seen *Cape Fear*?

The one with Robert De Niro?

Yeah. You know the very last scene? De Niro's feet are hand-cuffed, he's being dragged out to sea, and he's barely above sea level, barely breathing. That's what it is like to be The Roots sometimes. You really do have to be conscious of every move you make. And sometimes even our most sponta-neous moves are absolutely inaudible. I know it's somewhat disheartening to sort of destroy people's fantasies. There's no way that we could be, in this case, on a major label, on the same major label, and really just have thirteen winning lottery tickets. That's what we always tell cats that are mak-ing music. You have to be very conscious.

I'm surprised people don't use live drums rather than rhythm machines. Are you surprised?

No. Now with the sampling rates as gargantuan as they are... the reason hip-hop is going through such a creative drought right now isn't for a lack of creativity, because there is a lot of underground hip-hop that is exciting to me. But it's just not financially possible to execute this type of music. I guess the alternative to making the music that really defines hip-hop's creative period... if you want to talk about the Native Tongue period or the Public Enemy period, I guess the answer is they're making what they've called the keyboard beats, which basically sounds like Fisher-Price pop, which is what you've been kind of hearing as of late in hip-hop. I

think that's more of a financial issue because, whereas, let's say you wanted to do a song based on some Donald Byrd, you know back in 1988 or 1989 when it was under the ra-dar, hip-hop wasn't the industry's cash cow, you could pay a small flat fee like two thousand dollars. Nowadays, because hip-hop is the cash cow of the industry... rock music has all but faded away... most of rock's next movement people, The Strokes or whatever, aren't even reaching their poten-tial. And with hip-hop being the fortune, you would have to pay twenty thousand dollars. And because the royalty rates are huge... that's sort of like the financial pit and pendu-lum. But they have been utilizing instrumentation, but we are hip-hop's only quote unquote band... actually the weird-est thing is not only are we hip-hop's only band, we're black music's only band. We are the only group of musicians with a major label record deal. So we're kind of our own island. So what happens is because of this whole "hip-hop rule 101" of no biting allowed... the whole stigma of, "Oh, you guys sound like The Roots" has slowed the industry down. I mean it's flattering to hear, "Oh, you're not as good as The Roots," but that also hurts us because there's no one else to compare us to.

Rhythm, specifically, is in the foreground of your music. How much do you allow rhythm to influ-ence each track?

Well, rhythm is a very important thing to me simply because the way my mindset works I'm always trying to be all things to all people. I come from a town where there are a lot of musicians: Philadelphia. You look at major touring acts to-day, 60 or 70 percent of all of them come from Philly. The drummers who have established themselves out of Philly are what we call gospel drumming. The reason for this label is that there are no other venues for them to express them-selves but jazz clubs and jam sessions. Churches are the last venues left... because I'm in hip-hop, the hip-hop that really peaked my curiosity was the sample-based hip-hop. Hearing Public Enemy, De La Soul, Beastie Boys, I was always listening from a music standpoint. Those albums had songs on which there were at least fifteen to sixteen samples… so it was fun to pick out where each sample came from. I would go through my father's record collection and find the original records and study the breaks.

That's how I met Tarik. He was an art major student in Philadelphia and I was an instrumental major. In 1987 music in the backdrop of hip-hop was basically bare drums. Public Enemy really opened the door to making collages with samples, but that didn't happen till 1988, so in 1987 it was really, program a drum beat and start rhyming. Him and his friends would come up to me all the time and tell me, "Play some beat," and then I played the beat and, "Oh my God!" It was the equivalent of a billion back flips at a time. I knew that people kind of got off on the fact that I could play just like the beats, which requires immense discipline and concentration. When I'm creating music, I have to be ultra-disciplined. Because we entered the industry in a very crucial year, the year that Dr. Dre's *The Chronic* was released… which turned out to be a very pivotal year for hip-hop. The success of hip-hop is sort of defined by the quote unquote sell-outs of the industry. Rappers were proud not to make pop-based ten million-selling records like Vanilla Ice.

And why didn't you guys follow suit?

Well, because the hip-hop that we followed was like A Tribe Called Quest. We were like the caboose train of De La Soul, A Tribe Called Quest, and Jungle Brothers. And I guess the two artists that capped that whole movement off were Digable Planets and Arrested Development. By the time we finally got onto the train platform, the train had left already. We were left with a whole bunch of gangstas like, "Ah, you all soft." Again this whole Rudolph the Red-Nosed Reindeer theory I have. But our saving grace was the fact that musi-

cally, you couldn't think of us as soft because we knew how to play just like the samples, and that just comes from a lot of studio experimentation.

Your music is fundamentally a blending of styles. Is that a direct result of forcing yourself to play the music rather than sample the music?

I don't want to say forcing because it wasn't like, here, we gotta make our mark. The thing is… every member of The Roots has been doing his craft for over twenty years and been on path for over thirty years. My personal entry in hip-hop was the whole "I can play just like the samples that you hear on the records." I never thought of it as a marketing angle. The label followed it as a marketing device. But on *Phrenology* we finally got rid of that crutch as well. We didn't want to be just that.

So you weren't trying to be, but it turned out you were doing something original. How does somebody who doesn't have thirty years experience combat being unoriginal?

It's hard to do it in this marketplace. Which is kind of why we established ourselves as the Harriet Tubman of hip-hop. We established jam sessions, which kind of developed into various artists and groups in Philadelphia. These jam sessions started in my living room in 1998, and then the whole Philadelphia community. We know that not anyone's gonna have the guts to go through the GI Jane-esque basic training that we had to go through for the first six years of our career just to get to ground level and acceptance in the industry.

You collaborate a lot. Is that why?

That's absolutely why. It's kind of weird. The whole underdevelopment of our business structure is a whole other chapter. It's really hard to be on the road three hundred days out

of the year and to discover talent and nurture them at the same time. We're literally doing it by the skin of our teeth. It wasn't until *The Tipping Point* that questions started to get raised, like, "Okay, well, I've been coming to your jam sessions since 1998 and now it's 2004. Are you guys ever going to utilize this? Or just hang around in the studio a lot and do nothing?" That's when we decided really to up our community-based collaborations and start having jam sessions for our albums. All the songs on *The Tipping Point* are the result of eight-hour-a-day jam sessions that we used to organize. At the end of the week we'd listen to twenty to thirty hours worth of jams and say, is this worth developing or not, I like that riff, mark off three minutes and forty seconds. Toward the end of the listening sessions you go back to the marked points and then you start writing music from that. Kind of like how a sampler listens to an old record and gets his source for what he's gonna sample.

I read that you'd kind of gone back to that, to groups of people in the room while recording.

Sometimes it would get too crowded and we'd actually call the cops on ourselves [*in a woman's voice*], "Oh, there's a ruckus going on over there."

Outside of that situation, is it helpful to have that many minds?

It's absolutely helpful because I believe that there is sort of a creative ribbon. Again, we've been doing this since we were nineteen, and now most of us are in our mid-thirties, so our songwriting process was always the same thing like, "Okay, we've all got a good sound check. I know we didn't get no sleep. Let's go to sound check and just jam." *Things Fall Apart* got created based on all the sound checks we had. Now we don't have to be on the road that much… because our stock has risen. We're not doing shows for pennies anymore. It's normal for us to do 150 shows for an album.

Once we decided that Philadelphia had no outlet for us to perform at, we started busking, I guess that's what you call it. We'd set up on the street corners, play, put a hat out or a shoebox. That's really how we got our start. I consider that our start instead of 1987. But from 1987 to 1992 it's like, "Damn, okay, we're a band, what do we do?" We weren't doing any gigs. We were a group in name only. So that's how our first album got created. Our second album got created as a result of being in the studio writing.

Things Fall Apart was the neo-soul record that really established the whole Philadelphia sound, so to speak. The quirky drumming the beats, that neo-soul record. The *Phrenology* record was doing everything we weren't supposed to be doing. Kinda like the record I'd been dreaming of doing. *The Tipping Point* is the direct result of constant jamming.

Is there anything about rhythm in hip-hop that bothers you?

It doesn't bother me. The thing is… I can't say that the music of 50 Cent is basic. It's derivative of what early hip-hop was. Very primitive sounding. Snare rhythms. I really can't get mad. Most people today say that music sounds like Fisher-Price machines. Then I alert them that, you know, all you old-school flag bearers, groups that we definitely claim are the greatest groups of all time, early LL [Cool J]… those cats did snare arrangements. Hip-hop is, first off, an African thing. You have to understand the science of hip-hop. It took a college course for me to understand West African music and hip-hop's parallel lines. Hip-hop is a very rhythmic-based thing, which is why there's a lot of repetition… there is hip-hop that does challenge you artistically that goes to those levels.

My only problem with it is that the only hip-hop that's praised is the hip-hop that is so controversial that that is the story. The world doesn't know about Aesop Rock, the world doesn't know about LP, or Little Brother. That's my only gripe.

Eddie Rabbitt

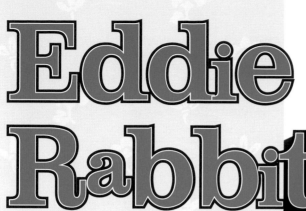

Eddie Rabbitt (1941–1998), the writer of Elvis's "Kentucky Rain" (1970), Ronnie Milsap's "Pure Love" (1974), and many hits for himself—including "Every Which Way But Loose"—was not exactly your typical Music Row tunesmith.

He was born in Brooklyn, New York. Not only is it almost one thousand miles from the Row, but also the longtime home of the Dodgers baseball team and countless Jewish comedians, and it could very well be a million miles away from Hillbilly Heaven musically. Rabbitt was raised in New Jersey, the son of Thomas and Mae Rabbitt, in a home that was filled with all kinds of music.

What separates Rabbitt, Gary Burr, Al Anderson, and other transplanted Northeastern songwriters from their southern competitors in Nashville is that they bring a rock/pop/bluesy feel to their work. Listen to the Connecticut native Burr's "I Try to Think About Elvis" (number three in 1994 for Patty Loveless), Anderson's thumping rocker "Unbelievable" (number two for Diamond Rio in 1999), or Rabbitt's "Kentucky Rain" as examples. The chord changes all three of these men wrote were rarely heard on country records before they used them, and they added crossover appeal to their records.

Tragedy surrounded Rabbitt's all-too-brief life and career. In 1985, he and his wife Janine saw their twenty-three-month-old son, Timmy, who had been born with severe defects, pass away. Eddie would succumb to cancer in 1998; he was just forty-six.

—PHIL SWEETLAND

Interview by
Vernell Hackett

American Songwriter,
July/August 1985

Do you remember writing your first song?

I was twelve years old, and it was a love song. I titled it "Susie." When I finished it, I went in the kitchen and played it for my dad.

How do you manage wearing both hats—artist and songwriter?

Being an artist sometimes over-shines the fact that you have written songs, too. Like Even [Stevens] and I have written so many hit songs together and my being an artist has overshadowed that.

Do you still write with Even?

Since I'm out on the road six or seven months a year we don't see each other for a while, but when we do get together it's like the good old days again. We still get a great kick out of writing with each other. In fact, we wrote just about everything that's on my new album.

How tough is the song selection process for your albums?

We probably write thirty or forty songs in order to get ten for the album. We may get through one hundred bad song ideas before we lock into a general idea of the type of thing we feel this year. We don't go in with a preconceived concept because I like all kinds of music—anything from "Two Dollars in the Jukebox" to "Suspicions"—so we never go in to write an album full of one style or another. We let it happen on its own time. During those six or seven months we haven't seen each other, we change and grow, and from year to year we have new ideas. So we go to write with whatever changes are in us that year, and we let the mood of that year find itself as we mess around with one song after another.

Do you write much on the road?

It's hard to write when you're in the Las Vegas glitter one day and mid-America the next. It's hard to nail down any mood when I'm traveling, so I wait to do the basic writing when I'm off the road. Then I go down and see Even, and we schedule times to write so you get a routine of sameness going. You need that discipline and routine when you write.

Where does your strength as a writing duo come from?

I'm sure that it's the fact that we're such good friends and our minds are in the same place. We have the same kind of ideas and principles and thoughts about songs. We like to write about the same things.

How well does criticism go over between co-writers?

A lot of new writers are afraid to say anything negative [in a co-writing situation] if someone comes up with a line they don't think is good. So they end up accepting a song because they're afraid to say, "I hate that line" or "I don't like your melody." Even and I know each other so well that when a bad line comes up, from either one of us, we can say, "That's awful" without offending the other guy.

Are you involved on Music Row when you're not touring?

I'm involved totally when I'm in town, seeing what's being cut and what needs to be sent to whom, listening to some of the songs the writers are coming up with.

Do you have any publishing advice for new writers?

At an established company, new writers get to meet and write with other writers and see the other songs coming into the office. They know what's going on in town and the songs that are happening at the time. Then as you become more diverse and you get to the point where you've pretty much got it figured out, you start your own publishing company and cross your fingers!

How about advice on the craft itself?

If you're already in town, keep writing. Listen to other writers and what they're doing and what's happening in town. Continue writing because out of quantity comes quality. I'm not saying that will happen all the time, but constant writing and listening to what's going on, keeping your finger on the pulse, so to speak, [will pay off]. After you write five hundred songs, I would think the next one you write would be better than the first one.

So quantity is really that important?

[For example], this new writer went by [a publisher friend's office], and he had a few songs that showed promise. So he told the kid to go home and write one hundred songs, and then come back with those songs and he'd sign him to the publishing company. So the kid did what the publisher told him to do, and when he showed up with the hundred songs, the publisher said, "Play me the last ten you wrote," because he figured they'd be better than the first ninety. His thinking was that in the first ninety, the kid got rid of all the junk, and he really had to think to write at least ten. Six out of those ten got recorded.

When you're a craftsman, then you don't become a craftsman by just doing it here and there; you need to be doing it all the time so you get good at it and stay that way.

How do you respond when a publisher or someone else wants you to critique a song or wants you to change it?

When you're a writer, you look for that type of input. You're always trying to add to what you already know, which is never enough, it seems.

How do you find time to write with your artist responsibilities?

If I were on the road twelve months a year, I think I would get kind of dingy. My manager and my agents go a little nuts when I take five months off, but if I'm going to write what I consider good or great songs, then I need that time to think about it. When you're a craftsman, if indeed we are, then you don't become a craftsman by just doing it here and there; you need to be doing it all the time so you get good at it and stay that way.

Do song ideas ever just hang around for a while before you actually write them?

I had the idea for "Warning Signs" for three years, and I kept messing around with the idea. I remember being in the kitchen at the office one day and I kept telling the guys there, "Let's get into writing this… it really has a nice feel to it and I really like it." They'd say "Well, it's okay but let's write something else," and I'd keep putting off writing it. Well, two years ago I brought the idea up again and they still didn't get excited about it. So finally I went and started writing it myself, and toward the end of the song Even Stevens kind of got into it and we finished it off together. But it was a song I had started three years ago and I kept telling the guys at the office, "This is really good… you guys better believe me… it's going to be a hit," but they never got interested. So I just decided to write it myself.

Lou Reed

Lou Reed has seen at *least* a good chunk of it all. Beginning as a house songwriter at Manhattan's Pickwick Records, he went on to found the incalculably influential—if unappreciated in their day—Velvet Underground, achieve massive solo glam-pop success with 1972's *Walk on the Wild Side*, bottom out through a sequence of almost hilariously disappointing albums during the eighties, and return to form in periodic bursts of creative reinvention ever since.

In the summer of 2004, Reed had just issued *The Raven*, a double concept album based on the work of gothic horror writer Edgar Allan Poe, and was also watching Dab Hands's remix of Reed's "Satellite of Love" climb to the dance charts in Europe. It would be affixed to Reed's latest (and completely remastered *again*) greatest hits anthology, *NYC Man: The Ultimate Lou Reed Collection*.

Both a certified proto-punk and a songwriter with an astonishing gift for sentimental melody, Reed is also an admitted gear dork. The sixty-two-year-old New Yorker is happiest when talking about the different ways that technology has affected both his songcraft and his performance. Indeed, he led the conversation back to this topic many times—clearly an ongoing source of inspiration over his incomparable five-decade career.

—JESSE JARNOW

Interview by Jesse Jarnow

The London Times, *2004*

You've been working with electronic music for a while now. Have the recent remixes inspired you to go further in that direction?

My electronic music is way different from *that* electronic music. My electronic music kind of goes back to something I did called *Metal Machine Music*. The premise there was, "What happens if you didn't have a steady rhythm and you didn't have a melody?" It was just amorphous, all guitars. That was the idea there. The electronic music I did for *The Raven* is still the same idea, essentially. When I was doing it with guitars, A harmonic hits B harmonic resonance and creates C harmonic. I was trying to figure out how to do that, 'cause you can go deaf doing that, and I didn't like that. I was trying to figure out how I could replicate that. I got some high-tech people… tell me when this makes you go to sleep [*laughs*]. You can do key-shifting by frame, and as you go further away, you're going to lose and degrade the sound. And all the sound won't sound like what you were able to do with analog. You can't do that. Not yet. Five years, okay, but not now. So, I wanted to find other ways of doing that. So I brought in a lot of guitar effects and hooked it up, and I played it as though it's a guitar, even though it's not. But then all these great sounds processed it, and making these things happen and feeding back and hitting against itself by producing guitar effects.

I know [Radiohead/Beck producer] Nigel Godrich makes people play all their plug-ins live…

Really? Are you serious? That's what this is. These are not expensive things either, by the way. The recording rig costs a bit, but anybody with a computer can do it. The plug-ins are not expensive at all. They're all guitar plug-ins. Once it's done, you can't undo it. It's not adjustable that way. You gotta get it right the first time. It's kind of like playing live, in a way. It's really fun. It's either there or it's not. If it's not,

you go back and do the whole thing over again. You can't go back and fix it because there's nothing to fix. That's it.

It's just a good take or a bad take.

It makes it really fun to do, but also—because you're doing all of that—it's tiring. [One of my favorites] on *The Raven* is "Fire Music," which is *Metal Machine Music* taken to some new… it's really a shame. People who get mp3s… *I* get mp3s, I understand. But it's kind of funny, because I [go] to all the trouble to get [the old] tapes to upgrade them, because they'll never hear that, because when you put it back down to mp3, everything you try to make better, well, that won't be there. That said, "Fire Music"… when we mastered, we did these amazing moves in mastering, where the sound actually advances at you, which you also won't hear on the mp3. It's kind of a weird situation. If you have a decent system, you have to pay for it. It's like, if you drive a really good car, you have to pay for it. I don't know whether people are into it. It doesn't seem like they care about good sound, particularly.

It kind of strikes me in the way that car radios were in the sixties, when the sound was all tinny, and Brian Wilson would master stuff just for that. That's what mp3s are today.

Oh, yeah. The thing is, now, you look at the radios you get now, and they have ones with enough bass to actually move a building. That's not an mp3. I don't think people are hooking their iPods to this system. I think they're playing CDs.

How often does a new piece of technology inspire you to try something new?

Well, these days, it's pretty exciting. Having said all that, I'm using a Telecaster. But all these other things I have are to the nth power, and there are little things in there that nobody would ever notice. It takes years and years and years to get these

things, to figure out a way to build it, or for me to find a guitar luthier to construct something. In other words, I'm using new guitars, but the neck's one-hundred-year-old maple. It's not gonna go anywhere. That's hard to come by. For playing, how can you get the harmonics you want and not get the ones you don't? How can you do feedback and not go deaf? How can you have power sound without hurting you and some of the people around you in the process? Things like that. There are some advances that have been made—the speakers in the cabinets. This guy up in Baltimore, Mark, has been working on this cabinet for ten years, so one thing can sound like two. It's kind of like a motorcycle. It's cubic inches, and you're doing that in cabinet space.

On *The Raven*, in places, it sounds as if you're taking a very different approach than you were on 2000's *Ecstasy*. Was that a conscious decision, or did it just sort of happen?

On the road, from all the exercising, and doing this and that, my voice opened up. Something happened. Something good. I was very astonished by it. A couple of extra notes and wider. That was a choice. Before, I had a choice of, maybe, three notes. And now, all of a sudden, I have nine. It's interesting. It just happened, finally. I've been singing a lot better ever since I went on tour with Little Jimmy Scott. After that tour, I think I learned to sing… from watching Jimmy. He worked with me. Not, "Lou, sit down and let's do scales" but, every night when we played, he would do something and I would advance; I'd learn from a true master. Suppose if I had Hendrix sitting and playing guitar with me and he said, "Turn your tone control all the way over to the bass—now try it."

What did that new approach bring to the older stuff? Do you keep finding new things to discover?

I've always… it's always been figuring out what a song is really about three or four years after, and figuring out these really great guitar parts that we could've done that we didn't do then. We always say that the way to do that is to go out on the road with the songs for two or three years and then go back. You can't really do that. But I also like the excitement of doing a song for the first time, and that's what you're hearing—us doing it for the first time. That's the fun of that. From a singing point of view, it's like suddenly having some distance on the lyrics saying, "Whoa, I thought that was about that, but it's really about *that*." Back to technology, I now have a seven-string guitar...

What's the seventh string? A lower B?

Yeah… you're the first journalist who's ever been able to say something like that. No offense. It's really amazing, just the most amazing sound. This guy in Brooklyn, Carl Thompson, built it. Incredibly beautiful guitar. The song "Guardian Angel" *is* that sound. We do that sound live. No small trick, that, with that B string. You can imagine some of the problems trying to get that to go through it. That changes the way you play. It changes your whole thought. Even just keeping in mind that you have seven instead of six strings is hard enough.

What makes an older song stick around for you?

We go back and we start playing, and if it doesn't feel right, we stop within about twenty seconds, or a minute, and just say, "Not really happening." What I do [is] I say—and this is a real band, these are not pick-up musicians—"What would you like to play?" and somebody like [cellist] Jane [Scarpantoni], who's the newest member, will say something like, "Well, I wanna try this, 'cause it has a cool violin part that I can adapt."

Jane and [trumpet player] Steve Bernstein are drawn from the New York jazz/downtown scene. I was wondering how often you go out and check out the players.

We're going around all the time. How did we find Antony, whose new album is called *I Am a Bird Now* [and who sings

"Perfect Day" on *The Raven*]? That's how you hear these people, saying, "Don't miss so-and-so," or "You should hear this," or "You should hear that." Or [longtime arranger Hal] Willner says, "Check out the Mingus Band at Fez," or "There's this new horn player... go down to Tonic..."

How often do you see bands that have supposedly been influenced by you?

Um, not very often. It's usually come and gone before anybody bothered to tell me, and I don't really totally understand when people say that, anyway. I've never really understood what anybody means by that. Seriously. It's two guitars, bass, drums... basic. I don't understand.

Somebody once said that if you take what you should from a musician you admire, you won't come out sounding anything like them.

Well, you couldn't anyway. I have been in awe and in love with Ornette Coleman since the first note I heard from him, and Don Cherry. It's influenced every cell in my body, but I'll never play like them. But the idea's in me. I do it, me, but I got the idea over there. I didn't think of that one. Those kinds of harmonies, those kinds of melodies, oh my God! Check out a cut called "Lonely Woman" on [Coleman's] *Change of the Century*. If I had to pick one song in the whole world... I hum that at least once a day and I'll say, "Oh, did I write that?" and the answer is, "No, I didn't," but I wish I did. If Ornette was smart, he'd ask me to do lyrics for it.

Well, I'll put that right through the proper channels, then.

Heh, I already played him... If you listen to the track "Guilty" on *The Raven*, listen to Ornette's horn part. He did seven of them. This is how crazy he is. He did seven. He said, "One is with your voice, then I'll do one with the guitar, then I'll do one with the other guitar, then I'll do one with the bass, then I'll do one with the drums, then I'll do two more just overall..." None of them are interchangeable, 'cause each has long thoughts. It's one shot, either you like it or you don't. I wanted to put [out] an album of all seven. They're all different, and they're all wonderful. But I had to pick one. That was a drag.

That would be a nice EP.

We were hoping to get a jazz label. It's fascinating. You hear the same thing seven times, but of course it was complete genius. One was really removed physically, and there was another that was so cerebral. There are moves he makes where you just [*gasps*]. Seven of them. We only put out one. And we tried. And not one person has ever noticed it or said, "Boo." Can you imagine? I mean, really, we know how good it is, where we want to hear all seven; maybe other people just aren't there for it.

Luke Reynolds
Blue Merle

*Interview by
Caine O'Rear IV*

American Songwriter,
March/April 2005

Despite being a mostly acoustic band, Blue Merle has no qualms about defying expectations and rocking out. After all, the mandolin, upright bass, and fiddle-loving musicians did take their name from a line in a Led Zeppelin song, namely "Bron-Y-Aur Stomp." The seeds of Blue Merle were sown when Vermont singer-songwriter Luke Reynolds befriended bassist Jason Oettel. The newly formed duo were cutting demos in a Sony-run Nashville studio when they caught the ear of the president of Sony Publishing, who offered them a production and publishing deal on the spot. Although they declined, the experience gave them the self-confidence to press on under their own terms. With the addition of drummer William Ellis and mandolin player Beau Stapleton, Blue Merle set out recording their 2005 Island Records debut, *Burning in the Sun.* The album reached number eight on the *Billboard* Heatseekers chart and led them to high-profile showcase gigs at Farm Aid and Bonnaroo. Blue Merle parted ways in 2006, and band members are currently exploring other opportunities.

—EVAN SCHLANSKY

How long have you been writing songs?

I've been writing since I was little. I started studying piano when I was four, and both of my parents are musicians.

Do you write most of the lyrics for the band?

I write all of the songs. In terms of the parts coming together, everyone writes their own part, and that's how a song as it appears on the record comes to fruition.

Who influences your songwriting?

In the blues, Willie Dixon. Paul Simon, and Sting. Lyricists, taking different aspects from different writers, like how prolific Woody Guthrie was. My mom and dad have a massive vinyl collection and my mom's kind of like a song plugger almost. She's always making me mix tapes and sending them down.

Had you planned on assembling the musicians that make up Blue Merle for some time?

The vision was meeting really great musicians that could play with a lot of restraint and subtlety. The thing that connected us was that all of us had played in all different types of bands, but really wanted to play in a song band, where a really good song was paramount to everything, followed by musicianship, subtlety, and restraint.

In contrast to senseless jamming, basically?

That has its place, too, if you can incorporate the two. Robert Cray is so much more than just a blues guitarist, because he's got great songs and phrasing, and total restraint. And he's like the whole package. People totally make it work. Dave [Matthews] makes it work really well. We're just trying to write good songs starting off.

Has constant touring changed the band?

We're always evolving. It's really been the songs that dictated change and development and growth. With us, a song gets brought in and it gets passed around the horn and if everybody's really moved and touched by it, then we commit 100 percent and get behind it.

Do you think it will it take time for the band to build a huge fan base, like it has for a lot of jam bands?

It will demand the time and patience from true music fans and listeners to spend a little bit of time with it. I definitely think that a real connection between audience and live show will occur when there's some sort of mixture with having already been familiar with the lyrics or songs, and then seeing them performed live. It doesn't totally hit you over the head. We'll play with every bit of commitment and strength and soul as we can on the road. At the same time, the subtleties demand a little bit of familiarity with the songs. And that's a tradeoff that we're excited to take and give.

The song "Part of Your History" seems to be a different kind of love song in that it's a positive look back at a past romance.

The song represents a strong and thoughtful effort to live in a mindful and thoughtful and very full way. I was really lucky because I grew up in a family that really encouraged full living. There is not a lot of room in my body or heart to hold grudges. It's almost a tribute, to truly love someone, you have to really let go, as full as you can. That's about as true an expression of love as you can give.

Josh Ritter

Interview by
Brian T. Atkinson

American Songwriter,
May/June 2005

Josh Ritter is one of America's most cerebral songwriters. A native of Moscow, Idaho, Ritter was inspired to start making music at age eighteen after becoming entranced with Bob Dylan and Johnny Cash's duet of "Girl of the North Country" on Dylan's *Nashville Skyline*. After college he moved to Boston, where he integrated himself into the local singer-songwriter scene. His self-titled 1999 debut and 2002's *Golden Age of Radio* demonstrated Ritter's gift for intimate story songs that employ both literary and historic allusions. In 2003, the critically lauded *Hello Starling* increased Ritter's profile in the United States and helped turn him into a pop star in Ireland, where contemporary folk music still resonates on the charts. In 2006, Ritter released his strongest album to date, *The Animal Years*, a collection of spiritually searching songs, such as the stirring "Girl in the War" and the nine-minute, apocalyptic "Thin Blue Flame," a masterful blend of surreal and topical imagery.

—EVAN SCHLANSKY

Many people think of you as a folk singer. Where do you feel you fit into the scope of contemporary folk music?

I think folk music these days is about history. I read a lot of Mark Twain. There's a lot about Egypt on *The Animal Years*. I write about Cairo, Illinois, and then Cairo, Egypt. Stuff about General Grant. I like getting a whole bunch of historical material together, taking it all apart and then putting it in a different order in a song. It was about getting a bunch of characters together, too. I was really interested in Twain and Thomas Jefferson and their philosophies about America. A lot of things they had to say are really pertinent today. Maybe they're worth remembering.

But I don't really care for songs that come in and try to recreate something that's happened, or music about somebody's feelings. There's enough about that already. If you want to talk about your feelings because your girlfriend left you, sometimes that can be helpful. But it's not the only thing. Like Neil Young can make a record that's supposed to be a folk record, but it's not. I feel like that's the direction that stuff has to move.

What's your songwriting process like?

Up to this point, I'd write a song and it'd work its way into the set because we weren't sure when we were going to record together again. This time, with the ones on *The Animal Years*, the songs came together fairly quickly. I had one—"Girl in the War"—that sort of set the mood for the record, and then it became really clear how I wanted to build on that.

We had a whole bag of songs, which was an amazing thing. When I did the last record, *Hello Starling*, we just made whatever we had sound as good as we possibly could. This time, we had more than we needed and it was a matter of bringing stuff in and weeding things out. I didn't know beforehand that all the songs would fit that well together. It was like finding pieces of the puzzle before you actually have the puzzle.

I feel like each song should be a chapter that builds on the one before it. This isn't a theme record, but there is an emotion or feeling when I sing a song or when I hear it, that for me, matches up with something else. It probably isn't noticeable to anyone else.

Talk about "Thin Blue Flame." It's such a massive song—so many ideas.

I had that going on in my head and I just wanted to get it out. All I had room for were images. It's an old, old American tradition to moralize in songs. I think that comes out some, but all I wanted to do was throw out as many images as possible. Not try and explain anything, just throw them out so fast that nothing can be explained. Along with horrible things, there are good things. One doesn't outweigh the other, it's just complete chaos.

The song's very nonlinear. What exactly is its message?

It doesn't have to have a purpose. It just has to have that fuel that pushes it forward and washes over. That was really fun to write, because when you get on a roll the words just jump out and you don't even know where they come from. Sometimes they come out and they're awful, and you leave them and come back and laugh at them. I wrote so much for that song, and then pared it down.

I was thinking about how the conservative Christianity and the anti-Christianity movements swirling around are in a lot of way moot points. What is there except the people around you that you can help? I feel like everyone's missing the boat if we don't remember that. Why is it that community is so undervalued? God isn't going to make things better. I don't understand spending all this time trying to be good in a certain way hoping to get to heaven. It is not doing any good for any of us if we're not doing good for other people. That's part of the song. It's impossible to imagine

that there's a God who's going to help you out if you're not going to help other people out.

The power of a song like that is that it shouldn't have a clear message. So many of those clear-messaged songs are just preaching to the choir these days. Is a song gonna make you go out and vote for Kerry when you were gonna vote for Bush beforehand? You just lose the beauty of words and emotion. Trying to fit them all into a moral sometimes does the poetry and the music a disservice. I'm a songwriter—I'm a writer—that's what I do. I'm not very comfortable writing straight political songs. I've tried it before and it never made me feel very good.

I know you were considering about fifteen songs for *The Animal Years*, and it ended up having eleven on it. Are there any songs on the album that almost didn't make the final cut?

I wasn't even going to put "Idaho" on the record. It had been a frustrating day, we were between takes, and I just set up the mike and sang that. [Producer] Brian Deck heard that and he knew where to take it and where to leave it. It turned the whole day around, and we came up with a bunch of other stuff. He was a great guy to see through the glass every day. "Idaho" was a first take.

"Good Man" is another we almost didn't record because I didn't feel right about it. I'd written love songs in the past, and it kind of hit me that all those songs were about me not being quite good enough. "Good Man" is the first time that I've been unsure about things, trying to push things in a direction that you hope people will come along and give it a chance. But I thought maybe it was time to step to the plate and give it my best shot.

What songwriters influenced you the most as you were thinking of seriously pursuing songwriting yourself?

Before I went to college, I was listening to Johnny Cash and Bob Dylan. I started listening to them pretty late, but that's who I was into when I went off to college. Then at Oberlin [College], there was a girl at the end of my hall who used to give me music, and one night she gave me Townes Van Zandt. The album she handed to me was *Rear View Mirror*, one of his live ones, and to me that was a total revelation. Townes was doing things that no one else was doing. Like "Snowin' on Raton," that's one of my favorite songs ever. I just love it. But it's really weird, when you write it down and read the lyrics and see how it's structured, it's just not typical.

So, I got into Townes Van Zandt, and then from him I found Guy Clark and songs like "The Randall Knife." People talk about those guys like they're poets, and they kind of are—like Raymond Carver, you know? There's a real sensibility to the way Guy Clark writes. It's incredible. But someone like Townes Van Zandt really blows your mind as a songwriter, and really as just a writer. The songs are just so… nice. When you listen to his songs, no one cares how many records Townes Van Zandt sells or how many people were at his shows. You just look at him as a writer and look at that incredible writing. He's making something that I feel lives beyond itself.

I think I saw him once. It was my freshman year in college and I was starting to think about getting into music. I went down to the Kerrville Folk Festival [in Texas]. They have these campfires and everybody plays around the fire. This was about a year before he died, and I didn't know all that much stuff about him. But I was sitting at this campfire and I believe Townes was there. I don't remember what song he was singing—but I believe that had to have been him. At least that's the way it is in my mind, anyway. I feel really close to him. He's kind of like one of the founding fathers.

Smokey Robinson

Bob Dylan once dubbed Smokey Robinson "America's greatest living poet." Perhaps the most moving artist to come out of the Motor City, Robinson earned the distinction by exploring every nuance of love in such magnificent soul classics as "My Girl" and "The Tracks of My Tears." Born February 19, 1940, in Detroit, Robinson began writing songs as a teenager for his high school doo-wop group, the Matadors. In 1958, they had a regional hit with "Got a Job," a musical response to the Silhouettes's then-popular "Get a Job." Motown Records founder Berry Gordy fell in love with them and made them one of his first signings, renaming them the Miracles. Their first national hit, "Shop Around," helped get the storied label up and running, reaching the number two spot on the pop charts and moving over a million copies. Robinson's timeless songs would find their way to into the Top Forty charts twenty-eight more times.

Robinson took on an active role at Motown, eventually becoming label vice-president in 1961. Robinson wrote and produced memorable hits for such artists as the Temptations ("My Girl"), Mary Wells ("My Guy"), and Marvin Gaye ("Ain't That Peculiar"). After splitting with the Miracles in 1972, Robinson embarked on a successful solo career, scoring two top five hits with "Cruisin'" and "Being With You." In 2004, he recorded an album of contemporary gospel songs, *Food for the Spirit*.

—EVAN SCHLANSKY

Interview by
Paul Zollo

American Songwriter,
September/October 2005

When you write songs, do you write words or melody first?

There's no set pattern for writing songs. Sometimes the melody will come to me, sometimes some words. I'll see a billboard sign, or maybe some words in a newspaper, and they will trigger something in me. My songwriting happens all different ways, and as long as a good song gets written, that's all that matters.

Your chords are chromatic and beautiful. Do you come up with them on the piano?

Yes. I always write on piano. I've always wanted to play the guitar, but it's hard for me. I can't do it. So piano is my main instrument.

Do you have favorite chords or progressions?

No, I don't. Usually when I start to write, I have a melody in mind. Sometimes the words start first. Usually, before I get to the piano, even when I have words, I have some sort of a melody in mind. I will write down the notes to a melody, if I'm on a plane or somewhere that I can't get to a piano. I do that so I won't lose that melody. I used to carry a tape recorder, but now, if I don't have one readily at hand, I will call my voice mail. If you're somewhere, and a song comes to you, and you don't have a tape recorder or a pen and paper with you, call your voice mail, man.

"Going to a Go-Go" starts with rhythm, then a drum beat, then bass, then a great riff. Did you write the riff first?

No, my guitar player, Marv Tarplin, wrote that riff. He did the riff on "The Tracks of My Tears" and "Ain't That Peculiar," and other songs, too. This guy is prolific, man. The Rolling Stones turned "Go-Go" into a rock 'n' roll song.

Did it surprise you that your songs, which are R&B, can be rock 'n' roll?

No, it doesn't. Because I try to start off with a *song*. And a song can be done any way. As a songwriter, if someone picks up one of my songs and records it, that's my dream come true. I want to write a song that people can record. I don't critique them; I don't have ones that I like better than others. I'm just flattered that somebody picked up one of my songs and said, "Hey, I love this song and I want to record it"—because most of the people who have done my songs and re-recorded them are songwriters themselves.

"You've Really Got a Hold on Me" starts with a great piano riff. Did you write that?

Yes. But the bass line was not mine. James Jamerson came up with that. But the song was written in a hotel room in New York. I was on the road. I'm not one of those writers who has to isolate himself and go to the beach for two months, or go to the mountains and be in a little cabin or something like that. I write every day, man—wherever I am. I write on the golf course, I write in the car. I am not an isolated writer.

"You've Really Got a Hold on Me" was inspired by Sam Cooke. I *loved* him. He had a song out at the time called "Bring It on Home to Me." It was a bluesy record, and I wanted to write something like that. I was vice-president of Motown at the time, and in a hotel room, and I wrote that in my room. So I imitated another song and came up with that one. Imitation in songwriting is okay; it's something I think every writer does.

The lyric of that song is "I don't want to kiss you, but I need you." It transcends sexuality.

What that song is saying is that here is a person who absolutely treats you wrong, but you love them. You don't really want to love them, but you can't *help* it. I don't really want to love you, but I do—because I can't help it. That's what that song is saying. It's everything: You've got a hold on me mentally, you've got a hold on me physically, you've got a hold on me emotionally, and so on.

The new album has new songs and many of your classic tracks. It also has "Shop Around," your first.

That was a lyric-first song. The rhythm for that song was Berry Gordy's idea. I recorded that in another version and put it out. It was out for about two weeks, and Berry called me at three in the morning and told me he wanted to change it to that particular beat. So we re-recorded it with Benny Benjamin on drums, and that's the version that you know now.

It's a story song. Was it hard to write a whole story in under three minutes?

No, you had to. You didn't have any choice, man. You had to tell a story and do it quickly. You had to get in there and get out quickly.

Is songwriting more a sense of following than leading?

Absolutely. Melodies will show you where they want to go. Your job as a songwriter is to follow them, and if you do it right, and not interfere, they will lead you to the right place. Almost all of my songs came as a result of following where the melody, and where the lyric, wanted to go.

"The Tracks of My Tears" is a happy song about being sad, as is "Tears of a Clown."

Interesting that you think so. That was based on a guitar riff by Marv Tarplin. He put that riff on a tape for me as he does whenever we write together. He puts his music on tape, and I just listen to it, listen to it, and listen to it until I come up with a song for it. That song was inspired through his guitar riff.

You're the first person I've ever heard call it a happy song. I've always looked at it as a sad song. Maybe the melody might seem happy. It's a song about faking happiness.

> *I write every day, man—wherever I am. I write on the golf course, I write in the car. I am not an isolated writer.*

The melody to "Shop Around" is purely soulful. What's the key to such a great melody? Is it the chord progression?

I had the whole thing before I ever went to the piano and figured out what the chords were. I just had to follow where that was going. So sometimes it's the melody, sometimes the harmony, sometimes the rhythm, or [sometimes] the words. There are all these separate elements that, when you combine them, add up to a good song.

"Tears of a Clown" is another song about faking happiness.

That was inspired by the music of Stevie Wonder. Stevie gave me that musical track. That riff that he has in there [*sings riff*] reminded me of the circus, so I wanted to write a heart-wrenching lyric about the circus. I thought about Pagliacci, the clown, who made everyone happy, though he himself was sad and couldn't get anyone to love him. I wanted to get him into the song.

You started out in Detroit as part of a vocal group, the Five Chimes, then the Matadors. Were you writing songs for your own voice or the harmonies of a quintet?

I was just writing songs, man. Then when I met Berry Gordy, he was a songwriter himself, and he showed me how to construct songs. I learned almost everything I know about songwriting from Berry. He's a beautiful guy and was my mentor for a long time.

Was it different having the sound of a woman in the group?

No, because she sang high, but the high voice was a natural sound. Most of the guy groups had high voices. So it sounded like a guy group, but with Claudette singing the high parts.

"Fallen" is a beautiful song.

When I got "Fallen," the track was already there. The demo track to "Fallen" and "My World" was all there. The chorus was in place, and I wrote to that track.

How about "I Second That Emotion"?

That was something I wrote from scratch. That was an accidental song and an accidental title. The guy who wrote that with me was a guy named Al Cleveland, and we were Christmas shopping, and we were in a store, and a young lady was waiting on us, and she said something. Instead of Al saying, "I second that motion," he said, "I second that emotion." We *laughed* about it when he said it, and when we walked away from the counter, we said, "Let's write a song with that title." And we did.

"Baby That's Backatcha"?

That's a song that I wrote because I thought about a person telling another person how much they loved them, and the person was just thinking, "Well, I love you the same way. However much you think you love me, *that's* how much I love you."

"A Quiet Storm."

"A Quiet Storm" was my comeback. I was going to the office every day, doing my VP of Motown gig, having retired from the Miracles. But after about three years of not playing music, I was climbing the walls. I guess I was making everyone miserable, so Berry and Claudette came to me, and said, "Man, you need to get back to music. You need to get back to music." And I always thought of myself as a quiet singer, and I wanted to go back and take show business by *storm*. That's why I did that particular album and that song.

After all these years, is writing a song still a joy for you?

Yeah. There's nothing like it. You write something that will touch people, and maybe make them feel romantic, and can last for years. That's something wonderful, man. It's really wonderful.

Josh Rouse

Josh Rouse is one of American music's best-kept secrets. He was born in Nebraska in 1972, but thanks to his father's military career, was raised alternately in California, Arizona, Utah, Wyoming, Georgia, and Arizona. An uncle taught him how to play guitar at age eighteen, and he promptly began writing songs, influenced by the soft rock stations he heard coming through the radio. As many good songwriters do, he moved to Nashville in the mid-nineties, where his music attracted the attention of Ryko/Slow River Records. His debut album, the subdued and folksy *Dressed Up Like Nebraska*, was released in 1998. A year later, Rouse put out *Home*, which saw him adding elements of soul and R&B to his literate lyrics. Rouse became a little less of a secret when his songs began appearing on TV show *Dawson's Creek* and his tune "Directions" was picked for the soundtrack to the Cameron Crowe film *Vanilla Sky*. In 2002, he released *Under Cold Blue Stars*, a song cycle about a troubled Midwestern couple, inspired in part by the movie *The Straight Story*. In 2003, he released *1972*, which drew its influences from classic seventies artists like Carole King, Curtis Mayfield, and Al Green. By 2004, Rouse's marriage was breaking up, and he left Nashville for the coast of Spain. The resulting album, 2004's *Nashville*, is the teary goodbye and thank you to the city in which he began his career. *Subtitulo* was released by Netterk America Records in 2006.

—EVAN SCHLANSKY

Interview by
Lacey Galbraith

American Songwriter,
March/April 2005

313

This is your fifth album in seven years. Since 1998, you've done one almost every year to year and a half. Is it safe to assume you don't suffer from writer's block?

Well, no, not too bad. Sometimes I do but usually I can do a record a year.

Are you able to write while on tour?

I come up with a lot of ideas when I'm on the road, but I can't really finish them. I need to be at home, focusing on it to finish it. I can't really work on the complete song there, but I get inspired by a lot of ideas.

What's your writing process like?

It comes in waves usually for me. Sometimes I can sit down and in a day come up with five ideas for [songs]. I'll work on them at different times, and so throughout maybe one week, I'll get five songs done but then I won't have anything for months.

You named your most recent album _Nashville_, in honor of a place where you say you really learned the craft of songwriting. What was it about the city?

Well, it was the age. I moved there when I was twenty-four, twenty-five. I was valet-parking cars down at the Renaissance Hotel and writing songs at night. That's when I really started focusing on it and learning how to do it, the first time I really wasn't in a band so it was just me making concise pop songs.

Was there anyone specifically who inspired or helped you?

Just [seeing] other people doing it and being around that environment, you know? I don't think there was one person in particular that I learned from, as I learned from a lot of different people. All the years of living there and writing songs… that's where I honed my skills, I'd guess you'd say. Kurt Wagner from Lambchop and I hung out quite a bit those first few years. I learned a lot from him—I don't know necessarily about songwriting in general—but just about the business or his philosophies on things. It was nice.

What about co-writing? That's such a Nashville thing and on this album you seem to have done a little bit more of it.

I've been doing a bit more of it lately. When I first started out I didn't really do any. I did some with Kurt Wagner a ways back but that was where I had the music and I gave it to him and he wrote lyrics for it. It just depends on what the song needs. Sometimes I can finish it and I have a clear vision of it myself. Sometimes it's a little blurry so I have to throw it to someone else and go, "Hey, what do you think about this?" It's usually where I have the song almost there and then need that something else. Daniel [Tashian] co-wrote a couple of songs on this album. I'd get together with him and go, "What about this part?" and he helped me out on that stuff.

So you're living in Spain now, right? Why there?

Yeah, I moved there in September [2004]. I tour there and I like it a lot. I just really wanted to learn the language to be honest, and I wanted to check out another culture for a while.

Have you been able to see yet how it will influence your writing?

I don't know yet. Maybe I'm too close to it to really see. I came up with some things when I first moved there but the majority of my time has been spent trying to learn the language. It's fun but it's definitely work.

Do you feel you're received differently over there?

Yeah, I kind of treat them as two different things. I always feel like I'm doing better over there than I am here, but I don't know if that's necessarily the case. I think they're a bit more artist-friendly. I don't think they're quite as obsessed with the pop culture, the kind of "here today, gone tomorrow" thing. There are a lot of people who are really focused on following an artist. I seem to have found an audience in almost every country over there that has my catalog, so it's been really nice. And [there's] a young audience that knows Neil Young and Bob Dylan. It's really cool. I have a following here, it's just taken a lot longer. America is just so spread out. I think it's going well here, too; it's just I don't have the competition. With all the R&B and hip-hop and stuff that happens [in the U.S.], it's not really that prevalent over there. It's around but it's not ruling the pop charts.

It just depends on what the song needs. Sometimes I can finish it and I have a clear vision of it myself. Sometimes it's a little blurry so I have to throw it to someone else and go, "Hey, what do you think about this?"

Who are some of your influences?

You know, Neil Young is the one I always think has been a big influence on me, although you may not hear it in the music. Just people I look up to as artists. Bob Dylan and Neil Young and Tom Waits. Paul Simon—people who have made thirty records and have been doing it for a long time and keep doing it... who aren't focused on making a masterpiece each time they make one. It's about the songs. I'm trying to follow in their footsteps.

What about some of the newer artists working today?

I think M. Ward is really good. I like the Kings of Convenience guys. They do some cool stuff. There's a guy named Adam. He's from England and he's really good. And I like Badly Drawn Boy.

Do you have any idea of where you want to go next musically?

I don't know. I'm kind of thinking about that now, I guess. I'm kind of a song guy. Sometimes I think, "Well, maybe I should re-invent myself, but I don't know what that's going to be until it happens. I don't want to do the whole Wilco thing and start deconstructing everything and just jamming out and saying, "Hey, I re-invented myself." I guess I'll figure it out when it happens.

John Scott Sherrill

Interview by
Robert L. Doerschuk

American Songwriter,
November/December 2005

One of John Scott Sherrill's most famous compositions, "Church on Cumberland Road" by Shenandoah (number one, 1989), created a little confusion for Sherrill when his music publisher, Woody Bomar, told him about it.

Bomar told Sherrill and the song's co-writers, Bob DiPiero and Dennis Robbins, that he had gotten a Shenandoah cut. "We said, 'A what?'" Sherrill asked, perplexed. Sherrill, who had never heard of that band, told Tom Roland a couple years later for *The Billboard Book of Number One Country Hits*, "Now we know to have a little more faith in Woody when he does that."

Sherrill clearly admires eccentrics. He's one of the only co-writers Dennis Linde ever uses. Linde, the writer of Elvis Presley's "Burning Love" and Joe Diffie's "John Deere Green," writes nearly all his songs alone.

Sherrill returned to number one with Brooks & Dunn in 1998 with "How Long Gone," which he penned with Shawn Camp. For many fans, though, Sherrill's "Some Fools Never Learn" (by Steve Wariner, number one, 1985) is his greatest work. Wariner himself said that "Fools" is the only song he's ever cut where he told his producer (Tony Brown in this case) the day they left the studio that the single would reach number one. It did exactly that, and thus gave John Scott Sherrill the first chart-topper of his career. Co-penned with frequent collaborator Shawn Camp, "Nobody But Me" (Blake Shelton) entered the top ten on the Billboard chart in 2006.

—PHIL SWEETLAND

316

You're still writing and working, but is everyday life different than it was ten or twenty years ago?

There have been many changes, lots of them cyclical—boom and bust periods. But it's very different now, compared to what it has been. I'm very fortunate to have actually had cuts in four decades: seventies, eighties, nineties, and oughts.

Is that what we call this decade we're in?

Yeah, because we *ought* to be doing something a little differently. We had that urban cowboy swell, which kind of reminds me of today, where all of a sudden people are rushing to town and trying to capitalize on country music, and country music disappeared on account of it for a little while. Then it came roaring right back and did great for a good long while. Then Garth and all the big guys came along, and all of a sudden we had another influx of people, and I don't know if they really even love country music or not, to tell you the truth. It seems like looks, presentation, and the way you move are more important than even how you sound, because they can fix that. The song is also taking a bit of a back seat, because a certain sound and a certain tempo are almost required now to get radio airplay. It's hard to sneak by all these barriers.

So we're back to the era of the pin-up country artist.

Well, don't you feel that we're on the tail end of that sort of thing?

I do, actually, because of this whole Americana movement.

Do you see signs of that?

It is a very insular community, so that's hard to say. But it has led people to ask what country music really *is* these days, whereas thirty years ago that was self-evident.

Well, if you go down to the Idle Hour and ask those boys in there, they'll tell you that they know what it is and that they don't hear it anymore. There's a certain crowd that has a very firm idea of what country music is: It kind of stopped with Waylon, as far as they're concerned, and everybody else is either imitating it or ignoring it.

So what is it that makes a song country?

Some of it is as simple as being able to hear an acoustic guitar. I had a fellow down there the other night, saying, "You know, when I listen to the radio [these days], all I really hear is a kick drum and a couple of guys singing really high." Country music is acoustic music at heart. To me, bluegrass is the most exciting thing happening right now, although I know it probably doesn't sell any better than Americana. But there's got to be something exciting going on, and there is a lot of that in bluegrass.

What about the lyrics?

That example of the acoustic guitar was just a simple way of putting it; it goes much further than that. Lyrically, country music has always been about pain and sorrow and suffering in some way, or celebrating the absence of suffering. There's a relentlessly upbeat attitude in these songs. And I find myself guilty of the same thing. I write these things in an attempt to get them cut [*laughs*]. I try to be as relentlessly upbeat as I can sometimes.

Well, there must be good days where you can do that with a clear conscience.

Absolutely! I'm very upbeat most of the time. But the songs we all grew up loving, the ones that made us fall in love with country music, touched a little deeper than that.

There are more nostalgic songs coming out these days, about when we were kids driving in our fast cars.

Every other song seems to be about that. But is that a reflection of yearning for better country music? It's all about being self-conscious: "I'm going to self-consciously talk about how great it was in Little League." When I came to town in 1975, there was an artistic fervor, if that's not too strong a word. Kristofferson and Lee Clayton took it really to heart and considered themselves artists in the deepest sense of the word.

Your background had very little to do with country music.

I'd been in hippie vans up in New Hampshire. We all lived together in an old commune, grew our own vegetables, made our own beer and wine, and when we ran out of money, we'd go play a gig. My songs were ten minutes long and they changed tempos and keys. I had a lot to learn. I remember going to my first writers' night at Franks 'n' Steins, a songwriters' club on West End. I heard these songs that emotionally grabbed you in three minutes and left you wrung out. I realized I had a long way to go.

Were those songs more about being frameworks for jamming, or were you thinking even then about doing lyrics that told compelling stories?

Here's a wild thing: Up there, especially in northern New Hampshire, the only popular radio stations are country. Country was the only thing all those old boys up in the woods listened to. I became deeply intrigued by all that stuff. I listened to a lot of Charlie Rich back then. If you couldn't play Charlie Rich in your band, you couldn't get any gigs. So Nashville wasn't too strange of a progression from that. Country music is more of a rural/urban divide than a North/South divide.

How hard was it for a commune refugee to adapt to the Nashville lifestyle?

That's an interesting question, but I felt like I'd stepped into my real community with all the songwriters. Half of them, probably, were Republicans, and the other half, if they didn't look like me, were just crazy. There was some of that going on. But it was incredible how much at home I felt. All of a sudden here were all these people trying to do the same thing I was. I'd never felt that at all anywhere else. There were just a few clashes. One time, when I had really long hair, I was standing in the hallway and Bob Beckham, who was the president of Combine Music, stopped and walked all around me in a circle. Johnny McCrae, the vice president, said, "Yeah, and when he wants to take a shit he has to climb up in a tree because his hair is so long." They gave me a good-natured ribbing. It was good for me; I enjoyed it.

You must have had contact with the old guard, too: Harlan Howard and Felice and Boudleaux Bryant?

Those guys were totally at the top of the game. I got to know Harlan after several years. I got to know Felice a little bit. I never got to know Boudleaux. It was a strange world. There was only a handful of publishing companies: There was Cedarwood, Tree, Combine, and the big one down on Eighth Avenue. And that was about it. There were enough writers to turn out enough songs for the number of artists there were in town at the time. I'm wondering now if there's such a ratio anymore.

Your relationship with these writers must have somehow been a combination of competition and mutual support.

It was, and Beckham ran Combine very differently than modern publishing companies are run. For one thing, he didn't pay his writers worth a hoot. When I signed down there I was climbing a tree as a tree surgeon, making twenty-one dollars an hour, which back then was really good money. I quit to make seventy-five dollars a week writing for Beckham. I took a lifestyle hit those first few years. At the same time, it was almost like a college. Lee Clayton used to lecture me up on the third floor. He'd pace back and forth, looking out the windows, and say, "You don't realize it, but you're in the middle of the world's most incredible college for songwriters. There's [nowhere else on] the planet like this. You've got to open your ears and you've got to pay attention to your heart." He'd go off on it. You had to get your songs past the vice president, Johnny McCrae, if you were to get them demo'ed.

What did that involve?

That involved going to play your song for Johnny McCrae. Those boys knew how to tear a song apart. It was very different from whatever it is now. If they'd heard it before, or if it was old hat, or if it was the same old stuff, they'd instantly turn it down. You had to do better than that. It's the young writers we're talking about; they didn't do this with Kris [Kristofferson].

The point is that they were expecting something new, rather than conforming to a formula, which is the approach now.

That's very true. It seems like they want to hear more of the same now. Maybe I'm wrong, but when I turn on the radio, it all sounds similar, sonically and thematically.

What was your first big cut?

Johnny Lee cut some stuff early on and that kind of opened the door. I wrote one of those songs with Steve Earle. He and I actually got into a knock-down fistfight at our first-cut-ever-released-on-country-radio drinking party, just the two of us. We were out in the gutter in front of Maude's, or it might have been before Maude's, arguing about [which of us] was the more dedicated, energetic songwriter.

There must have been a better way to resolve that question.

There probably was, but I don't think we ever did resolve it. Anyway, not too long after that, Jon Anderson cut "Wildwood Blues"; that was what started everything for me.

You performed a lot in the old days. Was there an issue with moving more toward writing behind the scenes and playing less?

Yeah. I had a fabulously eclectic band called the Wolves in Cheap Clothing, with shifting members coming into town and going out again. It was great fun and I don't think it interfered with the writing too much. After we were signed to Warner Bros. we were going to be called the Wolves in Cheap Clothing. We had the artwork drawn up. And then the Warner Bros. legal department found out there was already a band out in California called the Wolves—not in Cheap Clothing, just the Wolves. They said, "Well, we can't do that." So we had to come up with a new name for the band. I was on vacation and hadn't left anybody a phone number, which I found out was a no-no. I was down in Florida, at a state campground, and I spent my whole vacation talking on a telephone that was on a palm tree, nailed up there by the concession stand, on conference calls with Warner Bros. trying to come up with a new name for the band so we could release this record. Bob DiPiero finally came up with Billy Hill. That band did end up eating into some songwriting time, but we tried to do it for a couple of years.

What's your writing routine like on a normal day?

I usually write four days a week. Around ten or ten-thirty I show up here, hopefully knowing the name of the person

I'm co-writing with… just kidding, but it's almost that bad. No, it's pretty good. I've got some people who are very dear to me whom I like to write with on a more or less regular basis, and the newer writers are fine, too.

Writing a song is like pulling a rabbit out of a hat. It's a very ephemeral process. Do you have any insights into the process that you didn't have when you were new in the business, or is it still a mystery?

I'd say it's more of a mystery now than it ever has been, especially if you do it every day. It's hard to say where something comes from. You might have had an idea—some notion of a melody or a little spark of something—but if you write every day you don't have anything like that; you start from scratch all the time.

When you co-write, the first part of the session must be conversation rather than actual writing.

That's true, especially if it's somebody you don't know or have never met before. You've got to spend that first little while getting to know them a little bit. It's such an intimate relationship to do that with somebody you've never met. I won't say it's comparable to a love affair, but you're supposed to get down to a level where you can talk about something that matters to both of us. Well, that's an odd thing to do with a stranger.

Is it easier or harder to write with a brand-new person?

It's far easier to write with my dear friends, whom I'm used to writing with, because I know their style. Half the time, all you have to do is get into a groove and the song will emerge somehow or another. With somebody you don't know, you don't know what to expect. Sometimes it works out great

and you're so surprised: "Where has this person been all my life? What a great player. What a great writer. What a great singer." Other times it's like, "Why did this person get into the music business?"

Give me an example of some new person who worked out wonderfully as a writing partner.

The first time I met Shawn Camp I knew there was a kindred spirit and a real writer. I don't know if you know Michael Smotherland, but he was a California transplant who came way before any of these new guys. There are a couple of others, too, where I just knew right away that something was going on.

How do these new talents get to you? Are they recommended by folks who work here?

Yeah. Especially over these past couple of years, since I don't know any of the new kids. I'm getting so elderly… thank God I've got Carla Wallace, the president [at Big Yellow Dog Music] and Whit Jeffords—who are youngsters themselves and are in touch with the buzz on the street.

Do they bring in people who are talented but maybe intimidated by you? How do you put them at ease?

Oh, sometimes they'll say they're scared, but I always try to be my disarming self.

You mentioned that bluegrass is an area where you feel there's something going on from a songwriting perspective. This genre used to be dominated by traditional material, so why is that changing?

I'd love to see it happening more and more. There are some artists out there who are stretching the boundaries of bluegrass writing and recording other material that would not even be considered remotely bluegrass. But they put that undeniable bluegrassical musicality to it. Alison Krauss and Shawn Camp come to mind. Alison just recorded a song of mine, "If I Didn't Know Any Better," on her new album, and it's a perfect example of that; it's not a bluegrass song.

You wrote it simply as a song and she found a context for it.

I wrote it with Mindy Smith, an up-and-coming rocker, and Mindy and Alison got to know each other. Alison heard Mindy sing it and fell in love with it.

You did the folk and coffeehouse scene in Boston before you came out to Nashville. Did that background give you a different perspective on writing country material?

that I thought were folk songs. It turned out they were just rambling hippie songs.

But maybe Nashville was more open to this different approach to lyrics.

Those two things, country and folk, having blended up there in New Hampshire with all that rock 'n' roll, set me up pretty well for coming here. I didn't know it at the time, but looking back…

Do you have any upcoming cuts?

Other than Alison, the coolest thing I've got right now is the title cut on Dierks Bentley's new album, *Modern Day Drifter*. He's a very exciting, up-and-coming guy, and he's near to the bluegrass world as well.

It's hard to say where something comes from. You might have had an idea—some notion of a melody or a little spark of something—but if you write every day you don't have anything like that; you start from scratch all the time.

That came even before my New Hampshire days—before the commune and all that. I was going to try and make it in the coffeehouse scene. But I missed it by a year or two. The places were still open but the people had moved on. I still find it fascinating; it's almost like an old English fairytale world. So when I got up to New Hampshire, that's what I tried to interject into that band: these long, poetic things

The Statler Brothers

Quartet singing has long been a staple of gospel music, a style that attracted such diverse fans as Hank Williams and Elvis Presley. Artists like the the Statlers, who are all Virginians kept the longstanding tradition of quartet singing very much alive in country music for the last several decades.

The Statlers (original lineup: bass singer Harold Reid, born August County, Virginia, 1939; lead vocalist Don Reid, born Staunton, Virginia, 1945; baritone Phil Balsley, born Staunton, Virginia, 1939; and tenor Lew DeWitt, born Roanoke, Virginia, 1938) were named after a brand of tissues. It was DeWitt's offbeat composition "Flowers on the Wall" that gave The Statlers their first huge country and pop hit in 1965 on Columbia Records. Four years later, The Statlers signed with Mercury Records and stayed there over twenty years. At long last in 1978, the band achieved number one for the first time with "Do You Know You Are My Sunshine."

The ensemble nature of The Statlers, combined with their natural showmanship, made them a natural for television. They hosted a weekly TV program on The Nashville Network, which debuted in October of 1991. The Statlers were happy to make the program retro, modeling it after the great variety programs of the Golden Age of Television in the fifties. Their most recent album, *Farewell Concert* (2003) is filled with twenty-one live tracks.

—PHIL SWEETLAND

Interview by
Vernell Hackett

American Songwriter,
May/June 1990

322

What did "Bed of Roses" do for your career?

Phil: We took "Bed of Roses" to the producer at our first label, and he told us it wasn't our image. When we went over to Mercury and started working with [producer] Jerry Kennedy, we played it for him, and he said if you guys like it, do it.

Don: We had a problem early in our career with not having a direction. During the time we were on that previous label, we were writing our heads off, but they wouldn't let us record any of our own material; we couldn't get anybody else to record it [either]. All of a sudden, with the advent of "Bed of Roses," which was our first record at Mercury, we had the freedom to do our own material. We had direction and we had a catalog of material unheard and unrecorded.

Where do you guys draw your inspiration from to write?

Jimmy: It's kind of hard to come up with new things sometimes. Sometimes you try not to think about it too hard, at least I do anyway. Sometimes you sit down and you're inspired to write something and it comes out, or we'll come up with something that we'll want to work on for a project or something. That's the hardest thing for me to do. Harold and Don seem to come up with that a lot better than I do. I just can't seem to write that way very well, but I think that's the way it works a lot of times.

Can you do anything to help receive signals for songs?

Don: You have to constantly have your mind open for new ideas. You don't want to repeat yourself, but like Jimmy said, you can get yourself in trouble trying too hard. You try not to make a conscious effort, but at the same time you have to remember not to write in a certain direction because "We've done that before." We're always looking for something new,

something fresh, but without any drastic changes, and that's a very thin line to walk. Just sitting here talking to you, you might say something that has a musical catch to it, and we'll write that down mentally. Sometimes we'll all start fighting for a pencil at the same time.

What's an example of a burst of inspiration that occurred for you?

Harold: We were playing Buck Lake Ranch in Indiana, and we'd been having a really good time all day. There were a bunch of college students in the audience singing along to every song we were doing, so we got them up onstage to sing and I went down and sat in the audience. At that point, the audience started making requests. Some of them were just yelling them out, but this one girl walked up to the edge of the stage and very quietly called me over to the side and she [asked me], "Do you know 'You Are My Sunshine?'" I mean, I started looking for a pencil right there! I carried the title around with me for a couple of weeks, I guess, and finally I wrote the bridge or maybe just a portion of the beginning or something. I don't even remember. So Don and I got together one night and we worked on it, but we couldn't come up with anything. So we threw it back in the briefcase and forgot it.

Is it easy to get discouraged and think, "Everything's been written about?"

Harold: I think every writer, at some time or another, sits down and thinks he's said all he has to say, or he's dried up. The nicest thing that can happen to you during one of those dry spells is that somebody will say something or you'll suddenly have a thought which will inspire you to write down two lines of something that you know you will complete later. It's a nice feeling to think, "Hey, you know, I still have something going for me." Avoiding writer's block is just a matter of keeping your mind open. When we're

working on a project or an album, we know what we're looking for so we have the advantage over any outside writer. But the problem we really run into is that once we've recorded an album and start to look for other material similar to what we just had out. By that time, that's old hat and we're not looking for it anymore. So when writers send us material, judging by what's out at the time, they're always about six months behind what we're actually doing. So by the time someone knows what we want, we've already done it. It's kind of a vicious cycle.

Tell us about your recording of Roger Miller's "You Ought to Be Here With Me," from the Broadway show *Big River*.

Don: [*Big River* wasn't] released yet. We finally got a copy of it and sat down, and I mean there were ten choices of what we could have gone with. We finally decided on "You Ought to Be Here With Me." He really had some terrific songs on there. Roger is a great talent in everything he's ever tried.

going to duet, and when the harmony comes in. It's a total equal amount of input from everyone.

What's the story with "O Baby Mine"?

Phil: We talked about recording that song for four years. It had been on the list of songs that we oughta record one of these days. Finally, we pulled it out and decided it fit the album we were working on, and it came off really well and lo and behold, it became a single. There have been times when we worked on songs right down to the wire, right up to the time we were going in the studio, and we've just had to say, "Man, this doesn't feel right," and we've shelved it—then gone back later and put it on another album.

Do you have any advice for aspiring songwriters?

Jimmy: Songwriting is a talent that you have to have, but if you just let it lay there, it's not going to do anything for you. You have to keep working with it, constantly trying to improve and learn. If you continue to work with it, you'll find that you will be able to keep on writing good songs.

> *Songwriting is a talent that you have to have, but if you just let it lay there, it's not going to do anything for you. You have to keep working with it, constantly trying to improve and learn.*

Is it hard to decide how to record and produce songs?

Don: We all have input. No matter who has written it, when it comes time to write the arrangement and decide what and how it's all formed, we sit down and decide the key and who's going to sing it, how we're going to sing it, who's

Cat Stevens

The author of such contemporary classics as "Peace Train" and "Moonshadow," folk artist Cat Stevens has had a unique and distinguished career. Stevens was born Steven Georgiou in London, England, in 1947. He attended Hammersmith College in the sixties, where he immersed himself in the burgeoning folk music scene. His eclectic debut *Matthew & Son* (1967) was bolstered by Stevens' first radio hit, the quirky "I Love My Dog." His second album, *New Masters*, sold poorly but featured the well-known track "The First Cut Is the Deepest" (a hit for Rod Stewart in 1976 and Sheryl Crow in 2003). Stevens began to focus on more introspective material in the early seventies, releasing the classic albums *Mona Bone Jakon, Tea for the Tillerman,* and *Teaser and the Firecat.* In 1977, Stevens retreated from the spotlight, embracing the Islamic faith and taking the name Yusuf Islam. He ceased recording and performing western music, but in 2006 he announced his intention to release a new album of pop songs.

—EVAN SCHLANSKY

*Interview by
Ken Sharp*

American Songwriter,
July/Aug 2006

"On the Road to Find Out"…

"On the Road to Find Out" [*recites some of the lyrics*], "In the end I'll know but on the way I'll wonder…" So I was still in this phase of wondering. In "Peace Train" I never explicitly said where I thought it would end up. Interestingly, the word *Islam* itself is a derivative of the word *peace* in Arabic, which is *salaam.* So there were hints in my songs that I was a man of change. I loved trying out new ideas, thinking and pondering this world from different angles, and I suppose that all began for me back when I had my first crisis in life with getting tuberculosis. After an initial year of success and flashbulbs and adoring fans my seat was vacant. I was in bed thinking about this world whizzing by me and where I was going. It was my first brush with death. It made me think more seriously. At that point I started reading books about the self like *The Secret Path* by Dr. Paul Brunton. It's a very interesting book for anyone who's of western mind looking for a place of peace within his life. For me it was a revelation.

Did your spiritual beliefs help you deal with the initial onset of your phenomenal success?

For sure. My first period of success was an inoculation toward preparing me for the next phase of exposure to fame and fortune. I was on a secret mission, perhaps not everybody could see it but through my words they can kind of find my story and my longings and yearnings for peace and enlightenment. My albums illustrated that also. For instance, *Catch Bull at Four* was taken from a kind of ten-stage enlightenment process from Zen Buddhism. And my music evolved to that point, I suppose. I tried many different styles as well. I mean, *Foreigner* was one stage, it was me saying, "Look, you can't nail me down, I don't want to be nailed down in this particular style or format or package or box, I want to be free, and say it from another part of my soul."

Today you are finally embracing your musical career, not shying away from speaking about it.

When I finally discovered through receiving a gift of the Koran, when I finally discovered Islam, it opened up a whole new world of knowledge for me, which linked hitherto. It sort of turned them into realities. My belief in God became absolutely confirmed when I read this book. And in a way it was a confirmation of all the things that I instinctively felt and also those things of which I had been brought up with through the Bible, through my Christian education and upbringing. Even things from my Buddhist journeying, this Koran was weaving it all together in a wonderful picture of unity and oneness. I finally embraced Islam. I never read anywhere in the Koran anything to do with music; I couldn't see the word *music* in quotation marks. So I never thought it was a problem.

There were problems connected with lifestyle, frivolous and temporary relationships and obviously those kinds of things are not quite sanctioned by the Koran. So drinking, partying, all those things that really quite honestly gave me a headache anyway and were problems, things I wrote about. Like in "Hard Headed Woman" I sing, [*recites lyrics*] "I knew a lot of fancy dancers. People who can glide you across the floor. They move so smooth but have no answers when you ask them what do you come here for." But you know what they come here for. It's not the real thing, it's the fleeting life. So in other words, I realized there was a problem with remaining in the business and trying to purify my life.

Then I heard some severe warnings about the music business itself explicitly coming from scholars, people who were teaching me, so I decided to just quit. And I did in a kind of dramatic fashion which reflects my urge for 100 percent maximum commitment, whether I'm a musician, an artist, or a Muslim. At that point I couldn't see any place for music at that time in my life. It was not necessary. I had done that, been there, done that sort of thing. So that's when I sold my instruments for charity and walked off. It was a sad moment for many of my fans and perhaps it was one of those things I now regret, perhaps doing it in that way. But I needed to envelop myself in my new life and I had to learn basics like a child going to primary school again. I was just beginning at the very lowest level. And I wanted to be at that level, I felt it was my chance to escape the limelight and to get human again. Then after that a period passed of great experiences and turbulence.

Sometimes I'd be involuntarily asked to comment on major crises in the Muslim world and in the world generally and it was only because I was a Muslim celebrity. But I was not really prepared many times to answer those kinds of complex questions. Then more and more I saw the horrifying picture of Islam as it was projected in the media. People were turned off because of strange and unpredictable events in the Muslim world, which had nothing to do with the faith itself or like the experience I was living. The majority of Muslims actually live every day without much controversy. I was dragged into controversy.

It became clear that I should look again at the idea of communicating through the medium. The medium I knew best was recording. So I went back into the studio and said, "I'm going to record something to at least help people to understand this faith that I've grown to love and that I feel can benefit so many people if they just understood it." I began my Mountain of Light record label and the first recording I did was of the life of the lost prophet. Peace be upon him. Because so many people today, with all the amount of information flying all over the place through the Internet and satellite television and whatever, have no idea who this man was and what Islam means. When that happened I started softening my approach and started looking back at my own music. And even though I was not going to make that kind of music again I did decide to look back into it.

The remastered sound on the new reissues of your work is breathtaking. *Tea for the Tillerman* **sounds amazing.**

Yes I know. It's incredible. For that I have to thank Bill Levenson and his amazing dedication. Again there are personalities in there that help remind me of some of the treasures that still reside in those tunes, in those words. With that kind of encouragement, I suppose also with a little help from my older brother, David, who has always been an important figure in my life. I think he also wanted to help me maximize my ability to shape the musical inheritance I was going to hand over. When I pass away obviously that's what a lot of people are going to still remember. I remember in my song called "Sitting" I said, [*recites lyrics*] "I'm not making love to anyone's wishes only for that light I see. 'Cause when I'm dead and lowered low in my grave that's going to be the only thing that's left of me." I had an idea of the purity of the soul and the need to guard it against corruption, against becoming lost in the world. So coming back to that I realized looking at my songs that there is a value and an explanation in a way of why I am who I am today. If I don't fill in those gaps people will not read between the lines. And the lines that have been written are so scarce and often so distorted that nobody will ever understand. I felt that was almost criminal. I said, "No, I've got to get involved." Not only that, but there were a lot of friends and fans that I wanted to make amends with.

When was the last time you had a guitar in your hands that you actually played?

Good question. I would think it was the Year of the Child Concert in 1979, that was my last concert. I may have carried a guitar offstage that day but that was it.

I'm staying at a hotel in Piccadilly, very close to where you grew up in the West End. Bring

us back to your childhood and days of wonder growing up amid the bustling and vibrant theater district. Discuss how that impacted on you as a person and songwriter.

It was the backdrop. And in a way one of the major influences of my life and career was the fact that I grew up in the center of London and the hub of the West End where theatres and coffee bars and jukeboxes played throughout the night. So in a way it was natural that I fell into the entertainment world. It was a natural step. There were many great shows. Right across the road from us was the Shaftesbury Theatre, *Hair* was one of those shows. One of the first places I played was the Saville Theatre. I played there with Georgie Fame and Julie Felix back in 1967. It was strange to go out of my front door just down the road to the Saville Theatre. Some of my early gigs, some of my first shows, were at little kebab shops and pubs and folk clubs just outside my door, just a few hundred yards away.

You played at Les Cousins, a folk club.

It was an inspiring club. I never really played that often there, maybe only once. It was a very elitist folk club and I was one of the young trainees. I certainly was not ready to stand up next to Bert Jansch or John Renbourn or Davey Graham, who frequented that club. And Paul Simon also. It was an inspiring venue, but eventually I was looking at not necessarily being a performer and more of a songwriter. That's an important point really, which maybe some people don't know. I thought I could stay in the background, write songs, and have other people sing them. Unfortunately the songs that I wrote were so quirky.

Your version of "The First Cut Is the Deepest" sounds like The Small Faces could have done a bang-up job with it. Rod Stewart, of course, later covered it to great effect.

I always wanted someone like Percy Sledge to sing that song. I didn't know the song was that special when I wrote it. P.P. Arnold found it. Mike Hurst, my producer, and P.P. Arnold thought it was a great song and was particularly special. I had a kind of feel for that having a slow rhythm and blues type of thing. Again, I was writing songs that I thought other people would be singing. Eventually I had to sing them myself.

Your song "Here Comes My Baby" was a smash hit for The Tremeloes, proving your rising status as a songwriter.

That was amazing when that happened. It was extremely exciting to see my song going so high in the charts by another group. It was interesting when that whole thing happened. Brian Poole & The Tremeloes, I think they split. Brian Poole felt he was the tops and he just couldn't carry this group with him. And then The Tremeloes made a record and it went to number one.

Some of your early songs like "Matthew & Son" and "I'm Gonna Get Me a Gun" had a pop edge. Then there was a transformation for you in the seventies where your work became much more introspective and folky. What prompted this change in styles?

There were always hints of my folk roots anyway even in my early albums, songs like "The Tramp," "Blackness of the Night," and "Portobello Road." They're kind of folk songs in a way. It's only when the producer and the arranger got together that really my songs started changing. I was starting to write in a way for my arranger that became a bit too poppish. I wanted to get away from that. One of the last songs that I recorded with Mike Hurst, "Where Are You," was an attempt to get him on board with that kind of style. It never made it and so we parted. It was later that I met Chris Blackwell [the founder of Island

Records]. I had an idea of writing a musical on the Russian Revolution. One of these was "Father & Son" and suddenly he said, "Why don't you sign with Island Records?"

Tell me about the British tour you did with Jimi Hendrix, Engelbert Humperdinck, and the Walker Brothers. I heard they used to pull tricks on you by sending a wind-up toy out on the stage during your show.

I heard about that, too. I can't remember it for the life of me. Probably things like that happened so often that I wouldn't even remember it. It was exciting, that tour. I remember that I'd done my particular spot, gone back to the dressing room and suddenly someone was shouting, "He's started a fire on stage." So we all came dashing down and we saw Jimi Hendrix and his guitar on fire. I've never seen anything like that before; I couldn't imagine what was going to happen next. I didn't get to know Scott Walker, but Jimi and Engelbert were both human beings you could relate to, especially offstage. Jimi was a quiet man off stage. In some respects he was pushed by different people in different ways. And he was shaped by the public that loved him.

Tea for the Tillerman is a brilliant album, your first gold album, and one of your most popular to date. Share your recollections behind the making of that landmark effort.

For me it represented a picture of childhood and childish wonderment. And I would say also the spirit of inquiry. To me the childish picture on the front told the story.

How long did it take for you to create the artwork on the album cover?

Maybe four or five hours. I think the album had the feel of being homemade; it was minimalist when that word wasn't even known at that time. There was a lot of space, which was also kind of the touch of Paul Samwell-Smith, who gave a lovely aesthetic air to the studio and to the productions. So I think that was one of those special milestone albums, which conforms itself out of the blue.

Do you still draw for pleasure?

No, I'm happy with the productions I'm making for Mountain of Light. I'm involved in all these books and packages, which I take great delight in, making sure that the colors are right, the illustrations, the typeface, the spacing, the paper, everything to do with the feel and the presentation.

Your lyrics can stand on their own as poems and stories. What inspired you as a lyricist?

I suppose you'd have to go back to the musicals, which first of all influenced me. All of those musicals were part of the story. Painting stories with words was like my art. Influences? I suppose I loved the stories behind certain blues songs, Leadbelly's songs, songs about the days of slavery and the struggle for freedom. Those are real songs, real words. I think Dylan came in to make everybody think about how words can be used in a contemporary music genre. I think that helped. Along that vein came Paul Simon and various people. I think the biggest influence was maybe the musicals in the beginning.

Share your memories of some of your key tracks, starting with "Hard Headed Woman."

I suppose that was another yearning for the ideal partner in life when everything would be balanced. I'm talking about marriage, making a commitment.

"Where Do the Children Play?"

A song of, if you like, recording the destruction of this world and looking at what we're leaving for future generations.

How about "If You Want to Sing Out, Sing Out," a song that appears in the film *Harold and Maude?*

That was telling people, or saying to myself, that life is full of choices and it doesn't matter what you choose so long as it is true to you. I may have changed my point of view of course at this point because I think there are right and wrong choices.

"Father & Son"

It was about a son who was eager to join the revolution, to leave the farm of his father. And his father was trying to keep him home and telling him you shouldn't just grow up chasing dreams that [*recites lyrics*] "you still may be here tomorrow but your dreams may not."

Was your father supportive of your music?

I don't know if he even heard much of it so I'm probably sure he wasn't really supportive. He used to like the effect of my music because it brought a lot of customers into the shop. He had a restaurant very near to the West End called Moulin Rouge. Later I changed it to my father's name; we turned it into a Greek restaurant officially and called it Stavros.

"Morning Has Broken" was based on a hymn.

I found that in a hymn book when I was going through a sort of dry period. I hadn't written a song for a week or two. I was worried, I had to write something. I was looking for something to complete the album probably, *Teaser and the Firecat,* and then I discovered "Morning Has Broken."

How about "Oh Very Young"?

It's a very sweet song, again talking to the youth and indirectly asking ourselves, "What are we leaving our children?" and asking our children, "What are you going to leave your children on this Earth?"

"Wild World"

Again, it mirrors that kind of paternal advisor which you find in "Father & Son," giving words of caution to the young hearts going out to grab this world. So in a way, I don't know where some of these songs came from but maybe it was a reminder to myself about the need to be cautious.

The message of a song like "On the Road to Find Out" still resonates with so many people today.

The melody carried us forward. It had a driving feel to it and the words were reflecting the drive that I had in my life toward knowledge and understanding. And I was talking about all the options I was being offered, like the marketplace of ideas. I was listening to [*recites lyrics*] "Robins telling me not to worry, listening to the wind telling me to hurry." So it was that journey and listening to all the voices telling me which way to go.

Speaking of that journey, "Miles From Nowhere" fits that theme. In a song like that and with much of your work, you were able to instill a dynamic of building crescendos and emotion.

Usually I was aiming for a climactic moment; I suppose "Miles From Nowhere" has that. It's strange at that most climactic moment sometimes I would add a beat and throw the rhythm off so you wouldn't quite know exactly where you were. That would be a moment of questioning yourself and of surprise.

On *The Very Best of Cat Stevens* collection, it includes a wonderful and previously unreleased track, "I've Got a Thing About Seeing My Grandson Grow Old."

There were a whole lot of tapes, which in a way have been hidden and locked up for twenty years. When Bill Levenson got us to think about opening up those vaults we discovered all those hidden and unheard recordings. That song was one of them. For some reason it never got on any album, perhaps because I never played the mouth organ that well.

In the seventies, who were the contemporary artists mining a similar style of music that you personally enjoyed?

Probably James Taylor and Neil Young. At one point I think Neil was extremely unique with his sound and his laid-back mellow style. I used to admire James Taylor's guitar picking skills. He was a perfectionist in that area and he was so clean sounding and I love that kind of sound. His words were pensive so you could listen to them.

You said, "I used to be a singer of songs, my songs, a lot of the time I would be singing about finding the truth and about peace but I wasn't living it so I was a hypocrite." An interesting statement for an artist to say and admit to, again indicative of your spiritual quest for something more than fame and fortune.

It was very difficult to see it directly at the time. I was almost veiled from my own identity. It was only when I read the words of the Koran that I started becoming challenged and my soul was suddenly exposed. That's some of the power of the Koran. And I was beginning to discover and agree with that. I knew that life was full of, in some ways, deceit, people deceive themselves. The most explicit description of this in the Koran was in the chapter called "The Poets" where it says, "Don't you see the poets, how they say which they don't practice." Wow, bang on the head, that's me. And I was then able to realize that one doesn't have to act to create an illusion about one's self. To find peace and security you just have to be yourself. In fact I wrote that line once, I said "Come on now it's freedom calling, come on over and find yourself. " I can't remember all the words. "Eleven

apartments too and a house in Malibu," whatever. But until you know what inside you really are… In other words, you'll never have that freedom until you know who you are. That was the search I was on, the search for my identity. When I read the Koran I realized that I'm just one of your average human beings.

Lastly, "Moonshadow" is one of your songs of which there is a multigenerational appeal; kids love it as do adults and teenagers.

I never intended that. I was very much an instinctive writer and an instinctive recording artist. I used to go with the flow and sometimes I wouldn't know why. Something would feel right one way and not the other. "Moonshadow" is what I call the eternal optimist's anthem, which is fine. If that's the final word on my music, I think that's what should be remembered.

Even Stevens

Interview by
Vernell Hacket

American Songwriter,
January/February 1985

Even Stevens was graced with two very rare gifts—a nickname that is one of the catchiest in any genre of music and the ability to write songs that were radio-friendly, commercial successes, especially when Even teamed with Eddie Rabbitt. As a seventies artist for Jac Holzman's Elektra Records, Stevens was not as successful. His first single, "Let the Little Boy Dream" (1975), peaked out at number thirty-eight at *Billboard*. But when he finally teamed with the New Jersey tunesmith Eddie Rabbitt the following year (1976), they came up with the "Drinkin' My Baby (Off My Mind)," the first of Rabbitt's long string of number ones.

Stevens had come from Ohio, where he was born Bruce Stevens. He was a radio operator in the Coast Guard, and the other Coast Guardsmen gave him the nickname "Even" Stevens.

The way he made it is a true piece of Nashville history—the stuff of legend. Stevens had an uncle who played drums in one of the dives on Lower Broadway in Nashville. Stevens went to visit him and ended up playing one of his own tunes after his uncle's band finished the final set one night. Webb Pierce, the country legend whose fifties classics include "Slowly" (1954) and "There Stands the Glass" (1953), happened to be at the bar that night and heard Stevens's song, "Fair Weather Friends."

—PHIL SWEETLAND

Is it essential for songwriters to base themselves in Nashville?

Any music town is based in songs; there's no other way. If you don't have the song, it doesn't matter what else you have. And I'm not demeaning anyone else involved—a hit song is not a hit song unless it's done right. Nashville's music business is centrally located so writers run into each other a lot. In all the restaurants in this area… you always run into a writer or a publisher. The other towns may have as many songwriters and the towns are based on songs, but they just aren't as centrally located as we are.

In general, how have songwriters changed with respect to the business?

Writers today have a different idea about the business. When I first came here, I would have died to just get any tape recorder to use… anything to get my songs down. In this day and age, with the technology and people accustomed to Sony Walkmans, they want to be able to record their songs on a twenty-four track and do a whole session on them and everything. I guess writers are still obsessed, but they're just not crazy to do it any way they can. They want an easier way than before. There's nothing wrong with that. It doesn't make the songs better or worse, and it's just real interesting to me to watch the changes.

What should a songwriter expect upon moving to Nashville?

If you're gonna move here to make songwriting your profession, don't expect anything major to happen for three years. You can make a lot of contacts and learn a lot in three years. Before you move here, check out the publishers, set some appointments, and see if anyone's interested in signing you so you can get a small writer's advance to sustain you. Try not to have to work another job if there's any way at all to get by. I slept in my Jeep for six months so I could live on very little money, just so I could write and not have to work and be tired and not be able to write. I was going for it all the way—I was gonna make it or break it, I figured. Luckily, it's worked out pretty good so far.

How did your writing relationship with Eddie Rabbitt come about?

First if all we were real good friends before we became songwriting partners. We got to know each other's thoughts and how the other one felt about certain things. With most good songwriting teams, one has something the other needs and vice versa. Our situation has progressed from both sides, but when I first met Eddie, my background was California and folk music and I was writing real personal things. He had the hook idea down and knew how to structure a hook and more how to write country music. Eddie had already been a writer for a while in the business, and I never had been, so the combination worked out well.

How did your publishing company with Jim Malloy come about?

I went my own way and was placing songs on an individual basis with [Sony/]Tree and in the meantime, looking for a publisher who believed in me. I was walking down the street one day and this kid in a Porsche pulls up, stops, jumps out, and says, "Are you Even Stevens?" I asked why, because at that time I had a lot of bills and bill collectors were looking for me.

What happened then?

So I met with Jim the next day and played him some songs, and two days later we started the company.

The new material seems like it's classic Rabbitt/Stevens.

It's actually back to what Eddie and I were doing originally. It's something we've always talked about and we just did

it. We also tried to get back to the old style of writing we're known for. The first release of the album, "Burning Up With Love," was one of the demos we did in The Garage, our demo studio. We just restructured it. I just get an idea mapped out in my head and then come in the studio and create it and maybe even make up the words when I sing it on the mike.

How did you get involved with writing for films?

On Wednesday Kenny Rogers called and said he was calling all the writers he knew because he had a song he needed written for the movie *Six Pack*. He was gonna be in Knoxville the next night and David Malloy and I rented a Silver Eagle bus and got a drum machine and drove up to see him. We wrote a song on the way up, from the idea he'd given us when he told us about the script. So David and I watched the show and between every song, we would hum that melody back and forth because we were trying to remember it and we were hearing all those other songs. We got back on the bus and started the song and got about halfway back to Nashville—it was around two in the morning—and I said, "You know, Thom Schuyler would be great and would really help out on this song. So we called Thom and said, "Do you wanna write this song with us?" And he said, "Yeah," so we told him, "If you're any kind of writer you'll meet us at the office when we get there." So it was about 2:30 or 3:00 A.M. and Thom was there, and we hooked up the drum machine and we pretty much wrote the song by 5:00 A.M. That was Friday, and on Monday [Thom and I] got together in the studio. David was producing somebody over in another studio. We demoed the song and David jumped back and forth… and we would rewrite as we went. We got it out to Kenny on Tuesday. Wednesday they called us and loved it and wanted us to come out [to L.A.] with Kenny. So within a week we had met him, demoed the song, got it accepted, and were out producing it. We recorded it in several different ways, and when we had to rewrite, we'd get Thom on the phone.

As you've lived and learned in this industry, is your outlook the same as it was early on?

Someone told me a long time ago that those first few years would be the best times of all. And that's really the truth. That's when you're into it, and it's a magic time when you get people to start recording your songs. You see the ladder and steps you're going up. The excitement is not gone now. It's just different. It's like a love affair; when it's new it's always so romantic. Hopefully it's gonna be good later, but it's never gonna be just like those first few years.

What qualities do you have to have to make everything come together?

Blind ignorance and ego. I look back at the songs I pitched that I thought were really great, and I'd never pitch them now. You have to be obsessed with it and you have to have a little bit of an ego problem, in that *you* think they're great. Hopefully you get better.

Do you have a songwriting philosophy?

I think people who write songs are like plumbers; they have a knack for something. [And a songwriter's knack] is putting words and music together. I think any job should be something you love. Life's too short to work at something you hate. I think all great writers would write [even] if they never made a cent off it. If you feel that way, you'll probably make it as a songwriter.

Rob Thomas

photo courtesy Debbie VanStory

Like Beyoncé Knowles and Gwen Stefani, Rob Thomas has had the good fortune of being able to step away from a successful band and become a mega-popular star on his own. But the Matchbox Twenty front man has always been more than just a talented singer or pretty face—at heart, Thomas is a classic songwriter. Born on a German military base on Valentine's Day 1972, Thomas grew up in South Carolina and Florida. He first demonstrated his prowess for writing hooks with the Florida quintet Matchbox Twenty. Their grunge-pop anthems "Push," "Real World," "If You're Gone," "Bent," and "Mad Season" dominated rock radio in the late nineties and early oughts, and netted Thomas a host of songwriting awards that would prove to be prophetic. In 1999 "Smooth," a collaboration with songwriter Itaal Shur and Carlos Santana from the guitarist's comeback album *Supernatural*, made the pop world sit up and take notice of Thomas's abilities. Suddenly, superstars were knocking on his door. Thomas went on to collaborate with Mick Jagger, Marc Anthony, and Willie Nelson, contributing three country-tinged songs to Nelson's 2004 album *The Great Divide*. In 2005, Thomas was finally ready for his close-up. His debut solo album, *Something to Be*, showed off his stylistic versatility. It earned him the begrudging respect of the music press and spawned the hit single "Lonely No More."

—EVAN SCHLANSKY

Interview by David McPherson

American Songwriter,
July/August 2005

335

What gets Rob Thomas out of bed in the morning?

It's the little things in life. As a kid you think of the things that you might be lucky enough to be a part of, and working with Willie [Nelson] is one of those things. I like to know that I'm a guy that if I'm walking down the street and I pass Willie and I go, "Hey, Willie!" He'll go, "Hey Rob!" It's a good feeling because ten years ago I would have been like, "Hey Willie," and he would have been like, "Hey security!" That gets you out of bed in the morning.

What about your new crew cut?

I don't know if you call it a new image, I just got tired of having all that fucking hair [*laughs*]. That's a lot of hair after a while and during a hot New York summer that will kill you. I also liked the idea of becoming my own hairdresser.

How's your first solo record coming along?

It's completely consuming my time. I've always known that it's something that I wanted to try and do just because… all of us in the band are very aware of the fact that we spent ten years doing this at a level that we never expected we'd be able to do it. On top of that, we realized that all we had done was just us five. We had never really played with anybody else, never got to work with a lot of other people, and so I'm taking the opportunity. It wasn't that hard. I knew the kind of sound that I wanted to make and I had an idea of players already that I wanted to call. My biggest fear at the time was being worried that it was going to be hard to get them to say yes. You are always like, "Maybe if I call Mike Campbell [guitarist for Tom Petty and the Heartbreakers], maybe he will come and play." Getting everyone's schedules together and also trying to find not so much people that I think would play well together, but people that never in a million years would play together. I mean, can I get Tom Petty's guitar player and Dr. Dre's bass player and Mary J. Blige's drummer and Robert Ran-

dolph and Wendy from Prince and the Revolution. Can I get all of them on one track with me singing and make it sound like it all goes together? Diversity was the motto for the record. Everyone kept asking me over and over, "What's the difference going to be? Why do a solo record? If you write these songs and you're the front man, what do you have to say that you are not saying?" It's a testament to Matchbox Twenty because when we do something with Matchbox, it's a full band effort and every sound that we put on there is the result of an argument between five people. Being responsible for it all yourself was the difference. I don't take a lot of credit for it. The writing part of it always feels like the easy part. It seems like, "This is what I do," this is why I was born, so I write all the time. I'm just lucky enough that I get to do it for a living or else I would just have a lot of songs that nobody heard [*laughs*].

So, what inspires you to write songs?

The creation of something new. The idea that you walk into a room and there's nothing there… only a big, silent, empty room. Then there's a good chance of leaving that room with a song that never existed before… that's an amazing concept to me.

What songs do you think have left a footprint on musical history?

I take it all the way back to at some point, "Rock Around the Clock" did not exist and one day these writers went into a room and came out with this amazing song and now it's a piece of history… the same thing with Paul Simon's "Graceland" and Tom Petty's "Refugee." It's the one part of all of this that no matter how you try to fuck it up you can't… it stays pure. No matter what happens to it later, no matter where it goes, no matter how people decide to sell records or not to sell records, that part doesn't get changed.

Do you write mainly on guitar, or do you venture out to other instruments?

I'm a lot better piano player than guitar player. So a lot of times I start on the guitar, but I just kind of get stuck. I'll be like, "I know what chord I want to play, but I can't play it."

On the piano I'm not blocked by something simple like chord progressions. The only problem is that if you start on the piano a lot of times it seems you tend to go a lot mellower because anything that you play on the piano to try and rock just sounds stupid. No matter what you do it all just sounds like "Crocodile Rock."

How do you feel about collaborating with other artists and writers?

I've been really fortunate with Matchbox so any outside writing has been based on the idea: "Can I learn a whole lot from this?" or "Does this sound like something that is going to be a lot of fun?" I've been able to work with people that I'm a big fan of in some way. Everybody from Mick Jagger and Willie Nelson to people like [songwriters] Phil Vassar and Pat Green.

What was it like to work with Willie Nelson?

We spent two days together and he just wound up doing three of my songs. We sat down to write something together and we never actually wrote anything together, we just really got high for two days and played each other songs, basically. Willie's great because with him I was like, "You know what my favorite song is? I love 'Angel Flying too Close to the Ground.'" And Willie would go, "Yeah, well, 'If you're not falling,'" [*as Thomas puts on his best Willie Nelson voice and sings a couple of lines*] and I was like, "I'm in heaven right now."

And Mick Jagger?

With Mick Jagger it was a different thing altogether. It would be a couple of hours writing in the afternoon and then we would go out drinking. He was such an intense writer. I didn't expect that out of Mick Jagger. You think that everything just flows out of him or a misconception might be that he's such a big star and so busy being Mick Jagger that he doesn't care about writing and that's why I was there. But, to see him grab a guitar and run into the other room and start just beating a melody out, and even more importantly to see him doing it kind of the same way that I do it. See him just running at it and being really raw and [*makes inaudible noises*] not being afraid to make noises that don't make any sense. Seeing that as a young writer and seeing one of my idols doing that, that's a nice sense of, "Everything is right in the world, I'm doing things the way I should be doing."

When working with these legends, how does it feel to be the "young" songwriter?

That can carry you a long way in your head. It's a lot easier to shove off bad criticism that you read in a magazine. When I met Carlos [Santana] we had just finished coming off the road for our first record, we had sold all these records, and we were still very secure in the knowledge that we weren't that much better of a band than we were when we started. But, all of a sudden we were in this arena… literally in an arena… but in the arena of all these other rock stars and selling all these records that we were all of a sudden supposed to be at this level, and we weren't. We were standing there with our dicks in our hands going, "What do we do now? Is this it?" Because it didn't feel like it. And working with Carlos, it seemed like it had this really serendipitous perfect timing for him to come along and be like, "Hey listen, it's the fucking journey man… there is no destination." If you do all this and sell all these records then all you have done is buy yourself a chance now to be a better band… to buy yourself the chance to be better musicians, better songwriters, and realize that sooner or later if you have something that tanks that's fine. That just becomes part of your

repertoire… ten years down the road that might be people's favorite song…the one that didn't work. It's just a matter of doing this long enough that that could come to fruition.

Do you see yourself writing for the rest of your life?

I could probably quit everything else. At the end of the day, I get a bigger reward out of writing a great song than I do out of being a pop star. You know what I mean? That's something that I can see myself doing for the rest of my life. As opposed to the "the ass-shaking part."

How does your band react to you taking a break?

It's a good feeling… I talked to my drummer and we had a long conversation about it. We realized that we are so much more self-conscious around each other than we are anybody else in the world. So both of us working with other people, all of a sudden we were unearthing all these talents that we didn't realize we had because we had to take point and not sit back and bring it into the argument. Usually you would

> *I believe that all good art is brought from right in the heart of self-doubt.*

come in and say here's the idea I think and then you would go through everybody's idea and find the idea that makes everybody the happiest. And with this you come in and you have these people that are much better players than I am, they do this for a living, and they play with some of the best. So, your first fear is that you are going to walk in and they are like, "This guy doesn't fucking earn his paycheck, man, what are we doing here?" and then your second fear is that you are going to be like, "Shit, I don't earn my fucking paycheck, what am I doing here?" At some point you just click

and go, I'm making a record and I do know what I am doing and I do know how I want it to sound and I know exactly what I want them to play and then you just start doing it and it becomes an amazing thing… just on a selfish level it's great to tell your drummer to play this and he just plays it. I believe that all good art is brought from right in the heart of self-doubt. Even some of your most egotistical-sounding songs are brought because you don't feel that way. The distance between how you feel and how you want to feel, that's what the song's about.

Give us a brief list of who has influenced your songwriting.

Paul Simon, Tom Petty. Willie Nelson was it for me. He always is and always will be the greatest American songwriter…probably the greatest living songwriter. I mean, that man wrote "Blue Eyes Crying in the Rain." You know it's funny he didn't write "Mamas Don't Let Your Babies Grow Up to Be Cowboys" or "My Heroes Have Always Been Cowboys." I think that's the power of Willie, it's not just his songwriting; he takes these songs and makes them his own. We did a show with him in Nashville and he rehearsed until after midnight. When he was done rehearsing he went on his bus and there were all these people waiting outside his bus to talk to him and he stayed on his bus and brought everyone on his bus five at a time until 2 A.M. when he had signed something for everybody. He is the man.

Travis Tritt

photo courtesy Mils Fitzner, Travis Tritt, Quantum Management

Travis Tritt caught the music bug as a kid, teaching himself guitar at age eight and beginning to write songs at fourteen. He tried to settle down and put his musical aspirations aside, encouraged by his parents who felt that it wouldn't pay the bills. He married, worked several jobs—including one at an air conditioning company—divorced, and then began working the honky-tonk circuit. Danny Davenport, an executive at Warner Bros. Records, took Tritt under his wing and began to cut demos with him. He signed to Warner in 1989, the same year that two other young upstarts, Clint Black and Garth Brooks, signed on with Nashville labels. His debut, *Country Club*, produced two pivotal number one singles ("Help Me Hold On" and "I'm Gonna Be Somebody"), and Tritt became one of the hottest artists in town for the next three years. Though it didn't have as much impact as *Country Club* or *It's All About to Change*, his third album—*T-R-O-U-B-L-E*—kept Tritt rolling with the hit single "Can I Trust You With My Heart." 1994's *Ten Feet Tall and Bulletproof* gave Tritt a needed jumpstart with a powerful tale of parting ("Foolish Pride"), and the album soon went platinum. Tritt continues to write and record songs, and as of 2006, he signed to a new indie label called Category 5 Records—which includes such veteran superstars as George Jones and Sammy Kershaw.

—DOUGLAS WATERMAN

Interview by
Deborah Evans Price

American Songwriter,
May/June 1994

What do you think has made you a successful country artist?

Really good songs… good material. I think that's what it all comes back to. It all comes back to that. You can have great concerts, a great image, and all those other things, but you have to keep putting out material that is [going to] reach people emotionally. You have to have something to say. You have to have a song that is really special, that really means something to people. If you do good songs, you're gonna be in this business for a while. If you do material that for whatever reason doesn't hit home with the people, if it doesn't stir emotions, if it doesn't hit a chord with the audience, then you're just whistling in the wind.

Do you remember your first song?

I wrote my first song when I was fourteen years old as a result of a breakup with a girlfriend, and I didn't even realize what I was doing. I was just pouring out my heart on a guitar and basically sat down and wrote this song. It was called "Spend a Little Time." Years later, I was playing the song for some people and they'd say, "Gosh, that's really good. You oughta write some more stuff." I said, "Really? You think so?" Everybody I played it for loved it. I started thinking "Well, shoot, maybe I can write songs." More and more people started to like what I wrote. They'd say, "Yeah, I can relate to that… that works." So I began just experimenting around with it as a young songwriter, writing things that hopefully would make somebody cry or make somebody laugh or get some kind of response. I always hated to sit down and play a song for somebody and they don't respond at all… just not do anything. I like doing songs that make somebody laugh or make somebody cry or go, "Wow, I never thought of it that way." That's fun.

Did you pick up some good feedback about your writing early on?

When I first started, every song I wrote was about five minutes long. I was taught basically to shorten my thoughts so that they fit into three minutes and twenty seconds… or whatever… so you can get airplay. Most of the time [radio] won't play it if it's five minutes long. That was a major thing.

What about any other tips about how to improve your craft?

I think there are little tricks you can learn that can make you a better songwriter. But you know, there is no specific menu for writing a great song. I had people tell me for a long time that "I'm Gonna Be Somebody" would never be a hit. I said, "Why?" and they said, "'Cause it doesn't rhyme; a song has to rhyme." I said, "That doesn't have anything to do with it." They were wrong. It was a number one record. And then I've had people tell me, "You've got to get to the hook in the first ten seconds." All of that is somebody trying to be smarter than they really are. There's no such thing as a perfect recipe for a song. [It is] whatever makes sense to the audience and rings true with them. I think you can be taught certain things that will make you a better songwriter, little things that possibly young songwriters don't think about. You can learn those things, but there is no recipe for success. If there was, everybody would be using it.

What's your writing style like?

I'm very informal. I'm not a methodical writer at all. Sometimes I wish I could be, but I read a very interesting article one time about Bach. They asked him how he wrote all these beautiful concertos and melodies and he said, "I sit at my piano every day at 9 A.M. in a position to receive." I thought that was interesting because I look at [songwriting] the same way. Songs are a gift from God, I think, and when songs hit me, usually I get the whole song at once. I get the lyrics, melody, everything at one time. And you just have to be smart enough to go and write them down somewhere.

Do you have to discipline yourself to write, with your artist schedule already busy?

I do schedule time off the road to concentrate on my writing. I'll schedule a month where we're off and I'll say, "During this period of time off, I'm gonna relax, get my head on straight, and get ready to go back on tour again—but I'm also gonna take a one- or two-week period out of that time to focus on writing." I'll sit down and try to work on writing a little bit every day and that's when the ideas come to me. I don't get too many ideas when I'm out on the road, but if I'm at home and I'm alone and I'm away from all of the hustle-and-bustle stuff that's going on in the business, that's when my thoughts come together. That's when writing usually happens for me. Songs usually just kind of fall on top of me at that point.

> *Stay away from too many things that are unrelated to your audience.*

Do you write primarily from personal experience?

I do write from personal experience, and I find that's the only way I can really key in. I try to move *me* first, and if I can move *me*, I can move other people. I can't write about it if I haven't lived it. Romance, falling in and out of love, being involved so deeply and emotionally, being hurt in situations of love—that has a tremendous impact on you emotionally. If you can harness that energy and put it into songs, I think you really have something. So I write from personal experience. I write about the things that go on with me. The thing I try to stay away from is writing too much about the personal experiences that are going on in my life as a result of my success, because all of a sudden, you start out writing songs about the heartland and being close to your family and working out in the yard—the simple things in life and your loves. And then all of a sudden, you start real-izing there are songs where you've got the words "backstage" and "limo," and all of a sudden you've lost your connection to what got you [there] because [a lot of people out there] don't understand backstage and limo. They understand the simple things, the things that brought you there that you wrote about before. That's the thing that you should try to stay away from: Stay away from too many things that are unrelated to your audience.

Are there songs you are most proud to have written?

Yeah, I would say "Help Me Hold On" was one of those songs. I knew it really meant a lot to me at the time. I wrote it because I was going through a divorce and all those different things were happening to me, but I didn't know if other people were going to be able to relate. It was very personal. I wrote it with Pat Terry, and when we finished playing it back, I sat down and just cried. I thought, "This is a really personal song." I didn't know if other people were gonna accept it the way I did. It turned out that they did. That shows you what I know.

Do you make an effort to revise your songs?

Waylon [Jennings] sat me down and told me a long time ago about a song that he rewrote and rewrote. He wrote it about sixteen or seventeen different ways and finally ended up going back and doing it the original way. And it turned out to be one of his biggest hits. So I look at it this way—your first impression is usually your best—go with it. Don't try to over-think it. You study long and you study wrong, usually. That's my approach. I go with my gut and I go with my first instinct and let it go at that.

What makes a good co-writer?

Someone who is willing to put aside their ego and doesn't always have to be right about everything. They're willing to listen to your ideas and they're willing to throw some out at

you, too. It's a give-and-take situation. I've been in some sessions with some songwriters who were great writers, but for whatever reason, any idea you come up with they'd say, "No, no, no. I like this better." You can't have that. It's got to be a give-and-take situation. You've got to work for the good of the song and not the songwriter.

You've written some with Gary Rossington from Lynyrd Skynyrd.

Gary doesn't write lyrics a whole lot. I love having him around because he creates those memorable melodic little licks that you hear over and over. This is the guy who created the opening to "Sweet Home Alabama." You play three notes of that, and everybody in the world knows exactly what song it is. You hear the lick and you know. Or with "Freebird," you hear that lick and you know what song it is. Each song has its own individual lick. He's great at that.

What makes a song great?

It's basically how it hits that audience. There have to be songs that I have written that I thought were some of the deepest, most profound songs in the world, then you play them for an audience, and those songs go right over their heads. Then there are songs that I wrote that I don't think anybody's going to really care about—just a real simple thing—and people end up loving it. It becomes a monster. You have to find a way of saying things that have never been said before, something that will stir people's emotions in one way or the other. I think that's why "Here's a Quarter (Call Someone Who Cares)" was such a success, because of the fact that it hit a lot of people in a funny way. And it hit a *lot* of people. It was a mass-appeal thing. A lot of people out there wanted to say, "Here's a quarter, so call someone who cares" to their husband, their wife, their boss, to whoever. Having a term that's used that much, kind of like "Friends in Low Places," you know everybody can relate to that song.

I think mass relatability is what you look for in a great song, not a song that's just gonna be for the good ol' boys or rednecks or one specific group, but a song everybody can relate to. I think that's what makes great songs.

Do you have any advice for aspiring tunesmiths?

Every time you have the opportunity to play your songs, play them. Every time you have the opportunity to perform them in front of other people, perform them. Send them to everybody you possibly can and really believe in yourself and try to make yourself better. Realize that your competition is not the other guy down the street that's writing. It's the people that are having hits on the charts. That's your competition, and you have to write as good as those people do. You have to be honest with yourself and compare yourself to them constantly and say, "Is my stuff as good as I'm hearing on the radio?" If it's not, then you work to make it better. And if it is, then you work to get it to the people who can get it on the radio for you and get it recorded. You know, it's a tough business. It's a never-ending struggle, but if you believe in yourself, don't give up.

Jeff Tweedy
Uncle Tupelo, Wilco

Wilco is the type of band that has shed their skin so often, you're never quite sure what to expect from them next. There's no underestimating front man Jeff Tweedy's predilection for restless reinvention. Tweedy (born August 25, 1967, in Belleville, Illinois) began writing material in the band Uncle Tupelo, co-founded with high school friend Jay Farrar. Early songs like "Black Eye" and "Screen Door" used the barest economy of notes and lyrics, but Tweedy's dry delivery lodged them into fans' heads. Tupelo cut four seminal albums before the band split, and Tweedy gathered the remaining members to form Wilco.

Their 1995 debut, *A.M.*, was an overlooked collection of country-rock gems. They broadened their approach in 1996 with the ambitious double album *Being There*, an ode to the redemptive powers of rock 'n' roll. Wilco took an even bigger leap forward in 1999 with *Summerteeth*, which concealed its dark themes in abstract poetry and lush, soda-sweet arrangements. 2001's *Yankee Hotel Foxtrot* proved to be their watershed moment; after their label, Reprise, deemed the album commercially unviable and refused to release it, the band posted the master recordings on the Internet, where fans promptly declared it a masterpiece. After finding a new home on the Nonesuch label, *Yankee Hotel Foxtrot* was released and became their best-selling album ever. The adventurous *A Ghost is Born* was released in 2005 to further widespread critical acclaim. The band also released its first live album, *Kicking Television*, in 2005.

—Evan Schlansky

Interview by
Evan Schlansky

American Songwriter,
July/August 2004

343

How much of the new direction and sound on *A Ghost Is Born* is contributable to the new people you're playing with?

Well, the band that made *A Ghost Is Born* has been the band for the last couple of years. Mike Jorgensen made a lot of contributions, and a lot of the piano stuff that he did was a big part of the record. The new band dynamic, being a lot more interactive and a lot more communicative, contributes a bit to it. There's definitely a more unified, collaborative spirit with everybody than we've had in a while, and I'm sure that has a lot to do with it. I think the fact that we decided to really go for live performances as much as possible influenced the direction as well.

So *Yankee Hotel Foxtrot* was the opposite experience as far as playing live?

Kind of. There are core performances on *Yankee Hotel Foxtrot* that were… well, actually, on a lot of *Yankee Hotel Foxtrot* the original basis of it was the kind of thing that was interesting to strip away and just leave the ephemera, which is what we did a lot. *Yankee Hotel Foxtrot* was much more of a piecemeal-constructed-in-the-mixing-stage kind of record, kind of a montage, or a collage or something. This record was much more organic in its conception.

Did you want that because you wanted to record a record in a new way, or did you want that because you felt these songs would benefit from that?

Well, I think that once we made all of the changes in the songs for *Yankee Hotel Foxtrot* it evolved, and they ended up what they were after mixing and after all the final collaborative stages of it. After all that, we learned how to play those songs live with their sort of complex arrangements, and we got a lot more confident about attempting things. Then the thought occurred to us that we could keep recording and

do as much as possible, make the record, do all the evolutionary things that would happen over the course of time with making a bunch of songs that fit together, and then, the idea in the end was that we would relearn it and go perform it. Similar to what we did with *Yankee Hotel Foxtrot*, except have those performances be the record, instead of all the manipulated stuff. After we learned *Yankee Hotel Foxtrot*, played those songs live, and really put ourselves into it, we felt like a lot of it was more vibrant and a little bit more passionate than the way *Yankee Hotel Foxtrot* ended up. Which is part of *Yankee Hotel Foxtrot*—I don't dislike it, I just felt like over time, things that hold up to me usually have a lot more passion, and I wanted it to be a passionate record.

A Ghost Is Born, at first listen, seems less emotionally naked as *Yankee Hotel Foxtrot*. Would you agree or disagree?

Less emotionally naked? I disagree. I don't think I've written anything quite as emotional as "At Least That's What You Said." I think lyrically it's a lot more emotionally naked, so I don't really see it that way; it feels the most personal to me than any of them.

We'll get back to some of that. Of course, you play quite a few guitar solos on the record, which are awesome.

Thanks. Those are pretty emotionally naked to me as well.

What was it like to play them?

A lot of the guitar playing is live; I practiced a lot over the last few years, and I started to feel more comfortable than I've ever felt. Not with my level of technical proficiency, but with my level of how conversant I was becoming with the guitar and how I was able to say some things with the guitar that I wasn't able to put into songs lyrically. When there was a really expressive feeling, for me, it just felt really right to make a guitar statement.

Unlike a sort of wanky guitar solo, you're using the guitar solo to express things?

I like that idea, really that's my favorite kind of guitar playing, it sort of sounds like it's saying something, or trying to represent an emotion, and I don't think you have to be a great guitar player to do that, you just have to kind of turn off your mind and feel! And I really love doing that. I love it when I can get there.

I wanted to ask you about your singing on the album. At first listen, some of it sounds different. Was that a conscious decision?

I am different, I'm older. After having sinus surgery my voice has changed, probably. I was just trying to sing the same thing as my guitar playing, just trying to communicate; I didn't think about it being different at all. I sang a little softer on some stuff, we'd play live, and play pretty quiet in the studio, and kind of try and mix the sound in the room to be in a nice relationship between all the instruments, so with just one microphone it would sound like a mixed record. We worked really hard on having everything be in proportion to each other and so sometimes we were playing really quiet, and I had a little opportunity to sing a little bit airier, but mostly I was just trying to communicate the songs.

Could you tell me the significance of the album title?

Well, I don't know, it just sounded like what the record was expressing. Like letting go of identity, not trying to define yourself so hard by things. I look at it not as a bad thing—you know, as kind of contemplating death or something—but with the idea that if you can come to terms with that, you're probably a lot freer. I just thought it was a beautiful title.

In the press release you guys put out, you made the comment that the band wouldn't seem like Wilco without John Stirratt, the bass player.

Well, I've just been with John for a long, long time back to Uncle Tupelo, and I think that when new guys come in, like we said, Pat Sansone and Nels Cline come in now, and Mike in the past, and I just can't picture conveying to them what Wilco's all about by myself. I thought about it a lot since Nels and Pat have come in and how much John and I together could communicate it, but I don't know by myself; it would be something different, I think, without someone else there that knows what we've been through, that knows how everything has worked, especially the old songs; it's kind of hard to communicate those without a couple of people doing it musically instead of trying to tell people how to play. Plus, he's an awesome bass player, and more importantly, a really, really close friend.

I'm a songwriter, too, and I sort of got into Bob Dylan when I first started writing, and then Springsteen and Beck and R.E.M., and then I discovered your band, and it was a really important discovery. I feel a really strong connection to your songs, and I didn't mean to say that this isn't an emotional record.

No, I understood you. You were saying that on the first listens or initially it doesn't quite come out that way, and I can understand that. Because for one thing, the old records have been out for a long time and people like yourself, if you've cared about them or listened to them, you've had the opportunity to pour your emotions into them, and pour yourself into them—and that's what they're there for. It's what people do with songs, and that's why songs resonate with people, because they can pour themselves into it. I feel flattered and honored that anybody takes the time to do

that with any of my songs, but for me, it's obviously always going to be a different thing; I'm probably not going to make many songs that I'm not emotionally connected to.

That's the beauty of things that creep up on you slowly; you start to really get into them, and sometimes it's more rewarding than getting it right off. Are there any records like that for you?

Tons of them. [John Cale's] *Paris 1919*, [The Clash's] *London Calling*, [Nick Drake's] *Pink Moon*, [Television's] *Marquee Moon*, yeah, there are records that we think, "What the fuck?" I don't know. And then for some reason you keep being drawn to it, because there were holes in it that you couldn't understand. I believe part of our nature is to really want to understand something, and not just dismiss stuff because it's not worth listening to. Whatever compels you to want to understand something… that's what happens with a lot of great records that have meant a lot to me.

"Less Than You Think"—could you describe that a little bit?

We wanted "Less Than You Think" to be the longest song on the record, because of its title [*laughs*]. I also thought that after the subject matter of the song, and free will, and sort of contemplating death, that it would be interesting to hear a bunch of frequencies competing with each other randomly. Just a kind of structure-less chaotic sound of something being born, you know? Or dying, what's the difference?

Could you describe how that was created?

Everybody would set up a sound that would play itself. Either by a guitar feeding back, or a synthesizer with a key taped down, a snare drum sitting next to an amplifier that was feeding back so it would rattle, contact mics on fruit baskets, delay pedals that were repeating—anything that we could

walk away from and it would keep making a sound. We'd construct installations, then walk around the room and put microphones up, and then record it. We did that three or four times actually, the full version of that is a half-hour long—it's a whole reel of tape. Then we basically listened to it a couple times and made a rough sketch of how we wanted it to be shaped as far as, have an arc to it, and just set about making an arc.

Who are some of your favorite songwriters?

Ray Davies, Bob Dylan, Neil Young, the Beatles, Jeff Magnum of Neutral Milk Hotel, Leonard Cohen, Randy Newman, I could go on and on, Willie Dixon.

Is there one above any of the others that kind of follows you around?

Well, all the ones I mentioned follow me around, definitely. So many great songwriters, you know? Nick Drake. Dylan is probably the one that follows me around the most; he's had the longest lasting impact on my life, and then Neil Young.

It's the guys who create so many different kinds of songs… I read that when you would write some of these songs for *A Ghost Is Born* they would come from your notebooks, and you were improvising melodies and stuff… have you done that before?

[I've] improvised stuff on records before… "Sunken Treasure," a lot of the lyrics on that were improvised. We've improvised arrangements before, just let the tape roll, and play through stuff without talking, things have happened like that before. This is the first time we really used it as a discipline. We would do tapes, whole reels of tape, and the idea was: Okay, we're going to improvise our record, and get used to the idea that we're just making shit up, and that you can make a record in the time that it takes to listen to it. We did like nine reels of that and called them "The Fundamentals." I would just sit in a room with my acoustic guitar with a notebook, lyrics, and poems and journal entries and stuff. Flip through it all, stop and just start singing, or start playing the guitar first. A lot of those tapes are really incredible to me, I'll probably put them out someday—there were just completely weird shapes in the control room. Others would try to anticipate what was going to happen, but I wasn't listening to them, I was just making up songs. Over time through listening back to them, a lot of songs on the record emerged like "Company in My Back," "Muzzle of Bees," "At Least That's What You Said," "Hell Is Chrome," I don't know, over half of the songs on the record came from those sessions. The versions on the record aren't the ones from the sessions, but the songs themselves emerged from those sessions.

Are you saying that it was you, soloing at first?

I was playing by myself, to myself, but there are the versions of "The Fundamentals" tapes where everybody played along. So we would play along in the time it took to go through a reel, we'd listen to it once, and mix it as we were listening to a two-track. Then we would just listen to that and never go back, so there are all kinds of just haphazard stuff and really crazy beautiful synchronicities and things like that. It's really random and crazy sounding, but I love listening to them.

There's this sort of shape to them that nobody, at least I don't really hear how anybody could intend that to be there, and it's more interesting to me than just records. Records sometimes feel like chairs and those tapes to me sound more like trees [*laughs*]. I couldn't imagine how to make a tree; I could think about how to make a chair.

About the lyrics, which seemed to evolve over time, from *Summerteeth*, I don't know what the

word would be, maybe "surreal." Is that sort of a private language for you?

I think the lyric writing for me has just sort of evolved out of being, getting more pleasure out of it because I started putting more work into it and started writing a lot more, just for myself in notebooks and writing poems and stuff and just trying to get better at putting what I wanted on the page. At the same time, learning how to get out of my way, and just let what's going to come out, and over time, getting a little better at arranging what just came. I guess the raw material and the stuff that's aesthetically pleasing to me resonates longer than the stuff that I thought about too much.

On this album there are references to devils and God. Are there religious things happening on this record?

I don't know if there are any religious things happening on the record, but I think the record in itself is kind of about spirituality or there are some spiritual elements to the record, or there is some kind of quest for some spirit, and spirituality in the sense that religion is a set of rules, and spirituality is your relationship with the universe, your relationship with God, whatever you want to call it. How that gets muddled up in identity and ego and all that stuff, muddled up by our pursuit to feel better and to feel loved and all of that stuff. So yeah, I think that was another reason we wanted the record to be really passionately performed live, 'cause that's a lot of what it's about; it's about not being perfect, it's about being alive. It sounds really pretentious, but that's just what it's about.

What about the song "The Late Greats"?

It's a celebration of music and the acknowledgment that it's not all about the record, touring, and all of that stuff; it's all about being in a moment. I like the idea of the last lyrics on

the record at the end [are about] how the "best song never gets sung…" You gotta feel it, you gotta feel it first. If you can feel it, you don't have to make every feeling you have into something.

The song "I'm a Wheel" is more upbeat and rocking than we've heard for a while. Was it important for you to put it on there, to show that side, or was it the song itself that just needed to be on there?

There's a lot of material more like "I'm a Wheel." There's a song called "Kicking Television" that we tracked for the record. There were some really raucous early demos and things like that. At one point, I think there was the idea that we'd save them all for a really chaotic, scatological punk rock record, which might still happen, but that song, oddly enough, I don't know why, it just seemed to fit in the context of the record, even though it is kind of an anomaly.

You said your lyrics have evolved from more straightforward narratives on *A.M.* like "Passenger Side." Do you ever worry how people will perceive it or understand it?

No, I don't have any control over it. I still feel like I'm telling a story. I just feel like I'm leaving a lot more openings or doors for a listener to come in and interpret and feel stuff than just the straight narrative. Although, I don't think I've written many songs in my life as straight narrative as "Hummingbird," or even "Handshake Drugs." To me, this record has a lot more stuff that was going back to some of that, and using some of the things that I've learned over the years together. I think there are elements of both styles to me in a better balance than I feel I've done them in the past. "Hell Is Chrome" feels pretty narrative to me, "At Least That's What You Said" feels like pretty strong narrative, [also] "The Late Greats." I actually kind of concentrated on making the story a little bit more structured this time.

Do you have a favorite song on the record right now?

I think "Muzzle of Bees" means a lot to me. Otherwise, I don't know, it just came out so different than what I'd intended, and has this really unique shape to it. I always get some kind of emotion out of it when I hear it.

Is there a way you can describe "Muzzle of Bees": the imagery involved, what's going on in that song?

Not really, except it just sounded very painful. Maybe it's some kind of pain that you have from not being able to express yourself, or not being able to get things out.

I wanted to ask you about recently going to rehab. Do you feel it has affected your music at all, or did you write while you were there?

I did write a little bit while I was there, but I don't feel like it's affected my music at all. It's affected my well being quite a bit. I was in dual-diagnosis rehab, because I was self-medicating for migraines and for panic disorder for a long time. Dual-diagnosis rehab is all about not just focusing on addiction, but more importantly how it relates to, for me, how it related to the struggles I've had with depression, and generalizing anxiety and severe panic disorder for a long time. So it was a really great learning experience. It was just a really tough time, and I can't imagine how getting better and feeling better is going to have anything to do with the music that's bad [*laughs*].

Keith Urban

Since his arrival in America in 1992, the Aussie guitarist, singer, and songwriter has worked his way to the top of the country music industry. Urban carved his niche with an unriveled passion and musicianship that became his own blend of upbeat, carefree country/rock. This formula is what has given Urban musical consistency that has resulted in seven number one singles. From the 2004 record-breaking eight week number one hit, "Somebody Like You" as well as "Who Wouldn't Wanna Be Me" and "You'll Think Me," all from *Golden Road*, to the chartopping hits from his 2004 triple platinum award-winning album *Be Here*, Urban covers intimate and honest topics through melodic and well-crafted songs— the key for any successful musician. His third solo release, *Be Here*, debuted at number one on the Billboard chart with first-week sales doubling those of his previous album, *Golden Road*. The album's first single, "Days Go By," topped the charts and "You're My Better Half" followed closely behind. The album also spawned the number one singles, "Better Life" and "Making Memories Of Us." In November of 2005, Urban was awarded the Country Music Association's Entertainer of the Year. He also won the CMA's and The Academy of Country Music's Male Vocalist of the Year Awards.

—KRISTI SINGER

Interview by
Kristi Singer

American Songwriter,
March/April 2005

How did you get into country music?

My parents' record collection was all country. So, it really was the music I was exposed to the most at a young age. I started playing guitar when I was six, and consequently all of the songs I learned were Charley Pride, Dolly Parton, Tanya Tucker, Glen Campbell, and so on. It was all of those artists I heard first, and it just turned me on to the music right from the start.

It's not something that I consciously do, but when lyrics start to come and formulate a melody, it tends to have that theme about it.

Tell me about the first song you ever wrote.

I was nine or ten. I made a song up with my brother called "Good Ole Country Music" [*laughs*]. It was pretty bad.

Who are your songwriting influences?

There are so many. I just watched the movie *White Christmas* again last night, with Bing Crosby in it, and it just floored me… the kind of songwriting that used to be popular back in that day. Even a song like "White Christmas" or "Blue Skies." Guys like him and Sammy Cahn, some of the greats—they just had a flow of craft in lyric and melody. It's another era. And, I think it's hard to go past Paul McCartney as one of the all-time greats.

Did you realize you had a gift in songwriting, or did it take others to point it out to you?

I still don't feel like I do. It comes in waves. It's very sporadic; it's so elusive. I'm not one of those people that writes all the time. I can go for months and months and never write anything. Therefore, I work nicely when I take the time to write. Stuff just seems to come when I get into the path of writing and spend a month or so writing three or four times a week, especially co-writing.

So you're able to channel your songwriting energy when you make the time for it?

It's usually when I'm inspired by something or an idea sparks. Every now and then we'll come up with things at sound check. We did the *Billboard* awards Wednesday night. I played with Sheryl Crow. When we were sound checking in the afternoon, this whole melody and chord progression came to me. So I grabbed my phone and sang into it.

When writing songs, do you write lyrics or melody first? Or does it change from song to song?

It does change. Every now and then I'll scribble a bunch of lyrics out with really no melody to accompany them… just a meter. But mostly it's melody. Guitar riffs and melodies. Those are the things that usually come first. The lyrics usually come at the end of the process.

Do you need a certain writing environment? Alone? Quiet? Or do you prefer being around others?

I do a lot of co-writing. I write with John Shanks quite a bit. I'll go out to his studio in Los Angeles and we'll work out of there. Another guy, Monty Powell, I wrote with in Nashville a lot. He's got a little studio under his house, and we've had a lot of luck writing down there. So, nowhere in particular for me.

What is it about the co-writing process that you enjoy?

Just another creative person to bounce ideas off of. When you start writing with someone consistently like I do with John Shanks, Monty Powell, or even Rodney Crowell—guys I've written five or six songs with—you just find people that you click with. Your chemistry is really good. You tend to complement each other.

How do you find these co-writers? Do you have a selection process?

It's a lot of trial and error. You can write with someone and have it be quite disastrous, I've found. But then you do it again and it just works. I'm sure you hear it from other writers. It's even difficult talking about writing because it's such an elusive thing. Kind of like trying to describe an angel that you can't see.

> *The bottom line is that there are no rules in writing. There's no bad or good—just music that appeals to certain people.*

What do you find inspiration in? Are there topics you find yourself writing about more than others?

I write a lot about freedom in all its various forms. And again, it's not something that I consciously do, but when lyrics start to come and formulate a melody, it tends to have that theme about it. I've noticed that a lot when looking back at my songs.

Why freedom?

It's what we ultimately all are looking for in all forms. Freedom from the guilt and remorse that a lot of us carry around. Regret. Freedom from responsibility, and to some degree accountability. Freedom from expectations in life and what people demand and want from you all the time. I think we're all seeking that desert island somewhere.

I really felt that "freedom" in your first single from *Be Here*, "Days Go By." But the lyrics are about how quickly time goes by, which is kind of sad. What are your thoughts on that?

Yeah, well, we tend to be in such an age right now with so many technological inventions that are meant to help us have more free time and it seems like it has had a complete reverse effect. BlackBerrys and Sidekicks, e-mails, laptops, cell phones, voicemail—it just goes on and on. It seems that these things that are supposed to cut time from our work end up taking up all of our time, because they're all we devote our time to instead of people and instead of doing things for ourselves. We're always working toward life starting somewhere down the road instead of right now, instead of today.

What advice would you give to other songwriters?

I think the minute you start applying a formula, rules, or a general idea to writing, someone comes along with a song that defies all of it. I like a lot of songs that are stream of conscious lyrically, not so perfectly rhymed and symmetrical. Most of it's conversational, because it has a natural speech rhythm about it. I like all kinds of songs, so it's hard to define all that. I'd say just be as real as you can. That's really it when it comes to songs and songwriting, to a large degree. But then there's a bunch of songs that are a complete fabricated craft and they sound amazing. The bottom line is that there are no rules in writing. There's no bad or good—just music that appeals to certain people.

Tell me about the quote on the back of your liner notes in *Be Here*: "Life is a balance of holding on and letting go." Why did you put that there?

I was looking for a quote to put in the record somewhere that I think summed up how I look at life. Making a record is all about taking a photograph. It's all about capturing who you are at that time. That philosophy resonates with me currently, and I think it's a broad meaning because it's really up to the individual as to what it means to them. What do they hold on to and what do they let go of. Ultimately, it's all about balance.

> *I think I subconsciously keep songs a little ambiguous, again to not be too specific, and it lets people gravitate toward them in their own way.*

You thank God often in the liner notes. Are you a spiritual person? And how does your spirituality affect your songwriting?

Very spiritual. Not religious, but very spiritual. I don't know how it inspires my songs, but I just know that it does. I think that spirituality probably inspires it by the view of looking at lyrics. I find that a lot of songs I write I talk about "you" as opposed to "her," and it can have a spiritual connotation or personal connotation depending on who "you" is. "You" might be God, your girlfriend, mom, dad—it could be nature. It could be anything. I think I subconsciously keep songs a little ambiguous, again to not be too specific, and it lets people gravitate toward them in their own way.

Any final thoughts?

I'm really a fan of songwriters and honestly I'll never view myself as a songwriter in the way that I look at Rodney Crowell, Jimmy Webb, Paul McCartney, Bob Dylan, or Bruce Springsteen. I wasn't born to do it like those guys do it. Consequently, I'm just a real fan of songwriters.

Loudon Wainwright III

Loudon Wainwright III is one of America's funniest and most beloved folk singers. A keen observer and self-depreciating ironist, he has become—like his peers Randy Newman and the late Warren Zevon—a respected member of the songwriting elite. Born September 5, 1946, in Chapel Hill, North Carolina, Wainwright first became interested in folk music while attending St. Andrew's School in Delaware (the school that later became the basis for the film *Dead Poets Society*), and his early seventies albums for Atlantic and Columbia Records cemented his reputation as a cult favorite. 1972's album *III* spawned his biggest hit, "Dead Skunk," an offbeat tribute to roadkill. In 1971, Wainwright married Canadian songwriter Kate McGarrigle of the McGarrigle Sisters. They separated in 1977, but their marriage produced two talented songwriters in their children, Rufus and Martha Wainwright. The eighties earned Wainwright two Grammy nominations for his albums *I'm Alright* (1985) and *More Love Songs* (1986). Johnny Cash recorded Wainwright's "The Man Who Couldn't Cry" for his highly acclaimed 1994 album, *American Recordings*. Recent albums such as 2003's live *So Damn Happy* and 2005's *Here Come the Choppers* have left longtime customers deeply satisfied.

—EVAN SCHLANSKY

Interview by
Paul Zollo

American Songwriter,
November/December 2004

I know Dylan was a big influence on you, yet your songs are quite different from his.

I write much differently than Bob Dylan. It's true. My songs have a beginning, a middle, and an end. They're understandable and clear. That might be where my father influenced me the most—being a journalist. Clarity, detail, description, exploring a theme...

You are extremely funny onstage, and you write funny songs. Does live performance influence your use of humor?

Yeah. When I discovered I could make people laugh, too, I jumped on it. I started to write more novelty songs. The third album had "Dead Skunk" on it, and then I was definitely into the serious jungle of comedy songwriting. Now I'm trying to bounce the two off of each other. And in some songs, you can do both.

Is it hard to be funny in songs?

I've always enjoyed making people laugh, and I love to laugh myself. When I first started to play and sing, I sensed that people were amused by what I did. I went for laughs and I was criticized for it. It's almost involuntary on my part. I love it when people laugh. If there's any chance to elicit any laughter, you can be sure I'll go for it.

Do you have any kind of songwriting routine?

Not really. I don't have any form for it. I get an idea and I think about something. It's kind of like fishing: If you get a nibble, you hang in there. And if nothing happens after a while, you just shelve it. I know people who get up in the morning and sharpen pencils and sit down and write a song. I don't do it that way. There's a gestation period. I think a lot about it and then something pops out. I don't like to analyze it too much. It's a mysterious process that I

don't really understand too much myself, but I'm grateful when it happens.

Any hints how to make it happen?

No. There isn't really. I used to worry when it wouldn't happen for a while, but I don't do that either [now]. It comes when it feels like it. It's hard to do, but if you enjoy the process—whatever's happening—that's what I like. And I think the best songs come that way.

So songwriting is generally fun for you? It sounds like your songs are fun to write.

When it's going good, yeah. When the flow's on, when it's good, when the muse is there, it's a lot of fun. I can really feel something ready to come through, like waiting for a fax to come or a picture to develop. You watch it take shape, and you can actually feel it. It's hard to talk about, because it's something I don't understand. I don't want to dwell on it too much, because it's too painful when it doesn't come through.

So after all these years, you haven't found any way to control the process?

Not at all. I think I have less control of it. I realize more and more that it doesn't really have much to do with me. It has only to do with me in that it's filtered through me, my experience, my style of writing and what I bring to it. And that's craft, working, having a style, doing it twenty-five-plus years and having an audience to write for. But the actual *stuff* is mysterious.

Your songs seem truthful. Is it important to instill the truth into songs?

You have to write what you know about. I know about conducting my life and the relationships I've had. I'm very focused. I'm focused on me. It's a selfish kind of thing. I like sometimes to get out of myself. But yes, I certainly write about my swinging life.

Is it possible to write great songs and also be commercially successful?

It's possible to make a living. There are people who write songs who are incredibly successful. I'm marginally successful. I've been able to make a living at it for twenty years and I have an audience. I enjoy working and I'm happy and grateful about that.

Do you spend any time while writing songs thinking of commercial considerations?

No. I let myself off the hook. In the seventies, when I was on major labels, there was always pressure to make what I term loosely as a "radio record"—a record that is designed and intended to be played on radio. And that's what everyone wants to happen. Obviously, it affected production values, what you would put on an album. But I also think it seeps into the writ-

What words of advice, if any, would you offer songwriters?

It depends on what kind of songwriter it is. If it's a guy or gal who wants to write hits, then go ahead and work on that. I think my ambition and abilities were just to write what I'm obsessed by, what I'm amused by, what makes me angry… I just take my temperature, so to speak, and blurt it out in a song. If it's that type of thing you want to do, ignore everybody else and do what you feel.

I can really feel something ready to come through, like waiting for a fax to come or a picture to develop. You watch it take shape, and you can actually feel it.

ing of a song. And for me, personally, it made me very unhappy. What was happening was that I happened to have written one song in fifteen minutes that happened to be a successful single—"Dead Skunk"—but I'm not really that kind of artist… you know, a guy who makes great radio songs. And if I do worry about that, the quality of what I do diminishes.

Rufus Wainwright

Interview by
Paul Zollo

American Songwriter,
November/December 2004

Music is the birthright of Rufus Wainwright, son of
folk artists Loudon Wainwright III and Kate McGarrigle. Born in Rhinebeck, New York, in 1973, he started
playing piano at age six, and after his parents' divorce
was performing professionally with the McGarrigle
Sisters and Family Revue (starring his mother, aunt,
and sister Martha) at thirteen. Wainwright embraced both his homosexuality and his
musicality in his late teens. His love for opera led him to study at Montreal's McGill
University, and soon he was composing his own songs, crafting piano-based ballads
that owed as much to Edith Piaf as Elton John.

His recording career took off when his father passed along a demo of Rufus's
original material to famed producer and family friend Van Dyke Parks. Parks's
sophisticated string arrangements helped turn Wainwright's self-titled 1998 debut
into a theatrical carnival of musical delights. The album announced a stunning
new talent and landed Wainwright on several magazines' "Best New Artist" lists.

In 2001 he released his sophomore album, *Poses*, which found him experimenting with dark textures and electronic loops. Over the course of 2003 and
2004, he released his two-part opus, the ambitious *Want One* and *Want Two*.
Though no release date has been set, Wainwright has recorded new material in
New York, Berlin, and London, and plans to release a new album in 2007.

—EVAN SCHLANSKY

Want One **is so well executed in both song development and production.**

I really pulled out all the stops. I definitely felt that after the last record, which I really liked, it sort of opened the can to the different directions I could go in. Whether it was dance music, or folk music, or whatever. The last one was kind of a schizophrenic album. On the new one I decided to stay very firm and direct with the message I am trying to put across.

Did you have a lot of input into the production?

Yeah. There's no way I can really divorce myself from that process—only because I really think people can hear the difference between when the artist is involved in the production and when he is not. But I do not consider myself a producer, and I don't ever ask for a co-production credit because I think the idea of a producer is to realize the ideas… realize the vision of the artist. And Marius [de Vries], who I worked with, was *perfect* with doing that. He would really go for whatever I wanted to achieve. He was very much the producer of the album.

> *I think one of the major tactics of songwriting is dementia. And confusion. And unconsciousness.*

Are you someone who writes songs all the time, or do you write only for a specific project?

All the time. I like to have about five songs on the back burner that are going, so I can switch from one to the next when I get bored. I find it necessary to work on more than one song at a time. I don't see how someone can have just one song that they're concentrating all their ability on. I think overworking it can kill music.

Do you write on both piano and guitar?

Yes, I write on piano and guitar, and I also sometimes write on the sidewalk [*laughs*]… when I'm walking around on the street, without an instrument even. I think one of the major tactics of songwriting is dementia [*laughs*]. And confusion. And unconsciousness. One of the best ways to get in touch with that is to walk around the streets of New York, especially these days when there is an uneasy feeling in this country. I think it's really important to get inspiration from what's going on in the street, because there's so much happening.

Do you get both musical and lyrical inspiration on the street?

Yes, musical and lyrical. I think any songwriter, really, is basically a thermometer that's taking the temperature of society. Great songs are essentially already written. You just have to discover them—and be open to them, [which] requires action in life. It requires participating in life.

Is the process more discovery than invention?

Yes. I'm always amazed at the end of writing a song by the fact that I don't really remember writing it. It all kind of arrives. Often I am listening to my old records and wondering, "Where in hell did that idea come from?" So it's a very trance-like experience.

Is it more a sense of following where a song goes than leading it?

It's a bit of both. It is following. Music is a science, and there are certain laws that one has to respect in order to get their point across musically, and have it be comprehensible. A lot of those laws are dictated by what effect the song has on you, the writer, and on the listener. It's really hard gauging that. It really requires a kind of absence of will [*laughs*]… and an

ability to *feel*... to feel, because the music itself and the melody and the words are moving you. It's akin to flying. You've really got to feel like you're taking off.

Music is a science, and there are certain laws that one has to respect in order to get their point across musically, and have it be comprehensible.

It's interesting to me that you wrote a song called "11:11," because I tend to see that time a lot, and friends have told me they see it, too.

Yeah, it comes in waves. Sometimes you look at the clock, and it's always 11:11. It's very strange. I wrote that on guitar.

Do your piano songs and guitar songs come out differently?

There's a type of piano song I write that I don't write on guitar. My piano songs are either totally complicated or totally simple. My guitar songs are a little bit in between. That's my middle ground. I can strum simple things, but then also use very obtuse chords.

Do you write music first?

Yes. Music is much easier for me. But lyrics are much more rewarding. When I come up with a good lyric, it's intoxicating. A great lyric, with a melody that works, is the goal. Often what happens is that the music and a lyrical line will arrive together, but then the music will follow its natural course. When you introduce a measure and a formation and a range, that sets what the song is going to do. I like

to throw surprises in that serve the song. But once you've done that, the music usually arrives pretty quickly. And then I really have to work much harder on the lyrics. I definitely believe that great songwriters are primarily great lyricists. I think you can argue that Leonard Cohen, even though he has beautiful melodies, is great because of his words. Or even Hank Williams. And even Cole Porter in a way; his melodies are really dictated by the words. I tend to go a little crazy.

In what way?

With my music. I'm still very much tied to a musical eight ball. To me, it's the melody that really matters. But I have to match it with a lyric, which can be difficult. And that's why I hover around operatic and classical influences. That's a real marriage between intense melody and intense lyric.

That's interesting, because many of your structures are not typical pop song structures. You will have one section that extends throughout the song, with no repeats, and no verse or chorus.

I like playing with song structure. My main influence is opera and arias, which do not follow any structure. They try to convey a dramatic moment. I had a realization a long time ago that for me to do this job, I have to do that. It was intensely obvious to me that nobody was doing that, taking arias and making songs out of them. It became obvious that this would become my angle.

Even though you use these classic forms, your lyrical references are often quite modern, as in "Vibrate," which mentions a cell phone set to vibrate.

Yeah, you want to please the kids, you know [*laughs*]. That song came after a very depressing, failed love affair, which essentially ended with me trailing around bars looking for my lost love… primarily with my phone on vibrate, so that when it was really loud in the bar, I could feel the ring.

When you write melodies on the piano, do you experiment in places you've never been?

I try to experiment always. Or, I try to remain *completely* simple and not experiment at all. I'm either all or nothing, which is my motto. It's served me well, because it's allowed me to have these different branches in my career. I have very simple, easy-to-sing melodies, with accompaniment that is easy to pull off.

The song "14th Street" has kind of an old-fashioned, ragtime melody.

That one was definitely more about the melody being obvious… and being rousing. I didn't spend a long time on that melody. You can usually tell which songs are more complicated than others by the accompaniment. "I Don't Know What It Is" and "Vicious World" are good examples. Those two songs are somewhat out there, and then there are other songs where I am just playing the main chords, like "Harvester of Hearts."

Both your parents are songwriters. Would you play your songs for them?

Yes. I was always trying to please my mother. I was her joybox [*laughs*]. So I would always play my songs for her. For her praise, or for various criticisms.

It's interesting that you have the timbre in your voice of your father but the sustain and flow of your mother's voice.

Yeah, I got the best of both worlds.

When I come up with a good lyric, it's intoxicating. A great lyric, with a melody that works, is the goal.

How old were you when you wrote your first song?

Thirteen. I had written other stuff before that was more operatic, but my first song was then. It was called "I'm a Running."

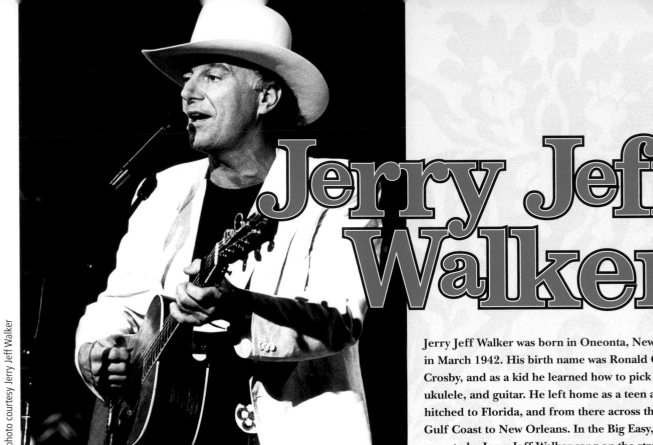

Jerry Jeff Walker

Interview by
Dorothy Hamm

American Songwriter,
May/June 1988

Jerry Jeff Walker was born in Oneonta, New York, in March 1942. His birth name was Ronald Clyde Crosby, and as a kid he learned how to pick banjo, ukulele, and guitar. He left home as a teen and hitched to Florida, and from there across the Gulf Coast to New Orleans. In the Big Easy, the soon-to-be Jerry Jeff Walker sang on the street for tips. He also did some jail time there, and one of his fellow cons was an unforgettable character with music in his soul and magic in his eyes—a man Walker so eloquently wrote about in "Mr. Bojangles."

By the mid-sixties, he returned to the Northeast and began working the folk clubs in New York's Greenwich Village. When he performed "Mr. Bojangles" on the radio station WBAI in the city, listeners were enchanted and called the station in droves. Walker quickly scored a record contract with Atco Records, the same label that housed Eric Clapton's band Cream at the time. By 1971, he split New York for Austin, where he and Guy Clark became pals. Clark wrote "L.A. Freeway," which Walker cut on Decca Records in 1972. By the eighties, Walker was still a legend but not always for the right reasons; like Mr. Bojangles, he could rarely turn down a drink and sometimes was intoxicated onstage. In 1985, he sobered up, started his own record label, and has been churning out new material ever since. *Jerry Jeff Jazz* and *Gonzo Stew* are two recent albums worth checking out.

—PHIL SWEETLAND

How long does it usually take you to write a song?

It varies. Sometimes it takes a few minutes and sometimes it takes a few months, because it changes when I'm working. I write it and play it some, and I make some notations usually. I play it over and over while I am writing it so it gets sort of honed to being performed. My songs breathe a little better when I play them all the way through. I have a lot of contractions that I put in songs so it sounds conversational. That's the way I write.

Do you ever get a verse and chorus and not finish it?

No, if I get a verse and chorus, I usually have a pretty good idea of what I'm doing at that point. I just finished one called "The Artist," and it's about writing songs and maybe being turned off by the business. This particular group of people quit playing music because they find that it's demeaning to be involved in a business that is cutthroat and so they quit. And I point out the fact that that's their right if they don't want to play the game, but we lose something for that.

I think songwriting should go on whether you're in the business or not. It should be like writing poetry. People write poetry to relax themselves. I don't think you should be discouraged by whether you're successful or not. I think you should write to enjoy yourself. That's what folk music has been about for years—people writing all kinds of songs about their lives. I work best, I think, when I'm not [performing] a lot, when I'm home and sitting around. If I take a month off or something, it's a much more productive period because I lay some sheets of paper out and leave my guitar there, and I'll go off and play a little golf and I'll come back and sit down and work on a song for a couple of hours. I won't play again until the next day when I come in. Coming back to it is much more productive than getting up and catching a plane and going some place and trying to write again. I think you have to seed yourself to flower a song later.

Do you ever co-write?

I've done a little bit but never a whole lot. I'm kind of headstrong about what I want to do. What happens when you co-write with other people is things go off on tangents that maybe you hadn't really seen in it. I like to keep homing in on what I was talking about in my own mind.

Are there other people who seem to energize you?

Other songwriters usually give me a perk when I hear something that really charms me. I like hanging around songwriters. Guy Clark is one of my all-time favorites. Mickey Newbury is a good friend and I like Mickey's stuff. Gary Nunn, if he doesn't have something he's just written, then he's got two or three songs in his pocket by someone else he's seen in New Mexico or Colorado. Another songwriter is Chuck Pyle. He wrote "Jaded Lover" and "Other Side of the Hill." John Prine is another songwriter I like. He charms me and makes me feel warm.

What is the most common mistake songwriters make?

I think it's the hook-line syndrome Nashville works around a lot. "The Last Word in Lonesome Is Me" is one of my favorites. Here a guy has told me a heart-warming thought and then he ends it with a line that's a play on words and I go "ahhh"—I feel like I've been suckered in. In "You're the Best Break This Old Heart Ever Had," the lyrics talk to me strong and then the chorus comes around and I think it almost had to have some sort of hook to start writing. I'd much rather see people talk about something they really want to say—about why they love someone or what it means to them. Talk to me in straight terms and not worry about whether it's got this great hook or not. I think it's why people started writing nonrhyming poetry. They wrote poems that had meter, which flowed but didn't necessarily have rhymes every other line like the roses are red, violets are blue type of

thing, because rhyming can sort of get you in a place where you're not really communicating what you feel. The Don Schlitz song "Give Me Wings" is a good example. I don't think it's a hook-line song. It's a song with a feeling—"give me freedom, give me wings." Then they go on and talk about giving space in a relationship.

I heard a song the other day about a house and I teared up… something about if a house could live on memories it would stand a thousand years.

Oh yeah, that's a good song. Thom [Schuyler] sang it the last time we were together in Austin. That's the thing, you get into a feeling about something and then you set about describing it and if you're a good songwriter, the lines will take shape. That's what I'm saying about writing about a feeling; he probably took a look at writing about it and it opened more and more doors, so to speak, in the song. He went places and found just what he needed in there, as opposed to just having a hook line and trying to write two or three verses just to fill up space and then get back to the hook again and then get out. There are some good songwriters today—Schuyler, Paul Overstreet, Don Schlitz. They really love songwriting. That song I sang tonight, "Last Night I Fell in Love Again With You," Don wrote with me. He came to Austin to visit—said he wanted to write something. He was telling me how they were all working on doing good songs and that they really want to write and do it right. Guy Clark is part of that whole group… integrity in songwriting.

If someone wanted you to change something in a song before they recorded it, would you change it?

No, I'd let them change it. I wouldn't change it. I didn't write a song for someone else to sing. I write it for me and the way I sing it is the way I do it. I did a song called "Gettin' By"; it's a kind of philosophical song. It says, "Gettin' by is my stock in trade, livin' it from day to day, pickin' up pieces wherever they fall, letting the high times carry the low." David Allan Coe did it for a while and he said, "You know I changed the verses in it," and I said, "You ought to." And I do that with other people's songs. If I find a song I like and a line in it doesn't suit me very well, then I change it. If they don't want me to record it that way then I'd probably have to do something else with it, but I would sing it the way it made sense to me.

Is songwriting an art form?

It should be. It's not just something to throw away. If everybody tries to express themselves, then we find out more about human nature. And if all songwriters wrote truly what they felt instead of what they think sells, I think we'd know more about human relations.

What is the most valuable lesson you've ever learned as a songwriter?

To stick to your guns. Do it the way you want to do it. If it's about a little subject or if it's a big subject or if it's funny to you, write it good and don't worry about who it's going to please as much as if it's going to please yourself. Then when you're done, see how many people like it.

But what about the people who say songs should conform to certain rules?

"Bojangles" broke all the rules. It was too long, was 6/8 time about an old drunk and a dead dog. [There were] so many reasons why it didn't fit anything. It would have never been a song if I had been living in Nashville and tried to take it through *there*. I recorded it in New York. I've always had my record deals through New York or L.A.

M. Ward

M. Ward is a busy man. After playing with his band Rodriguez for six years, he broke out on his own with great success. In addition to releasing critically acclaimed albums, the Portland-based singer/songwriter has been in high demand as a producer and co-writer, penning songs for Cat Power and Beth Orton's latest records, and co-producing Jenny Lewis's *Rabbit Fur Coat*. Ward also served as executive producer for *I Am the Resurrection*, a tribute album to the late acoustic guitar hero John Fahey. *End of Amnesia* garnered vast acclaim for its folk-rock virtuosity as well as its follow-up, *Transistor Radio*. At 32 years old, one can expect to see many more projects from Mr. Ward, a musician who offers a low-key posture that elevates the music above the artist. *Post-War*, his 2006 release, continues in the same vein of his previous work. M. Ward is well on his way to achieving the status of a modern-day master of song.

—MATTHEW SHEARON

Interview by
Evan Schlansky

American Songwriter,
May/June 2006

Can you take us through some of the collaborations you've done over the past couple of years? How did you end up working with Cat Power, Beth Orton, and Jenny Lewis?

I met Chan Marshall, of Cat Power, in 2002, I think. We did a tour together, got along really well, and then she asked me to do some recording with her. Then I went on tour with [Jenny Lewis's band] Rilo Kiley in 2003. They asked me to support them on an American tour and I asked them to be my backing band for a record I did called *Transfiguration of Vincent*.

That's been one of the pleasures of this job, getting the chance to tour with these amazing songwriters, singers, and instrumentalists. I went through this period where I didn't have a band and borrowed band members from whoever invited me to support their shows. It just ended up being a great way to meet amazing musicians, people who love to tour and make music. It's been great having the time and freedom to find out what each instrumentalist or singer does especially well, you know? Everyone has their own superpowers, and the collaborative aspect of it is one of the biggest joys of recording. Those are the things that always end up surprising me the most. It brings out the best x-factor possible.

How would you describe their different superpowers?

They're all great singers; they're all really different, though. I think Jenny's biggest strength is her ability to put a lot of muscle in her voice, and it still sounds amazing. She has this amazing vintage sound that she can get to without thinking about it. Whereas, I think Chan and Beth, I don't really want to compare them too much, because they're like night and day. They have this especially amazing expressiveness in quieter songs. That's kind of a sweeping generalization. I'm not sure I would stand by it tomorrow, but in general that's the truth.

The song you wrote with Cat Power, "Willie Deadwilder," is eighteen minutes long. It was featured on her 2004 DVD, *Speaking for Trees*, and a shorter version can be found on her album *The Greatest*. How did that song come about?

That happened completely off the cuff. She had a really long poem/song, and I had the idea of putting something simple underneath it, with ideally chords and melodies that wouldn't get in the way of the story aspect of the song.

Did you think eighteen minutes was excessive?

I like how it turned out, it's really unusual. How often do you hear a song that long? It has its ebbs and flows like any great song… this particular song has *really* long ebbs and *really* long flows. I can't tell you exactly the moment that it turned into a song. It's one of those great moments that you *can't* remember. It's been my opinion that the best songs come so quickly that the process is practically invisible.

When you worked with Beth Orton, was that a situation where she approached you to specifically do some songs for her record, or did it just come out of hanging out together?

Let's see… we toured in Europe together and got along really well and decided to go into the studio and turn some ideas into recorded ideas. I was playing lead guitar for her on this European tour. But it eventually turned into these recordings we did in a nice studio in Los Angeles and she was really great to work with—just a very soulful voice and full of energy all the time.

Was co-producing *Rabbit Fur Coat* the first time you've worked as a producer?

I've mainly produced my own records and little things here and there for friends. And before I worked with Jenny I worked with Beth and Chan and Conor [Oberst] from Bright Eyes.

Do you have a general philosophy about production?

The most important thing when producing a song is to try your best to follow where the song is taking you, and not necessarily where you want the song to go, or where you want your record to go, or what you want the video to look like. I'm talking somewhat about the subconscious. I think the subconscious is the best way to get tuned into the heart of the matter. It's hard to put in words, but I think a lot of times rational thinking can ruin production jobs because there is a constant temptation to re-create something that's already happened. There's also another part of the creative process that's impossible to chart, because you have no idea where certain ideas come from. That's also the exciting part of songwriting, being able to try to tune yourself in to where that part of your mind is taking you. Speaking personally, a lot of lyrics come without thinking about them, and I think there is a reason that's happening in your mind, and to be able to follow that path instead of some rational idea is the key to producing, following wherever the song takes you. Is this making any sense?

Everyone has their own superpowers, and the collaborative aspect of it is one of the biggest joys of recording.

Yes.

I have a feeling that that's the way great novels are written. It's not necessarily once you have point A, the next day you write the next few pages of the book. I think the best way to do it is to try to get in touch with whatever stimulus or impulse you had in writing that first paragraph and trying to go back to that place. It's really hard to put into words, but it has to do with the subconscious, and things that I don't understand [*laughs*]. Do you write songs?

Yeah, I do.

So *you* know what I'm talking about.

Yeah, I have a hard time, if I've written half a song and put it away, to go back and write the rest of it.

To redo, or to edit?

Yeah, or to come up with lyrics if they don't all come out in a rush.

I heard a good story one time, and I don't remember where I heard it or who read it, but the idea was, when you're performing live, if you can somehow return to the time or place of when you were writing the song, no matter what age you were or where you were, then it's going to keep the novelty of the song alive for you. And so it comes in handy when you're on tour for a long period of time and the songs start to get old. If you can return to the point of creation, then that can be sort of a wellspring when you're stuck in Dresden, Germany, bored out of your mind. And I think that does relate to the writing process, to be able to take your initial inspiration and let that be the cornerstone. I read an interview with [director] David Lynch where he talked about that.

Let's talk about doing covers for a second. You've recorded a healthy amount of cover songs over the years.

To me it's just as important as writing *original* songs. I have a little bit of an aversion to the word "cover song," because it

seems to be something that popular music has created, as if learning old songs is maybe somewhat lazy or unthoughtful. If you're a classical musician, people don't say, "Maybe we should cover that Mozart song." That's part of your education. I think that popular music would benefit from having a similar attitude toward digging up the past, if that makes any sense. In my opinion, that's an instrumentalist's best education, studying the game. And I have a feeling the farther back you go, the farther forward you're looking into the future. I think if you're a great athlete, then you're a student of the game and you're watching the tapes, and I think if you *want* to be a great musician, the most important thing is being able to listen and to *learn*.

> *If you're a classical musician, people don't say, "Maybe we should cover that Mozart song."*

Have you heard back from any of the artists you covered? Such as David Bowie, Daniel Johnston…

I haven't heard from either of those people, actually. Or maybe I did hear back from Dan Johnston through an e-mail, and I think my label got a call from David Bowie, but I don't know what he said. Maybe he hated it. I don't know. Most of the people that I cover are dead. I get most of my inspiration from old records. I do listen to a lot of new music, but it's definitely not something that's rotating a lot in my car or in my house. And there's good and bad things to that, but for some reason that's just the way it is.

What kind of old records are we talking about?

For some reason it seems to be records from the early part and the middle part of this past century. It tends to be American and I don't really understand why I've gravitated toward this, but for some weird reason I have.

Will you be doing more collaboration in the future? Do you have any dream collaborations?

I would love to collaborate with Tony Bennett. I think that would be a blast.

What would you do?

Oh, whatever he wanted to do. I think he's amazing. And I think Jimmie Dale Gilmore is amazing.

Do you have any aspirations to be as famous as Bob Dylan or Bruce Springsteen?

Not in the slightest. Most of my dreams involve non-musical aspirations, I guess. I love the position that I'm at right now, which is the freedom to wake up late and have other people pay for your weird recording experiments. It's hard for me to think of asking for anything more than that. Not that I'm a compulsive late riser! To have the time to spend with family and friends is a huge advantage that most careers don't give you.

When you were first fantasizing about a career in music, did you picture yourself collaborating with other artists?

When I was first starting my dream music career was to take a trip to Europe on somebody else's dime, and that happened in 2000, or maybe it was 1999. So I had to rethink it because I didn't know what my musical aspirations were.

Have you come up with a new goal?

Yeah, and that would be to continue doing what I'm doing at whatever pace is healthiest for me. It's been a great ride so far, I really don't have any complaints. I think if I thought about it any further I think I'd have quite a bit to complain about, but in general I feel really fortunate to not have to have a day job.

What attracted you to John Fahey's music? I read it was pretty inspirational for you when you were making *Transfiguration of Vincent.*

It was. When I first heard Fahey's music, I was twenty-one years old. I knew a little bit of biographical information about him. I had known that here was a guy, a guitar player, who created dozens and dozens of records playing solo steel guitar instrumentals, and just the idea of that was pretty fascinating to me. In my opinion, no matter what you do for a living, if you have that kind of focus and that kind of vision, good things usually come of that. If you can keep an original idea going for that amount of time then usually good things come of it. I had known that before hearing his music, and it just so happens the first record I heard, called *The Yellow Princess,* was brilliant. So there was that appeal to his music. In addition to that, the style of his record making, which is to basically create a thread between old songs and new songs, in a way that's historically interesting and emotionally exciting, that was a bit of a revelation to me—that you could make a record like that, that you could make *dozens* of records like that.

I like the idea of taking the best parts of your heritage, which… in my opinion, the best part of American heritage is the music we've been left with, and create something new. So there were all these different levels that really appealed to me, before *and* after I discovered his music.

I love the acoustic guitar, and when I was younger my uncle gave me the Leo Kottke *6- and 12-String Guitar* record, that I thought I would love, but it didn't do it for me, so maybe I was scarred by that.

Right! That's interesting. I'm not Leo Kottke's biggest fan either. I think Leo Kottke is more for extroverts, and John Fahey is more for introverts. And I'm more of an introverted person, so I think there was something unique there for me that was really hard to find. I think the fact that the amount of history that's inside of Fahey's records makes it really intellectually interesting for me, because so many songs that he covered were from the early part of the last century and beyond. He was the first one to combine classical arrangements with these blues idioms that you could ingest fairly easily, but it does take a little bit of time. But that's what all great music has to do.

Jim Weatherly

*Interview by
Lisa Wysocky*

HitWriters.com, 2005

Jim Weatherly, a native of Pontotoc, Mississippi, began writing songs when he was thirteen years old. During high school and college, he and his various bands played throughout the South. Upon graduation from high school, he entered The University of Mississippi, where he became an All-SEC quarterback for the Ole Miss football team.

Weatherly moved to Los Angeles soon after college and became involved in the songwriting scene. He had songs that not only became pop standards but also crossed over to R&B, country, gospel, and jazz. "Neither One of Us (Wants to Be the First to Say Goodbye)" was a number one pop/soul hit and won a Grammy for Gladys Knight & the Pips. "Midnight Train to Georgia" was also a number one pop/R&B hit and helped Gladys Knight & the Pips win another Grammy. Weatherly was nominated for a Grammy as songwriter in the R&B category.

Weatherly's songs have earned him more than thirty ASCAP writer awards, but he has also recorded seven albums of his own as an artist. "The Need to Be" reached number six on the pop charts during the mid-seventies. In 1974, Weatherly was named NSAI Songwriter of the Year.

Since moving to Nashville, Weatherly has continued to enjoy success. "A Lady Like You" was number one on the country charts for Glen Campbell, and "Where Shadows Never Fall," also recorded by Campbell, won Weatherly his first Dove Award. Bryan White had his first number one country hit with Weatherly's "Someone Else's Star."

—LISA WYSOCKY

What was your biggest moment as a songwriter?

You know the best thing that ever happened to me was the song that Gladys Knight & the Pips recorded ["Midnight Train to Georgia"]. It was an R&B and a pop hit for them. It was also a number one country record by Ray Price. And when I wrote the song, as I was writing it, Ray Price was the person I had in mind to sing the song. And that's probably the only time it has ever happened to me. I thought it just sounded like what he was doing at the time. I was very proud of that record as well. It has become one of Gladys's signature songs, which I am very pleased about. The song wasn't about anyone in particular at the time. I only thought, you know, I did remember a song title called "The Best Thing That Ever Happened to Me." So I wrote the song title based on that. And then later on, Rev. James Cleveland cut the song [and says], "Jesus, you're the best thing that's ever happened to me." So it's also become a big gospel standard.

What makes a song great?

You know, I try to write songs that have a universal appeal—songs that could be done R&B, pop, country… That's the way I used to write, with the approach that it felt like something that could be around for a long time. The writing changes over the years, and you get more specific. Attitudes are more specific in each of the categories now. So, universal songs don't get the crossover potential that they once had—to be cut in an R&B vein, a country vein, and a pop vein.

What was your background before "Midnight Train to Georgia"?

Before Gladys cut my songs, I had a few cuts, though nothing really major at that time. The first thing of mine that Gladys cut was "Neither One of Us (Wants to Be the First to Say Goodbye)." When I wrote it, I thought it was a country song. It was this little 4/4 time and more of a country feel. It's funny; I was just in a melancholy mood one night, and I walked into my room, sat up on my bed, and picked up my guitar and sang the first verse to that song. I didn't have the title. I didn't have the melody. I didn't have the lyrics or anything. I just picked it up and sang it. The song literally fell out of the sky. It was something that I knew after I said, "Neither one of us wants to be the first to say goodbye." I knew that I had a song idea. I wrote it in about thirty minutes. Also, it's really funny, because at the time I was trying to get publishers interested in my songs in L.A. It was an early stage in my career. They always say, "You write such sad songs," you know? And when I closed my book on "Neither One of Us," the first thought in my head was that there was another sad song nobody will want to hear… so thankfully I was wrong about that.

How did you get your career moving in Nashville?

When I first started writing, I was actually with a publisher that didn't want me to co-write, so I wrote everything by myself. I was kind of flying by the seat of my pants, 'cause I really didn't know how to craft a song. I think it was just a God-given talent—something that I was just supposed to do. I had written songs in high school and college, just off and on the whole time. I think that it was all just so amazing to me the way songs just came about to me at that particular point in time. All the songs that I wrote in the early seventies were written from a stream of consciousness; I'd just started singing and writing and playing and ideas would just fall in. And then later on, I started co-writing. I came to Nashville and started co-writing with a bunch of people. I actually learned the art of crafting a song. It's a much different process. But what I try to do when I write now is to really be my own editor. I was never my own editor before. I would kind of just write it and leave it as is. But now I go back and re-write.

Are there songs you are especially proud of?

I never envisioned the hits that I've had, especially in R&B, because I thought when I was writing them that I was writing country songs. I was really surprised when an R&B act—Gladys Knight & the Pips—would take the songs and take them to a whole new level. I didn't [have the] vision; I never even thought of it. I was totally amazed by it, and those songs are really special to me for that reason. There's another song I wrote years ago, when I first started writing in L.A., called "Mississippi Song," that's a very special song to me. It's been cut a few times but never been a big hit. It's one of those songs that's too specific, I think. As far as other songs, I don't know. I've been writing for so long, it feels like I have too many to choose from. I'm proud of all of 'em.

How do you keep songwriting fresh for yourself these days?

In writing today, I try to challenge myself. I really try to write something that I've never heard before… that I've never heard somebody else write… a title that I never heard somebody else write. [If it is a title that's already been written], I try to have a new slant on it. I get most inspired when I feel that I'm doing something that is unique. A couple of years ago… I had written two Christmas songs, and I thought, you know, it would be nice to make a Christmas album. Right after the first of the year, I sat down and wrote twelve Christmas songs from January to March. I recorded them and now they are on my Christmas CD. I was inspired more than anything that I've ever done. I was free to write. There were no boundaries. I just wanted everything to sound like it could have been written in the forties, fifties, and sixties… something that would fit in with a lot of the old classics. It was a lot of fun.

Do you prefer being a songwriter to an artist?

I was an artist for a while. I did three albums for RCA and three albums and two albums for Buddha, and I did three al-

bums, I think, for ABC. At that time, it was okay for artists not to perform. Harry Nilsson, for example, was a big-selling artist and he didn't really perform. I did a few things but I never went on the road for a concert tour or anything like that. My publisher really wanted me to concentrate on nothing but writing, and I was really glad to do that because the road can take you away from that. You gotta be really committed to it. I was really committed to being more of a writer than an artist. That's where I really found my happiness and my joy. I felt like I was much better at that. I do like to make records 'cause, [although] I don't have a real commercial voice, I think I sell the lyrics to my songs in a way that's unique.

Do you have any tips for young songwriters?

I really don't like to give advice. I'm so bad at it. The only thing I remember when people asked me, you know, what do I need to do to be a writer and all that… first of all I think that you have to have the gift. If you don't have the gift but you really want to be a writer, I think that you have to work your tail off to be a writer, to craft songs, to learn what the marketplace is in music at that particular time. I used to tell people to move to Nashville or move to L.A. or move to New York or somewhere, if you're really serious about it [to show] people that you're serious. I think that that's changed a lot now because there are other places in the country that are really becoming hot spots for writers. Writers don't really have to live in one of the major cities. I think that they can actually get deals… like the Internet has provided a place where people can find ways to place songs without actually moving to major cities.

What's an honor or award that you've received that stands out for you?

In 1974 I was NSAI Songwriter of the Year. That was at an early part in my career so I didn't really understand what that achievement was. I really had not been in a songwriter world. I had really been in my own world writing my songs. So, I really didn't understand all of the concepts of when you are presented things like that. Now looking back on it, I really think it was a great achievement, and I'm very honored that I was songwriter of the year in 1974. I'd like to do that again.

What else are you proud of in your writing?

I was nominated for a Grammy for "Midnight Train to Georgia" in the R&B field for Song of the Year. When I started writing, I never thought about awards. I just wanted to write songs and hoped somebody would like them enough to cut them. I didn't win. That was the year Stevie Wonder won practically everything. I remember the following year, Paul Simon thanked Stevie Wonder for *not* doing an album. Then I saw Gladys, and they won the award for best R&B vocal… something like that. The thing I'm proudest of is that some of my songs [have] lasted so long. I never envisioned that. I thought that once they became hits, maybe they would go away. As it turns out, three or four of the songs that I've written have

You were a football player in college. Was music a good career move?

I went to the University of Mississippi and played four years of football there. I'm gonna say this for the record because over the years people have made me [out to be] an all-American. But actually, I was an all-SEC quarterback. I won second team all-SEC quarterback behind Joe Namath. The things I studied, I was going to be a football coach. That's what I was gonna do. I never really thought about writing songs for a living. It's just something I did and enjoyed. So a lot of the things that happened to me I feel were supposed to happen, and it was out of my control. I'm just thankful that today I'm a songwriter and that I have been able to make a living for thirty years or more as a songwriter.

If you don't have the gift but you really want to be a writer, I think that you have to work your tail off to be a writer, to craft songs, to learn what the marketplace is in music at that particular time.

become classics. And they're still played today. That's probably the part of being a songwriter that I'm proudest of—the longevity. It shows me that I was thinking a universal song that had lasting power. I'm glad I stayed with that.

Bob Weir
The Grateful Dead, Ratdog

*Interview by
Jesse Jarnow*

Jambands.com, 2001

The Grateful Dead's Bob Weir, one of the strangest rhythm guitarists to ever play regular stadium gigs, is a thoughtful man. Weir developed his playing as the magnetic center for the Dead's cosmos-spanning improvisation, carving a bizarre place between Jerry Garcia's sweet Ornette Coleman-by-way-of-The Carter Family leads, Phil Lesh's serialist-influenced bass, Bill Kreutzmann's one-man snare dancing, and Mickey Hart's explosive world rhythms. And that's not to mention the acid. The Dead's de facto stage leader, Weir contributed a host of valuable songs to the band's considerable songbook, including the summer rock classic "Sugar Magnolia," the Western epic "Jack Straw," the reggae beat of "Estimated Prophet," and the pure angularity of "Victim or the Crime." In the years following Garcia's death in 1995, Weir has split his time between the decade-old Ratdog and various configurations of the Dead's remaining members.

—JESSE JARNOW

372

You've been playing these songs for quite a while now. What do you learn about a song like "Playing in the Band" after playing it for as long a period as you have? What new things come out of it?

"Playing in the Band" is a particular challenge, having been there so much. It's the key of D. And what can you do with the key of D? Where is it gonna want to go? That takes a lot of work, actually. We have to listen to each other acutely, and if somebody suggests something that sounds new, we have to understand what they're up to and we have to go there with them right away. That's the way you get a new occurrence, a new place to go visit. The possibilities having played the song God knows how many times… there are always gonna be more possibilities. But there's a huge backlog of places we've already been with it, and that just gets larger and larger as the years go by. We don't want to go back to any of those old places, 'cause that's where you find the joy of discovery.

What kind of historical sense do you have while playing? Are you acutely conscious of those places?

When we're playing—and I speak for myself, and I think I can speak for everybody—I go to an entirely other realm where the world and my life continuum is basically all the time I've spent onstage with these songs, and now [it's] with these guys [Ratdog]. Like yesterday, for me, becomes very truly the last time I was onstage; everything else just sort of falls away. Couched in that perspective, it's pretty easy to remember where you've been and what you've done. There's not a whole lot else to think about. For that reason, it becomes easy to remember where you've been, what you've done, and to, at least, have that there for reference.

When does that moment begin when you step outside your normal bounds?

It's hard to exactly say when, but generally within the first couple of tunes… sometimes, right off the bat, sometimes with the first note. Sometimes, it takes a little push and shove to get into that timeless space. We get there pretty regularly. But, like I say, it's hard to say when exactly that's gonna occur.

This obviously speaks a lot toward improvisation. How does it work toward a song? The singing of a specific lyric? Is it a similar kind of mental space?

Absolutely. Every time we play a tune we're gonna focus on a slightly different aspect, a slightly different facet. It's like light shining through a prism or something. Coming from one angle, it rainbows out in a certain way on the other side. But if light is coming from a different angle, it does a very different thing on a different side. For me, a song can do that, if I'm concentrating. For example, on a given night, I'm having a particularly swell time with my consonants—my *s*'s, my *t*'s, stuff like that. Maybe I can hear them well… they sound real distinct to me. At that point, I can use them percussively and emotively. That's gonna color my perception about the whole rest of the song and how I'm gonna deliver it. The whole rest of the song is gonna color my approach, or my touch, to my guitar playing. The lines that come out of me are gonna be really heavily influenced by just this one little thing. And then everybody else who is listening to me is gonna be influenced by this new perspective that I'm having on the song. Now, you take that and multiply it by six—because everybody's going through those little anomalies on a nightly basis—and you can see where a song would be very different from performance to performance.

How do you relate to the content of a lyric while you're singing it?

Ahhhh, I try to just let it reveal itself to me. Each song, every story, is multilayered. That's pretty much the nature of a story. On a given evening, one layer of the story will just

jump out of me, and I'm gonna live mostly there. I'm gonna be doing the story from that vantage point, from that point of view. Once again, that colors my perception.

You do tunes by a number of different lyricists, Dead lyricists John Perry Barlow and Robert Hunter and a fair amount of Dylan. Do you differentiate between lyric styles while you're singing, or does it just matter what song you're singing at that particular moment?

The lyric styles are most influenced by the guy that's singing the song. By that, I don't mean me. I mean the guy in the song, the character. They're character driven, for the most part. And, that character… I won't say on a nightly basis… but almost year to year, that character continues to grow and change. That character has a different sort of mode of expression, a different personality. If you check in, let's see, what's a good example of this… any of the tunes actually, you'll hear that—generally speaking, in my tunes—the characters in the tunes… their delivery is softening over the years. Maybe that's because I'm getting older and some of that is leaking into these characters. They get different.

Do you have a similar historical sense with the lyrics as you do with the music where you're entering the same kind of space?

Yeah, absolutely. I won't say it's a make-believe realm, because I'm not entirely sure it's make-believe. I think it's every bit as real as this realm we consider reality, but it's also every bit as fluid as this realm we consider reality.

How often do you find a lyric relating to your everyday routine?

Rarely.

Really?

Yeah. Well, until I go there and that's my everyday existence.

Do you consider yourself an actor, then, from time to time?

Yeah. [Anthropologist] Joseph Campbell actually called me a "conjurer."

You've integrated a number of Jerry Garcia's collaborations with Robert Hunter into your catalog over the past few years. How did you choose those specific tunes?

I was just lonesome for them. And there are more coming, for that matter.

Are there different qualities that make you want to do a Garcia/Hunter tune rather than a tune by another artist? Or is a good song just a good song?

Well, there's a little bit of that, that it's a good song. But with the Garcia/Hunter stuff… I know that stuff. I know where they live. I know where those tunes live. I grew up with them. They grew with me.

Does the nature of having a planned set list for a show tend to squash creative tendencies?

No, 'cause more often as not the set list ends up being a pack of lies, anyway.

In that case, what goes into calling a song?

If I hear something, or somebody else hears something, and just starts laying in a line that's suggestive of that song… or that place to take it, and if everybody's astute and listening, if everybody's on his toes, we'll go there.

How conscious are you of pacing the show in terms of song choices?

I take that into consideration a fair bit. A show has to breathe. You can't just keep slamming the audience all night. I once went to a Bruce Springsteen show, about three and a half hours, and it was one up-tempo tune after another. I was way ready to get out of there about two-thirds of the way into the show. He's good. The music was good. It was well rendered. Everything was excellent. It was just too much. That was, I'm told, a peculiar night for him and, in general, he paced it a little better than that usually. I was glad to hear that. You have to bring it up… you have to let it fall back down dynamically speaking, a fair bit to, in my estimation, create a complete experience.

How has your guitar playing changed in recent years? Do you perceive it changing?

Let me think about that [*long pause*]. I imagine it's changing a bit, but maybe I'm a little too close to the forest to be able to count the trees here. I do pretty much what I've always done, which is play architecturally. I try to paint with broad strokes, play big support lines for people to hang stuff off of. That has not changed. There are gonna be scales and modes that I play these days that I'm learning, say, from our sax player or whatever. But that's always gonna be in flux.

Continuing the metaphor of architecture, how do you envision this overall building as something different from the Dead?

[*Long pause*] Well, we got a sax; that's different. We've got one drummer, rather than two. [*Pause*] The biggest difference, I think, is that the Dead were—by and large—older musicians. I grew up with Jerry… I grew up with the tunes, with the influences that Jerry and I wordlessly could communicate about. "I'm going to a Bill Monroe kind of place here" as opposed to any of a number of other bluegrass kinds of places—those kinds of differentiations. I'm never gonna share that with anybody else, so we don't have quite that library, that archive, of influences.

How do you do you feel about Dead cover bands—Dead tribute bands? Every town seems to have one now.

I'm kinda tickled about that. I expect they're having fun, 'cause we really had fun with that format, when we did that. If they're taking up where we left off, they've gotta be having fun as well, which is good—that's the whole point. There's a line of thought that holds that the Grateful Dead were the authors of the jam band aesthetic. Really, the jam band aesthetic is an outgrowth of American musical tradition: State a theme and work it. You find it in blues, you find it in jazz, you find it in the heart of American music. For the last couple of decades, that aesthetic has kind of disappeared into the background of general popular musical offerings. It's great to see that coming back out.

Where do you see the form going?

I wish I could tell you. Actually, I'm not sure. I'm actually happy to let it just tell me.

Don Williams

Interview by
Kelly Delaney

American Songwriter,
January/February 1988

Known for hits like "I Believe in You," "You're My Best Friend," "Good Ole Boys Like Me," and "Tulsa Time," musician Don Williams has made an indelible mark on country music. In the seventies, he was arguably the most successful country artist in the world. Born in 1939 in Floydada, Texas, Williams's professional career began as a member of the sixties folk act the Pozo-Seco Singers, who scored a hit with "Time" in 1966. In the early seventies, Williams launched his solo career, beginning with his 1973 debut *Don Williams*. His first number one hit came with the 1974 song "I Wouldn't Want to Live If You Didn't Love Me." Williams continued to chart throughout the eighties and into the nineties—in 1991, he reached the top ten with the singles "Lord Have Mercy on a Country Boy" and "True Love." In 2006, Williams retired from the stage, embarking on an international farewell tour.

—EVAN SCHLANSKY

You're a successful songwriter in your own right; do you ask writers to make little changes in their songs so they might be better suited for you?

I have to do that fairly often and I'm always real concerned that it's acceptable to the writer. I never want to change someone's song, but I have to make it to where it fits me at the same time, or I can't do it.

Have you ever had someone object to making changes?

I've been real fortunate; I've never had it happen yet.

Do you subscribe to that old saying about songs being like children?

I think most writers when they start out can't stand the thought of someone else being involved in their thoughts. That's such a very personal thing with them. It's kind of like kids in a way. You go through a stage where your kids are perfect. There's just nobody who could ever say a thing about how they look or act. Then after you get a little older and they get older, you begin to realize—if you're realistic about it—they're people and nobody's perfect. I think a lot of songs are the same way. There are a lot of times when a writer won't see in a song what someone else may see. It may be a better song than the writer thought, or it may not be as good as they thought.

Are there are certain types of songs that you would simply not record?

I really don't know what kind of song it would be, if it was the old triangle song or a boozer song. I don't know what it would take for me to be interested in it. I'm not going to say I wouldn't ever be interested in a song that was dealing with that, but it would really have to be an unusual observation—something that I felt would benefit someone.

So you feel the artist has some responsibility not to endorse potentially harmful ideas through music?

I feel very responsible to that. I don't know of anything that's as small an industry as entertainment that affects so many lives. I think it's sad when people totally take an attitude that they shouldn't be responsible, that they don't need to be responsible for the way they act. It shouldn't be a crippling kind of weight. I think it's just awareness.

How do you go about listening to songs when you're looking for material to record?

I have one of those Walkman-type deals that I listen to. I listen at home, going down the road, or whatever. Basically, I listen when I'm alone. If I'm heavy into it, I go off by myself at home and do some serious listening.

Do you listen to songs all the way through?

It depends. There are some that I don't listen to all the way through because there are already so many things that have happened that are a little objectionable to me. Or, it's an interest level that isn't there. But if it's marginal, I'll listen to the whole song.

What common mistakes do you see in songs submitted to you?

I'm not really that interested in who wrote it when I'm initially listening to it. There are a lot of times when I do know who wrote it before I listen, but it's not an issue. For me, I think one of the biggest mistakes that I see people make is that part of writing where they're really plugged into a community. From each community of writers there emerges kind of an overview that is very successful. So, whether they realize it or not, they all start adjusting to this overview. I think it gets to a point where the overview is really dictating the terms of what a song is going to say or its basic structure.

Don Williams

So, you prefer songs that aren't contrived or formula patterned?

I like songs the best that are not a constructed effort in that arena. I like songs people write that they sit down, and it's a real personal statement because that's the way they felt at that moment and they don't care if anyone records it. It's that intense statement from a person. Those are the songs I love the best.

It's true that trends develop and hit sounds become kind of cookie-cutter patterned after each other.

It's not that they're not exemplifying their control of the craft. It's the same thing in the studio because you have at your disposal such an incredible array of electronics that you can lose the emotion of it all by becoming so technical. I guess that's what I'm saying about writing; when it becomes that technical, I hear very few songs that I care anything about. It feels contrived. It may be the cleverest thing and wonderfully put together, but it somehow loses the emotion of the thing.

people sit down and write for me are a reflection of something I've already done. I'm not interested in doing what I've already done if I can help it. I guess that's why it turns me off.

Do you like to be pitched full demos?

A lot of times I would prefer that it was not a demo—just a writer and his guitar or piano. Demos can go one of two ways for you. If it's a demo that helps, sometimes it'll help a lot. But by the same token, I think there are demos that close the door because it takes you in a direction maybe you don't want to go in.

So the song in its purest form is the key ingredient for you?

Without the song, you can be the best artist in the world and have the best production, but if you cut a bad song, it's just a bad song with incredible production. That's what it all boils down to.

You can be the best artist in the world and have the best production, but if you cut a bad song, it's just a bad song with incredible production.

Have you ever recorded any songs that were written expressly for you?

I could be wrong, but I don't think I ever cut a song that somebody sat down and wrote for me. Most of the ones

Song

Brian Wilson

There are a small handful of artists who have been labeled a "genius" in rock and roll. At the top of that list, you'll find Brian Wilson's name. As The Beach Boys' driving creative force, Wilson created a body of work in the 1960s that not only sparked a national surf craze but inspired numerous artists, including the Beatles, to reach for new creative heights. The Beach Boys' early hits like "Fun, Fun, Fun," "Surfin' Safari," "I Get Around," and "California Girls" attracted fans with their sunny vocal harmonies and buoyant melodies. Wilson's creativity as a writer, arranger, and producer reached a peak with 1966's classic *Pet Sounds*, which featured sublime tracks like "God Only Knows." The eccentric songwriter would retreat from the spotlight for several years but return with a self-titled solo album in 1988. In 2004, Wilson was joined by Elton John, Paul McCartney, and Eric Clapton on the album *Gettin' in Over My Head*. Later that year, he gave fans what they had long desired, a re-recorded version of his previously unreleased sixties masterpiece, *Smile*.

—EVAN SCHLANSKY

Interview by
Kristi Singer

Singer Magazine, *2002*

Going back to some of the earliest albums recorded by you with **The Beach Boys**, there were always very accessible melodies and harmonies. How did you put that all together?

Well, we started out with one chord, then we'd put a melody to that chord, then we'd add three voices of harmony to it, then we added two more, which makes five. And then we'd mix it all together and you have one big sound.

When you wrote those songs, did you have everyone's voices in mind?

Yeah, each song I wrote, I wrote specifically for different Beach Boys.

How did you decide who would sing lead vocals on each song?

I would take the melody, and I would find the right key for each singer and then they had to find the key that I found. And the key was the chord that they were singing in… they could sing four notes per measure, four beats per measure, and that's how it was done.

In 1990, when *Pet Sounds* **was re-released, you wrote in the introduction that your voice was turned up sweet this time. This implies that there were times when you weren't happy with your voice. Is this true and if so, how did you deal with that?**

What I did was, I didn't like the way I was singing, so I took singing lessons for three months… and after I got done with my singing lessons, I went back and it worked out fantastic; it really worked out good.

After recording "God Only Knows" with Carl Wilson, you both prayed asking God for guidance and "maximum love." Why for that song?

He and I kept praying for the highest love, love of the highest kind to bring to people.

Was that something you did often when you recorded?

We did that before we recorded.

Would you care to comment on your spirituality at all?

We all believe in Jesus and we believe in God and we believe that we were his messengers, so we followed through with our career as his messengers to the world. And that's how we did it.

Would you say that your spirituality helped you create some of these songs?

Spirituality is love, right? Love and spirituality are kind of like the same, but spirituality is like everlasting love. So we put everlasting love in our voices, and now we have everlasting albums that will live forever.

What do you think it is about the music on *Pet Sounds* **that has made it so immortal?**

The harmonies of the record… the sound of the record.

For the most part, the lyrics on *Pet Sounds* **expressed an innocence that maybe has been lost. How much of that reflected your views at the time, and how do you feel about the direction of rock music since the sixties lyrically?**

I think we've evolved lyrically. Some of our songs were about cars and surfing and then we did *Pet Sounds*, which was a big departure from our regular kind of music. Then we went back to the car songs and surf songs. Then we did "California Girls," which is a fantastic, great record.

You've said you were inspired to record *Pet Sounds* after hearing the Beatles' *Rubber Soul* album.

That's true. That's very true.

What was it about *Rubber Soul* that captured your attention so much that it drove you to create *Pet Sounds*?

Because the Beatles' *Rubber Soul* was like a collection of folk songs. It was like a little collection of songs that all seemed to go together in some magic way. So, I wanted to capture that magic with *Pet Sounds* and make a great album just like *Rubber Soul*.

When you were finished with *Pet Sounds*, did you feel that you achieved your goal? Did you feel it inside or were you not sure?

I was very relieved afterwards. I thought it was an experience that I would never forget for as long as I lived. And it was just a real, spontaneous, loving, spiritual album. That's how it's gonna be remembered.

Would you say that your goal at the time was to "out-write" Lennon and McCartney?

You know what, I didn't try to out-write Lennon and McCartney at all. I didn't try at all. I just did my thing. I wasn't in any competition with John and Paul at all.

How much of a challenge has it been to perform *Pet Sounds* live?

Every time we do that, it brings back the moment when I recorded the album in the studio—the original album. And it just takes off. It just does this thing in my brain. It's just amazing how when we do it on stage, people love it just as much as they do the original record. People love the record. They love it!

How do you feel about it being called "the greatest album ever made"?

I don't believe it. I think *Phil Spector's Christmas Album* is the greatest album ever made. That's my opinion; maybe I'm wrong. Maybe I shouldn't say anything, but I have to tell it like I feel it. That Christmas album was number one as far as an album is concerned. *Pet Sounds* is number two, *Rubber Soul* is number three, and *Sgt. Pepper's…* is number four.

How do you feel about the fact that, after creating *Pet Sounds*, the Beatles did *Sgt. Pepper's Lonely Hearts Club Band*, trying to get up to your standards with *Pet Sounds*? How did that make you feel?

I was honored that they could make such a great album. When they heard *Pet Sounds* they probably said, "Oh boy, we're going to have to beat those Beach Boys. Let's go into the studio and do *Sgt. Pepper's…*" They probably said to each other let's go, that kind of thing.

Do you feel that recording *Pet Sounds Live* brings new energy to it? Are you able to give something to your audience and listeners that you can't give in the studio?

It has *more* energy than the original record. The record has just so much energy to it, but the live version has so much more energy in the instruments and in the background singing and in the leads. The lead singing is fucking unbelievable.

I've heard that you have dealt with some stage fright in your career. I wondered how you deal with that now that you're out there performing on your own. Have you overcome that fear?

It's hard to overcome it, but every time I go on stage… about a half hour before I go onstage… I feel like I want to

Brian Wilson

vomit. I'm afraid that I feel like I'm going to throw up, and then when I finally go out there it's like a shock. And then when the band first hits the first notes I just relax and start singing and it works. I go through that all the time. Every time I get stage fright I go through the same thing and I always say to myself, "Come on, you know it's going to be okay. You know you can do this. You've done it before and you can do it again." That's my attitude.

You've written so many number one hits. What inspires you the most, and what is your songwriting process like?

My wife and my kids and my manager and my fans around the world [inspire me]. I'm so dedicated to my music, I could get lost in it somehow. I'm so dedicated that I feel a little bit afraid… a little scared of how much into it I am, but I can get through it just as easy as I can.

Do you usually start with your lyrics?

First there's the chord, then the melody, then the lyrics—in that order.

I'm so dedicated to my music, I could get lost in it somehow.

Do you have any advice to offer any other artists, singers, or songwriters entering the music business?

My advice to them: I would recommend that they follow through if they have an idea. Follow through with it. Don't quit halfway through like a baby. Go through the whole shebang and carry it through instead of quitting halfway. That's my advice to young people.

Through your years with The Beach Boys, what's one thing that sticks out as something valuable you learned?

We learned with "California Girls" that if we put our heart and soul into it, it will come off really good. And "Good Vibrations"… we learned a lesson that when we go in to record a great record, we all vowed to each other that we'll keep going until we get it done.

Bill Withers

Soul. You either have it or you don't. Revered in music circles as one of the seminal and influential artists in soul and R&B, Bill Withers didn't have to work it; he plain had it.

Raised in Beckley, West Virginia, Withers's path to stardom was an unlikely success story. After an almost decade stint in the Navy, Withers relocated to Los Angeles in 1967, where he worked in an airplane factory plant. But on nights and weekend Withers woodshedded, mixing the stylistic ingredients that would create his unique musical stew of soul, R&B, gospel, and folk. On the brink of giving up on music altogether, fate intervened—as it often does—and Withers was signed to Sussex Records.

Withers recorded his debut solo LP, *Just As I Am*, in 1971. The record is a model of uncompromised aesthetic purity and elegant simplicity, and today is recognized as a soul classic. It also deeply connected with the public at large, sending "Ain't No Sunshine" to the top of the charts and earning Withers a Grammy for Best R&B Song.

Withers then released 1972's *Still Bill*, which contained two watershed moments in soul: "Lean on Me" and "Use Me." Withers continued to carve out chart success in the seventies and eighties with "Just the Two of Us" (another Grammy win for Best R&B Song), a duet with Grover Washington, Jr., and a string of well-received albums. He is still writing songs with artists such as Jimmy Buffett—two songs were included on Buffett's last album.

—KEN SHARP

Interview by
Ken Sharp

American Songwriter,
March/April 2006

Thirty-four years after its release, *Just As I Am* is hailed as a classic. Listening back to the record, can you explain why it still connects and resonates?

First of all, I don't listen to that stuff that much. It's like if you made something that was distinctly disco then, it would probably be most functional during that time. I think the style that we did was kinda folky. The people that were involved, from Booker T. to Stephen Stills… you've got some genres covered right there. And then Graham Nash sat in front of me, encouraging me. The subject matter, too. "Grandma's Hands" was on that record. I mean, grandmas ain't never gonna go out of style. Kanye West said, "Is there anybody here that didn't like their grandmother?" He said, "Sometimes you don't like your mom, but everybody likes their grandmother." [*laughs*]

Do you view yourself more as a songwriter than an artist?

I never was able to separate. It's like asking somebody who's ambidextrous, "Are you right-handed or left-handed?" Probably now I would think of myself more on the songwriting side, but there's a reason for that; at this age I don't really need that kind of vanity. I'm not trying to attract girls or anything. But at that age, I probably felt I could find more use for the attention I would get as a singer.

The material you recorded lent itself to a very sparse, organic approach.

Probably that… and the fact that the record company didn't have any money. We did that whole album in about three sessions—the last of which we did like half the album on. We got through two sessions and we got kicked out of the studio because the record company couldn't pay the bills. I had to wait six months until somebody came up with enough money to finish recording that thing.

How did you come to write "Ain't No Sunshine," and did you know it was special at the time?

I was watching a movie called *The Days of Wine and Roses* with Lee Remick and Jack Lemmon. They were both battling alcoholism, and at one point, one of them would be up and one of them would be down. They kept leaving each other. Then I looked out the window and probably a bird ate a peanut, and that just crossed my mind [*laughs*]. The song was written pretty quickly. It's a very short song anyway. It has no introduction. They put it on the B-side of another song because they didn't think it was suitable. When you put out singles in those days, you put what you thought you're never gonna need again on the B-side. The people turned it over and started playing it. How many songs can you think of that have no instrumental introduction and just, bam, somebody starts singing? And then not only that, a song that has no words in the chorus, just "I know, I know, I know." In fact, I was gonna write something in there and Booker said, "Nope, just keep it like that." The song has no introduction and a two-word chorus. I think people still like "Ain't No Sunshine" because a lot of people left a lot of people in there [*laughs*]. More people get left than want to admit it, and they can identity with the song. Years ago somebody told me this; it might not have been true. They found this person who had committed suicide somewhere in Northern California. Remember those old 45 record players that would just keep playing over and over again? They kept hearing "Ain't No Sunshine" over and over again. They broke in there and the guy had killed himself listening to that song. The only thing that I thought was special when we did that album was telling Booker T. about "Grandma's Hands." I said, "If anybody remembers me, they're gonna remember me for this." And now when people come up to me, they usually sing "Grandma's Hands." Johnny Cash came to see me once in Hawaii, and I was surprised Johnny Cash knew who I was. He said, "I'd like to meet your grandmother."

Paul McCartney covered "Ain't No Sunshine" in the nineties. Could you ever imagine in 1971, when you recorded your version of "Let It Be," that twenty-something years later he would be doing a cover of a song you wrote?

First of all, I couldn't have even imagined then that Paul McCartney would even *know* that I existed. That was very interesting. I liked his version. I like anybody's version of something that I've written because it's another point of view. Women will ask you constantly, "How do I look?" You can go out with the most beautiful woman in the world and before the evening is over, she's gonna ask you, "Do you think I'm pretty?" Everybody's told her she was pretty from the day she was born so most of us, even though we don't admit it, we all want to know how we appear to somebody else. When somebody covers one of your songs it's sort of reassuring that the appearance you gave to them made enough of an impression on them that they wanted to interpret it for themselves.

The lyrical content on *Just As I Am* reflects the times, the social and cultural upheaval. Was that conscious?

I'm satisfied when I've written a song if it makes me see something—if something visual comes to mind. So I think those songs on that album, first of all, weren't tainted by any mercenary reasons because it's your first album. You don't know if you're gonna make any money or if anybody's ever gonna hear this stuff again. But I think you can see things when you listen to it. I think it brings images to mind. That's the cutoff point for me; if you can see something in my songs, I've succeeded.

Another key track on *Just As I Am* is "Harlem," and it resounds with very powerful imagery. Had you been to Harlem to witness the surroundings before you wrote it?

I had been to New York, once when I was in the Navy and once when I was trying to get into the music business. I thought, "Maybe I'll meet somebody if I go to New York." So there was this guy that was the cousin of a friend and he used to take me to Harlem. At that time there were still clubs like Count Basie's club. I remember seeing a nineteen-year-old George Benson playing with a trio there. So I got to spend some time in Harlem. This was around 1965. During that period was probably the last time Harlem was like that. Nobody thought of Harlem as a ghetto then. It was a lively place that was the birthplace of a lot of stuff. Langston Hughes. James Baldwin. The days of Joe Louis, the fighter. That was where everybody wanted to go.

Sometimes I'll start a song and [put] it away and then finish it later when I get around to it. "Harlem" is a good one. Things come fairly quickly to me or not at all. I don't think that I labor over stuff that long, which is why I like songwriting because it's a short form. I've had it suggested to me that I write a book or a screenplay, but I haven't been inclined to do things that take that long. My whole mind could change between page 1 and page 206; I'd be a whole different person. With a song, you're challenged to say what you gotta say within that amount of time. And you also stay focused on that subject. "Harlem" captures what I saw at that time. "Harlem" is just kind of figurative in that sense because that whole process went on almost everywhere if you were black, but more so in the big city.

Recall how you came to write your number one hit, "Lean on Me."

I remember writing "Lean on Me." Since I'd started, I [had] made a little bit of money and I figured I could afford a little piano. So I bought one of those Wurlitzer pianos. I screwed the legs on it and sat down and just started running

my hands up and down. That's a song that most children find is the first song they learn to play because you don't have to change your fingers; you just go up and down. Then the lyrics are what crossed my mind. The message of the lyrics [is] just what it says. That's what I wanted to say. As to why I wanted to say it, it was an accumulation of subtle things that had buried themselves in my psyche over time. I think that would be the best explanation of why you would call something a gift… when something occurs to you, like in "Lean on Me," and you don't know why. If I knew why, I'd get up every morning and I'd push that song button and I would do it every day. And I would just dominate the whole genre. I've always said that I think some of the best stories about how songs were written are made up after the song is written, and people start asking you, "How did you do it?" That's just my little private theory. So the song lyrically deals with the two positions that people find themselves in most often. One of the most noble and self-fulfilling things to do in your life is to be able to offer help to somebody, 'cause it does wonders for your ego. It makes you the stronger half of something. The other is people who are in need of help and want to believe that there are people who care enough to give it. When you do that EKG exam and the thing is going up and down, very seldom are our lives in that middle position where we don't need to give or receive help. Sometimes we need to give help just to validate some kind of importance we need to feel. Sometimes we need help because we find ourselves in that position.

Your subject matter, straying from the generic love songs of the day, was a bit more insightful than much of the early seventies soul.

I got some complaints when I turned in "Lean on Me," not from my immediate record company but from the parent record company. There's a very famous record executive who is no longer with us… his response to my *Still Bill* album was, "Who let you go in and do this stuff?" Everybody was thinking boy/girl stuff and [that] I've gotten away with songs like "Lean on Me" and "Grandma's Hands," [which] don't have anything to do with romantic love. Romantic love is the most fickle thing in the world. The consistent kind of love is that kind that will make you go over and wipe mucus and saliva from somebody's face after they become brain dead. Romantic love, you only want to touch people because they're pretty and they appeal to you physically. The more substantial kind of love is when you want to touch people and care for them when they're at their worst.

You must be proud that "Lean on Me" means so much to people.

Yeah. It certainly would fall into the category of things that I was not sorry that I did [*laughs*]. What's interesting to me is all the places I've run into "Lean on Me." I remember visiting a prison and I happened to walk by where the prison choir was practicing and they were singing that song. They didn't know I was there. I remember the kids put me in the sixth grade play when my son graduated from elementary school. I had to sing "Lean on Me" with the kids. They got me there [*laughs*]. It's like it was something that was there before I got here. If you ask somebody they might tell you that "Lean on Me" was one hundred years old.

What are your memories of writing another big hit, "Use Me"?

That's fun stuff. That's just talkin' trash. That's just a song about being a little playful, a little arrogant, and a little cool. Unless you were one of those people born popular… I was a chronic stutterer until I was twenty-eight. I avoided the phone. So I wasn't this popular guy. I remember being young and I would have girls tell me, "You're too nice." I didn't understand that. What kind of twisted world are we in? Women like bad boys, I guess. There is no more confusing form of rejection than for somebody to tell you that you're not interesting to them because you're too nice. So over the course of time, you say, "Okay, you wanna play? Okay, let's play." "Use Me" taps into that. I tried to be nice, now let's get nasty.

As a songwriter, was there a time when you found your voice and weren't just mimicking what you had heard?

I don't think I'm similar as a writer to many people. I wasn't overly influenced by anybody. First of all, I grew up in a house where it was very religious so there was no secular music in the house. I can't say I sat around listening to the blues

> *I think the greatness of a song is directly proportionate to how many people want to think it is, and how long they think it is.*

or whatever. You couldn't bring any blues into my house growing up. I didn't have any money to go out and listen to music on jukeboxes, so I heard whatever inadvertently came on the radio, from Ella Fitzgerald to Frank Sinatra to Hank Williams. So whatever leaked through the radio into my psyche probably left a composite. I never felt equal enough to whomever I liked to try to sound like them. There were always a lot of songs [where there was] something about them I didn't like. Either I wished somebody would have said something different or whatever, so I had my own points I wanted to prove and my own things I wanted to say. The people that I admired, I always thought were so far out of reach that it would be pointless to try and imitate

anybody… If you talked about people you liked, you would have to be crazy to listen to Ray Charles and think that you could sound like that, or Aretha Franklin, or later on Whitney Houston… or Barbra Streisand—people that have these breathtaking sounds. I used to laugh when somebody would say, "Yeah, I got the next Aretha Franklin." And I thought, "You've got to be out of your mind! There ain't *never* gonna be another Aretha Franklin." [*Laughs*]

When you started having success, were there any songwriters you admired?

Yeah, people like Hal David. I'm a very lyric-based person. One of the most flattering things to me was that Hal David knew *my name* and was standing in my hallway by the bathroom, and Hal David was talking to me. We were having this little private conversation. This was at the event where he informed me that I had been elected to the Songwriters Hall of Fame. The event was secondary to me. The most fun was having Hal David pull me aside in a hallway and talk to me.

What are the elements that make a great song?

I'm gonna give you an answer you probably don't expect. I think the greatness of a song is directly proportionate to how many people want to think it is, and how long they think it is. I mean, you've got all kinds of stuff that becomes a hit. "Disco Duck" was a hit. But it was only useful during that time. When a lot of people find use for something over a long period of time, that means it's a great song. It's a subjective thing anyway; it's not like sports where you keep score by points. It's like who appreciates it. People who like one genre of music might not appreciate a great song in another genre of music. Let's take a great country song like Kris Kristofferson's "For the Good Times." It's a great song, but somebody whose taste is hip-hop might not sit there long enough to hear it. Or some of that fun stuff that Dr.

Dre does, like "California Love"... that is a great song in that genre. But somebody whose taste is jazz wouldn't want to hear that. So it's all so subjective. The only way we can assign any kind of rating to it is if lasts over the years.

You've been blessed to have had quite a few songs endure over a thirty-year period.

Yeah, that's probably what I like about what I did more than anything else. There still seems to be some use for my songs. I was tickled pink when Kanye West used a sample on his album of my song "Rosie" that wasn't really released. It was a demo and it was added to one of those endless greatest hits of mine. A few years ago, the group Blackstreet had a song called "No Diggity," which was a big hit and they used a sample of "Grandma's Hands." It's just satisfying when something can live on. The best thing I can say about anybody's songs is if I wish I had written it. I wish I had written "For the Good Times" by Kris Kristofferson. I wish I had written all of the Chuck Berry songs, which I thought were lyrically brilliant... "Sweet Little Sixteen," "Brown Eyed Handsome Man"... I mean, come on, man. Chuck Berry was a *brilliant* lyricist for that genre! I wish I had written "The First Time Ever I Saw Your Face." And all those Burt Bacharach, Hal David songs like "A House Is Not a Home." Another song I wish I had written is Billy Joel's "Just the Way You Are." I mean, come on, man!

Tell us about writing recently with Jimmy Buffett.

That was fun. Talk about crossing genres. There was something that Jimmy Buffett did last year; he had his first number one album ever in his life. There's a song called "Simply Complicated" that I wrote with him. "When you find out things about yourself that you hadn't ought to know, and your grandma calls and books you on the *Jerry Springer Show*." [*Laughs*] You don't get to say stuff like that normally in a song. And it was Jimmy's first country album. We were on

the phone and he used the phrase "simply complicated" and I thought, "Oh boy, Jimmy, we can do this." We just basically communicated over the phone and wrote it. The intent of what Jimmy does... it was fun to mess around with that because he doesn't take himself overly seriously. He's not trying to do serious, break-your-heart kind of music. Buffet's audiences are very bright people and it's a chance for a judge to come out and put on a grass skirt and some coconut breasts and a balloon hat on his head, drink some margaritas, and be silly. Buffett is probably the most successful touring artist over time than anybody else. I was surprised when he recorded something I had written years ago called "Playing the Loser Again." When people put those kind of labels on you... I never understood why Tom Jones would be called a pop singer and Otis Redding would be called an R&B singer. Tom Jones was trying his ass off to do everything that Otis Redding did [*laughs*]. I didn't like it when I was categorized. I think you really cheat yourself when you allow somebody to limit your interest because they have some kind of preconceived notion of you.

Photo Credits

American ★ songwriter
magazine

celebrating the craft of music

inspire • educate • transcend • create

If these interviews inspire you…
it's only an introduction.

Subscribe today to receive the world's
#1 resource on song since 1984.

www.americansongwriter.com

More Great Songwriting Titles From Writer's Digest Books!

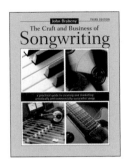

THE CRAFT & BUSINESS OF SONGWRITING
3rd Edition
By John Braheny

This insightful guide teaches you the craft of songwriting, and then goes behind the scenes of the music business to unearth insider secrets that will make your songs stand out. Features the industry secrets and technology information you need to make you more competitive in the crowded songwriting marketplace.

ISBN 13: 978-1-58297-466-8
ISBN 10: 1-58297-466-7
paperback
400 pages
#Z0525

THE NEW SONGWRITER'S GUIDE TO MUSIC PUBLISHING
3rd Edition
By Randy Poe

Provides insider knowledge and advice that's easy to understand, so you can get the best deals for your songs. With informative sidebars, sample forms, and amusing anecdotes this must-have guide gives aspiring songwriters a leg up on the competition.

ISBN 13: 978-1-58297-383-8
ISBN 10: 1-58297-383-0
paperback
160 pages
#11007

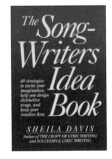

THE SONGWRITER'S IDEA BOOK
By Sheila Davis

This book takes you step by step through the songwriting process. You'll discover 40 proven songwriting strategies guaranteed to spark your imagination—all proven methods that songwriter/teacher Sheila Davis uses in her classes and national workshops.

ISBN 13: 978-0-89879-519-6
ISBN 10: 0-89879-519-2
hardcover
240 pages
#10320

These and other great Writer's Digest Books titles are available at your local bookstore or from online suppliers. Visit us at www.writersdigest.com.